60 HIKES WITHIN 60 MILES

3rd Edition

RICHMOND

Including Williamsburg, Fredericksburg, and Charlottesville

Dedication

I dedicate this book to my wife, Trish; my son, Mitchell; and my daughter, Carly, who joined me on many of these hikes, even the ones where I made them camp overnight.

60 HIKES WITHIN 60 MILES: RICHMOND
Including Williamsburg, Fredericksburg, and Charlottesville

Published by Menasha Ridge Press
Distributed by Publishers Group West
Third edition, first printing
Library of Congress Cataloging-in-Publication Data for this book is available at catalog.loc.gov.
ISBN 978-1-63404-312-0
ISBN 978-1-63404-129-4 (ebook)

Project editor: Kate Johnson
Cover and interior design: Jonathan Norberg
Cartography: Scott McGrew
Photos: Philip Riggan except where noted on page
Copy editor: Dianna Stirpe
Indexer: Rich Carlson

MENASHA RIDGE PRESS
An imprint of AdventureKEEN
2204 First Ave. S, Ste. 102
Birmingham, Alabama 35233

Visit menasharidge.com for a complete listing of our books and for ordering information. Contact us at our website, at facebook.com/menasharidge, or at twitter.com/menasharidge with questions or comments. To find out more about who we are and what we're doing, visit blog.menasharidge.com.

Front cover photo: Pocahontas State Park (see page 106). © vastateparksstaff (CC BY 2.0 [https://creativecommons.org/licenses/by/2.0])

Back cover photos:

DISCLAIMER This book is meant only as a guide to select trails in the Richmond area and does not guarantee hiker safety in any way—you hike at your own risk. Neither Menasha Ridge Press nor Philip Riggan nor Nathan Lott is liable for property loss or damage, personal injury, or death that result in any way from accessing or hiking the trails described in the following pages. Please be aware that hikers have been injured in the Richmond area. Be especially cautious when walking on or near boulders, steep inclines, and drop-offs, and do not attempt to explore terrain that may be beyond your abilities. To help ensure an uneventful hike, please read carefully the introduction to this book, and perhaps get further safety information and guidance from other sources. Familiarize yourself thoroughly with the areas you intend to visit before venturing out. Ask questions, and prepare for the unforeseen. Familiarize yourself with current weather reports, maps of the area you intend to visit, and any relevant park regulations.

60 HIKES WITHIN 60 MILES

3rd Edition

RICHMOND

Including Williamsburg, Fredericksburg, and Charlottesville

Philip Riggan
Prior edition by Nathan Lott

MENASHA RIDGE PRESS
Your Guide to the Outdoors Since 1982

60 Hikes Within 60 Miles: Richmond

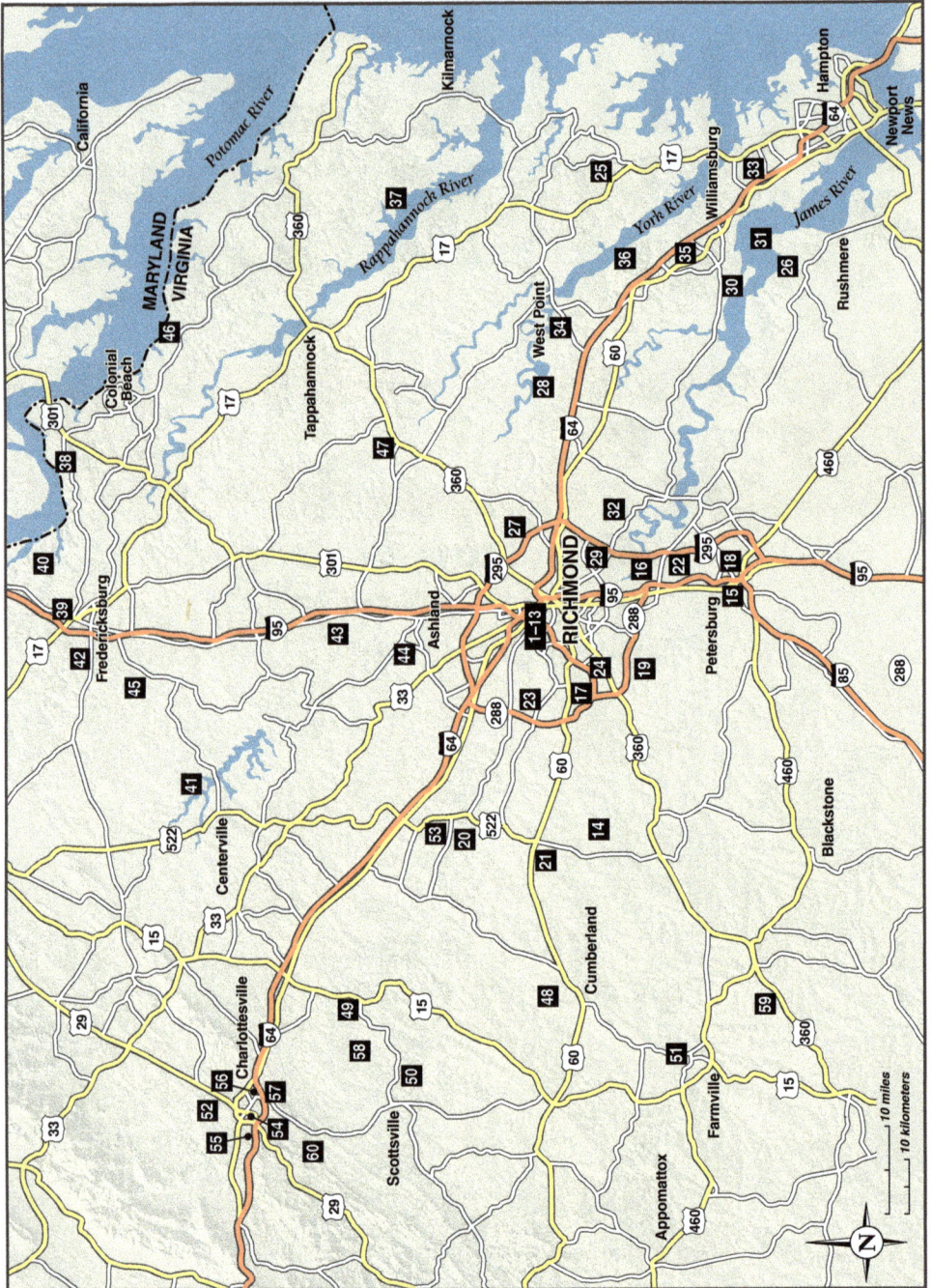

TABLE OF CONTENTS

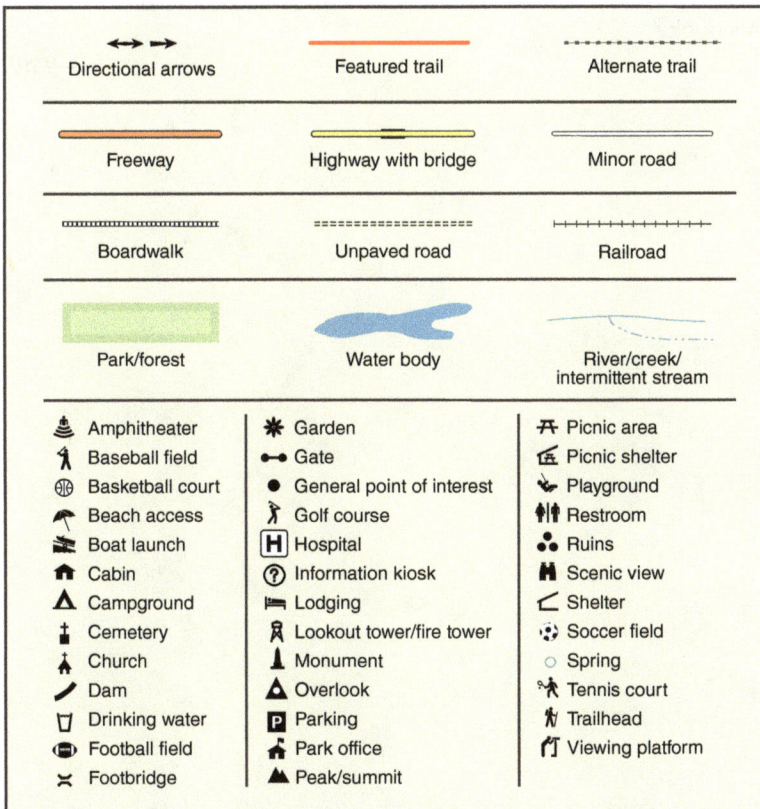

←→ ⇢ Directional arrows	Featured trail	Alternate trail
Freeway	Highway with bridge	Minor road
Boardwalk	Unpaved road	Railroad
Park/forest	Water body	River/creek/ intermittent stream

🎪 Amphitheater	✳ Garden	🌲 Picnic area
🏃 Baseball field	•– Gate	⛺ Picnic shelter
⛹ Basketball court	● General point of interest	🛝 Playground
☂ Beach access	Golf course	🚻 Restroom
🚤 Boat launch	H Hospital	Ruins
🏠 Cabin	ⓘ Information kiosk	Scenic view
⛰ Campground	⛏ Lodging	Shelter
✝ Cemetery	Lookout tower/fire tower	Soccer field
⛪ Church	Monument	○ Spring
Dam	⛰ Overlook	Tennis court
Drinking water	P Parking	Trailhead
Football field	Park office	Viewing platform
✂ Footbridge	▲ Peak/summit	

ACKNOWLEDGMENTS

As a child, I remember family hikes along the Blue Ridge Parkway and long days exploring creeks, pastures, and woods on family farms. I didn't realize how special that free time was until my grandfather sold his Pittsylvania County farm near the end of his life. His land supplied me with many of my most treasured adventures and outdoor memories.

I appreciate the help from my wife, Trish, and my children, Mitchell and Carly. They accompanied me on many hikes (and campouts) or allowed me the time away from home to visit all of these great parks and public spaces. Special thanks to the volunteers, land managers, planners, preservationists, and philanthropists who safeguard the parks profiled in this guide. Similar gratitude goes to the authors, ecologists, friends, and amateur historians who rewarded our research with fascinating stories and insights.

Many thanks to Nathan Lott for supplying more than a decade of guidance to the best hiking trails in the Richmond area in the first two editions of this guide. Finally, thank you to Menasha Ridge Press for allowing me to add my voice. As a reader, I have a great respect for Nathan's work, and I was thrilled to be invited to revise this book.

—*Phil Riggan*

FOREWORD

Welcome to Menasha Ridge Press's *60 Hikes Within 60 Miles,* a series designed to provide hikers with the information they need to find and hike the very best trails surrounding metropolitan areas.

Our strategy is simple: First, find a hiker who knows the area and loves to hike. Second, ask that person to spend a year researching the most popular and very best trails around. And third, have that person describe each trail in terms of difficulty, scenery, condition, elevation change, and other categories of information that are important to hikers. "Pretend you've just completed a hike and met up with other hikers at the trailhead," we told each author. "Imagine their questions; be clear in your answers."

An experienced hiker and writer, author Phil Riggan has selected 60 of the best hikes in and around the Richmond metropolitan area. This third edition includes new hikes, as well as additional sections and new routes for some of the existing hikes. From casual strolls through manicured suburban parks to history-rich explorations of Colonial and Civil War sites, from bird-watching excursions in Chesapeake Bay marshes to long backcountry treks through Piedmont forest, Riggan provides hikers with a great variety of routes—all within roughly 60 miles of Virginia's capital.

You'll get more out of this book if you take a moment to read the Introduction, which explains how to read the trail listings. The Topographic Maps section (page 4) will help you understand how useful topos are on a hike and will tell you where to get them. And though this is a where-to, not a how-to, guide, readers who have not hiked extensively will find the Introduction of particular value.

As much for the opportunity to free the spirit as to free the body, let these hikes elevate you above the urban hurry.

All the best,
The Editors at Menasha Ridge Press

Hikers in Richmond and central Virginia enjoy a wide variety of choices for a long walk outdoors. They have their pick of urban parks, suburban treasures, and rural getaways; of tidal wetlands, rolling hills, and riparian forest; of Colonial homes, Civil War battlefields, and many Virginia state parks.

This book combines opinions from Nathan Lott, author of the first two editions, and from me, Phil Riggan. We don't ask that you drive 3 hours west just to go for a Sunday afternoon stroll. We don't provide a multitude of curt trail descriptions and ask you to choose without maps. This is, above all, a *guide*book. Our intent is not only to get you to the trail but also to keep you on the path and help you appreciate the sights along the way. We provide lengthier descriptions to better equip novices, and we have peppered each profile with anecdotes and insights to enhance your experience.

Richmond has been my home since 1988, and the first park I visited was the beautiful Pony Pasture Rapids. The James River Park System has always been my favorite, but as my curiosity increased, I began to branch out and explore more parks, especially for hiking and mountain biking. Reading the first edition of this guide inspired me and my family to venture out to many more parks. Our goal remains to enable you to discover more in the Richmond region. What better way to explore the storied Old Dominion than on foot, just as the first English speakers and the local American Indians before them did? How else can one fully appreciate Virginia's ecological diversity and beauty?

In writing, I attempted to make this guide as serviceable as possible. A few notes on my approach: A hike's listed mileage is generally a minimum distance, with optional extensions provided. Many of these hikes can be significantly lengthened. As a rule, these are circuit hikes; that is to say, you start and stop at the parking area. Only the longest nonloops are profiled as point-to-points. Even parks and forests with extensive trail networks are not divided into multiple profiles. Thus, the guide provides 60 distinct destinations; though some may be adjacent to others, they are unique in that they are administered by different agencies (that is, a state park versus a state forest). Finally, in order to include a broad range of hiking experiences, the "60 miles" criterion was interpreted as "within 60 miles of metro Richmond as the crow flies." Thus, a few hikes require a noticeably longer drive. This makes the guide more useful to residents of peripheral communities such as Charlottesville, Fredericksburg, the Northern Neck, and Williamsburg and helpful to Richmonders planning weekend trips.

Researching this edition—for which we added 13 new parks—took me a year. I had never visited half the parks before this assignment, but I love discovering new places. To get to them, I drove approximately 3,400 miles and biked another 450. I biked another 100 miles exploring in the parks. According to my estimates, I spent about 95 hours hiking and burned nearly 38,000 calories. My family enjoyed the hiking time together as well, even on the three overnight campouts.

Forest Hill Park in South Richmond is registered as a Virginia Historic Landmark (see page 32).

So while I don't purport to have included every worthwhile trail east of the Blue Ridge, I believe you'll be surprised to learn which trails are in your proverbial backyard. We also think you'll find ones geared to your personal needs and interests. Whether you're out for an after-work hike or a trail runner's half marathon, a romantic weekend getaway or a serious overnight backpack, our suggestions will help you choose. Find a trail near your home and make a brisk walk part of your routine. Take the kids; take the dog. Watch the changing seasons paint your favorite trail in new colors. Learn to identify the trees and birds. Build your way up to a campground stay centered around hiking. You'll find yourself healthier for it, in both mind and body.

REGION Hike Number/Hike Name	Page	Mileage	Difficulty	Biking	Running	Kid Friendly	Less Busy	Heavily Traveled
RICHMOND CENTRAL								
1 Brown's Island/Potterfield Bridge Loop	18	2.4	E	✓	✓	✓		✓
2 Byrd Park/Pump House Park	23	1.6	E	✓	✓	✓	✓	
3 Deep Run Park	28	2.2	M	✓	✓	✓		✓
4 Forest Hill Park	32	2.2	E	✓	✓	✓		✓
5 James River Park Loop	37	6.4	M	✓	✓			✓
6 James River Park Main Area	43	2.5	E	✓	✓	✓	✓	
7 Joseph Bryan Park	48	2.2	E	✓	✓	✓	✓	
8 Lewis G. Larus Park	52	2.3	E	✓	✓	✓	✓	
9 North Bank Park	56	2.3	E		✓	✓	✓	
10 Pony Pasture Rapids	60	2.2	E	✓	✓	✓	✓	
11 Powhite Park	65	2.4	E	✓	✓	✓	✓	
12 Richmond Slave Trail	70	6.2	E		✓	✓	✓	
13 Virginia Capital Trail	75	3.1	E	✓	✓	✓		✓
SOUTH OF THE JAMES								
14 Amelia Wildlife Management Area	82	4.3	M				✓	
15 Appomattox River Trail	87	2.8	E	✓	✓		✓	
16 Dutch Gap Conservation Area	92	5.6	E	✓	✓	✓	✓	
17 Mid-Lothian Mines Park	97	1.7	E	✓	✓	✓	✓	
18 Petersburg National Battlefield Park	101	7.0	E		✓	✓	✓	
19 Pocahontas State Park	106	5.8	M		✓	✓	✓	
20 Powhatan State Park	111	6.8	M	✓	✓	✓	✓	
21 Powhatan Wildlife Management Area	116	5.0	M				✓	
22 R. Garland Dodd Park at Point of Rocks	120	1.7	E		✓	✓	✓	
23 Robious Landing Park	124	1.8	E	✓	✓	✓	✓	
24 Rockwood Park	130	2.1	E	✓	✓	✓		✓
EAST TO WILLIAMSBURG AND TIDEWATER								
25 Beaverdam Park	136	5.9	M	✓	✓	✓	✓	
26 Chippokes Plantation State Park	141	5.3	E	✓	✓	✓		✓
27 Cold Harbor Battlefield Park	146	3.3	E		✓	✓	✓	
28 Cumberland Marsh Natural Area Preserve	151	4.1	E		✓	✓	✓	
29 Dorey Park	156	2.1	E	✓	✓	✓	✓	

#		Page	Miles	Diff.					
30	Greensprings Greenway	160	3.3	E	✓	✓	✓	✓	
31	Hog Island Wildlife Management Area	165	3.8	E	✓	✓	✓	✓	
32	Malvern Hill Battlefield Park	170	3.0	E		✓	✓	✓	
33	Newport News Park	175	4.2	E		✓	✓		✓
34	Wahrani Nature Park	180	3.6	M	✓	✓	✓	✓	
35	Waller Mill Park	185	4.2	M		✓	✓		✓
36	York River State Park	190	6.4	M		✓	✓		✓

NORTH TO FREDERICKSBURG AND THE NORTHERN NECK

#		Page	Miles	Diff.					
37	Belle Isle State Park	198	5.2	E	✓	✓	✓	✓	
38	Caledon State Park and Natural Area	203	4.0	M		✓	✓	✓	
39	Canal Path/Rappahannock River Heritage Trail	208	3.5	E	✓	✓	✓		✓
40	Crow's Nest Natural Area Preserve	213	5.5	M		✓	✓	✓	
41	Lake Anna State Park	218	7.0	M	✓	✓	✓	✓	
42	Motts Run Reservoir	223	2.2	M		✓	✓	✓	
43	North Anna Battlefield Park	228	4.8	M		✓	✓	✓	
44	Poor Farm Park	233	2.3	M	✓	✓	✓		✓
45	Spotsylvania Court House Battlefield Park	237	5.4	E		✓	✓	✓	
46	Westmoreland State Park	242	3.3	M	✓	✓	✓		✓
47	Zoar State Forest	247	3.2	E		✓	✓	✓	

WEST TO CHARLOTTESVILLE AND CENTRAL VIRGINIA

#		Page	Miles	Diff.					
48	Bear Creek Lake State Park	254	5.0	M		✓	✓	✓	
49	Fluvanna Heritage Trail	259	6.7	M	✓	✓	✓	✓	
50	Hardware River Wildlife Management Area	264	2.3	E					✓
51	High Bridge Trail State Park	268	8.1	E	✓	✓	✓		✓
52	Ivy Creek Natural Area	273	4.0	M		✓	✓	✓	
53	Leakes Mill Park	278	1.6	E	✓	✓	✓	✓	
54	Observatory Hill	282	2.1	M	✓	✓	✓		✓
55	Ragged Mountain Natural Area	287	6.5	S		✓	✓	✓	
56	Rivanna Trail	291	3.0	E	✓	✓	✓		✓
57	Saunders-Monticello Trail	295	4.3	E	✓	✓	✓		✓
58	Scheier Natural Area	300	2.7	E		✓	✓	✓	
59	Twin Lakes State Park	305	4.7	M		✓	✓	✓	
60	Walnut Creek Park	310	7.9	S	✓	✓	✓	✓	

DIFFICULTY RATINGS		
E = Easy	M = Moderate	S = Strenuous

Hikes by Category (continued)

REGION Hike Number/Hike Name		Page	Urban	Lake, River	Scenic	Historical Interest	Wildlife	Wildflowers
RICHMOND CENTRAL								
1	Brown's Island/Potterfield Bridge Loop	18	✓	✓	✓			
2	Byrd Park/Pump House Park	23			✓	✓	✓	
3	Deep Run Park	28		✓				
4	Forest Hill Park	32		✓		✓		
5	James River Park Loop	37		✓	✓	✓	✓	
6	James River Park Main Area	43		✓		✓	✓	✓
7	Joseph Bryan Park	48		✓		✓	✓	✓
8	Lewis G. Larus Park	52					✓	
9	North Bank Park	56		✓	✓	✓	✓	
10	Pony Pasture Rapids	60		✓	✓		✓	✓
11	Powhite Park	65					✓	
12	Richmond Slave Trail	70	✓	✓	✓	✓	✓	
13	Virginia Capital Trail	75	✓	✓	✓	✓		
SOUTH OF THE JAMES RIVER								
14	Amelia Wildlife Management Area	82		✓			✓	✓
15	Appomattox River Trail	87		✓	✓	✓	✓	
16	Dutch Gap Conservation Area	92		✓	✓	✓	✓	
17	Mid-Lothian Mines Park	97	✓	✓	✓	✓		
18	Petersburg National Battlefield Park	101			✓	✓	✓	
19	Pocahontas State Park	106		✓	✓		✓	
20	Powhatan State Park	111		✓	✓		✓	✓
21	Powhatan Wildlife Management Area	116		✓			✓	✓
22	R. Garland Dodd Park at Point of Rocks	120		✓	✓	✓	✓	
23	Robious Landing Park	124		✓			✓	
24	Rockwood Park	130		✓				
EAST TO WILLIAMSBURG AND TIDEWATER								
25	Beaverdam Park	136		✓			✓	
26	Chippokes Plantation State Park	141		✓	✓	✓	✓	
27	Cold Harbor Battlefield Park	146		✓		✓	✓	
28	Cumberland Marsh Natural Area Preserve	151		✓	✓		✓	✓
29	Dorey Park	156		✓			✓	

#	Hike	Page						
30	Greensprings Greenway	160		✓	✓		✓	
31	Hog Island Wildlife Management Area	165		✓	✓		✓	✓
32	Malvern Hill Battlefield Park	170			✓	✓	✓	✓
33	Newport News Park	175		✓	✓	✓	✓	
34	Wahrani Nature Park	180				✓	✓	
35	Waller Mill Park	185		✓	✓		✓	
36	York River State Park	190		✓	✓	✓	✓	✓

NORTH TO FREDERICKSBURG AND THE NORTHERN NECK

#	Hike	Page						
37	Belle Isle State Park	198		✓	✓	✓	✓	✓
38	Caledon State Park and Natural Area	203					✓	
39	Canal Path/Rappahannock River Heritage Trail	208	✓	✓	✓	✓		
40	Crow's Nest Natural Area Preserve	213		✓	✓	✓		
41	Lake Anna State Park	218		✓	✓	✓	✓	
42	Motts Run Reservoir	223		✓			✓	
43	North Anna Battlefield Park	228				✓	✓	
44	Poor Farm Park	233					✓	
45	Spotsylvania Court House Battlefield Park	237			✓	✓		✓
46	Westmoreland State Park	242		✓	✓	✓	✓	✓
47	Zoar State Forest	247					✓	✓

WEST TO CHARLOTTESVILLE AND CENTRAL VIRGINIA

#	Hike	Page						
48	Bear Creek Lake State Park	254		✓	✓		✓	
49	Fluvanna Heritage Trail	259				✓	✓	✓
50	Hardware River Wildlife Management Area	264					✓	✓
51	High Bridge Trail State Park	268		✓	✓	✓		
52	Ivy Creek Natural Area	273			✓		✓	✓
53	Leakes Mill Park	278				✓		
54	Observatory Hill	282				✓		
55	Ragged Mountain Natural Area	287		✓	✓		✓	✓
56	Rivanna Trail	291	✓	✓	✓		✓	✓
57	Saunders-Monticello Trail	295			✓	✓	✓	
58	Scheier Natural Area	300		✓		✓	✓	✓
59	Twin Lakes State Park	305		✓	✓	✓	✓	
60	Walnut Creek Park	310		✓	✓		✓	✓

Welcome to *60 Hikes Within 60 Miles: Richmond.* Whether you're new to hiking or a seasoned trail veteran, take a few minutes to read the following introduction. We'll explain how this book is organized and how to make the best use of it.

How to Use This Guidebook

The following information walks you through this guidebook's organization to make it easy and convenient for planning great hikes.

OVERVIEW MAP AND MAP LEGEND

Each hike's number appears on the overview map, opposite the table of contents; in the table of contents; in the list of hikes at the beginning of the corresponding regional chapter; and in the hike profile itself. As you flip through the book, a hike's profile is easy to locate by watching for the number at the top of each left-hand page.

A map legend that details the symbols found on the trail maps follows the table of contents, on page vii.

REGIONAL MAPS

The book is divided into regions, and prefacing each regional section is an overview map. The regional maps provide more detail than the overview map, bringing you closer to the hikes.

TRAIL MAPS

A detailed map of each hike's route appears with its profile. On each of these maps, symbols indicate the trailhead, the complete route, significant features, facilities, and topographic landmarks such as creeks, overlooks, and peaks.

To produce the highly accurate maps in this book, the author used a handheld GPS unit to gather data while hiking each route and then sent that data to the publisher's expert cartographers. However, your GPS is not a substitute for sound, sensible navigation that takes into account the conditions that you observe while hiking.

Further, despite the high quality of the maps in this guidebook, the publisher and author strongly recommend that you always carry an additional map, such as the ones noted in each entry's listing for Maps.

THE HIKE PROFILE

Each hike contains a brief overview of the trail, a description of the route from start to finish, key at-a-glance information—from the trail's distance and configuration to

OPPOSITE: The Pipeline Rapids walkway under the CSX railway viaduct
(see Brown's Island/Potterfield Bridge Loop, page 18)

contacts for local information—GPS trailhead coordinates, and directions for driving to the trailhead. Each profile also includes a map (see Trail Maps, page 1). Many hike profiles also include notes on nearby activities.

KEY INFORMATION

The information in this box gives you a quick idea of the specifics of each hike.

DISTANCE & CONFIGURATION *Distance* notes the length of the hike round-trip, from start to finish. If the hike description includes options to shorten or extend the hike, those round-trip distances will also be factored here. *Configuration* defines the trail as a loop, an out-and-back (taking you in and out via the same route), a figure eight, or a balloon.

DIFFICULTY The degree of effort that a typical hiker should expect on a given route. For simplicity, the trails are rated as easy, moderate, or strenuous.

ELEVATION The elevation at the trailhead and at the high or low point of the hike.

SCENERY A short summary of the attractions offered by the hike and what to expect in terms of plant life, wildlife, natural wonders, and historical features.

EXPOSURE How much sun you can expect on your shoulders during the hike.

TRAFFIC How busy the trail might be on an average day. Trail traffic, of course, varies from day to day and season to season. Weekend days typically see the most visitors. Other trail users that may be encountered on the trail are also noted here.

TRAIL SURFACE Indicates whether the trail surface is paved, rocky, gravel, dirt, boardwalk, or a mixture of elements.

HIKING TIME How long it takes to hike the trail. A slow but steady hiker will average 2–3 miles an hour, depending on the terrain.

SEASON The time of year and hours the trail is open.

ACCESS Fees or permits required to hike the trail are detailed here—and noted if there are none.

WHEELCHAIR ACCESS Indicates whether there are paved sections or other areas for safely using a wheelchair.

MAPS Resources for maps, in addition to those in this guidebook. (As previously noted, the publisher and author recommend that you carry more than one map— and that you consult those maps before heading out on the trail to resolve any confusion or discrepancy.)

DRIVING DISTANCE FROM THE CAPITOL The Virginia statehouse is a convenient frame of reference for the distance of these hikes from central Richmond.

FACILITIES This item alerts you to restrooms, water, picnic tables, and other basics at or near the trailhead.

CONTACT Phone numbers and websites for checking trail conditions and gleaning other day-to-day information.

LOCATION The address for the trail.

COMMENTS Assorted nuggets of information, such as whether dogs are allowed on the trails.

IN BRIEF

Think of this section as a taste of the trail, a snapshot focused on the historical landmarks, beautiful vistas, and other sights you may encounter on the hike.

DESCRIPTION

The heart of each hike. Here the author provides a summary of the trail's essence and highlights any special traits the hike has to offer. The route is clearly outlined, including landmarks, side trips, and possible alternate routes along the way. Ultimately the hike description will help you choose which hikes are best for you.

NEARBY ACTIVITIES

Look here for information on things to do or points of interest, such as nearby parks, museums, or restaurants. Note that not every hike has a listing.

DIRECTIONS

Used in conjunction with the GPS coordinates, the driving directions will help you locate each trailhead. Once at the trailhead, park only in designated areas.

GPS TRAILHEAD COORDINATES

As noted in Trail Maps, page 1, the author used a handheld GPS unit to obtain geographic data and sent the information to the publisher's cartographers. The trailhead coordinates—the intersection of the latitude (north) and longitude (west)—will guide you to the trailhead. In some cases, you can drive within viewing distance of a trailhead. Other hiking routes require a short walk to the trailhead from a parking area.

You will also note that this guidebook uses the **degree–decimal minute format** for presenting the GPS coordinates:

N42° 20.827'   W83° 02.134'

The latitude and longitude grid system is likely quite familiar to you, but here is a refresher, pertinent to visualizing the GPS coordinates:

Imaginary lines of latitude—called parallels and approximately 69 miles apart from each other—run horizontally around the globe. The equator is established to be 0°, and each parallel is indicated by degrees from the equator: up to 90°N at the North Pole, and down to 90°S at the South Pole.

Imaginary lines of longitude—called meridians—run perpendicular to latitude lines. Longitude lines are likewise indicated by degrees. Starting from 0° at the Prime Meridian in Greenwich, England, they continue to the east and west until they meet 180° later at the International Date Line in the Pacific Ocean. At the equator, longitude lines are also approximately 69 miles apart, but that distance narrows as the meridians converge toward the North and South Poles.

To convert GPS coordinates given in degrees, minutes, and seconds to the degree–decimal minute format shown above, divide the seconds by 60. For more on GPS technology, visit usgs.gov.

Topographic Maps

The maps in this book have been produced with great care and, used with the hike text, will direct you to the trail and help you stay on course. However, you'll find superior detail and valuable information in the U.S. Geological Survey's 7.5-minute series topographic maps. At mytopo.com, for example, you can view and print free USGS topos of the entire United States. Online services such as Trails.com charge annual fees for additional features such as shaded relief, which makes the topography stand out more. If you expect to print out many topo maps each year, it might be worth paying for such extras. The downside to USGS maps is that most are outdated, having been created 20–30 years ago; nevertheless, they provide excellent topographic detail. Of course, Google Earth (earth.google.com) does away with topo maps and their inaccuracies, replacing them with satellite imagery and its inaccuracies. Regardless, what one lacks, the other augments. Google Earth is an excellent tool, whether you have difficulty with topos or not.

If you're new to hiking, you might be wondering, "What's a topo map?" In short, it indicates not only linear distance but elevation as well, using contour lines. These lines spread across the map like dozens of intricate spiderwebs. Each line represents a particular elevation, and at the base of each topo a contour's interval designation is given. If, for example, the contour interval is 20 feet, then the distance between each contour line is 20 feet. Follow five contour lines up on the same map, and the elevation has increased by 100 feet. In addition to the sources listed previously and in Appendix B, you'll find topos at major universities, outdoors shops, and some public libraries, as well as online at nationalmap.gov and store.usgs.gov.

Weather

Virginia's weather is often dynamic but rarely extreme. It's been said jokingly that the state has four distinct seasons but that they do not occur in any particular order. Hence, a modicum of planning should precede a hike of any significant distance— or of any significant distance from home. Obtain a reliable weather forecast, dress appropriately and in layers, and bring a raincoat just in case.

The following table lists average temperatures and precipitation by month for the Richmond region.

MONTH	HI TEMP	LO TEMP	RAIN or SNOW	MONTH	HI TEMP	LO TEMP	RAIN or SNOW
JAN	47° F	28° F	3.03"	JUL	90° F	69° F	4.49"
FEB	51° F	31° F	2.72"	AUG	88° F	67° F	4.65"
MAR	60° F	37° F	4.02"	SEP	81° F	60° F	4.09"
APR	70° F	46° F	3.23"	OCT	71° F	48° F	2.95"
MAY	78° F	55° F	3.78"	NOV	61° F	39° F	3.23"
JUN	86° F	65° F	3.90"	DEC	51° F	31° F	3.23"

Source: usclimatedata.com

In general, as the accompanying temperature chart shows, central Virginia summers and winters are relatively mild. As a rule, the eastern periphery of the area covered by this guide stays a few degrees warmer in the winter and a few degrees cooler in the summer than the rest of the state. The area to the west is typically a few degrees cooler during the winter than the rest of Virginia. Precipitation in Richmond peaks during July, which averages 4.5 inches of rain, but it is a year-round possibility. Other warm months average 4 inches, and cool months average 3 inches.

Blizzards and thunderstorms aside, a well-equipped, well-prepared hiker can enjoy these trails year-round. In fact, hiking in the wake of a snowfall rewards the intrepid with stunning scenery. Nevertheless, you'll find that trail traffic spikes in the spring. To avoid the crowds, head east of Richmond, where you'll find blossoms— particularly mountain laurel—on Tidewater riverbanks and migratory birds returning north along the Atlantic flyway. In the autumn, head west to the hardwood forests of the Piedmont and Appalachian foothills. You'll find stunning foliage and sweeping vistas near Charlottesville, without the throngs that flock to Skyline Drive.

Water

How much is enough? Well, one simple physiological fact should convince you to err on the side of excess when deciding how much water to pack: a hiker walking steadily in 90° heat needs approximately 10 quarts of fluid per day. That's 2.5 gallons. A good rule of thumb is to hydrate prior to your hike, carry (and drink) 6 ounces of water for every mile you plan to hike, and hydrate again after the hike. For most people, the pleasures of hiking make carrying water a relatively minor price to pay to remain safe and healthy. So pack more water than you anticipate needing, even for short hikes.

If you are tempted to drink found water, do so with extreme caution. Many ponds and lakes encountered by hikers are fairly stagnant, and the water tastes terrible. Drinking such water presents inherent risks. Giardia parasites contaminate many water sources and cause the dreaded intestinal giardiasis that can last for weeks after ingestion. For information, visit the Centers for Disease Control and Prevention website at cdc.gov/parasites/giardia.

In any case, effective treatment is essential before using any water source found along the trail. Boiling water for 2–3 minutes is always a safe measure for camping, but day hikers can consider iodine tablets, approved chemical mixes, filtration units rated for giardia, and UV filtration. Some of these methods (for example, filtration with an added carbon filter) remove bad tastes typical in stagnant water, while others add their own taste. As a precaution, carry a means of water purification to help in a pinch.

Clothing

Weather, unexpected trail conditions, fatigue, extended hiking duration, and wrong turns can individually or collectively turn a great outing into a very uncomfortable one at best—and a life-threatening one at worst. Thus, proper attire plays a key role in staying comfortable and, sometimes, in staying alive. Here are some helpful guidelines:

➤ **Choose silk, wool, or synthetics** for maximum comfort in all your hiking attire, from hats to socks. Cotton is fine if the weather remains dry and stable, but you won't be happy if that material gets wet.

➤ **Always wear a hat,** or at least tuck one into your day pack or hitch it to your belt. Hats offer all-weather sun and wind protection as well as warmth if it turns cold.

➤ **Be ready to layer up or down** as the day progresses and the mercury rises or falls. Today's outdoor wear makes layering easy, with such designs as jackets that convert to vests and zip-off or button-up legs.

➤ **Wear hiking boots or sturdy hiking sandals with toe protection.** Flip-flopping along a paved urban greenway is one thing, but never hike a trail in open sandals or casual sneakers. Your bones and arches need support, and your skin needs protection.

➤ **Pair that footwear with good socks.** If you prefer not to sheathe your feet when wearing hiking sandals, tuck the socks into your day pack; you may need them if the weather plummets or if you hit rocky turf and pebbles begin to irritate your feet. And, in an emergency, if you have lost your gloves, you can use the socks as mittens.

➤ **Don't leave rainwear behind,** even if the day dawns clear and sunny. Tuck into your day pack, or tie around your waist, a jacket that is breathable and either water-resistant or waterproof. Investigate different choices at your local outdoors retailer. If you are a frequent hiker, ideally you'll have more than one rainwear weight, material, and style in your closet to protect you in all seasons in your regional climate and hiking microclimates.

Essential Gear

Today you can buy outdoor vests that have up to 20 pockets shaped and sized to carry everything from toothpicks to binoculars. Or, if you don't aspire to feel like a burro, you can neatly stow these items in your day pack or backpack. The following list showcases never-hike-without-them items, in alphabetical order, as all are important:

➤ **Extra clothes** (raingear, warm hat, gloves, and change of socks and shirt)

➤ **Extra food** (trail mix, granola bars, or other high-energy foods)

➤ **Flashlight or headlamp** with extra bulb and batteries

➤ **Insect repellent** (For some areas and seasons, this is vital.)

➤ **Maps and a high-quality compass** (Even if you know the terrain from previous hikes, don't leave home without these tools. And, as previously noted, bring maps in addition to those in this guidebook, and consult them prior to the hike. If you are versed in GPS usage, bring that device too, but don't rely on it as your sole navigational tool, as battery life can dwindle or die, and be sure to compare its guidance with that of your maps.)

➤ **Pocketknife and/or multitool**

➤ **Sunscreen** (Note the expiration date on the tube or bottle; it's usually embossed on the top.)

➤ **Water** (As emphasized more than once in this book, bring more than you think you will drink. Depending on your destination, you may want to bring a container and iodine or a filter for purifying water in case you run out.)

➤ **Whistle** (This little gadget will be your best friend in an emergency.)

➤ **Windproof matches and/or a lighter,** as well as a fire starter

FIRST AID KIT

In addition to the aforementioned items, those below may appear overwhelming for a day hike. But any paramedic will tell you that the products listed here—in alphabetical order, because all are important—are just the basics. The reality of hiking is that you can be out for a week of backpacking and acquire only a mosquito bite. Or you can hike for an hour, slip, and suffer a bleeding abrasion or broken bone. Fortunately, these listed items will collapse into a very small space. You may also purchase convenient, prepackaged kits at your pharmacy or on the Internet.

- **Adhesive bandages**
- **Antibiotic ointment** (Neosporin or the generic equivalent)
- **Athletic tape**
- **Benadryl** or the generic equivalent, diphenhydramine (in case of allergic reactions)
- **Blister kit** (such as Moleskin/Spenco 2nd Skin)
- **Butterfly-closure bandages**
- **Elastic bandages or joint wraps**
- **Epinephrine in a prefilled syringe** (typically by prescription only, for people known to have severe allergic reactions to hiking occurrences such as bee stings)
- **Gauze** (one roll and a half dozen 4-by-4-inch pads)
- **Hydrogen peroxide or iodine**
- **Ibuprofen or acetaminophen**

Note: Consider your intended terrain and the number of hikers in your party before you exclude any article cited above. A botanical-garden stroll may not inspire you to carry a complete kit, but anything beyond that warrants precaution. When hiking alone, you should always be prepared for a medical need. And if you are a twosome or with a group, one or more people in your party should be equipped with first aid supplies.

General Safety

The following tips may have the familiar ring of your mother's voice as you take note of them.

- **Always let someone know where you will be hiking and how long you expect to be gone.** It's a good idea to give that person a copy of your route, particularly if you are headed into any isolated area. Let them know when you return.

➤ **Always sign in and out of any trail registers.** Don't hesitate to comment on the trail condition if space is provided; that's your opportunity to alert others to problems you encounter.

➤ **Do not count on a cell phone for your safety.** Reception may be spotty or nonexistent on the trail, even on an urban walk—especially if it is embraced by towering trees.

➤ **Always carry food and water, even for a short hike.** And bring more water than you think you will need. (That cannot be said often enough!)

➤ **Ask questions.** State forest and park employees are there to help. It's a lot easier to solicit advice before a problem occurs, and it will help you avoid a mishap away from civilization when it's too late to amend an error.

➤ **Stay on designated trails.** Even on the most clearly marked trails, there is usually a point where you have to stop and consider which direction to head. If you become disoriented, don't panic. As soon as you think you may be off track, stop, assess your current direction, and then retrace your steps to the point where you went astray. Using a map, a compass, and this book, and keeping in mind what you have passed thus far, reorient yourself, and trust your judgment on which way to continue. If you become absolutely unsure of how to continue, return to your vehicle the way you came in. Should you become completely lost and have no idea how to find the trailhead, remaining in place along the trail and waiting for help is most often the best option for adults and always the best option for children.

➤ **Always carry a whistle,** another precaution that cannot be overemphasized. It may be a lifesaver if you do become lost or sustain an injury.

➤ **Be especially careful when crossing streams.** Whether you are fording the stream or crossing on a log, make every step count. If you have any doubt about maintaining your balance on a log, ford the stream instead: use a trekking pole or stout stick for balance *and face upstream as you cross.* If a stream seems too deep to ford, turn back. Whatever is on the other side is not worth risking your life.

➤ **Be careful at overlooks.** While these areas may provide spectacular views, they are potentially hazardous. Stay back from the edge of outcrops, and make absolutely sure of your footing; a misstep can mean a nasty and possibly fatal fall.

➤ **Standing dead trees and storm-damaged living trees pose a significant hazard.** These trees may have loose or broken limbs that could fall at any time. While walking beneath trees, and when choosing a spot to rest or enjoy your snack, look up!

➤ **Know the symptoms of subnormal body temperature, known as hypothermia.** Shivering and forgetfulness are the two most common indicators of this stealthy killer. Hypothermia can occur at any elevation, even in the summer, especially when the hiker is wearing lightweight cotton clothing.

If symptoms present themselves, get to shelter, hot liquids, and dry clothes as soon as possible.

➤ **Know the symptoms of heat exhaustion (hyperthermia).** Light-headedness and loss of energy are the first two indicators. If you feel these symptoms, find some shade, drink water, remove as many layers of clothing as practical, and stay put until you cool down. Marching through heat exhaustion leads to heatstroke, which can be fatal. If you should be sweating and you're not, that's the signature warning sign. Your hike is over at that point—heatstroke is a life-threatening condition that can cause seizures, convulsions, and eventually death. If you or a companion reaches that point, do whatever can be done to cool the victim down and seek medical attention immediately.

➤ **Most important of all, take along your brain.** A cool, calculating mind is the single-most important asset on the trail. It allows you to think before you act.

➤ **In summary:** Plan ahead. Watch your step. Avoid accidents before they happen. Enjoy a rewarding and relaxing hike.

Flora & Fauna Precautions

Hikers should remain aware of the following concerns regarding plants and wildlife, described in alphabetical order.

BLACK BEARS Sightings of black bears in central Virginia are not uncommon. Attacks by black bears, however, are uncommon, though the sight or approach of a bear can give anyone a start. If you encounter a bear while hiking, remain calm and avoid running in any direction. Make loud noises to scare off the bear, and back away slowly. In primitive and remote areas, assume bears are present; in more-developed sites, check on the current bear situation prior to hiking. Most encounters are food-related, as bears have an exceptional sense of smell and not particularly discriminating tastes. While this is of greater concern to backpackers and campers, day hikers may plan a picnic or munch on an energy bar from time to time, so remain aware and alert.

BLACK FLIES Though certainly a pest and maddening annoyance, the worst a black fly will cause is an itchy welt. They are most active from mid-May to June, during the day (especially before thunderstorms), and in the early morning and late evening hours. Insect repellent has some effect, though the only way to keep out of their swarming midst is to keep moving.

MOSQUITOES Many of the hikes in this book are along waterways, which attract these pests. In some areas, mosquitoes are known to carry the West Nile or Zika virus, so all due caution should be taken to avoid their bites. Ward them off with insect repellent and/or repellent-impregnated clothing.

Poison ivy   Photo: Tom Watson

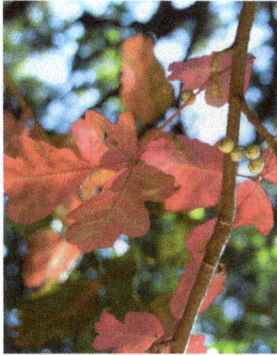
Poison oak   Photo: Jane Huber

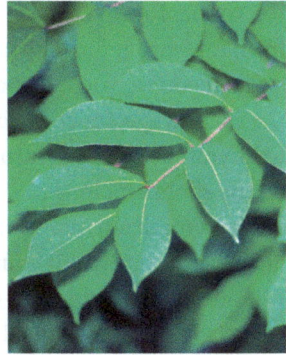
Poison sumac   Photo: Norman Tomalin/ Alamy Stock Photo

POISON IVY, OAK, AND SUMAC Recognizing and avoiding contact with poison ivy, oak, and sumac is the most effective means of preventing the painful, itchy rash associated with these plants. In the mid-Atlantic, poison ivy occurs as a vine or ground cover with 3 leaflets to a leaf; poison oak appears as either a vine or a shrub with 3 leaflets to a leaf; and poison sumac grows in swampland as a shrub with 7–13 leaflets per leaf. Consult a field guide to learn how to identify these species and distinguish them from benign counterparts like Virginia creeper.

Urushiol, the oil from these plants, is responsible for the rash. Thus, you may contract a case of poison ivy either by direct contact with the plant or by touching something—your clothing, boots, or pets—that brushed against it. Within 12–24 hours of exposure, raised lines and/or blisters appear, accompanied by a terrible itch. As with insect bites, scratching makes the situation worse, and bacteria under your fingernails may cause an infection. Wash and dry the rash thoroughly, applying calamine lotion or other desiccant to help dry it out. If the itching or blistering is severe, seek medical attention. Remember that oil-contaminated clothes, pets, or hiking gear can easily cause a the rash on you or someone else, so wash not only any exposed parts of your body but also anything that has come in contact with the oil.

SNAKES If you hike enough of these trails, you'll eventually spot a snake, usually sunning on the trail ahead or perhaps slithering into the underbrush at the sound of your footfalls. The odds that you'll happen upon a venomous snake are significantly lower. Still, you should give a wide berth to all legless reptiles—and other wildlife as well.

Canebrake rattlesnake   Photo: Savannah River Ecology Laboratory at the University of Georgia

Among the snakes native to central Virginia are the nonvenomous garter, black rat, and king snakes and the venomous water moccasin, copperhead, and canebrake (or timber) rattlesnakes. Snakes like warm—but not hot—weather and are active from midspring through midautumn.

If you're worried about snakes, you may want to spend a few minutes studying the various species and their habits before heading into the woods. A field guide may help you feel more informed and empowered. Basic precautions, such as wearing sturdy shoes and long pants and carrying a cell phone, should also assuage your fears while minimizing more-likely risks, such as twisted ankles and poison ivy. When hiking, do not step or put your hands beyond your range of detailed visibility, and avoid wandering around in the dark. Step *onto* logs and rocks, never *over* them, and be especially careful when climbing rocks. Always avoid walking through dense brush.

TICKS Ticks tend to lurk in the brush, leaves, and grass that grow alongside trails. May–August is the peak period for ticks in the mid-Atlantic, but arachnids can remain active all year. Scientifically, ticks are ectoparasites, living on the outside of a host for the majority of their life cycles in order to reproduce.

Of the two varieties that may hitch a ride on you—wood ticks and deer ticks— extensive research suggests that both need several hours of actual bloodsucking attachment before they can transmit any disease. Deer ticks, the primary vector for Lyme disease, are very small (often as tiny as poppy seeds), and you may not be aware of their presence until you feel the itchiness of their bites. The best avoidance strategy is to wear light-colored clothing (so you can spot the ticks more easily); tuck the bottoms of your pants legs into your socks (it looks geeky, but it helps); slather your ankles, wrists, and neck with a DEET-rich insect repellent; and remain on the beaten path, avoiding trails overgrown with tall grass. At the end of the hike, check yourself thoroughly before getting in the car; later, when you take a shower, do a more thorough check of your entire body.

When hiking with your dog, take precautions to ensure its safety. Regularly apply a topical anti-flea and -tick medication (such as Frontline Plus or K9 Advantix), and brush your dog after hiking to look for ticks, which tend to crawl up to the head and chest. Ticks that haven't bitten are easily removed but not easily killed unless you burn or crush them. Tweezers work best for plucking off attached ticks.

Hunting

Separate rules, regulations, and licenses govern the various hunting types and related seasons. Though there are generally no problems, hikers may wish to forgo trips during big-game seasons, when the woods suddenly seem filled with orange and camouflage. In Virginia, the majority of hunting seasons are scheduled for October–January, and most of the hikes in this book are in parks that prohibit hunting, except for wildlife management areas and certain special hunts in state parks.

Regulations

Though the hike profiles note some restrictions (generally in the Access category of the Key Information), it is your responsibility to learn and obey the rules of any park or preserve that you visit. Here are some common regulations that apply to most of the sites listed in this guide:

➤ **Use or display of alcoholic beverages is not allowed.**

➤ **All state and local ordinances apply,** including those governing fishing and hunting.

➤ **Pets must generally be leashed when allowed on the trails.** Pets are not allowed at most nature preserves.

➤ **Though hours vary, most parks generally close at sunset.**

➤ **Camping is not allowed without the permission of park management.** Established campgrounds are often closed in the off-season.

➤ **Fires are not allowed without the permission of park management.** Even campfires are subject to seasonal bans.

➤ **Swimming is not allowed unless otherwise specified.** Many rivers, lakes, and ponds are closed to swimmers, and some lake beaches are open only in summer.

Trail Etiquette

Whether you're on a city, county, state, or national park trail, always remember that great care and resources (from nature as well as from your tax dollars) have gone into creating these trails. Treat the trail, wildlife, and fellow hikers with respect.

Here are a few general ideas to keep in mind while on the trail:

➤ **Hike on open trails only.** Respect trail and road closures (ask if unsure), avoid trespassing on private land, and obtain all permits and authorization as required. Leave gates as you found them or as marked.

➤ **Leave no trace of your visit other than footprints.** Be sensitive to the dirt beneath you. This also means staying on the trail and not creating any new ones. Be sure to pack out what you pack in. No one likes to see the trash someone else has left behind.

➤ **Never spook animals.** An unannounced approach, a sudden movement, or a loud noise startles most animals. A surprised snake or skunk can be dangerous to you, to others, and to itself. Give animals extra room and time to adjust to your presence.

➤ **Plan ahead.** Know your equipment, your ability, and the area where you are hiking, and prepare accordingly. Be self-sufficient at all times; carry necessary supplies for changes in weather or other conditions. A well-executed trip is a satisfaction to you and to others.

➤ **Be courteous to other hikers** and to bikers and horseback riders you meet on the trails.

Tips on Enjoying Hiking in Richmond

HIKING WITH CHILDREN

WHILE THERE ARE NO AGE REQUIREMENTS FOR HIKING, use your best judgment. Flat, short trails are probably best if you're bringing along an infant. Toddlers who haven't quite mastered walking can still tag along, riding on an adult's back in a child carrier. Use common sense to judge a child's capacity to hike a particular trail, and always expect that the child will tire quickly and need to be carried. Many of the trails in this book are shared with mountain bikers, runners, and even some equestrians.

When packing for the hike, remember the child's needs as well as your own. Make sure children are adequately clothed for the weather, have proper shoes, and are protected from the sun with sunscreen. Kids dehydrate quickly, so make sure you have plenty of water for everyone.

THE BUSINESS HIKER

Whether you are in the Richmond area on business or are a resident, many of these hikes offer quick getaways from the demands of commerce. The city of Richmond is home to some of the best urban parkland on the East Coast. Instead of eating inside, you can pack a lunch and head out to picnic on a boulder beside the James River at Belle Isle or along the Virginia Capital Trail. Or plan ahead and take a small group of your business partners on a nearby hike in Pocahontas or Powhatan State Park.

THE TOURIST HIKER

A wealth of historical sites, homes, and battlefields are scattered across Virginia's Tidewater and Piedmont regions, with Richmond at the hub. Many of these destinations offer trails of their own; others lie en route to hikes profiled in this guide. Each year, thousands of visitors flock to Williamsburg, Monticello, Petersburg, and the Richmond National Battlefield parks. Sadly, many never leave their vehicles. America's history unfolded on Virginia's soil, and this guidebook invites you to tread in the footsteps of English settlers, American revolutionaries, slaves seeking freedom, Civil War soldiers, and Civilian Conservation Corps workers. Don't pass up the opportunity to walk a mile in their shoes.

OPPOSITE: View of the Appomattox River from High Bridge trestle (see High Bridge Trail State Park, page 268)

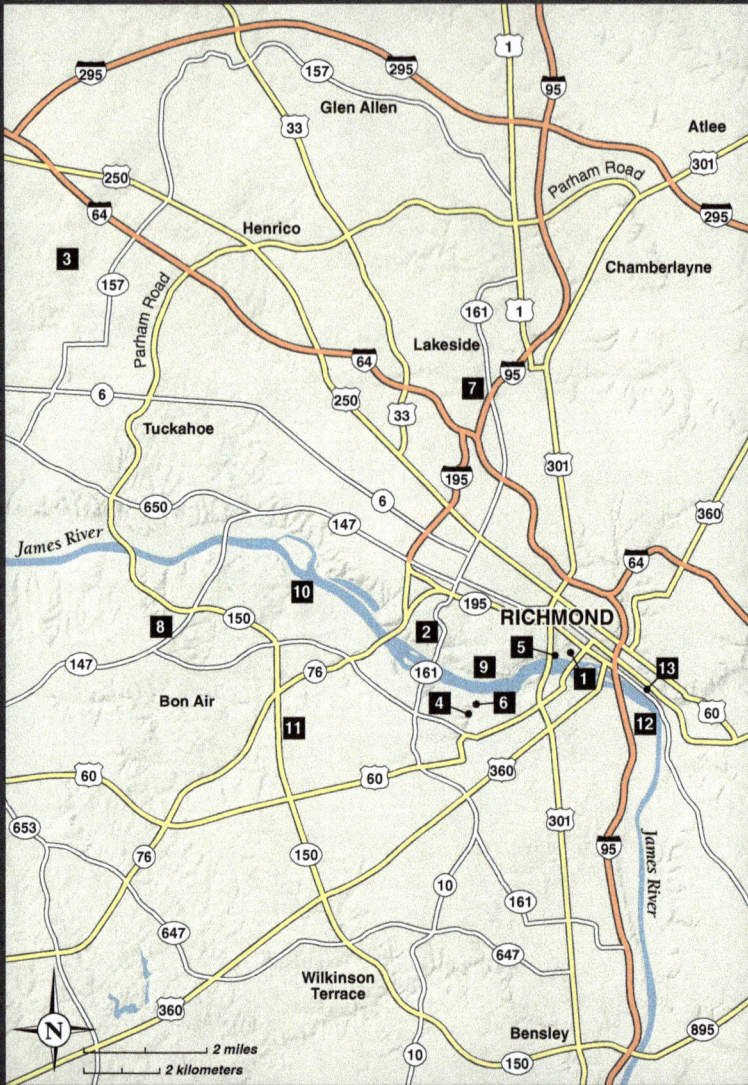

RICHMOND CENTRAL

1 BROWN'S ISLAND/ POTTERFIELD BRIDGE LOOP

View of downtown Richmond from the Floodwall Walk on the south bank of the James River, above Second Break rapid.

IT'S NOT AN OFFICIAL HIKE mapped or promoted by the City of Richmond, but with the opening of the T. Tyler Potterfield Bridge, this route opens up an easy and safe loop for viewing the James River and the downtown skyline.

DESCRIPTION

We suggest starting your visit at Brown's Island, which features a park where many of Richmond's premier outdoor events take place along the riverfront. Park for free on Fifth Street or in the Belle Isle parking lot just west on Tredegar Street. Tredegar Iron Works also has a paid parking lot. The bridge is across the street from Tredegar and is a great place to start this hike.

Runners, walkers, and hikers can now complete a scenic 2.4-mile loop that includes the Potterfield Bridge, Floodwall Walk, 14th Street (Mayo) Bridge, and Pipeline Rapids walkway. The surface is mostly gravel, sidewalk, or pavement, with a handful of grass, sand, or dirt patches in between. Walk the loop in either direction; you won't be disappointed, and it is easy to follow the route. For this hike, we will go counterclockwise.

The T. Tyler Potterfield Memorial Bridge is named in honor of a senior planner for the City of Richmond who died in 2014 at age 55. He spent years advocating and

DISTANCE & CONFIGURATION: 2.4-mile loop

DIFFICULTY: Easy

ELEVATION: 20' at trailhead, no significant rise

SCENERY: James River, floodwall, city skyline

EXPOSURE: Exposed most of the route

TRAFFIC: High, especially on Potterfield Bridge and Mayo Bridge

TRAIL SURFACE: Gravel, metal walkways and pedestrian bridge, paved path

HIKING TIME: 1 hour

SEASON: Year-round; Potterfield Bridge lit at night

ACCESS: No fee

WHEELCHAIR ACCESS: On Brown's Island and Potterfield Bridge

MAPS: See page 20.

DRIVING DISTANCE FROM CAPITOL: 1 mile

FACILITIES: Portable toilets on Brown's Island

CONTACT: City of Richmond Department of Parks, Recreation, and Community Facilities: 804-646-5743, richmondgov.com/parks; James River Park: 804-646-8911, jamesriverpark.org; river-level information for paddlers: 804-646-8228

LOCATION: Seventh and Tredegar Sts., downtown Richmond

COMMENTS: Brown's Island is located on the City of Richmond's Liberty Trail. While you're there, stop by the Richmond National Battlefield Park Visitor Center at Tredegar Iron Works as you complete your hike. For more information, visit nps.gov/rich.

planning for the bridge, which opened in December 2016. The former bridge was built in 1901 on top of a industrial dam from Brown's Island to the south bank of the James River in Manchester. At nearly 0.3 mile long and less than 20 feet above the river, the new bridge offers plenty of places to take in the views and hear the roar of the rapids. It has become one of Richmond's most popular outdoor attractions, a hub for gawkers and adventure seekers. It combines a picturesque location spanning the natural beauty of the James River in the middle of downtown, with fantastic views of the city's skyline. You'll be in the center of the action both on and off the river.

While crossing the bridge, the approach to the south side offers views of the Manchester Climbing Wall and the overlook above, both worth a look if you have time and there is access down to the base of the wall from the bridge. Just remember not to bother the belayers, who are concentrating on supporting a climber. The 60-foot cut-granite block wall is a remnant of the Richmond and Petersburg Railroad Bridge, which spanned the James River for much of the 19th century. Affectionately dubbed the Mayan Ruins due to its triangular shape, Manchester offers more than 40 routes that have evolved since the 1980s. Several matching remnant piers are lined across the James, and three are also marked and routed for climbs, according to the James River Park website.

Continue along the paved path past the first wooden staircase to climb up to the top of the Manchester Climbing Wall. For this hike, take the next staircase to the top, and if you want to see the downtown skyline from the overlook, follow the trail to the left. Retrace your steps and follow the paved path down to the gravel trail under the Manchester Bridge. (If you skip the staircase, the path wraps around the hill.)

Brown's Island/Potterfield Bridge Loop

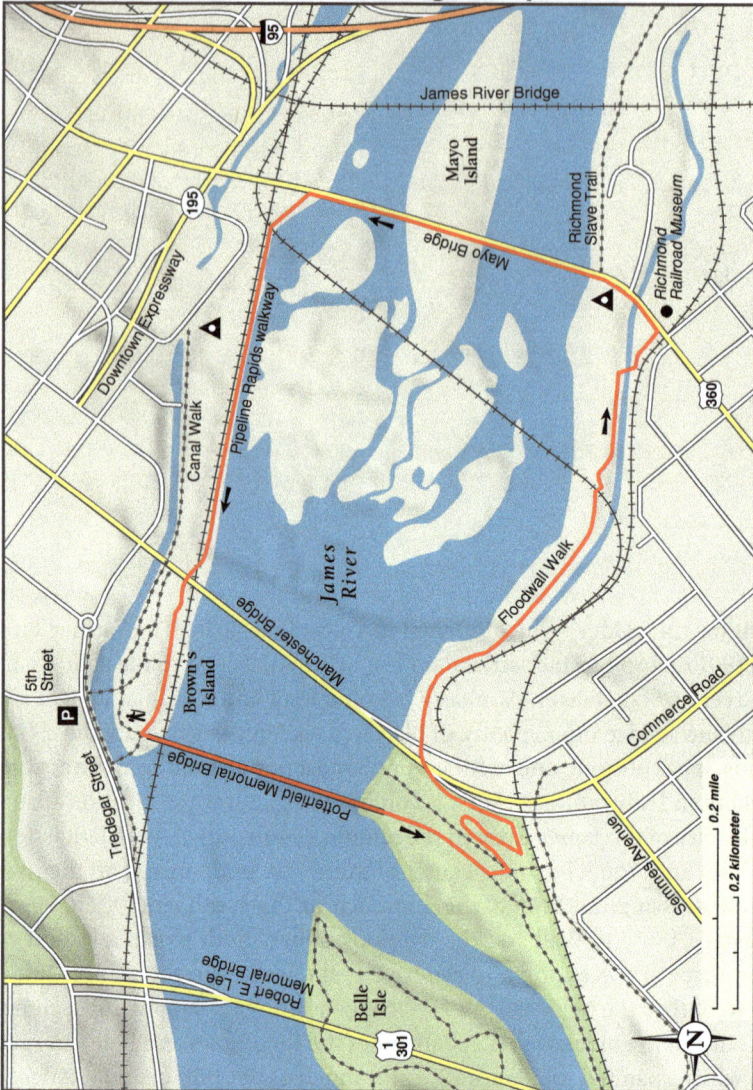

As you walk down the path, you will see eight 17-foot-tall welded steel rings called *The Path Untraveled* by artist Joshua Wiener lined across the hills on the south side of the trails. They were installed in 2017 as part of the unveiling of the Potterfield Bridge.

Follow the trail under the high concrete pillars of the Manchester Bridge, and pick up the winding trail over the gravel trail atop Floodwall Walk about 0.5 mile. This portion of the trail also offers panoramic views of the city skyline and the James River. The rapids through this section of the river are known as Second Break

(Class IV) and Southside (Class III) rapids. Depending on the water levels, you may spy some whitewater kayakers out enjoying the James.

The floodwall opened in 1994 and is designed to protect Richmond from floods of up to 32 feet with an average recurrence interval of 280 years, according to the City of Richmond. It is one of the largest flood-protection systems in the nation, and it opened miles of the James River to public access, with river walks, trails, and scenic overlooks. The total length is 3.2 miles, with 1.2 miles on the north bank of the river and 2 miles on the south bank.

The trail will cross over Norfolk Southern railroad tracks by way of a staircase and bridge then descend to a paved trail that leads to US 360/Hull Street. Take a left once the paved trail meets the sidewalk, and pass through the floodwall.

Watch for traffic as you cross the 14th Street Bridge, which is actually two spans with Mayo Island in the center. The sidewalk is narrow, and there is no buffer from the roadway. You will pass a recycling center on the left, and then the second span begins. The trail turns left and crosses train tracks before descending at a short staircase and ladder to the Pipeline Rapids walkway under the CSX railway viaduct. I suggest checking the water levels of the James (web search "Richmond Westham Gauge") before attempting to walk along the metal Pipeline catwalk, as it and portions of the trail can be inundated with water if the river is above 12 feet. This is a great place to watch kayaks and rafts playing in the rapids.

Due in part to the health of the James River, it is not unusual to see wildlife in downtown Richmond. You can find bald eagles, peregrine falcons, ospreys, and great blue herons, all likely to prey on the fish that migrate up the Falls of the James each year. Great blue herons are slender, grayish birds with sharp beaks, skinny legs, and huge wingspans. For several years, a large rookery could be found on Vauxhall Island, across from Pipeline Rapids walkway, but in recent years the herons appear to have moved elsewhere to raise their offspring.

Once the catwalk ends, take caution as you walk about 100 yards atop a narrow, uneven concrete section of the pipeline. There are no handrails, and if you have to pass oncoming walkers, it might be best for one person to stop and let the other pass. The trail passes along the sandy and rooted shoreline among volunteer trees about 300 feet before climbing up to Brown's Island under the Manchester Bridge. Follow the concrete walking trail back to the west side of the island to complete the loop.

NEARBY ACTIVITIES

If the Pipeline Rapids walkway is not to your liking, continue along the Floodwall Walk, and as you reach the pavement, look for the **Canal Walk** (804-788-6466, rvariver front.com). There will be a monument with a large cross commemorating Captain Christopher Newport's first visit, on May 24, 1607, to the place that would become

Richmond. Continue along the Canal Walk to the east end of Brown's Island, and follow the concrete path and bridge of your choice to get back to your vehicle.

• •

GPS TRAILHEAD COORDINATES N37° 32.119' W77° 26.606'

DIRECTIONS Brown's Island is accessible from Second Street by heading south on Brown's Island Way or from Byrd Street by taking South Fifth Street. Turn right onto Tredegar. You may park along the road on South Fifth Street or in the gravel and paved Belle Isle parking lot on the right (under the CSX railway viaduct). Tredegar has a paid parking lot, which might be best on a crowded weekend along the riverfront.

Several GRTC bus routes stop within one to three blocks of the park entrance. The island also has bike racks.

View from the Floodwall Walk on the south bank of the James River

The Pump House was built in 1882 under the supervision of city engineer Colonel Wilfred E. Cutshaw.

THIS HIKE TAKES VISITORS through two connecting Richmond parks: Byrd Park and Pump House Park, which is part of the James River Park System. This hike can be combined with one along the North Bank Trail, part of the James River Park Loop (page 37).

DESCRIPTION

Since the 1870s, William Byrd Park has been an outdoor recreation destination for Richmonders. The 200-acre park has three lakes; a 240-foot World War I memorial, the Carillon; Dogwood Dell; tennis and baseball facilities; a 1-mile fitness course walking track; a reservoir; plenty of trees; green spaces; and more. It is named after William Byrd II, whose family owned much of the area when Richmond was founded in 1737. The park was listed on the National Register of Historic Places in 2016.

Dogwood Dell is a 2,400-seat amphitheater owned and operated by the City of Richmond. Since 1956, it has been home to the Festival of Arts; a summer-long celebration of the arts featuring concerts, dance, and theater. Annual Fourth of July concerts and fireworks displays are also held there.

From the Carillon/Dogwood Dell parking lot, the large brick-and-concrete tower you can see is the Carillon, the commonwealth's monument to the approximately 3,700 Virginia men and women who died as a result of World War I. Dedicated

DISTANCE & CONFIGURATION: 1.6-mile figure eight, plus optional spurs

DIFFICULTY: Easy

ELEVATION: 215' at trailhead, 90' at low point

SCENERY: Hardwood and mixed forests, James River and Kanawha Canal, World War I memorial

EXPOSURE: Shaded except segments along the canal and the Carillon

TRAFFIC: Low; chance for mountain bikes on Dogwood Dell trails

TRAIL SURFACE: Dirt singletrack, grass

HIKING TIME: 45 minutes

SEASON: Year-round during daylight hours

ACCESS: No fee

WHEELCHAIR ACCESS: Wheelchairs not recommended except around the Carillon

MAPS: At park kiosks

DRIVING DISTANCE FROM CAPITOL: 4.5 miles

FACILITIES: Portable toilets at the Carillon and Pump House Park, baseball diamond, exercise trail, playground, tennis courts, Contact: City of Richmond Department of Parks, Recreation, and Community Facilities: 804-646-5743, richmondgov.com/parks

LOCATION: 1300 Blanton Ave., Richmond

COMMENTS: There is a small playground behind the Carillon. Barker Field, a park for dogs, is near the Dogwood Dell concert stage.

in 1932, the 240-foot tower houses fixed bronze bells that are played for special occasions. The design is an interpretation of the Italian campanile in Georgian classicism. A commission was formed about 1922 to study a design and a site, but public campaigns altered the initial proposal and delayed construction until 1931. It is listed on the National Register of Historic Places and is a Virginia Historic Landmark.

In 2017, the Department of General Services closed the Carillon for renovations, including exterior repairs, elevator replacement, masonry repointing, and window restoration. The first phase was completed in November 2018, in time for an Armistice Day Festival to celebrate the 100th anniversary of the end of World War I. Following the festival, the Carillon was closed again for further renovations, which are expected to be completed in 2020. Take a few minutes to walk around the Carillon, noting the long, tree-lined grassy mall in front. This area is filled with people during annual events like Arts in the Park and the Fourth of July celebrations.

To begin the hike in earnest, follow the trail behind the building toward the line of trees. Take a left down a granite staircase. This short trail leads behind Dogwood Dell and passes a spring before leading to a trail into the woods. Follow the signs for the Dogwood Dell hiking trail. This trail is separate from the other shared-use trail, which brings many mountain bikers to this hillside. Follow the Dogwood Dell trail as it steps along a series of cut-granite stepping-stones and then descends along a ravine, crossing a creek on a narrow, wooden hiker-only bridge.

As you walk this trail, keep an eye out for English ivy and other invasive species. These trails were designed and installed with volunteer labor, and much of the removal of invasive and nonnative plants has also been done by people who give their time to improve the parks.

As the trail reaches Pump House Drive, you can either walk along the roadway to Pump House Park or continue along a connector trail within Dogwood Dell. For

Byrd Park/Pump House Park

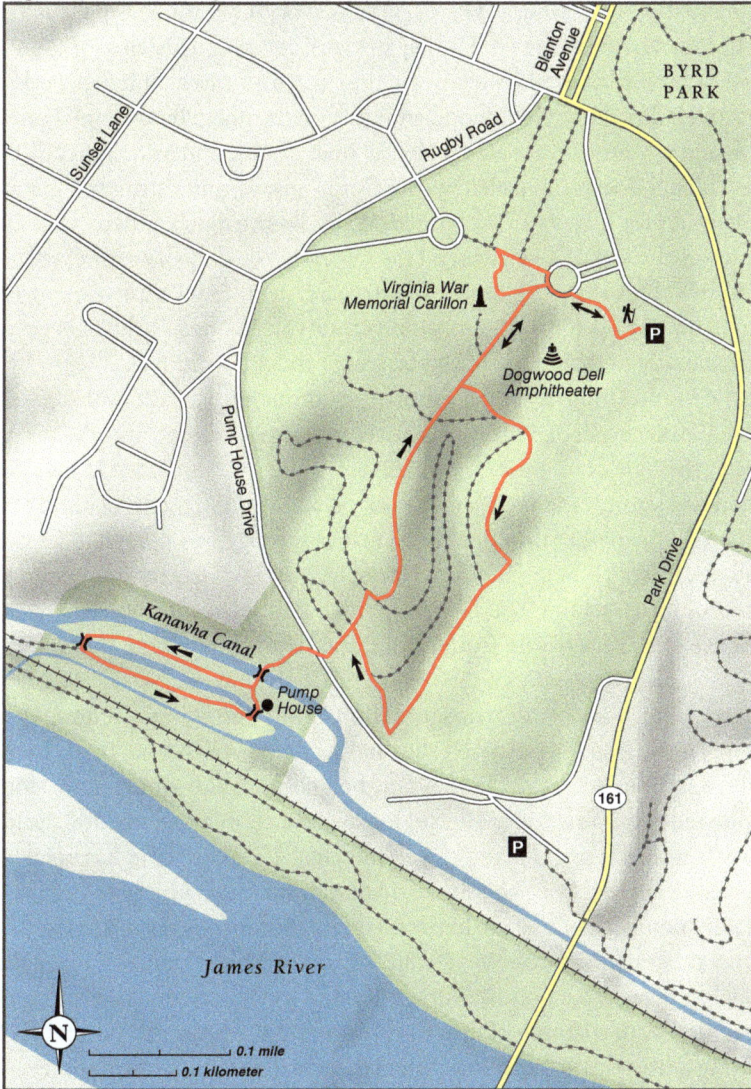

this hike, we stayed in the woods, turning right along the next trail, taking care to watch for mountain bikes. Once the trail reaches a somewhat steep decline with a partially covered pipeline, follow it down to the trailhead and cross the road to enter Pump House Park.

Cross the metal footbridge over the James River and Kanawha Canal. Two main sections of the canal meet at the Pump House. The watered section of the Lower Canal begins west of the Robert E. Lee Memorial Bridge along the North Bank Trail, connecting to the Pump House. The Upper Canal begins at the Pump House and connects to Bosher's Dam (west of the Willey Bridge), covering a distance of about 8 miles. A series of locks once carried vessels down the canal from Great Shiplock Park on Dock Street, through downtown Richmond and west on the north bank of the James River.

Turn your attention to the Pump House. Built in 1882 under the supervision of city engineer Colonel Wilfred E. Cutshaw, the Gothic gray-granite structure was designed to provide water for the city of Richmond. Water was channeled there from the James River, entering the canal from a dam on the north side of Williams Island, which is near Pony Pasture Rapids Park. For more than 40 years, the Pump House transported water up the hill you just hiked to a 26-foot-deep reservoir in Byrd Park. This water went, untreated, directly to Richmond businesses and residences until 1909.

But the Pump House also had a more glamorous side. Cutshaw designed an elegant open-air dance hall on its sweeping balcony. The space became a bustling venue, in use from the ballroom era to the swing era. By 1924, the Pump House no longer functioned as a pumping station, and the city sold the building's machinery for scrap metal during World War II. In the 1950s, just as the city was poised to demolish the Pump House, First Presbyterian Church bought it for $1. The city eventually regained possession of it but seldom used it. In the mid-1980s, the city officially established Pump House Park as separate from Byrd Park, further removing the gem from the public's gaze.

Retired James River Park manager Ralph White took on the Pump House as a project. He considered it a stabilized ruin and worked hard to raise funds to patch the roof, build handicap access, and clean out the debris. "With Gothic gray stone and a steeply pitched roof, [the Pump House] looks like a church or cathedral," said White. "That's what makes it distinctive—the architecture." The building has been used as a wedding venue and has been the site of many volunteer picnics, but as of this writing has not been renovated enough to be granted a full occupancy permit for larger events.

Follow the trail away from the Pump House past the bridge, following the canal. You will soon reach a part of the Three Mile Locks. The channel to the right of the locks provided both a source of drinking water and the power to pump it. That section was dug between 1880 and 1882 when the canal was closed to commercial transportation after the railroad tracks were laid on its towpath. The locks on the left with the cascading water are the former canal.

In 1785, the James River Company worked to build and maintain a canal system to allow bateaux (canal boats) passage around the 8 miles of the Falls of the James in Richmond. The locks would fit a boat measuring 91 feet long and 14.5 feet wide. Able to accommodate bulk cargo like grain and tobacco, canal boats were the safest and fastest way to move heavy freight. Smooth and stable, allowing both sleeping and dining, they were also the epitome of passenger travel for nearly 100 years. The canal ran nearly 200 miles from Richmond to Buchanan. Originally, it was intended to reach the Kanawha River in West Virginia, creating a water highway between the Atlantic Ocean and the Ohio Valley.

Cross over the wooden bridge and onto a wooden deck overlooking an old cut-granite arch. This is the Lower Arch, or George Washington's arch. This was the entrance to the main section of the canal. Built in 1786 with slave labor, it regulated water flow into the canal, allowing large, flat-bottomed bateaux to enter from the James River. According to park signage, George Washington stopped at the arch during his 1791 tour of Virginia when he was president of the James River and Kanawha Canal company. The sign reads: "Attended by a livery of servants dressed in red satin uniforms, he waited under the arch for a delegation of Richmond City Council members to join him for lunch. They arrived late and Washington dined alone." The stone wall below you was built in the late 1830s to hold up the high embankment of the canal towpath, located to your right. The railroad was laid in the towpath in 1880. It was moved to its present location, on a man-made ridge beside the river, in 1901 to accommodate a second set of tracks.

Follow the former towpath (and railway) about 0.2 mile back toward the Pump House. Take a few minutes to observe the flow of water through the locks and admire the stonework of the Pump House. Climb the staircase back up to the metal footbridge to exit the park. Cross the road and reenter the Dogwood Dell hiking trail. Retrace your steps back up the pipeline trail, this time continuing all the way to the top of the hill and back to the Carillon and eventually the parking lot where you began.

NEARBY ACTIVITIES

If you brought your dog on the hike, consider stopping at **Barker Field,** located in the Dogwood Dell parking area. It is a fenced, multiacre, wooded site and offers water, shelters, and seating. There are separate areas for large and small dogs. Barker Field opened in 1998 as Richmond's first off-leash dog park.

GPS TRAILHEAD COORDINATES N37° 32.458' W77° 28.981'

DIRECTIONS Byrd Park has a parking area next to Dogwood Dell and Barker Field. From downtown, take West Main Street (one-way) to South Boulevard Street. Turn left and cross over the Downtown Expressway (VA 195) into Byrd Park. South Boulevard becomes Blanton Avenue. Turn left onto Park Drive and immediately right into the park roadway for the Carillon and Dogwood Dell. The gravel parking lot will be in a wooded area to the right, just after a circular drop-off access road.

GRTC bus route 4 passes three blocks north of the Carillon. There are bike racks at Dogwood Dell near the trailhead.

Fall foliage along the trail in Deep Run Park

AN OASIS IN the busy western Henrico County suburbs, Deep Run Park is a welcome retreat, and the throngs of soccer players, families, dog walkers, and couples who flock here on sunny weekends attest to its popularity.

DESCRIPTION

The 167-acre Deep Run Park sits on land that in the 1800s was part of the railroad network that carried coal from the Deep Run and Springfield coal pits, located about 2 miles northeast of the park. The line ran south about 6 miles to the James River and Kanawha Canal, which facilitated the transportation of coal to downtown Richmond.

The centerpiece of the park is a bilevel pond encircled by a paved trail. Couples stroll by as youngsters timidly cast breadcrumbs to a gaggle of Canada geese that has made a permanent stopover of the small pond. Rambunctious schoolchildren frolic on the playground uphill, and teens play three-on-three on the adjacent basketball court after class. Fitness-conscious suburbanites tackle the exercise trail on their way home from work, and after-dinner dog walkers make their daily rounds.

A sign at the upper pond forbids swimming, boating, and ice-skating. Another instructs those fishing that there is a two-catch limit. Most fishing on this small body of water is probably catch-and-release, although the nearby picnic shelter often hosts weekend barbecues, so no one goes hungry.

DISTANCE & CONFIGURATION: 2.2-mile loop

DIFFICULTY: Moderate

ELEVATION: 175' at trailhead, 260' at high point

SCENERY: Suburban woods, duck pond

EXPOSURE: Mostly shaded; open around pond

TRAFFIC: Moderate; higher near pond

TRAIL SURFACE: Paved, dirt

HIKING TIME: 1 hour

SEASON: Year-round during daylight hours

ACCESS: No fee

WHEELCHAIR ACCESS: On the paved sections

MAPS: At henrico.us/rec

DRIVING DISTANCE FROM CAPITOL: 14 miles

FACILITIES: Restrooms, picnic shelter, fitness trail, playgrounds, ponds (fishing allowed), nature center with boardwalk, recreation center

CONTACT: 804-652-1430, henrico.us/rec

LOCATION: 9900 Ridgefield Pkwy., Henrico

COMMENTS: Feel free to explore the additional dirt trails that zigzag among and around the paved routes. The park is relatively small, so you can't get lost for long. Contact Henrico County Parks (804-501-7275) for details.

A wooden walkway bisects the pond atop a dam, which splits the pond into two levels. A gazebo and deck allow for gazing out upon the lower level, and bridges cross the creek that flows from the pond to join Deep Run in the marshland along Gaskins Road. The nature pavilion on the pond's northern shore is girded with extensive decking, complete with a second gazebo and a lofty boardwalk leading northeast for perhaps 100 yards to a wildlife-viewing station overlooking Deep Run.

At the center of the nature pavilion is a small building (restricted to park staff), the walls of which feature several dioramas and posters. These educational displays describe the habitats and wildlife of the mid-Atlantic.

Though the pond sees most of the action at Deep Run Park (excluding the soccer fields, which teem with participants and parents in spring and fall), the network of trails circumnavigating the park totals approximately 2 miles. The route mapped here begins at the second parking lot and heads north, away from the entrance. No need to lace up your hiking boots; tennis shoes will do on the paved trails. In a few spots, seeps wet the trail but are easily avoided. Deep Run is a handy spot for runners who would rather avoid the traffic of nearby modern suburbs, which seldom feature contiguous stretches of connected sidewalks. You may also spy a band of mountain bikers lapping the 2-mile trail around the outer boundaries of the park. Note, however, that the gravel fitness trail alone totals a meager 0.3 mile.

Unofficial dirt singletrack trails crisscross the woods in the park's eastern, northern, and western sections. You can readily stray from the route described here for an up-close glimpse of nature with little fear of getting lost. You may well arrive in an apartment complex or someone's backyard, but you'll never have to backtrack far to hit one of the paved loops again. Through the winter-bare woods, hikers can glimpse the roofs of surrounding suburban homes on even a few of the paved trails. When thick with summer vegetation, however, the forest becomes a verdant cloister, a delightful respite just a short drive from the much-vaunted shopper's paradise at Short Pump.

Deep Run Park

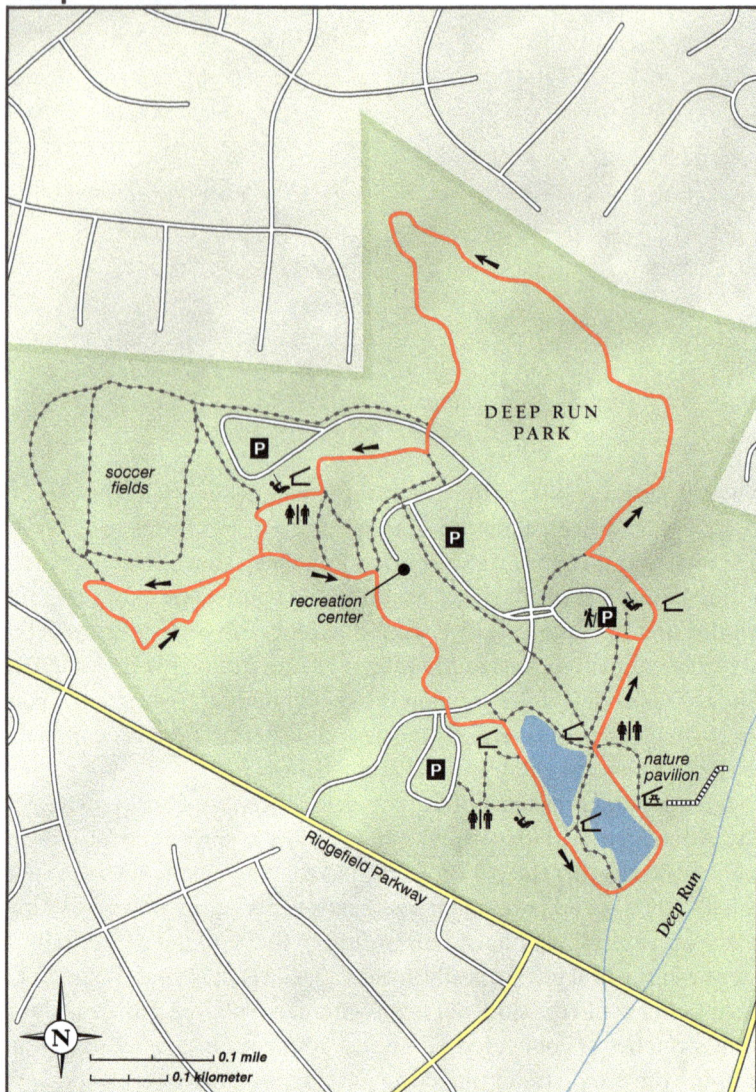

American holly is scattered throughout the understory of this relatively mature, largely red-oak forest. Trees en route are identified with signs, providing budding botanists a chance to test their tree-identification skills. Species include red and white oak, pignut hickory, loblolly pine, red maple, dogwood, red cedar, sweet gum, yellow poplar, and the less common ironwood, named for its hefty, solid wood. The relatively short (20- to 30-foot-tall) ironwood is also referred to as the eastern hophornbeam because of its hopslike seedpods. The tree's scientific name, *Ostrya*

virginiana, is one of many that early naturalists coined in honor of the common-wealth, despite such species' presence throughout the eastern United States.

Begin at the second parking lot (see Directions, below), tracking clockwise uphill along the paved path behind the family picnic shelters and a small playground. After meandering through a heavily wooded section, the trail turns sharply left and descends slightly toward the center of the park and its main access road. Cross the road carefully, and bear right back into the woods. You'll soon pass more picnic shelters, restrooms, and an elaborate playground that fronts a large parking lot, which serves the soccer fields in the park's western corner. For this hike, we took a gravel path into the woods for an optional 0.5-mile loop, which passes along a wooden boardwalk constructed by volunteers from the rvaMORE (Mid-Atlantic Off-Road Enthusiasts) organization over an area prone to staying muddy. Volunteers installed other such crossings to make the trail network less damaging to the environment.

When the trail comes to a T off the boardwalk, take a left to loop back to the main paved trail. The trail crosses over a small, sometimes dry creek. Bear right at the upcoming intersection and descend along a rocky rivulet flanked by cedars.

From the park's westernmost trail, you will descend toward the first parking area and the pond, crossing the main park road again and passing the parking lot on your right. By hiking the trails in this order, you save the pond and nature pavilion for last, allowing you to take a load off on a bench overlooking the pond to watch the ducks and geese beg for handouts. If you're hiking with kids still full of vim and vigor, let them romp at the playground or perhaps make a quick loop of the fitness trail. Numerous pathways diverge from, but quickly rejoin, the pond loop.

To return to your car, follow either the park road or the pathway just beyond the restrooms northwest of the nature pavilion. It is a short stroll from the pond through a primarily pine wood dotted with cedars.

• •

GPS TRAILHEAD COORDINATES N37° 37.564' W77° 35.429'

DIRECTIONS From Richmond, take I-64 to Exit 180A and follow Gaskins Road south past Three Chopt Road to Ridgefield Parkway. Turn right and then right again into the park. You will pass one parking lot on the right upon entering. This first lot is most convenient to the fitness trail, basketball court, playground, and pond. A second lot, also on the right, is closer to restrooms, a second playground, shelters, and the nature pavilion, and the lot where the trailhead of this hike is located. A third lot for the recreation center is across the park road, and a fourth lot provides access to soccer fields, more restrooms, and a very elaborate playground.

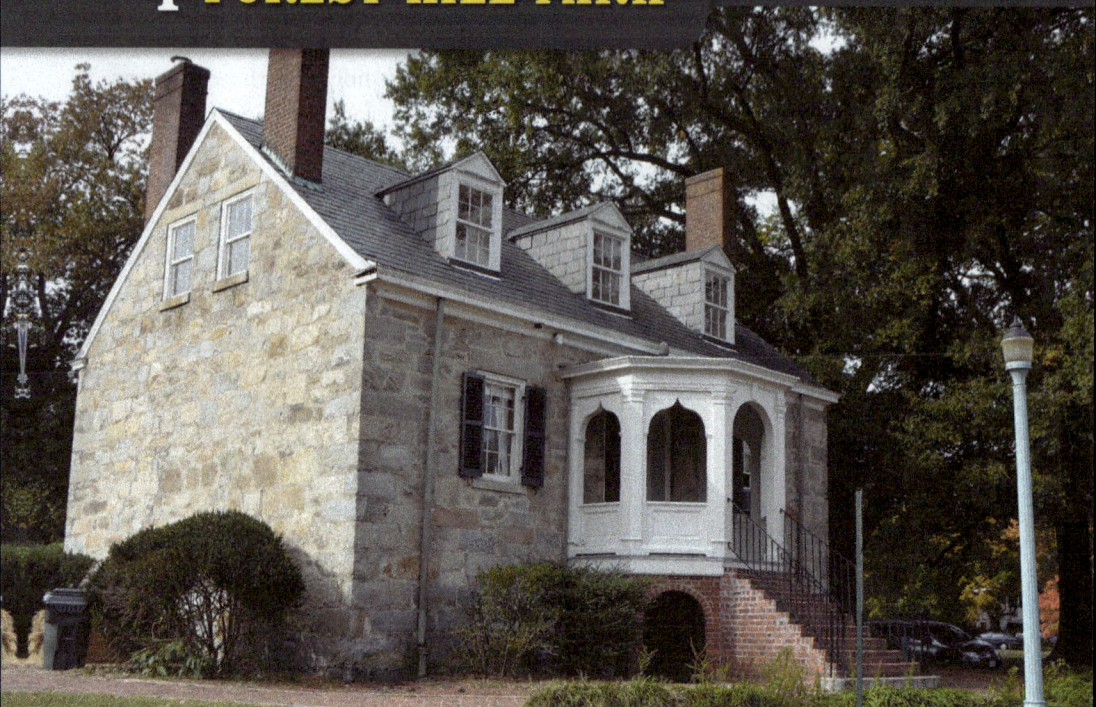

The Old Stone House was built in the 1800s with granite quarried on the property.

IN THE 1880S, a trolley terminus was established and an amusement park was built on the site of storied Forest Hill Park. The park has had many iterations over a long history, but the network of trails in this former quarry site has played a large role in its return to glory.

DESCRIPTION

This 105-acre park in South Richmond has an interesting history. It was once a granite quarry, one of dozens on the banks of the James River. The Old Stone House in the southwest portion of the park was built in the 1830s and '40s with granite from the quarry, which operated where the man-made lake is now. The house was once the residence for an old country estate known as Boscobel. In the heyday of the city's streetcar development, the park was an amusement park, according to the nonprofit volunteer group Friends of Forest Hill Park. In the 1880s, it was called Woodland Park and was part of the marketing strategy for a new streetcar subdivision called Woodland Heights. This part of South Richmond was still pastoral in nature at that time, but the area was a favorite destination for city dwellers seeking an escape from the clutter and smell of the city. In the 1930s, after the Great Depression led to the amusement park's closure, the land was purchased by the city and became a public park. The entire park is now registered as a Virginia Historic Landmark.

DISTANCE & CONFIGURATION: 2.2-mile loop, plus optional spurs

DIFFICULTY: Easy

ELEVATION: 160' at trailhead, 83' at low point

SCENERY: Hardwood and mixed forests, pond, Reedy Creek

EXPOSURE: Shaded, except segments along pond

TRAFFIC: Moderate; expect mountain bikes on much of the trail network

TRAIL SURFACE: Dirt singletrack, gravel, paved

HIKING TIME: 1 hour

SEASON: Year-round during daylight hours

ACCESS: No fee

WHEELCHAIR ACCESS: On the paved sections

MAPS: At park kiosks and at rvamore.org/trails

DRIVING DISTANCE FROM CAPITOL: 3.6 miles

FACILITIES: Restrooms at the large parking area near the shelter on West 42nd Street (additional portable toilets at the Reedy Creek parking lot at the Riverside Drive trailhead), shelters, playground, pond, old stone house, tennis courts

CONTACT: City of Richmond Department of Parks, Recreation, and Community Facilities: 804-646-5743, richmondgov.com/parks

LOCATION: 4021 Forest Hill Ave., Richmond

COMMENTS: Portions of the trail are shared with mountain bikers and runners, although pedestrians have the right-of-way. Take time to explore the huge boulders in Reedy Creek, and visit Forest Hill Park's Saturday farmers market.

These days, Forest Hill Park is still an attraction. During the growing season, it is home to the Saturday South of the James Market, the best farmers market in town, and on snowy days the hill along Forest Hill Park Avenue is the most popular spot in South Richmond to sled. The trail network connects with the James River Park System and brings in plenty of mountain bikers. After heavy downpours, kayakers can sometimes be found paddling down the raging, swollen waters of Reedy Creek.

Forest Hill Park has a wealth of singletrack trails, but this hike will only briefly share those pathways. They are all good for hiking, as long as you are aware that faster-moving mountain bikes may pop up from time to time.

The hike begins from the large parking area accessed from the New Kent Avenue entrance off West 42nd Street. Pass the first shelter, and park near the lower shelter. Opposite, a stone staircase with a brick walkway descends through the woods toward Forest Hill Park Lake. Take care; about halfway down, a trail frequented by mountain bikers crosses the walkway.

Some of my favorite details of Forest Hill Park are the granite walkways, staircases, and retaining walls along the trails, which recall the park's origins as a quarry. You'll find many hidden grottoes and trails along the edges of the bedrock, and in many shaded areas, a deep-green mossy hue covers the mortar lines and cracks of exquisite stonemasonry. The work was done in the same style as can be seen in Joseph Bryan Park in Richmond's Northside.

When you reach the lake, walk clockwise around the wide, paved pathway lined by large trees, including many sycamores. In 2009 more than 30,000 cubic yards of muck were dredged from the Forest Hill Park Lake, sediment and debris that had

Forest Hill Park

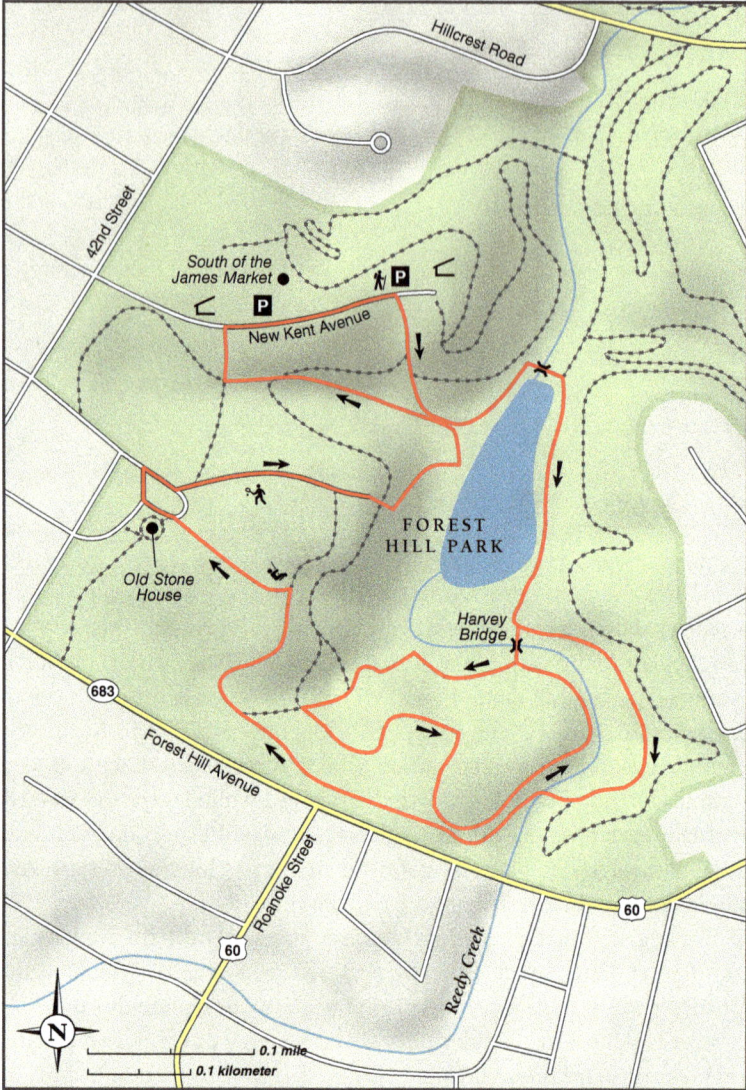

washed down Reedy Creek and settled in the lake since the 1970s, turning it into a silted, cattail-choked marsh. Walkways and water channels that had been buried for years suddenly reappeared, to the delight of ducks, turtles, and fish. A gazebo, a shelter, and several picnic tables and benches now dot the shoreline.

Cross a spillway bridge above the dam at the north end of the lake. If you prefer to connect to the James River Park Loop at Reedy Creek, take a left and follow the path along the creekbed to a tunnel under Riverside Drive; walk through or over the tunnel to connect to that wonderful trail system. Otherwise, take a right and continue along the path until you see a shelter and the Harvey Bridge. Take this footbridge over Reedy Creek, which feeds into the lake near this spot.

Park signage near the bridge says that a full loop around the lake is 0.46 mile round-trip, completed using the Harvey Bridge near the point where Reedy Creek reaches the lake. The bridge was dedicated in 2010 in memory of four members of the well-respected Bryan Harvey family, nearby residents who were murdered on New Year's Day in 2006. After crossing the bridge, take a right and begin looking for a trail cut into the quarry wall to climb to the higher levels of the park's interior. This path is narrow and has several ruts, so take precautions, and if you are hiking with children, keep a close eye on them, as there is a drop-off to the right of the trail.

At the top, turn left and follow the path through a forest of pines and hardwoods. This portion of the trail merges with the path most popular with mountain bikers, so again be alert. Take a right at trail junction marker FH12.

You will soon come upon a mysterious 9-foot-tall granite-and-stone pyramid that is somewhat hidden under a canopy of holly and pine trees and is located not far from the intersection of Forest Hill Avenue and Roanoke Street. As the story goes, the pyramid was a forgotten relic. It had been covered with ivy and weeds for decades before volunteers from Friends of Forest Hill Park cleared away the invasive menace in 2011.

Why is it there? Speculation is that the pyramid marks a slave burial site or that it is a distinctive feature of an azalea garden that once graced the park. Perhaps it is a memorial to Confederate soldiers, like the 90-foot-tall Monument to the Confederate War Dead in Hollywood Cemetery. A more plausible conclusion, endorsed by Friends of Forest Hill Park, is that it marks the grave of a "pet" bear that inhabited the park around the turn of the 20th century when it was an amusement park.

When the trail reaches a paved park road, take a left. Slowly wind back down to the lake and recross the Harvey Bridge. Take a right to walk along the trail on the other side of Reedy Creek. As you venture along this part of the trail, watch for old and crumbled park drainage and stonework damaged by erosion, tree roots, and neglect. The huge, smooth granite boulders in the creek are a great place to stop and admire the beauty of this park feature. The flow of water is normally just a trickle, but after rainstorms it can be a raging torrent.

The path continues along a fenceline and then opens to the right at a rocky crossing of the creek in a flat section around the boulders. Cross here and carefully walk up the dirt path to the main park road. Take a left and follow the road to the playground. Another left, across the grass, will take you to the Old Stone House, which still hosts functions and has some historical maps and photos of the park.

If you are ready to stop, follow the path directly across from the front door of the house to a brick, tree-lined trail, which leads over a brick patio and past a seating area for an old spring to a double staircase. Take the stairs up to return to the parking lot. This should put you at the first shelter in the New Kent parking lot; take a right to find your vehicle.

If you have another 0.5 mile in you, walk down the tree-lined roadway that passes to the left of the tennis courts through the park maintenance buildings. There will be a grand stone staircase; follow it down to the first landing and take the left path back down to the lake (either path leads down to the waterway). Briefly walk along the lake, and as a shelter comes into view on the left at a junction, take a left up a paved roadway back to the New Kent parking lot at the first shelter. Take a right back to your vehicle.

· ·

GPS TRAILHEAD COORDINATES N37° 31.260' W77° 28.379'

DIRECTIONS If driving from downtown, take Belvidere Street or South Ninth Street across the James River, and travel along Semmes Avenue. Turn right onto West 41st Street and follow the road to the park's large parking area, accessible from West 42nd Street at New Kent Avenue. If you cross the James River on Belvidere (Robert E. Lee Bridge/US 301), immediately upon reaching the southern end of the bridge, you can exit onto Riverside Drive, heading west (right). Take a left onto West 42nd Street and turn left into the park at New Kent Avenue.

GRTC bus routes 2A and 2B stop on Forest Hill Avenue near the Old Stone House. The park has bike racks.

Water cascades down large granite boulders in Reedy Creek at Forest Hill Park.

The pedestrian bridge to Belle Isle is suspended under the Robert E. Lee Memorial Bridge.

THE JAMES RIVER PARK SYSTEM is the best natural asset in the Richmond area, and Belle Isle is the wild centerpiece in the heart of urban downtown. There are dozens of entry points to this loop, including from North Bank Park, Maymont, Pump House Park, Reedy Creek, and Belle Isle (both banks of the river).

DESCRIPTION

Begin this hike from the Belle Isle parking trailhead and take a counterclockwise loop. Through experience and word-of-mouth, more mountain bikers ride the trail clockwise, which could help diminish the chances of a rider surprising you from behind. Keep in mind that this well-worn singletrack is very popular with cyclists and runners, which travel in both directions. Heavy vegetation will block neighborhoods and views of the James River for most of the trail loop. Except for occasional trains and automobile noise, you may feel like you're hiking along a mountain trail, far away from urban trappings.

To follow the route mapped here, begin by ascending the gravel trail under the Robert E. Lee Memorial Bridge. Cross the dry bed of the James River and Kanawha Canal by a wide footbridge, and take a left onto the North Bank Trail. This gravel doubletrack will pass below the Oregon Hill neighborhood, with the canal to the left (trees and underbrush grow in this abandoned, unwatered section).

DISTANCE & CONFIGURATION: 6.4-mile loop, plus optional spurs

DIFFICULTY: Moderate

ELEVATION: 48' at trailhead, 174' at high point

SCENERY: James River, mixed woodlands, abandoned quarries

EXPOSURE: Mostly shaded on the north side; open along bridges and Belle Isle

TRAFFIC: High

TRAIL SURFACE: Dirt singletrack, except wide gravel pathways at Belle Isle

HIKING TIME: 2.5 hours

SEASON: Year-round during daylight hours

ACCESS: Parking at several lots along the route (for this hike, we chose the Belle Isle parking lot)

WHEELCHAIR ACCESS: On Belle Isle

MAPS: At jamesriverpark.org/visit-the-park/maps

DRIVING DISTANCE FROM CAPITOL: 1.2 miles

FACILITIES: Portable toilets in parking area and on Belle Isle

CONTACT: City of Richmond Department of Parks, Recreation, and Community Facilities: 804-646-5743, richmondgov.com/parks; James River Park: 804-646-8911, jamesriverpark.org

LOCATION: 300 Tredegar St., Richmond

COMMENTS: The trail is heavily trafficked by runners, mountain bikers, and hikers. Take precautions and remember that pedestrians have the right-of-way.

You'll reach the gate of a chain-link fence, with the CSX railway and Dominion Energy headquarters on the left. On the right is the historic Hollywood Cemetery, the final resting place of two US presidents, the only Confederate president, and thousands of well-known Richmonders. Follow the gravel doubletrack under a shaded section before reaching a wooden ramp and a rock garden that climbs up along the ridgeline above the canal. The trail passes through a low area full of invasive species like kudzu and English ivy before reentering a wooded stretch. After traversing a maintenance area for the cemetery, you'll cross a wooden bridge that climbs through a series of switchbacks to reach Riverview and Mount Calvary Cemeteries.

The North Bank Trail was built largely by volunteer labor, beginning in the 1990s, and often travels just below the top edges of bluffs. This terrain was quarried for its granite, which was used to build much of Richmond. You'll see a brown park sign with an option to take a hiking-only trail; use this shortcut to avoid a series of switchbacks and continue west on the trail.

After crossing a wooden bridge in a ravine, the trail climbs a long rock garden, the result of an effort to curb trail erosion. Volunteers used a pulley system from the cemetery above to deliver many of the stones to the trail here.

The trail soon reaches another chain-link fence, signaling that you have reached North Bank Park (see page 56). The metal pedestrian bridge would take you over the canal and train tracks to Texas Beach, a well-known hangout for Richmonders, but take the series of wooden staircases up to the parking lot to continue our hike. If you prefer, you may instead continue along the trail through switchbacks designed to allow mountain bikes to progress up at a lower slope than the passage at the staircase.

From North Bank, the trail for this hike follows an off-trail urban section to connect to Maymont. Follow Texas Avenue for one block, then take a left on Kansas

James River Park Loop

Avenue and walk five blocks. Since my hike, city trail-building staff and volunteers built a 0.4-mile connection from North Bank to Maymont that follows the bank along the canal. This wooded, natural-surface path flows along below the hilltop of the Maymont neighborhood. It crosses a small brook, passes an old granite quarry, and eventually tunnels through a large stand of 30-foot-tall bamboo before connecting to a wooden ramp on the eastern edge of Maymont. This new segment would likely make for a more enjoyable hike; just keep an eye out for mountain bikers.

From the street route, you'll see a trailhead on Hampton Street at Maymont to reconnect with the trail. Descend the trail through a rock garden laid by volunteers. A long wooden ramp will connect down to the flat gravel path that runs between the canal and the park. This wide area of the canal was a turning basin for bateaux and provided access to Maymont, the former home of James and Sallie Dooley, who lived on the 100-acre Victorian estate overlooking the James River from 1893 to 1925. From the trail, you'll be able to see the Japanese Gardens and the black bear enclosure before passing under the Boulevard Bridge to climb up to the Pump House (see page 23) parking lot and trailhead.

Follow the trail to the right out of the parking lot, and take a right across the Boulevard Bridge. Formerly known as the Nickel Bridge, due to the cost of the toll long ago, it provides beautiful views to the west of the river below and the high-arching Atlantic Coast Line Railway Bridge in the distance. The walkway is narrow, but there are railings, so it is safe for children. Pedestrians have the right-of-way, but watch for runners and cyclists. Once you reach the south end of the bridge, take a right to continue on the loop trail on a section known as the Buttermilk Trail.

Climb another rock garden as you pass under the bridge and continue along the western section of the trail, known as Buttermilk Heights; it has steep embankments and is rooty and eroded in spots, so watch your step. The trail is also almost completely shaded, while the roadway above, Riverside Drive, is designated as a Richmond Scenic Byway. The trail and road both wind and undulate along ridgelines and ravines; the terrain in this section was heavily altered by granite quarries.

As the trail approaches the West 42nd Street access for the main section of James River Park, it descends to pass underneath the staircase tower. East of the tower is the Neatherwood Quarry, which offers a 0.3-mile loop trail. For this hike, we continued to the left where the trail climbs a stone staircase that has an accompanying ramp for mountain bikes.

The trail continues about 0.3 mile before reaching the Reedy Creek parking lot and trailhead, which offers a water fountain and portable toilet. You can connect to the gravel park road beyond the park headquarters to reach Belle Isle or follow the loop route, crossing Reedy Creek and continuing along the Buttermilk Trail. If you want to add a 2.5-mile loop, pass through the tunnel under Riverside Drive to connect with Forest Hill Park (see page 32).

This section of the Buttermilk Trail has many large hardwoods but is under attack by invasive plants, especially English ivy. There will be several narrow sections along the trail, and a couple of bridges cross springs from the hillside to the right of the trail. Soon you'll come upon the old spring that gives the Buttermilk Trail its name. It hearkens back to when there were farms on the south bank and milk was kept cold in the spring before being taken to market in Richmond.

The trail crosses the entrance road to the 22nd Street parking lot before climbing to the trailhead and staircase tower that connects to Belle Isle. You'll find a portable toilet, a water fountain, and a kiosk with a trail map here. Follow the granite staircase to the tower.

From atop the tower, take in the view of Belle Isle, dubbed Broad Rock by city founder William Byrd II. The 54-acre island was once known as Bell's Isle in homage to a resident Scotsman who operated a horse-racing track on the site. Upon his departure, the island's nomenclature was recast in French for respectability's sake—or so the legend has it.

Take the staircase down and, from the base of the tower, find your way through the Southside Rocks area of Belle Isle. The rounded rocks are a popular side trip for park visitors who explore the pools and lounge on the large, smooth stones. Rock-hop your way across the field of boulders, looking for a concrete wall with a metal ladder. After you climb the ladder, you will pass over a metal walkway and a strainer gate that still gathers debris, although the hydroelectric plant is no longer in service.

In the course of your hike on the island, you will see numerous remnants of industrial operations that were housed on Belle Isle in the 19th and early 20th centuries—for instance, the ruins of the hydroelectric plant once operated by Virginia Electric Power Co. (VEPCO), a precursor of Dominion Energy, and the ruins of an iron foundry. On the east end of the island, you'll find the ruins of the Old Dominion Iron and Steel Company, which operated metalworks on Belle Isle well into the 20th century.

Take a left onto the wide, crushed-stone path that loops around Belle Isle. As you round the island's western edge, the rocks below are a good spot to relax and watch the whitewater kayakers playing in the First Break rapids. Next you will pass a pond, complete with a fishing pier, on your right. Granite cliffs tower over the pond, the product of a bygone quarrying operation. Rock-climbing enthusiasts have a series of routes on the quarry walls.

Continue along the path, looking to the left at all the huge granite boulders along the river. On most days, the rocks will have plenty of people out enjoying this outdoor paradise. Soon you'll pass Class III–IV Hollywood Rapids, on the left. Kayak and raft guides are the island's modern entrepreneurs. Keep your eyes peeled for their colorful crafts darting about in the whitewater. In its history, these granite shoals were the site of the island's first industry, fishing. American Indians who inhabited the island relied on the James for sustenance.

As the trail emerges from the shaded path at a junction, find the informative sign that outlines the island's past and its role in the Civil War in particular. The flat expanse of land on Belle Isle's eastern shore (now mostly beneath the Lee Bridge) was the site of a Confederate prison. Earthen berms are visible reminders of the prison, which housed upward of 8,000 Union prisoners of war. Two or three times that number passed through the mostly tent brig during the course of the war. Many perished from disease and were interred on the island, their remains later moved to Richmond National Cemetery.

Walk up the long concrete ramp under the Lee Bridge to access the 1,040-foot suspended pedestrian walkway that has connected Belle Isle to the north bank at Tredegar Street since 1991. Take in the views of the downtown skyline, river, CSX train trestle, and more. The ramp on the north bank leads back toward Tredegar Street, and it's a short walk to the Belle Isle parking lot.

• •

GPS TRAILHEAD COORDINATES N37° 32.062' W77° 26.914'

DIRECTIONS Access Belle Isle from Second Street by heading south on Brown's Island Way or from Byrd Street by taking South Fifth Street. Turn right onto Tredegar. You may park along the road on South Fifth Street, at the main visitor center for Richmond National Battlefield Park, or in the gravel Belle Isle parking lot on the right. The lot is under the CSX railway viaduct. The footbridge is suspended under the Robert E. Lee Memorial Bridge and extends from Tredegar Street to Belle Isle.

Several GRTC bus routes stop within one to three blocks of the park entrance. Belle Isle has bike racks.

Great blue herons can frequently be spotted along the banks of the James River.

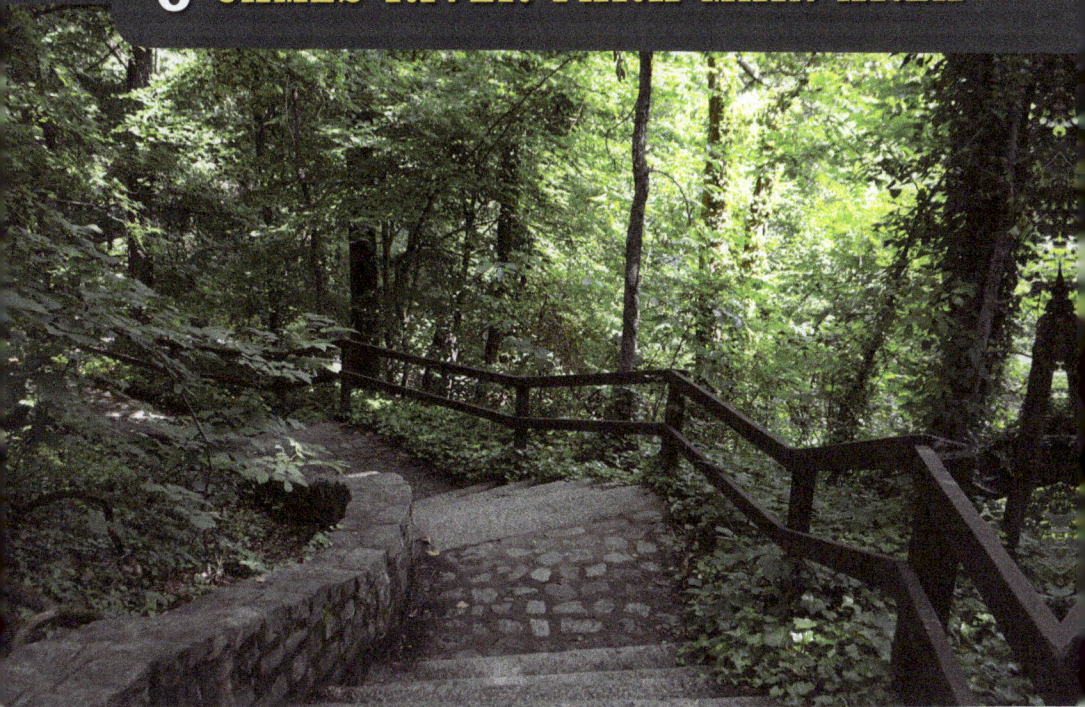

A granite staircase leads to the trail from the parking area.

BISECTED LENGTHWISE BY A RAILROAD TRACK, the main section of James River Park retains a distinctly urban character. In addition to providing up-close views of boulders and islands along the banks of the James, this route passes under the Boulevard Bridge at its western terminus and crosses a lofty walkway that doubles as an observation deck. When the river is low, this hike could also be done via rock-hopping alongside the river.

DESCRIPTION

Richmond's James River Park consists of nearly 20 noncontiguous parcels, which together significantly multiply the outdoor-recreation options of Richmond residents. Besides providing water access to anglers and paddlers, the almost 550-acre park offers waterside trails for walking, running, and cycling and is home to a surprising diversity of wildlife—a testament both to nature's persistence within the modern city and an urbanite desire to escape into the outdoors.

This is particularly true of James River Park's Main Area, where the park headquarters stands a short distance from the Norfolk Southern Railway tracks, which are still active. The tracks run east–west through the park's Main Area and have necessitated the construction of two concrete footbridges with towers and a spiral staircase to cross them. Yet the river frontage remains popular despite the occasional

DISTANCE & CONFIGURATION: 2.5-mile out-and-back, with a balloon and optional trails

DIFFICULTY: Easy

ELEVATION: 140' at trailhead, 66' at low point

SCENERY: James River, Boulevard Bridge

EXPOSURE: Shaded; open along the river

TRAFFIC: Moderate; higher along Buttermilk Trail

TRAIL SURFACE: Gravel, dirt

HIKING TIME: 1 hour

SEASON: Year-round during daylight hours; best avoided after rainfall

ACCESS: No fee

WHEELCHAIR ACCESS: Not recommended for wheelchairs

MAPS: At visitor center and jamesriverpark.org

DRIVING DISTANCE FROM CAPITOL: 3 miles

FACILITIES: Portable toilets, water fountain, park headquarters and visitor center, picnic shelters, canoe and kayak put-in, mountain bike trail

CONTACT: City of Richmond Department of Parks, Recreation and Community Facilities: 804-646-5743, richmondgov.com/parks; James River Park: 804-646-8911, jamesriverpark.org

LOCATION: 4301 Riverside Dr., Richmond

COMMENTS: Dogs are allowed but subject to a leash ordinance. Picnicking is permitted, but glass containers are not. Paddlers can call 804-646-8228 for river-level information.

rumble of passing freight, and some visitors come primarily to gawk at the skyline from atop the walkways.

Within the Main Area, a wide gravel path north of the railroad tracks leads to spur paths connecting to the river. Mountain bikers frequent the winding dirt singletrack known as the Buttermilk Trail, which is pressed against the hillside below Riverside Drive. Dog walkers, hikers, and runners tend to gravitate toward the river along the doubletrack road, away from cyclists. Making use of Buttermilk Trail at the end of this loop route will minimize backtracking, but be mindful of approaching cyclists.

It's possible to begin this hike from the Reedy Creek trailhead and parking area, which is linked to the river by the aforementioned walkways. However, the route mapped starts at the West 42nd Street parking lot and trailhead. The lot is not open at all times of the year, so if the gates are closed, park on Riverside Drive.

Take the granite staircase located past a kiosk from the parking lot. The stairs lead down to a bridge across the railroad tracks and a concrete tower with a spiral staircase. Descend to the gravel trail along a side channel of the river and the islands and rocky shoreline of the James. Take a left at the base of the tower to go west along the main path.

After periods of rain, muddy spots develop and little brooks from the hillsides above often trickle across the road. A few rough concrete patches where the roadway narrows allow vehicles—such as whitewater rafting companies—to pass without causing more damage and erosion to the path. In periods of heavy rainfall, the James swells over its banks. Look closely and you will see debris and detritus wrapped about tree trunks and lodged amid rock formations in the channel. Hydrophilic species, such as beech, sycamore, and birch, grow along the shore, often entwined with vines. In periods of drought, the river recedes to reveal rocks and pebbles, the

James River Park Main Area

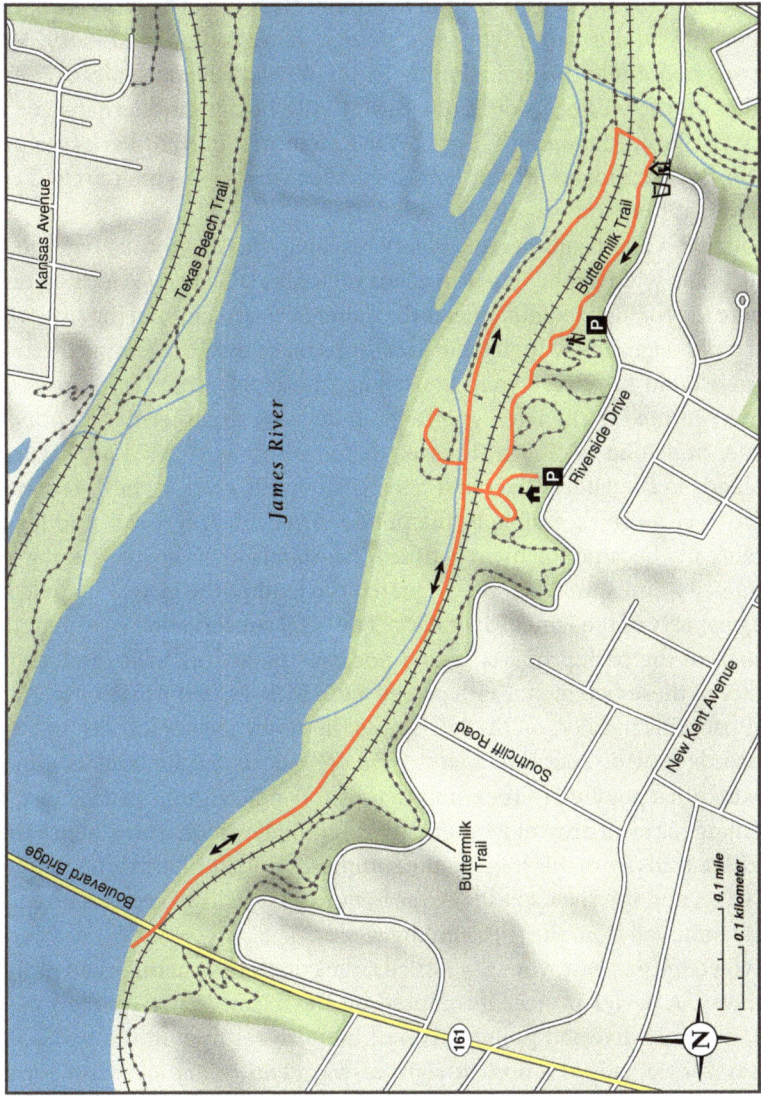

remnants of larger stones churned to bits by torrential waters then smoothed by the river's continuous flow.

When you see an opening and a picnic shelter, a rough spur leads to the water's edge, where rafting companies drop off equipment for guided trips. If you'd like, you can take this spur trail along the riverbank and rejoin the main path just before it passes under Boulevard Bridge. For this hike, I continued along the main path due to excessive mud.

Pass under the Boulevard Bridge to admire the view. The steel span measures 2,030 feet long and is set on concrete pilings. It was completed in 1925 and has been renovated a few times, including in the 1990s, when a pedestrian walkway was added on the western side. Look beyond the bridge and perhaps you can see the lofty Carillon, Richmond's World War I memorial in Byrd Park (see page 23), visible on the north bank of the James. Farther west is the high-arched concrete Atlantic Coast Line Railway Bridge.

Though it widens considerably before reaching the Chesapeake Bay, the James is almost 0.5 mile wide by the time it reaches Richmond. The city is located on the fall line, where the rolling Piedmont meets the flatter coastal plain, and the river's boulder-dappled rapids signal its swift descent as it drops more than 100 feet in elevation.

Turn around to retrace your steps along the main path. As you pass the concrete tower, notice to the left a granite boulder with a marker that honors Charles J. Schaefer and John W. Keith Jr., two friends who investigated the ownership of many islands in the James River and parcels along the river in the 1960s, hoping to make the river more accessible to the public. After much research and legal work, they eventually became the owners of several islands in and parcels along the river within the city limits. In 1972, they donated the land to the city so it could become the first property of the James River Park. The 2009 conservation easement that protects much of the park property would not have passed without the foresight and generosity of these two men. Keith passed away in 2008, and Schaefer in 2014.

Just past this marker, on the left across the rocky channel, trails on two of the larger islands provide access to a large field of smooth granite boulders. In periods of low water, it's possible to rock-hop to these islands without getting wet. But the risk of falling, or even drowning, is greatly magnified by high water, hence the exclusion of these trails from this hike. In the summer, sunlight filters through trees at the water's edge, and the river splashes over minute waterfalls to create a serene setting distinctly removed from the surrounding city.

As you continue east, you may notice large concrete structures and piping along the pathway. A sewer project, prompted by the Clean Water Act and completed in 1972, not only diverted polluted runoff but also resulted in the park's first land acquisition—originally the project right-of-way. This is one overflow location for the city's Combined Sewer Overflow (CSO) system. During dry weather, the CSO system carries all sanitary flow to wastewater treatment plants, according to the city website. During times of heavy rainfall, however, overflow can occur. Excess water is released into a stream or river.

Though scarred by heavy use and periodic flooding, the riparian woods along this hike retain their allure for many Richmonders. And while the park is worn, the river is now significantly cleaner than it was three decades ago, when municipal and industrial pollution kept residents away.

Just a bit farther down the main trail, you'll see a small meadow. In the spring and summer months, this meadow is often a big attraction for butterflies and birds. Just a bit farther is the Reedy Creek takeout and launch, where kayaks, canoes, and rafts often line the gravel path.

If you want to add another 1.5 miles to your hike, continue along the gravel trail to pass the park headquarters and down to the 22nd Street tower at Belle Isle. If you climb the staircase, that route also returns along the Buttermilk Trail. For this hike, before you reach the park headquarters, take a right through the gates and cross the railroad tracks. Pass the water fountain, portable toilets, and changing area for Reedy Creek before you take a right at the kiosk to begin the return trip along the Buttermilk Trail (see page 37).

You're now on a singletrack trail that twists and turns with the topography under towering trees and dense vegetation. There are additional boardwalks along this stretch, where water seeping downhill tends to muddy the trail. Watch for mountain bikers and runners along the narrow path. A stone-and-wood staircase takes you over a steep hillside that descends into the former Netherwood Quarry, one of dozens that dot the banks of the James River in Richmond.

There is a 0.3-mile spur trail through this quarry, or you may continue along the trail to the right and pass under the tower that this hike first crossed. The pathway winds uphill to the left, and a spur trail to the left will take you to the granite staircase that will return you to the West 42nd Street parking area.

• •

GPS TRAILHEAD COORDINATES N37° 31.382' W77° 28.252'

DIRECTIONS From downtown Richmond, cross the James River on the Robert E. Lee Memorial Bridge (US 1/US 301). To reach the bridge from I-95/I-64, take Exit 76 and head south on Belvidere Street. Immediately upon reaching the southern end of the bridge, exit onto Riverside Drive, heading west (right). You will pass the 22nd Street parking lot (often gated) on your right near the eastern terminus of the Buttermilk Trail. The Reedy Creek trailhead lot is the next right, with a sign for the park's headquarters and visitor center. A third parking area farther west along Riverside at West 42nd Street is an optional trailhead (recommended for this hike).

From the south via US 1/US 301 (Jefferson Davis Highway), turn left onto Semmes Avenue, which becomes Forest Hill Avenue just before passing Forest Hill Park on the right. Turn right onto West 42nd Street and proceed to a T intersection. Turn right onto Riverside Drive; the lot is just ahead on your left.

GRTC bus routes 2A and 2B stop 0.5 mile from the West 42nd Street parking lot.

Azaleas in bloom at the garden in Joseph Bryan Park

ABUTTING HENRICO COUNTY in North Richmond, Joseph Bryan Park offers wide-ranging amenities, including disc golf, soccer fields, closed paved roads popular with cyclists, and state-park-style group-picnic shelters. Its streamside woods along Jordan's Branch are pleasantly rustic, despite the roar from the nearby interstate exchange.

DESCRIPTION

Confederate veteran Joseph Bryan never resided on, or even owned, the land that was to become his namesake park. The end-of-the-19th-century publisher of the *Richmond Times,* which he merged with its main competitor to form the *Times-Dispatch* in 1903, lived instead at two of North Richmond's most famous addresses. When Joseph wed Isobel "Belle" Stewart in 1871, they moved into her family's posh estate, Brook Hill, which had served as a Confederate hospital and inn during the Civil War. Although his father-in-law added a Gothic Revival wing to better accommodate the young couple, the Bryans purchased the Laburnum estate, 2 miles east, in 1883. Perhaps Joseph was inspired by his close friend Lewis Ginter's success as a real estate developer. It was Ginter who gave Joseph, then his personal attorney, the struggling *Richmond Times* in 1887.

The original Laburnum, a many-gabled brick Victorian featuring elaborate ironwork and gas lighting, burned in 1906, but the Bryans resolutely set about

DISTANCE & CONFIGURATION: 2.2-mile loop, plus other optional paths

DIFFICULTY: Easy

ELEVATION: 174' at trailhead, 204' at high point

SCENERY: Riparian woods, rolling hills

EXPOSURE: Mostly shaded; open along paved internal park road and along Young's Pond

TRAFFIC: Light; higher in summer and on weekends

TRAIL SURFACE: Dirt trails, grass, paved roads

HIKING TIME: 1 hour

SEASON: Year-round during daylight hours

ACCESS: No fee

WHEELCHAIR ACCESS: Wheelchairs not recommended except in paved area near Azalea Garden

MAPS: On signboard near parking lot and at friendsofbryanpark.org

DRIVING DISTANCE FROM CAPITOL: 6.9 miles

FACILITIES: Restrooms, tennis courts, disc golf course, soccer fields, picnic tables, grills, group shelters, wildlife-viewing area, nature center, Azalea Garden

CONTACT: City of Richmond Department of Parks, Recreation, and Community Facilities: 804-646-5743, richmondgov.com/parks

LOCATION: 4308 Hermitage Rd., Richmond

COMMENTS: With a playground and duck pond en route, this is a good hike for families with children. The Azalea Garden is a feature in April and May. Consider bringing your disc golf equipment for a round while you are here.

constructing a 50-room Colonial-style mansion with towering limestone columns that stands to this day. Joseph died in 1908, shortly after the house was completed.

Soon thereafter, his wife purchased the Rosewood estate at a public auction. (The land was acquired by William Young in the 1700s and bequeathed to his daughter Rosina in 1832.) In 1909, Belle donated the Rosewood land to the City of Richmond in honor of her late husband, specifying that it remain "a free park for the use and benefits of all its citizens." Over the next few decades, the city reshaped what was a large tract of farmland into the wooded, rolling hills and duck pond that visitors see today. The rustic shelters, bridges, and stonework were constructed during the Great Depression by the Works Progress Administration (WPA).

Of the park's 262 acres, some 180 are forested. The pond and adjacent marsh (on the pond's northern, upper portion) offer welcome respite to migratory waterfowl, although ducks and geese, fattened by breadcrumbs, maintain a presence year-round. Contemporary visitors will also find a playground, tennis courts, and soccer fields, as well as an azalea garden. Those seeking to stretch their legs will want to bypass these features and head to the parking lot closest to main entrance at Shelter 1. The signboard near the parking lot features a map, but not all trails are included. The intrepid need not worry: stick to well-worn paths and you'll soon reemerge on pavement.

Begin by walking down the paved road past Shelter 1 and Young's Pond. At the base of the hill, you can walk across the spillway bisecting the two-tiered pond. For our hike and wooded trails, instead head left by Shelter 1. A short walk will unveil a bridge, which evokes a Parisian *pont* with its wrought-iron lampposts. Across the bridge, a short trail bears right along the pond then uphill to Shelter 2 and the park's

Joseph Bryan Park

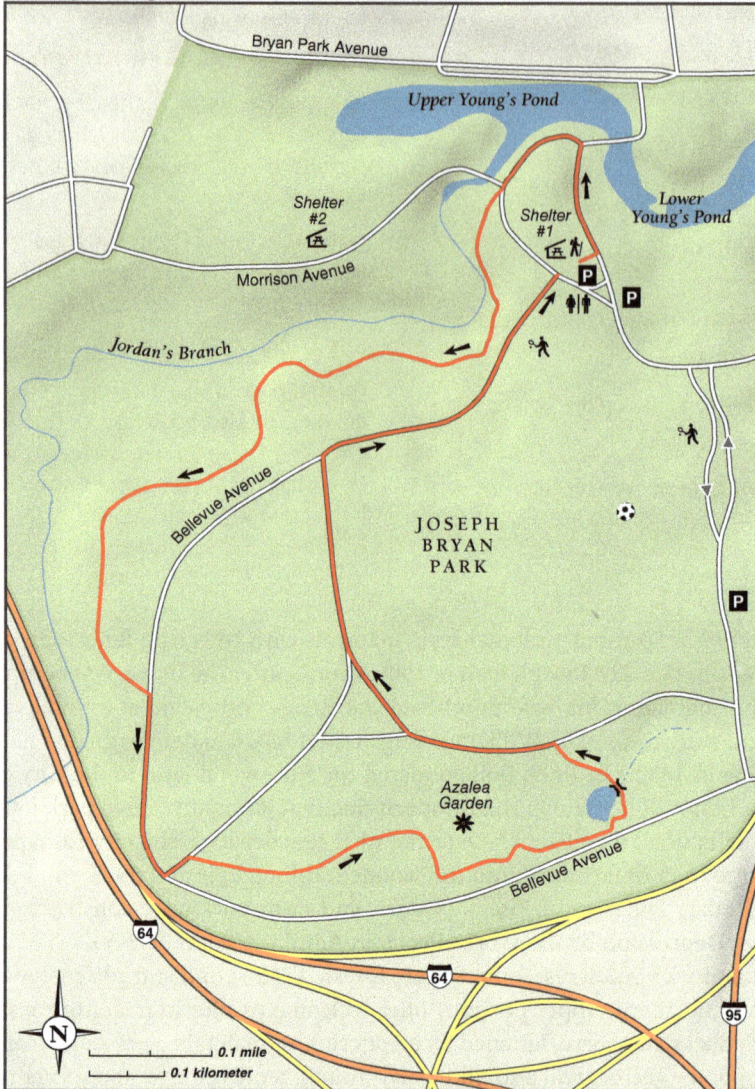

Bryan Park Avenue

Upper Young's Pond

Lower Young's Pond

Shelter #2

Shelter #1

Morrison Avenue

Jordan's Branch

Bellevue Avenue

JOSEPH
BRYAN
PARK

Azalea
Garden

Bellevue Avenue

64

64

95

N

0.1 mile

0.1 kilometer

nature center. A worthwhile side trip for those interested in Depression-era park construction, this small loop suffers from infrequent maintenance.

Next, bear left (facing the bridge) into the woods. Follow the earthen path as it drops to parallel Jordan's Branch, which feeds into the pond. Grills along the stream will beckon you to return with the family for a picnic. The trail offers a path back to Shelter 1, but bear right to continue into the woods along Jordan's Branch Trail (it may be unmarked). Meander through woods of white oak and water-loving birch trees. Towering oaks felled by previous storms and hurricanes may block the trail.

Upon intersecting a wider path, turn right then left. Enjoy this lengthy stretch of woodland. In winter, the deep-green holly interspersed among deciduous trees lends life and color to the forest. Soon the trail draws near I-64, and the drone of traffic temporarily overpowers birdsong and the babbling of Jordan's Branch. The trail emerges on a paved road, one of several in the park rarely opened to vehicles. Turn right and continue until you reach a trail on your left. Follow it through vine-strewn woods to emerge on another road. Cross the pavement and continue into a section on the western side of the old Azalea Garden that is being reforested.

Every year the Azalea Garden is open to driving visitors from April 1 to May 15, but it is closed to vehicular traffic the remainder of the year. The garden was begun in 1952 by Robert E. Harvey, a former Richmond parks superintendent, with a donation of 5,000 azaleas from the City of Norfolk, according to the Friends of Bryan Park website. With the help of many volunteers, 45,000 azaleas—50 varieties— were planted throughout 17 acres. When the azaleas were at their peak, the garden attracted as many as 400,000 people each spring.

Walk through the garden and around a granite-walled pond with a fountain in the center. Turn left to cross a small bridge and continue west along the garden or along the paved road to return to Shelter 1.

If you prefer, there is also a spur trail to connect to the park's meadow. Bear right once you see a doubletrack trail with signs for the meadow. The undulating surface of the meadow (formerly a city stump-dumping site) is mowed annually. In the summer, its tall grasses teem with birds and insects. Up a short, steep hill are the soccer fields. Bear left across them toward the playground to return to your vehicle.

After finishing your hike, you may wish to take the park tour described on the Friends of Bryan Park website, friendsofbryanpark.org. It includes several points of historical interest in the park's western half, removed from the trails described here.

• •

GPS TRAILHEAD COORDINATES N37° 35.762' W77° 28.252'

DIRECTIONS The park lies at the crux of and is hemmed in by I-64 and I-95. The main entrance is on Hermitage Road (which is Lakeside Avenue north of the park), at the park's northeast corner. If you're coming from I-64, follow the signs for I-95 N before exiting at Hermitage (Exit 80) and heading a short distance north.

GRTC bus route 14 stops one block from the main park entrance. The park also has bike racks.

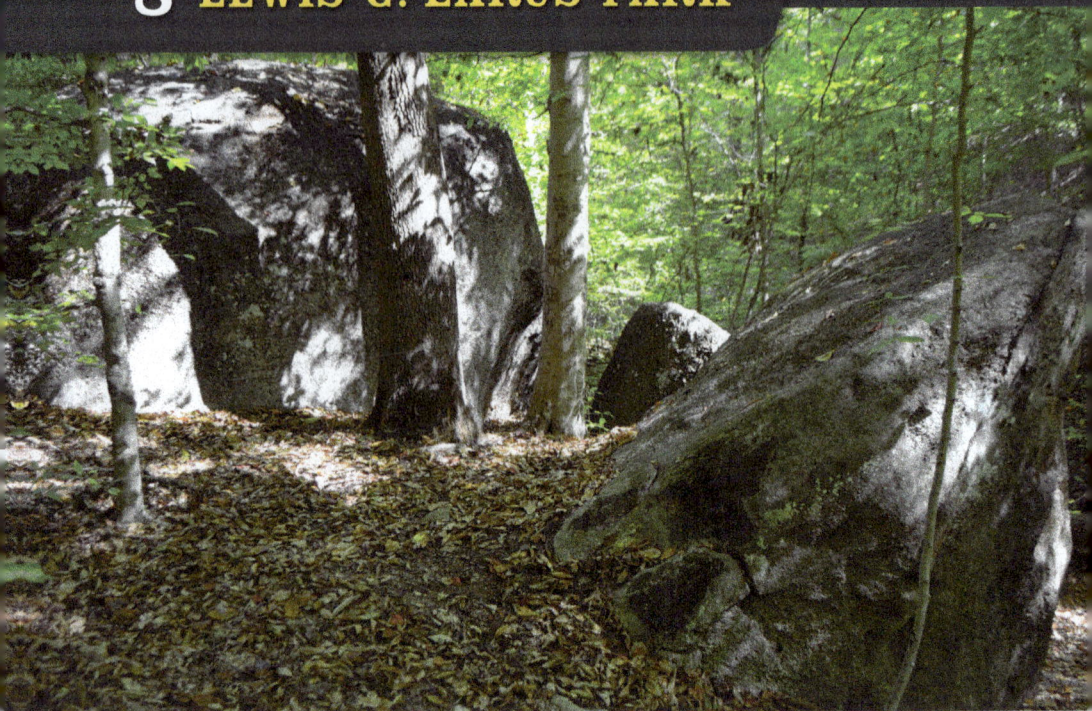

Large granite boulders in Larus Park are so tempting to climb.

LARUS PARK'S 106.5 ACRES are situated in the western tip of the city, bounded by Huguenot Road, Chippenham Parkway, and Stony Point Fashion Park, yet the park manages to remain relatively unknown to most Richmonders. It is heavily wooded with no open green space (except a power-line easement north of the Chippenham) with approximately 3 miles of unsigned trails. There are a few tiny brooks, but they can run dry in times of drought. The central water feature, Dancing Creek, flows through the heart of the park and through a tunnel under the parkway on its way to the James River.

DESCRIPTION

In 1915, Lewis G. Larus bought the plot of land that now includes the park and Sabot at Stony Point School, which sits on a bluff on the western edge of the property. This property was once part of Chesterfield County before the City of Richmond annexed the land in 1970. Signs acknowledging the park were posted by the city in 2006, but the land has been city property since its purchase in 1978.

The school sits near the northwest corner of the park, perched above Stony Point Fashion Park. Chippenham Parkway passes through the center of the park, and office buildings and housing developments border the southeast and southwest portions.

DISTANCE & CONFIGURATION: 2.3-mile balloon loop, with optional spurs

DIFFICULTY: Easy

ELEVATION: 327' at trailhead, 145' at low point

SCENERY: Mixed hardwood forest, streambeds, rolling hills

EXPOSURE: Mostly shaded

TRAFFIC: Low

TRAIL SURFACE: Loose rock and dirt, combined mountain bike trails

HIKING TIME: 1–2 hours

SEASON: Year-round during daylight hours

ACCESS: No fee

WHEELCHAIR ACCESS: None

MAPS: See map on page 54.

DRIVING DISTANCE FROM CAPITOL: 9 miles

FACILITIES: None

CONTACT: City of Richmond Department of Parks, Recreation, and Community Facilities: 804-646-5743, richmondgov.com/parks

LOCATION: 8760 W. Huguenot Rd., Richmond

COMMENTS: This is a great park for dog owners. Alternate trailheads are on Stony Point Road, Hayden Hill Lane, and on Beechmont Road. Trails are not marked, and there are no restrooms at the 3 main entrances. A spur trail connects to Stony Point Fashion Park through a parking lot.

Larus Park is a good place for exploring and wandering. A network of dirt and rock singletrack trails traverses the park. If you were to hike the entire area, you could probably cover 3–4 miles, but that would require a substantial retracing of steps. The variety of paths crisscross and split in different directions, but this hike forms an elongated counterclockwise loop that covers the majority of the park's main trails and interior.

Larus offers a mixed deciduous hardwood and pine forest, with a central rocky stream (Dancing Creek) running through the middle of the park. Despite the near constant noise from Chippenham Parkway, which splits the park, it is a peaceful space for a walk, hike, or run, with its patches of ground cedar, loblolly pines, chestnut oaks, pawpaws, blueberries, and wild ginger.

Our hike begins at the trailhead on Hayden Hill Lane behind Richmond Fire Station 25 (located on West Huguenot Road). The central connecting trail through the park to the Beechmont Road trailhead is known as Wukong's Path, a wonderful and thought-provoking name for a 1-mile connector route. (I'm sorry to say I was not able to find information to explain the moniker.)

The trail enters into a narrow corridor of cedar and pine. A long wooden boardwalk spans a brief wet area, and a long stretch of the trail is perennially covered in pine needles, so be careful not to slip. After a short distance, the trail meets a fork; follow the trail to the right.

As the trail widens into a brief opening in the tree canopy, a multitude of small rocks and sticks is revealed. For most every hike I've taken through Larus Park, this is where children get most excited about exploring. From here the trail begins a gentle descent into the central ravine of Dancing Creek.

Larus has so many beautiful trees and very little underbrush to clutter the forest floor. As the trail winds along, many of the twists and turns follow a worn path that

Lewis G. Larus Park

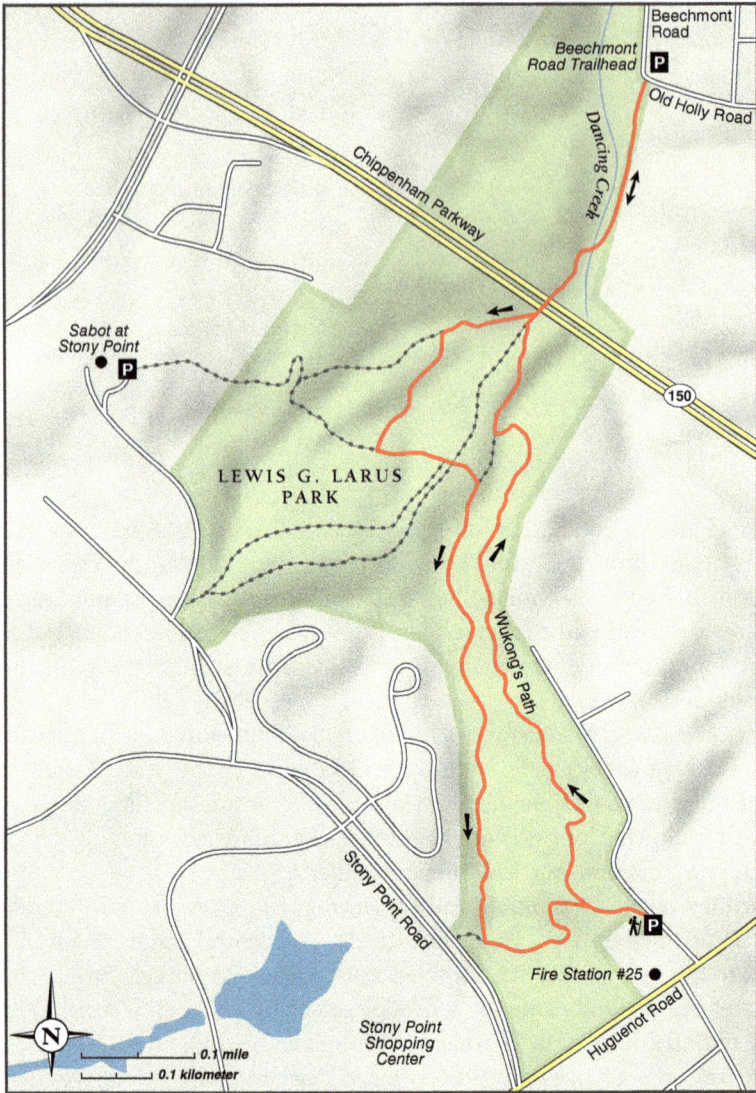

has migrated left and right at times to navigate around fallen trees, which generally are left in place to rot away, unless they block the trail. This leaves even more fun places for children to climb and to discover insects, moss, and more.

As the trail approaches Dancing Creek, follow the path right instead of taking a sharp left. This short path will take you farther down the creekbed along the south bank. A left will cross the creek as well, but you will cross at that spot on the loop back.

Cross the creek and notice the large boulders that form the creekbed, which may appear dry. The water flows below the surface between these boulders when it has been too long between periods of rain. If the creek is dry during your hike, just walk across the boulders. If water is flowing, there should still be plenty of places to cross.

Follow the trail as it continues to the right, and soon you'll reach a wide trail crossing. This is the main east–west trail that connects to the trailhead at Sabot at Stony Point school. At this point, Chippenham Parkway should be in view to the right. A wooden staircase leads down to another trail crossing; follow it to the right to pass through the tunnel under the Chippenham Parkway and to the Beechmont Road trailhead. This out-and-back will add 0.6 mile to your walk and is very flat, following above the banks of Dancing Creek a good portion of the way. Turn around at the trailhead and double back to rejoin the loop.

After returning to the base of the staircase, cross the creek to follow the trail uphill. You'll find a couple of giant boulders the size of a dump truck sitting on the forest floor. They beckon to be climbed, and their size alone provides a good reason to pause to admire them.

Continue past the boulders and follow the trail up the hill as it climbs a series of steep sections before meeting another trail. Take a left to meet the wide east–west trail again, then cross the trail and descend toward Dancing Creek once more. If needed, cross the tiny waterway by way of an old footbridge. Head right and begin looking for a hiking path marked by logs and stones at its entrance.

This trail follows above and along the banks of the creek behind several homes and a preschool as it meanders uphill. The path crosses the creek and will likely have a couple of large trees lying over it in this ascent, so be prepared. As the trail approaches the top of the hill, it veers left to circle back to Wukong's Path. A water tower and two cell towers are just behind the fire station at the trailhead.

• •

GPS TRAILHEAD COORDINATES N37° 32.345' W77° 33.678'

DIRECTIONS Larus Park is located near the western tip of the City of Richmond's boundary with Chesterfield County. Take Chippenham Parkway to Huguenot Road and travel south on West Huguenot Road, or cross the James River by way of the Huguenot Bridge. If driving north on Huguenot Road from the Midlothian Turnpike (VA 60), take the first left past Buford Road/Stony Point Road, which is Hayden Hill Lane. The entrance can be easy to miss. There's a sign for the park at the intersection of West Huguenot and Stony Point Roads, but enter instead via Hayden Hill Lane, which runs between Richmond Fire Station 25 and a Shell gas station off West Huguenot Road. The trailhead sits at the edge of a private road to Sneed's Nursery. Parking is limited to about five vehicles.

GRTC bus route 2A stops along Stony Point Road.

Granite boulders line the shore of Texas Beach at North Bank Park.

TEXAS BEACH IS POPULAR with people taking in the day just sitting by the river. The wild James River is a big draw, and this hike along the sandy trails of North Bank Park explores some beautiful scenery and a little history.

DESCRIPTION

North Bank Park is one of the best places to visit the James River Park. It's known to many Richmonders as Texas Beach, thanks to the avenue that leads into the park and the sandy beaches that line the banks of the river. Retired park manager Ralph White used to say that North Bank might be the best of all the parks in the system at giving visitors a feeling of being lost in nature and away from urban Richmond.

Begin this hike at the Texas Beach parking lot. As you follow the trail into the woods, keep in mind that this first short section is shared with the North Bank Trail, the northern section of the James River Park Loop that opened in 2005 (see page 37). Traffic on the singletrack trail flows in both directions, connecting from Boulevard Bridge along Maymont, through North Bank Park, and below the scenic and beautiful hilltop resting places at Mount Calvary, Riverview, and Hollywood Cemeteries. Sections of the trail separate hikers from mountain bikers, and the trail offers fantastic views of the James River in certain areas.

DISTANCE & CONFIGURATION: 2.3-mile out-and-back

DIFFICULTY: Easy

ELEVATION: 159' at trailhead, 62' at low point

SCENERY: James River, mixed forest, James River and Kanawha Canal

EXPOSURE: Shaded, except segments on the rocks and Texas Beach (optional)

TRAFFIC: Moderate

TRAIL SURFACE: Dirt singletrack, wood staircases, wood and metal pedestrian bridges

HIKING TIME: 1.5 hours

SEASON: Year-round during daylight hours

ACCESS: No fee

WHEELCHAIR ACCESS: None

MAPS: On park kiosks and at jamesriverpark.org

DRIVING DISTANCE FROM CAPITOL: 3.7 miles

FACILITIES: Portable toilets and bike rack at the parking lot; no trash service beyond the parking area, so take out what you take in.

CONTACT: City of Richmond Department of Parks, Recreation, and Community Facilities: 804-646-5743, richmondgov.com/parks; James River Park: 804-646-8911, jamesriverpark.org

LOCATION: 1907 Texas Ave., Richmond

COMMENTS: This park often has dogs off leash, even though city ordinance requires leashes.

Take a left down a series of wooden staircases, which were installed in 2013 as an Eagle Scout project to replace a well-worn trail that was eroding the hillside because it was too steep for cyclists and pedestrians. This is the first of several volunteer projects in North Bank that we will highlight. Volunteers continue to have a tremendous impact on the quality of people's experiences in James River Park.

As you reach the landing before the pedestrian bridge, notice another wooden staircase and the trail below. This is the North Bank Trail. Cross over the CSX railroad by way of the metal pedestrian bridge, which dates back to the early 1970s, when James River Park first opened. If you are lucky enough to catch a train rolling through, look for railcars loaded with coal. This route follows along the banks of the James across Virginia and into West Virginia.

Make your way down from the pedestrian bridge to the trail below. In late 2014, a notoriously damp section of the trail here was finally tamed by volunteers from James River Hikers who constructed a footbridge over the mud with the guidance of city trail staff. The supplies and wood were delivered across the James by bateaux from the Reedy Creek takeout.

After crossing the footbridge, the trail soon reaches the shallow waters and calm sands of Texas Beach. This is an excellent setting for exploring. People who frequent this park generally are more laid-back, the type who play guitars, bring their dogs, and find a rock to call their own for an afternoon of fun. As you follow the trail to the right, watch for many spurs that access more beaches, boulders, or the water. The trails along the river are not marked, but there is one main spine route, and it is unlikely you'll get lost along the way.

The next 0.25 mile will have a few openings with good vistas of the river but few rocks to hop to. Look for sycamore and birch trees as you hike west along the sandy

North Bank Park

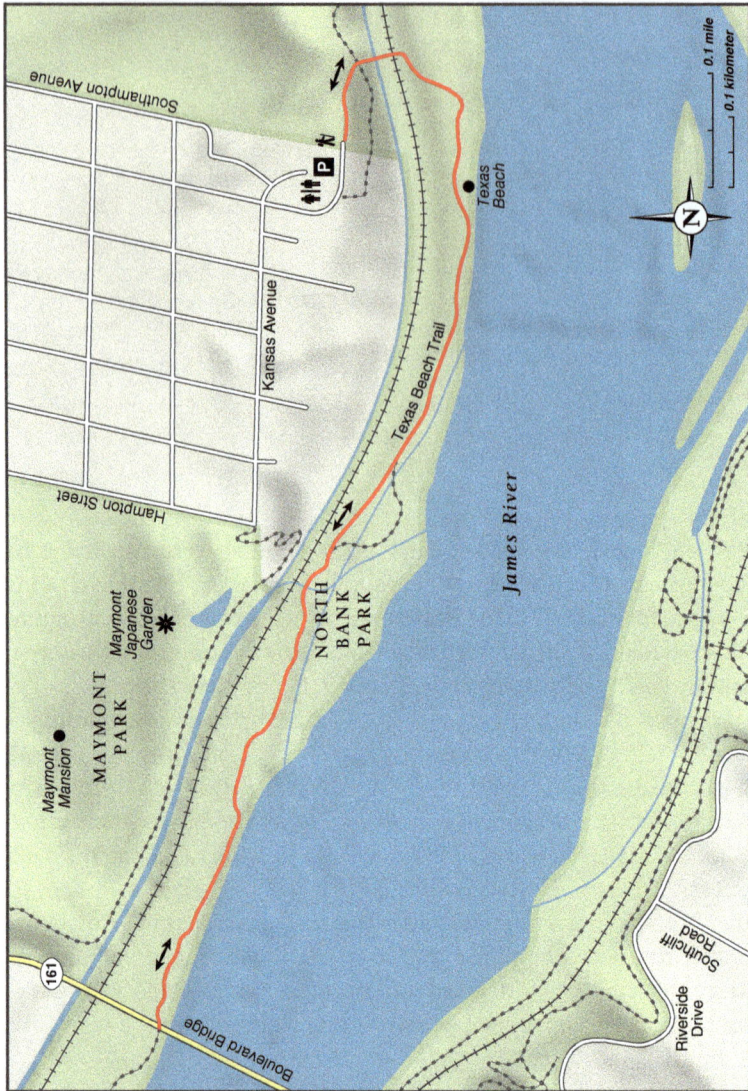

path. The woods are thick, as are the invasive species. James River Park is in a constant battle with invasives, many of which have washed down the river over the years or were dumped or even escaped from people's yards.

Soon the trail approaches a series of large boulders and a spillway from the James River and Kanawha Canal that runs under the CSX tracks. This area is directly south of Maymont, but you'd hardly know it because the thick trees and high train tracks block the sights and sounds. Maymont is a beautiful park with lovely gardens, trails, and animal enclosures. It is definitely worth paying a visit.

This section of the hike used to be treacherous if water levels were high, but a series of wooden bridges was installed in late 2016 to help parkgoers more safely cross the boulders below the spillway. Tragedy inspired Charlie's Crossing, named for a dog that was killed by a train while attempting to cross the tracks above the spillway. Donations from a fundraiser helped supply the necessary materials, and volunteers installed the new crossings, which replaced temporary board placements that would wash away during heavy rains.

On the other side of the bridges, the trail bends left before winding through a series of trees. You'll find the Foushee-Ritchie Mill site about 100 yards west of the spillway. The two-story gristmill was constructed in 1819 using granite quarried nearby. Remains of the millrace that powered the mill can still be found if you look carefully.

The mill is named for Dr. William Foushee, who served as Richmond's first mayor when it became a city in 1782. He sold the mill to his son-in-law, Thomas Ritchie, in 1824. It did not last long, as it was destroyed by flooding in 1832. Unfortunately, in recent years, the site has been a target for graffiti tagging and has often had to be painted with granite-colored paint to diminish the blight. It is also under constant attack from invasive species and volunteer trees that tend to grow in between the granite blocks of what's left of the crumbling structure.

While Foushee-Ritchie Mill is an interesting destination for most hikers, the trail continues another 0.5 mile through a few stands of pine trees and large hardwoods to the Boulevard Bridge. Watch for muddy sections, especially following periods of rain. The bridge is a good spot to turn around, as the trails continuing west of it are not as well defined or maintained.

You may retrace your steps to the trailhead or, for adventure seekers, if the river level is low consider walking out among the boulders and rock-hopping your way east back along the shoreline. There are good access points closer to Foushee-Ritchie Mill. From my experiences rock-hopping, there is an art to finding the best routes without getting wet. It is all part of the fun. There are also trails on the small islands that are strung along Texas Beach, but these are inconsistent and sometimes less reliable.

• •

GPS TRAILHEAD COORDINATES N37° 31.862' W77° 28.149'

DIRECTIONS From downtown, take East Main Street, then turn left onto South Meadow Street. Follow it until the road ends at Kansas Avenue. Take a left and travel four blocks before taking a right onto Texas Avenue. The park entrance will be at the end of the dead-end street on the left. The parking area can accommodate 30 cars.

GRTC bus route 10 stops six blocks from the park entrance. The park has bike racks.

10 PONY PASTURE RAPIDS

These granite boulders at Pony Pasture Rapids are a popular spot for rivergoers on warm days.

DESPITE THE SWAMPY NATURE of its ragtag woods, Pony Pasture Rapids remains a popular outing for Richmonders. Take time to admire the James River. The granite rocks near the parking area are packed when the weather is warm and the river level is less than 5 feet. The parks' central, Southside location and well-marked trails attract dog walkers, joggers, and families. Crickets drown the sound of traffic, and riparian wildlife thrives among the vine-swathed trees.

DESCRIPTION

For many Richmonders, Pony Pasture Rapids is an urban paradise. Situated along the south bank of the James River, it offers a staycation opportunity for the region, a cheap way to make the best of a day for those who don't have the time or money to leave the city. The scenery alone is a big draw—the huge boulders have plenty of unique nooks shaped by years of erosion from the rapids. A typical visit to Pony Pasture involves jumping from rock to rock all the way across the river or sitting in the shallow water to enjoy a relaxing cooldown from the heat. Get there early on busy summer days to stake your claim to a rock.

Pony Pasture doesn't actually have ponies, but there was once a pasture here, and ponies were kept in it. Retired park manager Ralph White once told me that the

DISTANCE & CONFIGURATION: 2.2-mile figure eight, plus multiple side trails

DIFFICULTY: Easy

ELEVATION: 95' at trailhead, no significant rise

SCENERY: James River, hardwood swamp, marsh

EXPOSURE: Well shaded

TRAFFIC: Moderate; highest along river

TRAIL SURFACE: Gravel, optional dirt trails and boardwalk

HIKING TIME: 1–1.5 hours

SEASON: Year-round during daylight hours

ACCESS: No fee

WHEELCHAIR ACCESS: On gravel sections but may be muddy

MAPS: On kiosk in main parking lot and at jamesriverpark.org

DRIVING DISTANCE FROM CAPITOL: 6.7 miles

FACILITIES: Restrooms, kayak takeout, wildlife-viewing area

CONTACT: City of Richmond Department of Parks, Recreation, and Community Facilities: 804-646-5743, richmondgov.com/parks; James River Park: 804-646-8911, jamesriverpark.org

LOCATION: 7310 Riverside Dr., Richmond

COMMENTS: The Captain John Smith Chesapeake National Historic Trail connects to Pony Pasture. In the summer months, this is an extremely popular park, and as a day progresses, the parking lot can fill. If you bring a dog with you, city ordinance says it should be leashed. Paddlers interested in using the park as a put-in or takeout can call 804-646-8228 for river-level information.

name came from the 1960s when the area was suburban and people housed their horses near the river. This land was also once a granite quarry. A park sign (written by White) declares, "Quarries were a big business in Richmond in the 19th and early 20th centuries." There were a couple dozen quarries in the area, and the granite was quarried for the construction of Richmond for more than 100 years. Much of the stone was moved by railcars, and Riverside Drive used to be a railroad bed.

There are two main trails across the mostly flat terrain. The River Trail parallels the James River, and Pleasant's Creek Trail follows its namesake as it grows from a bubbling stream on the park's western edge to a 20-foot-wide creek where it enters the James. Most visitors stick to the River Trail, which offers the best views and access points to the river. The two paths converge before a bridge across Pleasant's Creek. On the opposite side is the Wetlands Trail, an additional gravel loop by which the wildlife-viewing area is reached.

As you leave the main parking area, take either of the main trails. Then cross the bridge over Pleasant's Creek to follow the wetland circuit. On the return trip, take the other trail to get the full experience of Pony Pasture. Of course, you'll be tempted to stray from the wide gravel paths onto the numerous side trails that crisscross the park's interior. These easily double your mileage, but the risk of getting lost is minimal. Besides extending your hike, the side trails offer up-close views of flora and fauna and an open meadow with high grass that provides sanctuary to birds and wildlife.

Even along the heavily trafficked River Trail, mud puddles dot the gravel pathway for days following any substantial rain. Likewise, fluctuations in the level of the

Pony Pasture Rapids

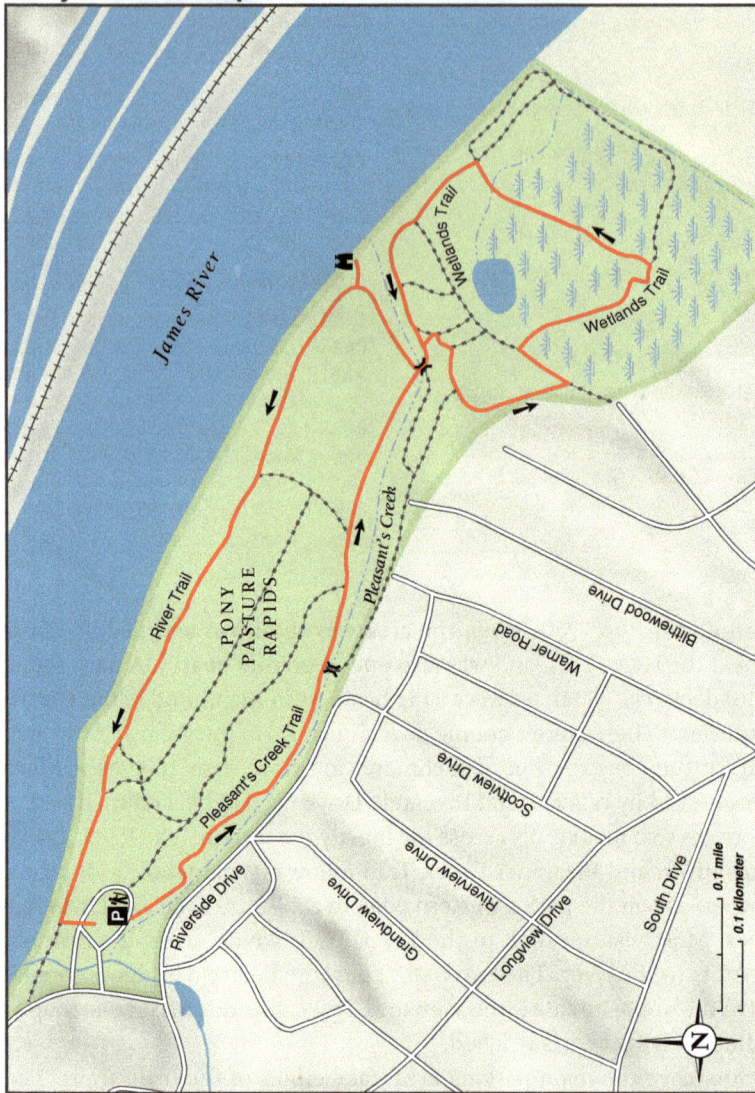

James River determine its proximity to the trail, which can range from 20 to 50 feet inland. Waves lap the shore along the route, but the rushing rapids about 100 feet away are ever audible, as are occasional trains across the river. On the weekends, you are likely to catch a glimpse of canoeists or kayakers darting downstream through the Class II rapids.

No visitor should miss sunset at Pony Pasture. But don't just look west. The real show is across the James, particularly in autumn, where the sinking sun sets the trees aglow and glints from the windows of riverside estates. A full harvest moonrise completes the scene. Some of the best river (and swamp) views are from spur trails, so give yourself time to explore—and wear appropriate attire. Follow Pleasant's Creek from its wide mouth at the James riverbank upstream to where it dwindles to a mere trickle. Dragonflies dart about in warmer months, and honking Canada geese pass overhead in the spring and fall. The park's wet soil accommodates a host of vegetation but few of the mid-Atlantic's more common hardwoods. Here sycamores tower over a deciduous mix thick with underbrush; shaggy-bark birches and ivy ground cover are common.

If you're going to flout the city's leash law, know that thick vegetation makes it easy to lose sight of your pet. Many visitors bring dogs to Pony Pasture, but fewer ride through the park on a mountain bike. Tire tracks, however, testify to the riders' persistence. New gravel was laid along the main paths in 2017, providing for more separation from the mud.

At the adjoining park, The Wetlands, expect fewer people, fewer river boulders, calmer waters, and a number of people walking their dogs along the shaded trails and boardwalks. In the center of The Wetlands, wooden blinds—facades with short, wide windows and animal- and plant-identification placards—facilitate views of wildlife across a small pond. Bird-watching is particularly good here. Visitors may be fortunate to spot a downy woodpecker or a pileated woodpecker, its telltale red crest visible from its treetop perch. Beavers may be found along the banks of Pleasant's Creek or the James.

Note that the trail in the southwestern portion of The Wetlands passes along a few dirt mounds or small hills. This area was once part of Chesterfield County before being annexed by the City of Richmond in 1970. The land at the end of Landria Drive was once a dumping ground for the county. Those mounds are what's left of those piles, which included leaves and yard debris, after everything decomposed and turned to dirt.

From The Wetlands, return to the wooden bridge over Pleasant's Creek, and choose a path to return to the parking lot.

NEARBY ACTIVITIES

Huguenot Flatwater, the westernmost portion of the James River Park and a popular canoe and kayak put-in, offers another mile or so of trail easily linked to Pony Pasture via Riverside Drive, which is designated as a Richmond Scenic Byway and is a popular spot for runners, cyclists, and walkers. Along the way west, you'll find another part of the park system, a 2-acre parcel called the **Riverside Meadow Greenspace,** which offers a beautiful open vista of Williams Island and the James above Pony Pasture and access to the Z-Dam, which is popular with anglers and whitewater kayakers.

• •

GPS TRAILHEAD COORDINATES N37° 33.014' W77° 31.212'

DIRECTIONS From the southern terminus of the Huguenot Road Bridge (VA 147), follow Riverside Drive east. At 2 miles, the main Pony Pasture Rapids parking lot is on your left, just after the road curves away from the river. It's equally feasible to access the park via Forest Hill Avenue, which intersects Chippenham Parkway (VA 150) to the southwest and Powhite Parkway (VA 76) to the southeast. From Forest Hill Avenue, turn north onto Hathaway Road, which is roughly equidistant from the parkways. Proceed to a Y inter-section and veer left onto Longview Drive. Travel two blocks then turn right onto Scottview Drive, which turns sharply left in a few blocks to become Riverside Drive. Turn right again in a few blocks to remain on Riverside. The parking area will be your next right. A smaller eastern parking lot is accessible from Forest Hill by veering right, at that Y intersection, from Hathaway Road onto Wallowa Road. Take the second left onto Landria Drive, which dead-ends adjacent to the park by the Wetland Trail.

GRTC bus route 2A stops about a mile from the park entrance. Pony Pasture Rapids has bike racks.

Park volunteers constructed this wooden boardwalk over a marshy area.

Fungi growing on a fallen tree in Powhite Park

THIS FUN AND RELATIVELY EASY HIKE has many boulders and fallen trees to sit on along the way. Powhite Park is rarely crowded, and most hikers and mountain bikers may have the trails to themselves. It appears to be a great place for dogs to get their outdoor fix.

DESCRIPTION

Depending on where you're from and your perspective, how you pronounce the word *Powhite* may say something about you. Do you say "Pow-hite" or "Po-white"? Before you answer, let's look at where the word comes from.

Chief Powhatan, whose proper name was Wahunsenacawh, lived circa 1550–1618 at the time of European colonization of the New World. He was chief of a confederation of Algonquian tribes in what would become Virginia, the founder of the Powhatan Confederacy, and the father of Pocahontas. He made his headquarters at Werowocomoco, near the York River 15 miles from Jamestown, and he lived at the falls of the James River, near what eventually became Richmond. His home was known as Powhata, which is why the English colonists called him Powhatan.

When Europeans colonists first began to settle in Virginia, they interacted with many Native American tribes, including Chief Powhatan's people. Let's assume that

DISTANCE & CONFIGURATION: 2.4-mile balloon interwoven with other optional routes

DIFFICULTY: Easy

ELEVATION: 200' at trailhead, 125' at low point

SCENERY: Powhite Creek, wetlands, hardwood forest

EXPOSURE: Shaded

TRAFFIC: Low

TRAIL SURFACE: Dirt

HIKING TIME: 1 hour

SEASON: Year-round during daylight hours

ACCESS: No fee

WHEELCHAIR ACCESS: No

MAPS: On kiosks at trailheads (off Jahnke Road across from Chippenham Hospital and at the end of Greenvale Drive) and at rvamore.org/trails

DRIVING DISTANCE FROM CAPITOL: 7 miles

FACILITIES: Portable toilet at the Jahnke Road entrance

CONTACT: City of Richmond Department of Parks, Recreation, and Community Facilities: 804-646-5743, richmondgov.com/parks

LOCATION: 7200 Jahnke Rd., Richmond

COMMENTS: This is a good park for dog owners. The trails are not marked, and there are no restrooms at the 2 trailheads.

when Powhite Creek was named, the reference was to the Native American *Powhite* (likely derived from Chief Powhatan, his people, or their confederacy).

In the Richmond area, people say the name different ways. Do you say "Pou-uh-tan" or "Pou-hat-n"? We have Powhatan County (and Powhatan State Park), Powhatan Hill (with Powhatan Park and Powhatan Recreation Center), Powhite Creek, and Powhite Parkway. The name comes up often, but the debate will rage forever, as I don't believe there is an established correct pronunciation. For the record, I usually say "Po-white" but believe it should be said "Pow-hite" to best honor Chief Powhatan.

The land for Powhite Park was once part of Chesterfield County before the City of Richmond annexed it in 1970. In my research, I was not able to locate the exact year the park opened, but it appears to be the late 1990s.

This little-known 92-acre park in South Richmond is popular with mountain bikers. Plenty of people hike here as well, but the well-worn singletrack trails are clear evidence that riders frequent Powhite Park. The 8 miles of intertwined trails are a great place for beginners to work on their riding skills or intermediate riders to get their legs into shape and have a lot of fun, especially riding in the Ravine, which skilled riders have turned into their own version of Mother Nature's half-pipe.

Outside of the cyclists, hikers often have Powhite Park all to themselves. It is difficult to escape the droning of automobile traffic from Powhite and Chippenham Parkways, which form the western and northwestern boundaries of the park. Once you get accustomed to it, your mind will likely block out the sound.

While I'm on the subject of the highways, Powhite Park's proximity to high-speed traffic corridors does have some unintended consequences. You will most likely find litter, especially along the waterways, and much of it is blown or thrown from the nearby highways. It ends up in Powhite Creek and gathers as it washes downstream.

Powhite Park

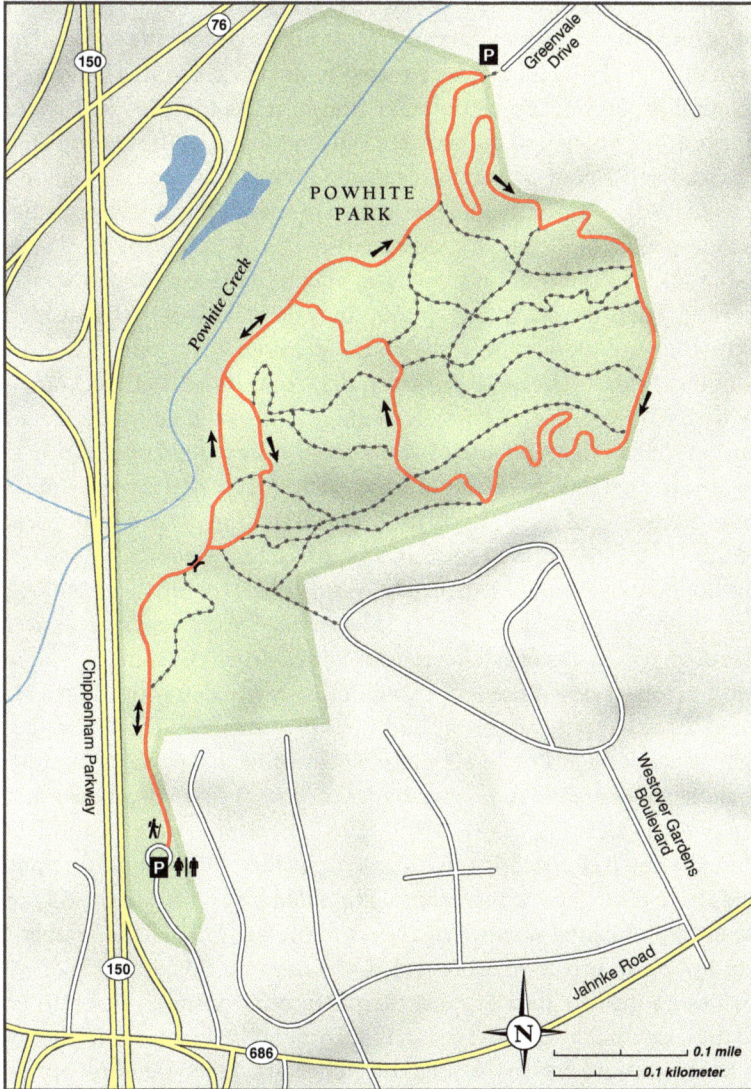

Volunteer cleanups can be challenging in the marsh and wetlands, but there are enough plastic bottles, Styrofoam, tires, and aluminum cans to make regular cleanups worth the effort. Consider bringing a bag with you on your hike to collect trash.

Begin this hike from the Jahnke Road parking lot trailhead. The trail starts to the right of the traffic circle at the end of the lot, along the fenceline. This section has seen plenty of erosion and has many exposed roots, so watch your step. The path parallels Chippenham Parkway before reaching the top of a knoll and a small opening in the tree canopy. The trail has options to the left and right; both lead to the same point at the bottom of the ridge. Most hikers choose the left, and mountain bikers take the right, which has a very rutted switchback. For this hike, we took the left. Be careful as you walk down the steep trail, as it has some loose gravel.

At the bottom, you'll find the wooden Wilson Memorial Bridge, which was built in 2002 as an Eagle Scout project. This single span is the one connection across a marshy, wide creekbed within about 0.25 mile of the trailhead that must be crossed to access the majority of the park. After crossing, the junction offers several trail options, but stick to the trail on the left, as this route takes you clockwise around the outer trail. There are also many spur options that take you to the park's interior.

Follow the trail along a wet lowland and eventually along the wide, grassy marshes of Powhite Creek. You'll see sycamore, American beech, hickory, elm, and a variety of hardwoods in this sandy lowland. Many of the fallen trees are covered in a beautiful shade of green moss or white fungi. The many large, exposed granite boulders are covered in lichens and moss as well. This park has plenty of spaces for children to discover and learn. Look for bugs among the downed trees. Play in the sand and mud in the creek. Find rocks. Climb trees. Enjoy nature.

I have found that Powhite Park can be a good place for bird-watching. Also look for turtles, deer, raccoons, and skinks. Most of all, the signs of beaver activity are everywhere; gnawed nubs of small trees dot both sides of the trail.

As you progress down the path, you'll cross a wooden footbridge. More spur trails climb into the park's interior, and the hilly terrain in the higher reaches of the park makes hiking at Powhite a more worthwhile challenge. If you just stick to the trail along the marshes and watershed, you'll miss the switchbacks and climbs to the top of the ridge.

Eventually the trail reaches a 90-degree right turn then continues uphill to the Greenvale Drive trailhead. At this point, I stumbled into a herd of deer. I counted at least five of them bedded down. I'm always impressed that so many deer can find a place to live in an urban environment, but I imagine this Powhite Creek greenway provides enough food to support them. On other visits to Powhite Park, I've explored the sandy banks of the creek in that corner of the park, which has pathways through wetlands but isn't maintained. Stretches of tall grass and plenty of vegetation provide hiding places for deer and other wildlife.

Watch your footing as you climb the loose gravel toward Greenvale Drive. The trail cuts to the right and will progress through a series of switchbacks as it makes its way up the ridge in the higher elevations of the park's interior. This is an area to watch for mountain bikes, but at least you should have good visibility and see them coming. Remember, pedestrians have the right-of-way on trails, but be prepared in case the rider doesn't adhere to the rules.

The trail follows along the park's eastern boundary, which is clearly marked as private property. A new housing development planned for this area is expected to bring more than 370 new residences to a 55-acre plot that connects to Jahnke Road. Enjoy the solitude in Powhite Park while you can; soon there may be many more visitors to share it with.

During this hike, I took a right at an unmarked trail in an effort to get to a bluff that provides at least a glimpse of the creek watershed and Chippenham Parkway, but I missed the correct path and ended up back on the main trail along the creek. I doubled back briefly, though, before taking a steep, rocky spur trail up the side of the bluff to recover this route.

Atop the ridge, the view is somewhat obscured but sufficient. This area is safer from mountain bike interaction due to the steep hillside. Take a left off the rocky bluff down a trail that reconnects with the Eagle Scout footbridge, and take the path back to the Jahnke Road trailhead.

• •

GPS TRAILHEAD COORDINATES N37° 31.036' W77° 31.635'

DIRECTIONS From I-195 S, take the exit to Chippenham Parkway, then take the Jahnke Road exit and head east. The main park entrance will be immediately before the on ramp to Chippenham Parkway N. Or take Forest Hill Avenue to Jahnke Road and drive west 6 miles. The entrance is on the right, just before the on ramp to Chippenham Parkway.

GRTC bus route 2B stops near the park entrance. The park has bike racks.

An Eagle Scout project helps park visitors cross a long stretch of wetlands in Powhite Park.

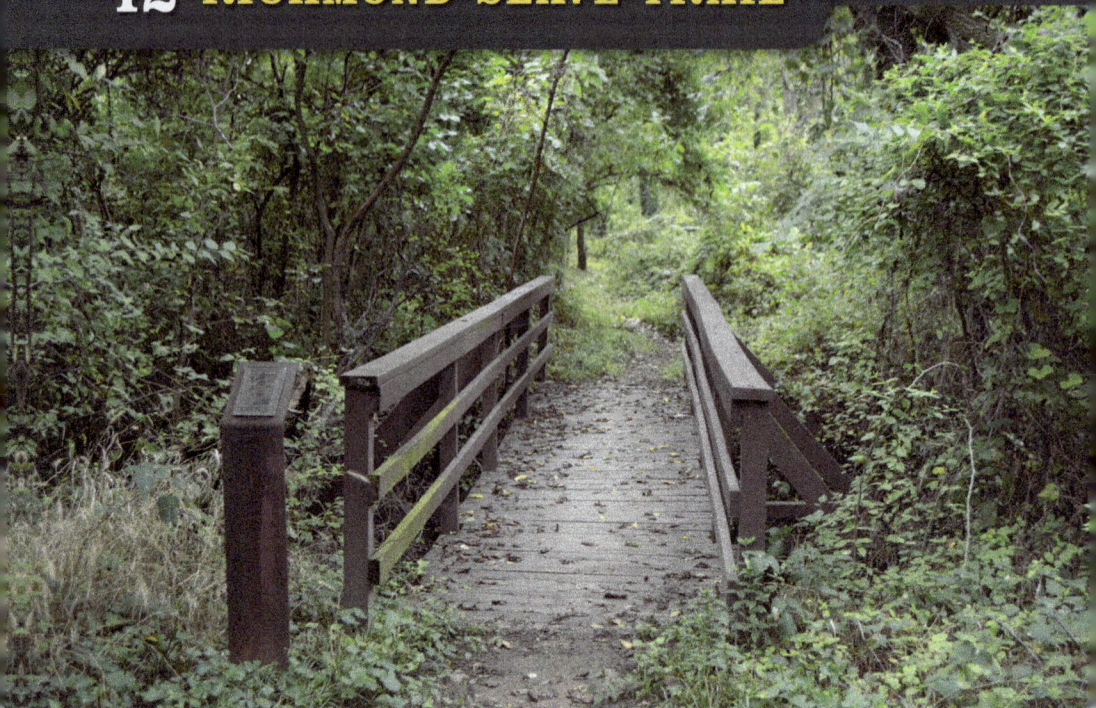

A footbridge near the Manchester Docks along the Richmond Slave Trail

THIS IS THE MOST URBAN HIKE presented in this book. It follows a route traveled by some of the thousands of enslaved Africans who made their journey to America in ships. They were marched along the banks of the James River on a route through the slave markets of Richmond. This route passes the Slavery Reconciliation Statue, the site of Lumpkin's Slave Jail, and the Negro Burial Ground, among many other important sites.

DESCRIPTION

The Richmond Slave Trail is a self-guided walking trail that chronicles the history of the trade in enslaved Africans in Virginia until 1775 and other locations in the Americas until 1865. After more than 10 years of planning, the City of Richmond and the Slave Trail Commission unveiled markers at 17 key historical sites along the Richmond Slave Trail in April 2011. (Note that the majority of the historical information from this hike comes from signage and the trail map.)

The trail begins at the Manchester Slave Docks, part of Ancarrow's Landing in the James River Park System. Combined with Rockett's Landing on the opposite side of the river, the Manchester Slave Docks was a major port in the massive downriver slave trade, making Richmond the largest source of enslaved Africans on the East Coast between 1830 and 1860. For this hike, follow the signs from the parking area to the

DISTANCE & CONFIGURATION: 6.2-mile out-and-back, or 3.1 miles one-way

DIFFICULTY: Easy

ELEVATION: 10' at trailhead, 110' at high point

SCENERY: James River, Canal Walk, statues, historical sites, Negro Burial Ground

EXPOSURE: Mostly open

TRAFFIC: Moderate

TRAIL SURFACE: Dirt and paved, including sidewalks

HIKING TIME: 2.5 hours

SEASON: Year-round

ACCESS: No fee

WHEELCHAIR ACCESS: On paved areas

MAPS: At jamesriverpark.org and richmondgov.com/commissionslavetrail

DRIVING DISTANCE FROM CAPITOL: 3.2 miles

FACILITIES: Interpretive signage

CONTACT: Richmond Slave Trail Commission: 804-698-1070, richmondgov.com/commission slavetrail

LOCATION: Ancarrow's Landing, 1400 Brander St., Richmond

COMMENTS: Portions of the Slave Trail are part of the City of Richmond's Liberty Trail. The Slave Trail can be done in segments, but the best way to experience it is with a guided tour, especially during the annual Juneteenth celebration. For more information, contact the Elegba Folklore Society at 804-644-3900 or visit efsinc.org.

docks. Today this is a popular fishing area, as it consists of a granite block wall about 5 feet above the tidal waters of the James River. Look for the interpretive sign, and follow the trail to the left along the docks. At a second interpretive sign, begin the Slave Trail and enter a wooded path. Keep an eye out for the trail medallion, visible at many spots along the trail, including embedded in sidewalks and parking lots where needed, as a way-finding marker.

To best understand the suffering that captured and enslaved Africans had to endure, consider taking a guided, torchlit tour at night with the Elegba Folklore Society. It is stirring and emotional. At that time, slaves were mostly transported at night so as not to disturb the citizens of Richmond. Famed and now retired James River Park manager Ralph White had the best advice for people hiking the Slave Trail: To help set the scene, envision as you enter the woods that you are being marched by torchlight, chained to other captives. You may have emerged from a ship after being imprisoned in a tiny holding space belowdecks for weeks. You are malnourished, sick, likely beaten, and covered in your own filth, and you have no idea where you are or how to get away. You are being forced to march more than 2 miles alongside and across a wide, unknown river in a foreign land. Keep this in mind during your hike.

The next 0.5 mile is the only wooded portion of this hike. Volunteer groups help maintain this section, under the guidance of James River Park staff. The trail runs 10–15 feet above the James, and there are several spots from which to view Libby Hill and the downtown skyline across the river. The trail emerges under the I-95 bridge at the floodwall gate on Brander Street. Take a right and follow the gravel doubletrack road to the next interpretive sign before reaching a paved section of

Richmond Slave Trail

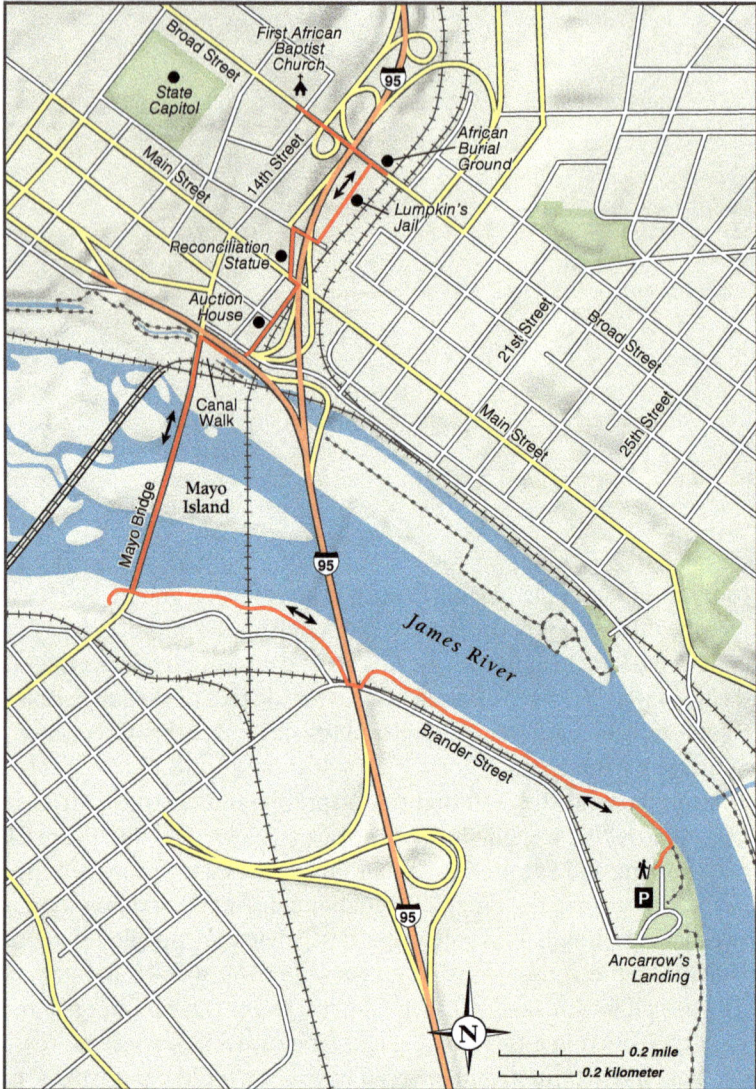

the trail that runs between the floodwall and the river. Look for fishermen dropping anchor near the falls of the James, watch for the occasional freight train, and pause to admire the Richmond skyline before you continue.

The floodwall was dedicated in 1994 and is designed to protect Richmond from floods of up to 32 feet, which would have stopped all of the recorded floods except Tropical Storm Agnes, which hit 36.5 feet in June 23, 1972. As this trail crosses to the north side of the river, you will pass through the floodwall again.

The trail passes under the Mayo Bridge (14th Street Bridge) and turns left, winding up onto the sidewalk on top of the bridge. Continue left across the current Mayo Bridge, which has been in service since 1913. There has been a bridge crossing below the falls here since the late 1700s. During the time of the slave trade, the bridge would have been wooden, less sturdy, built much closer to the water, and likely frightening to cross. As you continue along the sidewalk, take care, as traffic on the bridge can be intense. Look for another trail marker about halfway across the bridge on Mayo Island.

After passing through the floodwall gates, under the CSX railway viaduct, and over the Norfolk Southern tracks, take a left down a staircase to the Canal Walk, which opened in 1999 after a long period of renovation. An optional side hike along a 1.25-mile walkway will take you west to Tredegar Iron Works by way of Brown's Island and east to 17th Street in Shockoe Bottom. It features a series of markers and signs that interpret Richmond's history and provides a link to many of downtown's best attractions and restaurants. As for the James River and Kanawha Canal, African Americans provided much of the labor in the construction. Numerous African American boatmen traversed the canal, while black Richmonders carted cargo to and from the boats. The canal became another means for shipping slaves.

Walk east along the canal and cross over it via a footbridge. You should see a black box on display in a small plaza. That display is in honor of Henry "Box" Brown, who in 1849 shipped himself to Philadelphia in a wooden crate to escape slavery. Follow the signs and cross Dock Street to continue on 15th Street. Stop to read about the auction houses in this area, where slaves were sold.

Cross Main Street and stop to see the Richmond Slavery Reconciliation Statue. The 15-foot, half-ton bronze sculpture depicting two people melded in an embrace was unveiled in 2007. It is identical to statues in Liverpool, England, and in Benin, West Africa, that memorialize the triangular transatlantic slave-trade route.

Cross 15th Street and read marker 14 about the Odd Fellows Hall. Note Main Street Station just a couple dozen feet away. Take a left into the parking lot of the train station, and look for Winfree Cottage and the site of Lumpkin's Slave Jail. The notorious "Devil's Half Acre," owned by Robert Lumpkin, was a holding facility (a prison for slaves) and an auction house. Two years after the Civil War, Lumpkin's widow, Mary—a black woman—leased the complex to an institution that would eventually become Virginia Union University, a historically black college.

Continue along the parking lot to a tunnel that passes under Broad Street. As you pass through, you'll be at the edge of the African Burial Ground. There was once a hillside gallows where many escaped slaves were hanged and buried along Shockoe Creek. Local enslaved blacksmith Gabriel Prosser was executed after the discovery of his elaborate plan of revolt in 1800. The unmarked graves of free and enslaved Africans were paved over to provide a parking lot until protests led city and state officials to reclaim the historic area, leaving a grass field in memory of the dead.

Follow the path to the right to ascend to the sidewalk, and turn right to walk up Broad Street and over I-95. Take care crossing the on and off ramps to reach First African Baptist Church, which was founded in 1841 after the white members of First Baptist Church sold the building to the black members of the congregation, both free and enslaved. The building is now part of the Virginia Commonwealth University School of Medicine.

This is the last of the 17 stops of the Richmond Slave Trail. Retrace your steps to return to Ancarrow's Landing and the parking area.

• •

GPS TRAILHEAD COORDINATES N37° 31.177' W77° 25.134'

DIRECTIONS From downtown Richmond take the Maury Street exit off I-95 S and turn right. Or cross the James River by way of the 14th Street Bridge (Mayo Bridge) and take a left on East Third Street through an industrial area. Take a left onto Maury Street. Cross over train tracks, and the road becomes Brander Street at the floodwall gate. Drive until the road dead-ends at the parking lot of Ancarrow's Landing. The signs will include Manchester Slave Docks.

Several GRTC bus routes stop near the middle portions of the trail, and there are bike racks at Ancarrow's Landing.

The African Burial Ground, one of the stops along the Richmond Slave Trail

The Low Line is a linear park under the CSX viaduct along the Virginia Capital Trail and the James River and Kanawha Canal.

A LONGTIME DREAM of bicyclers and hikers in eastern Virginia, this 52-mile dedicated multiuse trail connects Richmond and Williamsburg along the beautiful and historic VA 5 corridor. After more than 25 years, the Virginia Capital Trail became a reality thanks to the coordinated efforts of citizens, tourism officials, the Virginia Department of Transportation, and local governments along the route.

DESCRIPTION

The Virginia Capital Trail parallels VA 5 between Jamestown and Richmond and has achieved its goal of making this historic corridor just as accessible to cyclists and pedestrians as it is to motorists. This state scenic byway is lined with famous plantations, including Sherwood Forest, home to President John Tyler.

The Virginia Department of Transportation (VDOT) oversaw the trail's construction, which began in 2008. The trail officially opened in October 2015. VDOT also maintains the trail, while the nonprofit Virginia Capital Trail Foundation continues to add amenities, including trail maps, educational kiosks, interpretive signage, mile markers, bike racks, restrooms, and benches.

The paved, 10-foot-wide path is the first long-distance, separated, multiuse trail in the Richmond region. It is lined with beautiful trees and a lush agrarian landscape

DISTANCE & CONFIGURATION: 3.1-mile out-and-back

DIFFICULTY: Easy

ELEVATION: 14' at trailhead, no significant rise

SCENERY: James River, Richmond skyline, Rockett's Landing

EXPOSURE: Open, with little shade

TRAFFIC: High

TRAIL SURFACE: 10 feet wide, paved

HIKING TIME: 1 hour

SEASON: Year-round during daylight hours

ACCESS: No fee

WHEELCHAIR ACCESS: Yes

MAPS: At trailhead and virginiacapitaltrail.org

DRIVING DISTANCE FROM CAPITOL: 1.8 miles

FACILITIES: Parking, portable toilet, fishing, and paddleboat access, all at Great Shiplock Park

CONTACT: Virginia Capital Trail Foundation: 804-788-6453, virginiacapitaltrail.org

LOCATION: Great Shiplock Park, 2803 Dock St., Richmond

COMMENTS: There are several trailheads along the 52-mile Virginia Capital Trail. For a longer jaunt, consider hiking from Four Mile Creek Park in Henrico County, Charles City Courthouse, or Chickahominy Riverfront Park in James City County. The Captain John Smith Chesapeake National Historic Trail also connects at Great Shiplock Park.

and is open year-round, just like any other public roadway. It is a big draw for trail users of all ages because it allows them to relax, enjoy the view, and feel safe with little intrusion from vehicles. For most of the trail's length, the James River will be nearby but not visible. Richmond offers your best bet to hike alongside the river.

For this hike, I suggest Great Shiplock Park as the best place to begin. The park, part of the James River Park System and dedicated as the Richmond trailhead for the Virginia Capital Trail in October 2013, is located near the western terminus of the trail along Dock Street in Shockoe Bottom. The park has a nonmotorized boat launch, a 0.5-mile trail, and enhanced access to the 5.6 acres of riverfront parkland.

From the trailhead in the park, walk east along Dock Street toward the Intermediate Terminal. Stone Brewing has a lease on the building on Wharf Street but is planning to demolish it to build a restaurant and beer garden. The City of Richmond is working on plans to renovate the former Lehigh Cement site, just west of the Intermediate Terminal. This project may slightly alter the current route of the Virginia Capital Trail as it passes through this development.

Located across the James on the south bank of the river is Ancarrow's Landing. The infamous Manchester Slave Docks are a part of that park, which is where the Richmond Slave Trail begins (see page 70). Just south of Ancarrow's is Richmond's Wastewater Treatment Plant, which on certain days with certain wind patterns may put a stink in the air as you hike on the Virginia Capital Trail.

Next up is the Rockett's Landing mixed-use residential development, which includes a few restaurants, a marina, sand volleyball courts, and more. It is also the home of the Virginia Boat Club, a nonprofit organization that promotes rowing in the Richmond area. They store many of their boats alongside the trail and often practice in the tidal waters of the James here.

Virginia Capital Trail

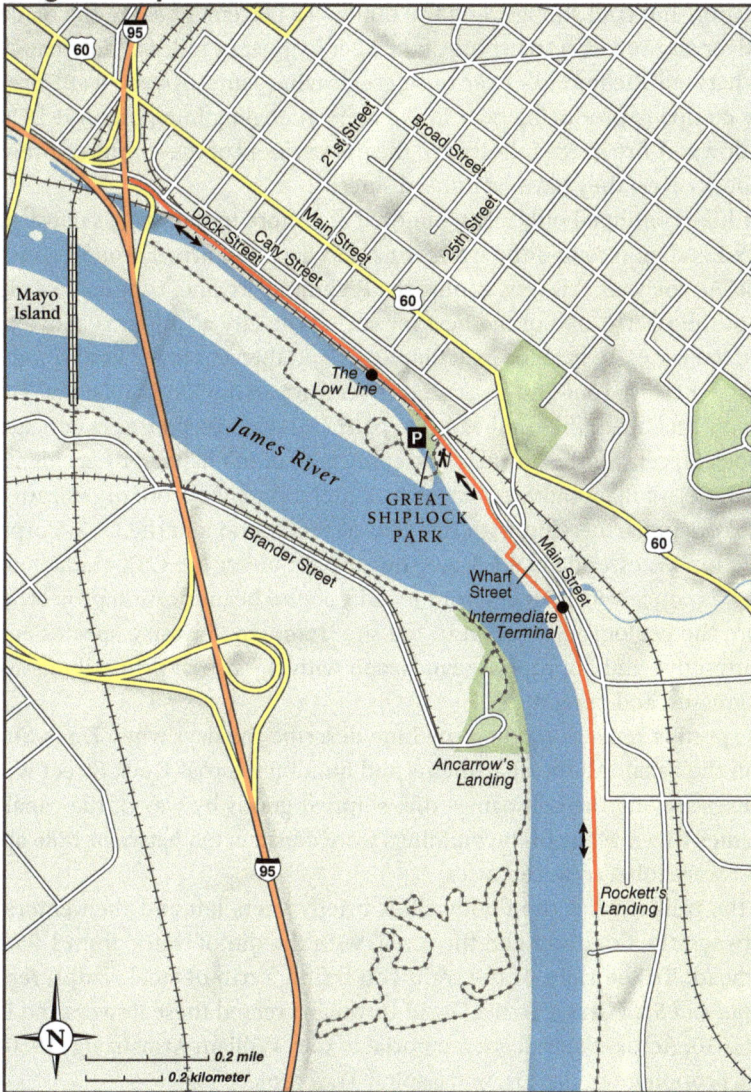

As you walk along the trail, once you pass the Conch Republic restaurant, begin looking on your left for an old stone building with an arched entrance and bricked-in arched windows, likely blocked off by chain-link fencing. These are the former beer "caves" of the James River Steam Brewery, which were built in 1868 by D. G. Yuengling Jr., son of brewery founder D. G. Yuengling. According to *Richmond Beer: A History of Brewing in the River City* by Lee Graves, the building was 80 feet high, with five stories aboveground. The beer caves, or tunnels, were used for both fermentation and cold storage, and the building's placement along the banks of the James River allowed easy transport of the beer by boat or railcar. The financial crisis of 1873 harmed Richmond's beer business, leaving James River Steam Brewery as the only company producing beer in the area. Yuengling hung on until 1879, when he shut down. A fire in 1891 destroyed the upper floors of the shuttered brewery but left the beer caves; they have sat unused since.

Our hike continued only a few hundred feet more to the east, as construction at Rockett's Landing rerouted the trail for us that day. We turned around and retraced our steps. As you walk this way, admire the Richmond skyline. Especially at night, this section of the river is one of the best for seeing the city as it looms above the calm waters of the James. Return to Great Shiplock Park, then continue west to add another 1.4 miles to this hike (out-and-back) and cover more of the Virginia Capital Trail.

As you again pass the trailhead, the path crosses railroad tracks and again runs along Dock Street. The beautiful landscaping here didn't happen by accident. This is the Low Line, a collaborative effort led by a Richmond nonprofit organization called Capital Trees in partnership with the City of Richmond and the CSX Corporation. The Low Line is essentially a 5.5-acre linear park under the CSX viaduct along the canal. It was conceived as an environmentally sound beautification project, an effort to restore the ecological function of the site, removing invasive species and creating an attractive and appropriate landscape with the use of primarily native trees, shrubs, grasses, and perennials.

Interpretive signs along the Low Line describe the days when Dock Street was a port on the canal. All the apartments and buildings across Dock Street were once warehouses serving the companies that shipped goods by way of the canal system or the James River. Many of the buildings were constructed between 1886 and 1929, and most were tobacco warehouses.

As the trail reaches the floodwall, it briefly veers left and then enters a wide area between the floodwall and the canal, with the din of traffic from I-95 droning on overhead. To the right of the trail, you'll find a trio of steel sculptures known as *The Bud and Seed Group.* Artist David Boyajian created these flowers and installed them in 2010. Across the trail is a memorial to Carl William Armstrong (1950–2009), "a strong proponent of the Virginia Capital Trail project."

If you wish to continue, walk through one of the two doors through the floodwall to begin the Canal Walk, which offers a 1.25-mile walkway that connects to Tredegar Iron Works by way of Brown's Island from this point. On that side of the wall, markers show the highest floodwater levels in Richmond's recorded history. Dedicated in 1994, the floodwall was designed to protect Richmond from floods of up to 32 feet, which would have stopped all of the recorded floods except Tropical Storm Agnes, which hit 36.5 feet in June 23, 1972.

Retrace your steps along the trail back to Great Shiplock Park.

NEARBY ACTIVITIES

If you want to explore other sections of the Virginia Capital Trail, about 10 miles east of Richmond, **Dorey Park** (page 156) and **Deep Bottom Park & Four Mile Creek** (henrico .us/rec/places/deep-bottom) are part of a 3.5-mile trail diversion around the I-295 interchange with VA 5. Park at either location and enjoy eastern Henrico County. As the trail continues west into Charles City County, take in the magnificent rural and agrarian scenery. Several historic plantations are accessible: Shirley, Edgewood, Berkeley, Westover, and Sherwood. All are worth a visit to see stately homes, beautiful gardens, and views of the James River.

At the eastern terminus of the Virginia Capital Trail is the **Jamestown Settlement** (888-593-4682, historyisfun.org), with its kid-friendly re-creations of the Colonial settlement circa 1607 and the three sailing vessels that brought English settlers to the New World. Just beyond is the actual Jamestown site, known as **Historic Jamestowne** (757-856-1250, historicjamestowne.org). It is home to ongoing archaeological excavations, and a museum showcases artifacts found at the site, including coins, ceramics, and a suit of armor.

• •

GPS TRAILHEAD COORDINATES N37° 31.557' W77° 25.259'

DIRECTIONS From Richmond, take I-95 S to Exit 74B (Franklin Street) onto 15th Street. In about 0.2 mile, turn left onto Dock Street and follow it less than a mile to the entrance of Great Shiplock Park on the right. From I-95 N, take Exit 74C (Broad Street) onto Oliver Hill Way. Take a left onto East Broad Street and an immediate right onto 18th Street. After four blocks, turn left onto Dock Street and follow it less than a mile to the entrance of Great Shiplock Park on the right.

GRTC's Pulse line stops along East Main Street and at Rockett's Landing. Great Shiplock Park has bicycle racks.

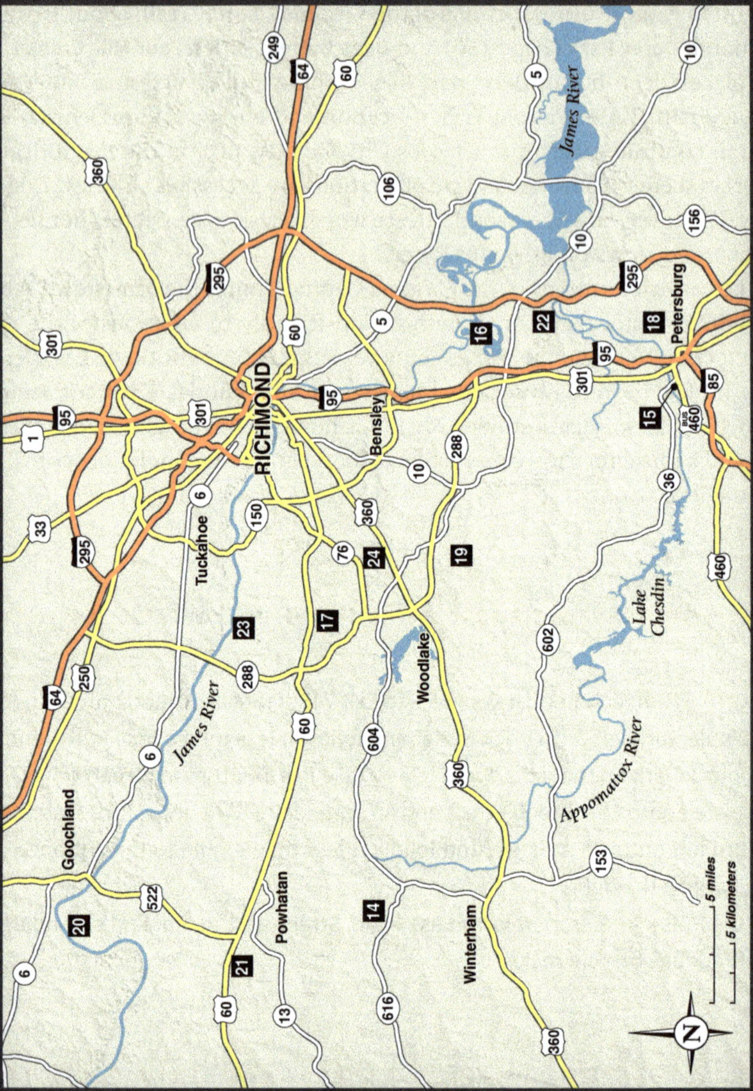
RICHMOND
Petersburg
Bensley
Tuckahoe
Woodlake
Goochland
Powhatan
Winterham
James River
Appomattox River
Lake Chesdin
14
15
16
17
18
19
20
21
22
23
24
5 miles
5 kilometers
N

SOUTH OF THE JAMES

14 AMELIA WILDLIFE MANAGEMENT AREA

Amelia Lake is an attractive destination at the wildlife management area.

THE 2,217-ACRE AMELIA WILDLIFE MANAGEMENT AREA encompasses forest, rolling fields, and wide hedgerows that offer great bird-watching. The 100-acre Amelia Lake and a smaller pond entice anglers with largemouth bass, channel catfish, walleye, redear sunfish, and other species.

DESCRIPTION

The commonwealth's wildlife management areas (WMAs), operated by the Virginia Department of Game and Inland Fisheries (VDGIF), greatly expand outdoor recreation options in central Virginia. With no national forests east of the Appalachian Mountains, avid hikers look to WMAs to effectively double the state-owned land at their disposal. And while these areas lack the conveniences associated with state parks, they are, as the name suggests, great for wildlife-watching.

If you have more than watching in mind, you can bring your fishing pole (and fishing license) anytime. Hunting is allowed in season, and the seasons vary with the game. They typically begin with bird hunting in September and continue intermittently through February. It's advisable to avoid hiking in Virginia's wildlife areas during the popular deer and wild-turkey hunting seasons.

But don't let the preceding caveat dissuade you from visiting, particularly if you're one of the many Chesterfield County residents just half an hour away. In actuality,

DISTANCE & CONFIGURATION: 4.3-mile loop, plus options

DIFFICULTY: Moderate

ELEVATION: 331' at trailhead, 238' at low point

SCENERY: Mostly hardwood forest, fishing lakes, fields, hedgerows

EXPOSURE: Moderate

TRAFFIC: Low

TRAIL SURFACE: Dirt and gravel doubletrack, mowed-grass paths

HIKING TIME: 2 hours

SEASON: Year-round during daylight hours, but avoid trails during fall and winter hunting seasons

ACCESS: No fee; horseback riding and mountain biking allowed; no ATVs

WHEELCHAIR ACCESS: Not for the mapped route; boat launch and fishing pier are accessible

MAPS: At dgif.virginia.gov/wma/amelia

DRIVING DISTANCE FROM CAPITOL: 35.5 miles

FACILITIES: Pier, boat launch, shooting ranges, informational kiosks, resident staff

CONTACT: 804-561-3350, dgif.virginia.gov/wma/amelia

LOCATION: 15841 Kennons Ln., Amelia Court House

COMMENTS: The grassy trails here are mowed sporadically. If you plan to hike in summer, call to inquire about trail status. All wildlife management areas are open to hunting. Check with the Virginia Department of Game and Inland Fisheries (804-370-1000, dgif.virginia.gov/hunting) for annual hunting seasons.

aquatic wildlife constitutes the main draw at Amelia, and you'll inevitably spot anglers casting from the shore or from small watercraft. If it's not hunting season, you may hear gunshots from the firing ranges northeast of the lake. This loop takes you past them along a gravel road—a short, necessary link between the trails on either side of it.

The north–south road bisects the area, with Amelia Lake and the firing ranges in the western half and the much smaller Smith Lake and former farm buildings in the east. Placid Amelia Lake reflects the tall trees along its shore, while the cumulative effect of the fields and buildings—which include barns still used by the VDGIF and a decrepit abandoned manor—is one not of wilderness but of bucolic decay. Come in the winter and you may fancy seeing the old manor, on an abandoned Dust Bowl farmstead—there's even a Model T rusting in the woods. In the summer, the pastoral scene is positively shaggy with greenery. At any time of year, this loop presents an intriguing and endearing dichotomy.

In contrast to trails in nearby Powhatan WMA, where equestrian use keeps overgrowth at bay, Amelia's trails are sometimes shrouded in waist-high grass. With that in mind, the loop described avoids the easternmost trails in favor of the westernmost one, which is easier to follow because it traces the shoreline of Amelia Lake.

The VDGIF elected to maintain the fields and hedgerows of this former farm, as they constitute an ecosystem unto themselves. The hedges provide habitat for rabbits and other woodland mammals, which in turn draw the owls and raptors you may see circling overhead. Smaller birds, like doves and quail, forage in the fields and nest in the hedges. Rotund long-billed woodcocks reportedly favor the banks of the Appomattox River, which forms the WMA's northern and eastern borders but is not along the trail network. You're more likely to spot wild turkeys feeding near the

Amelia Wildlife Management Area

many stands of oak. According to the VDGIF, healthy deer and turkey populations exist on this management area. Hunted nearly to extinction a century ago, the wild turkey is now a conservation success story.

Begin by crossing the park road to a yellow metal gate that signals the trail's departure westward toward Amelia Lake. The path winds along the mowed boundary of a meadow before picking up a dirt doubletrack trail that flows in and out of tree cover. After 0.5 mile of mostly level walking through hardwood forest, the trail descends steeply toward a marshy wetlands area where I was able to spot a young buck standing in the waterway having a drink. It was early enough in the year that he still had velvety nubs for antlers. I was about 50 feet from the trail and watched him for about 10 seconds before he raised his head and spotted me. He turned to dart away, deeper into the cover of the marsh, with a handful of other deer scampering away with him. It made me wonder if they were accustomed to people hiking in the park or if they assumed I was a hunter.

The trail meets the lake at the end of the first mile and then traces the lake-shore northward, looping occasionally into the woods but promptly returning to the waterside. The lake does not have many convenient access points on the west side, especially if the grassy buffer between the forest and the lake has not be bush-hogged. The trail can be very crunchy along this way; wear boots or sturdy hiking shoes to protect your feet, especially along this section.

Bear right when spur trails head left, and you'll soon reach the earthen dam at the lake's northern edge. The grassy slope with views across the lake is a pleasant spot to catch your breath. The dam and shoreline were covered in a variety of beautiful wildflowers during the time of my June hike. Ascend east through a parking lot for a trailhead, and follow the gravel road past the firing ranges. Turn right at a sign-board that signals Marsh Point Trail (also known as Milking Parlor Trail), and follow the gravel roadway approximately 1 mile back to the parking lot and trailhead.

If you prefer to hike Marsh Point Trail, it would add at least 2 miles to your trip. Shaggy cedars border the gravel doubletrack, which is closed to vehicles. Cedars commonly line the state's rural roads, indicating that the road predates the establishment of this WMA. Ahead on the left is the trail's namesake, an open-sided milking barn that now houses maintenance tractors. A newer cinderblock structure nearby serves as a seasonal hunting headquarters and has restrooms. Turn sharply right onto another doubletrack before passing the building.

Head south past a series of fields and hedgerows. The bands of brush between fields have been allowed to widen beyond those of a working farm to increase animal habitat. A hardwood forest of oak and hickory towers at the periphery of the field. You'll descend to reach a small pond abutting peaceful Smith Lake on the right. Its twin lies across that lake to the south. Pass a spur path to a nearby parking area on your right, and continue uphill past the water.

Soon the old grain silos and abandoned manor of the former farmstead rise into view on the horizon. The VDGIF now uses the barns, including a quaint red one, for storage and workspace, but vines are overtaking the brick manor house, which is shaded by a mammoth oak. The manor's shutters still hang despite missing windowpanes, and its roof, though rusted, appears to be intact. The house fronts the Woodcock Trail, a gravel road that leads past a quail-restoration demonstration and back to the trailhead parking area. To follow the route as it's shown on the trail map, continue southward.

You'll soon reach the newer manager's residence, passing directly beside the domicile. A few hundred yards ahead, a dirt doubletrack veers left. Turn here and look for the rusted car that has collapsed in the leaves to the left of the trail. Proceed between two stands of hardwoods to see a field opening on the left. Look for a narrow dirt path on the right. Though brief, this lone stretch of singletrack is Amelia's best footpath, wending past some younger pine forest and through more-mature trees back to the parking area.

• •

GPS TRAILHEAD COORDINATES N37° 27.168' W77° 55.012'

DIRECTIONS From Richmond, go west on US 60 (Midlothian Turnpike) 20 miles and turn left onto VA 634 (Stavemill Road). In 2.5 miles, turn left onto VA 622 (Dorset Road), which becomes VA 604 (Genito Road) at Dorset Market. From the market, follow VA 604 for 6 miles, then turn right onto VA 616 (still called Genito Road). Continue about 1.5 miles, until you reach VA 652 (Kennons Lane), which enters Amelia WMA after less than a mile. Park in the first lot, immediately on the right as you enter the WMA.

Wildflowers in bloom in Amelia Wildlife Management Area

A southbound Amtrak train passes over the Appomattox on the Seaboard Coast Line Railway Bridge.

THE LOWER APPOMATTOX RIVER CORRIDOR has a long history and many natural, cultural, and social amenities to explore. In 1997, volunteers devised a plan to develop the corridor, and the cities of Petersburg, Colonial Heights, and Hopewell, together with the counties of Dinwiddie, Chesterfield, and Prince George, were identified as stakeholders. Friends of the Lower Appomattox River (FOLAR) was formed in 2000 by the volunteers and consists of representatives from the six stakeholder localities and Virginia State University. The six localities now work with FOLAR to develop and maintain the Appomattox River Trail, a 22-mile trail system with 12 miles of riverside trails, 11 riverside parks, and seven boat access points.

DESCRIPTION

This hike first heads west along the Appomattox River Trail from the trailhead at Campbell's Bridge by Patton Park and Fleet Street. As of this writing, the trail was not well signed, and there are no markers along the route for this out-and-back hike.

The rapids were an immediate draw for me as soon as I hit the trail. The flow of the Appomattox River is somewhat controlled along this section by the dam at Lake Chesdin, but when the water is up, you can clearly hear the rapids west of Campbell's Bridge. The river is also much narrower in this section, and you'll find the flow more

DISTANCE & CONFIGURATION: 2.8-mile out-and-back, with optional offshoots

DIFFICULTY: Easy

ELEVATION: 29' at trailhead, 60' at highest point

SCENERY: Riparian banks of Appomattox River, remnants of dam network, railway bridge

EXPOSURE: In and out of shade

TRAFFIC: Low

TRAIL SURFACE: Dirt doubletrack

HIKING TIME: 1.5 hours

SEASON: Year-round during daylight hours

ACCESS: No fee

WHEELCHAIR ACCESS: No

MAPS: At park kiosk and folar-va.org

DRIVING DISTANCE FROM CAPITOL: 25 miles

FACILITIES: Pier, boat launch, shooting ranges (open daily except Monday), informational kiosks, resident staff

CONTACT: Petersburg Parks and Leisure Services: 804-733-2394, petersburgva.gov/facilities

LOCATION: 515 Fleet St., Petersburg

COMMENTS: Friends of the Lower Appomattox (FOLAR) is a volunteer organization working with the regional localities to plan the trails, parks, and boat access points along the river corridor. Contact them at 804-861-1666 or visit folar-va.org

dictated by human influences, scars of Petersburg's industrial past. Many spur trails head through openings in the trees down to the rocky shoreline. There are also a few picnic tables and benches along the trail.

Continuing west along the gravel doubletrack, look for sycamore, bitternut hickory, pawpaw, and green ash trees scattered along the shoreline. There is a heavy concentration of invasive species and undergrowth along the trail and shoreline, so look for clear, well-used spur trails to avoid contact with any poisonous plants.

Soon the trail meets Battersea Dam, a crescent-shaped concrete dam that was designed to redirect water into the South Canal (left of the trail, now dry) and the North Canal, which runs along the north bank of the river. Until 2008, this was the end of the trail because of the challenge with the waterway, but FOLAR volunteers, after their first major fundraising effort, installed two steel bridges at the dam. The first bridge spans about 80 feet, crossing the rapids to a rocky island, and the second spans about 40 feet at almost a 90-degree angle to direct the trail back to the shoreline. The separation between the bridges provides an opportunity to relax on a rocky island that connects to the dam. There is plenty of shade, and the setting is beautiful.

After crossing the second span and rejoining the trail, begin looking to the right for a clearing with two stone arches. These are the ruins of the Pocahontas Mill. The old mill, also known as Battersea Mill, was constructed in 1840 at the end of North West Street and was in use during the Civil War. The water rights for the millrace (now filled) were acquired in 1901, and the mill closed in 1918. The cut stones are interesting to examine up close. Be sure to identify the keystone if you have children with you so they can learn how a stone structure can support itself with good craftsmanship.

Though it is not visible, historic Battersea is about 0.25 mile west on the other side of the trail, over the train tracks and through the trees. This Palladian villa was

Appomattox River Trail

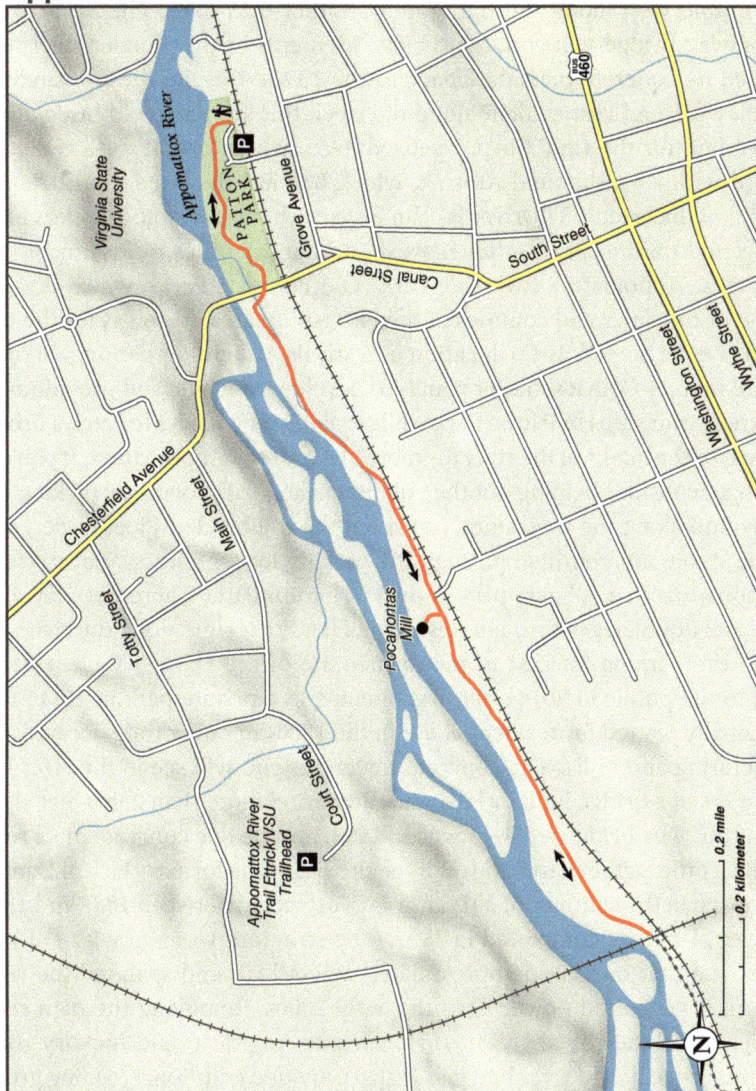

built in 1768 by Colonel John Banister, the first mayor of Petersburg. Efforts are under way to restore the house and estate, and there is potential to connect Battersea to the Appomattox River Trail.

Along this route, you may be able to see more former mill sites, including remnants on Strawberry Island, located in the center of the river. As with much of the Appomattox in this stretch, the landscape has been altered by heavy industrialization.

Continue west along the trail about another 0.25 mile. The Seaboard Coast Line Railway Bridge will come into view. Elements of this slender steel structure supported by concrete piers date back to the 1890s. Despite the ivy hanging from the framework and rust evident along the steel, this attractive old bridge is part of an active line for the CSX Corp. I paused here awhile to wait for a train and was rewarded with a southbound Amtrak, which had just departed the Ettrick station just north of the bridge. The river is calm here, with several large boulders to hop to.

The trail unofficially continues west another 2.5 miles to eventually connect with trails at Appomattox Riverside Park (Old Ferndale Park), which is a valuable amenity for the cities and counties of the Petersburg area as well as for the trail system and river. The park is the location of festivals, watercraft parking, hiking, running, and more. FOLAR's master plan is to develop this route and provide signage.

Retrace your steps to Patton Park while looking for chances to catch a fishermen's trail down to the banks of the river for more views of the Appomattox. If you brought a spare bag, consider helping out the volunteers and park lovers by picking up litter you may find along the way. Once you reach the trailhead at Fleet Street, carefully cross the street and continue through the parking lot for an easy, flat stretch along the Appomattox to a 3.4-acre park known as Patton Park. There are a few big trees and a gravel doubletrack through this strip of land that runs along the river, stretching from the parking lot east to the former site of the Harvell Dam. Patton Park opened to the public in 2014 after first opening as a private park in 2011. The land was originally platted for residential use in the 1700s but over time became a site for manufacturing and mills. The concrete structures you will see in the river here are former piers of a bridge built in 1931 and measuring more than 2,000 feet across the Appomattox. The bridge was removed in 1983, but the five concrete piers remain.

Walk a little farther east and you'll see the site of the former Harvell Dam, which was removed in the summer of 2014. It was constructed between 1885 and 1891, and the power plant was completed in 1927. The structure was a gravity-fed concrete buttress dam that measured approximately 9 feet high and spanned the river in a Z pattern. It generated power until the early 2000s. Removing the dam reopened 127 miles of habitat for migratory fish, such as American and hickory shad, alewife, American eel, and river herring. It also provided additional feeding ground for striped bass and other predators that consume the aforementioned species.

Take in the view, read some of the history of the area on interpretive signs, stop at the picnic shelter for a snack, and then retrace your steps to the parking lot.

NEARBY ACTIVITIES

If you want another short hike nearby, on the north bank of the river in Chesterfield County, the **Ettrick/VSU Trailhead** of the Appomattox River Trail was dedicated in 2016. It is the first phase of a project that is expected to eventually connect the town of Ettrick with the Skinquarter community in the western part of the county, 20 miles upriver. The trailhead is located beyond a 12-space parking lot at 3801 Main St. in Ettrick. As of this writing, you cannot connect from Petersburg by trail, but the hope is that there will someday be a connection to the Chesterfield trail network from Campbell's Bridge.

• •

GPS TRAILHEAD COORDINATES N37° 13.881' W77° 25.004'

DIRECTIONS From Richmond, take I-95 south to Petersburg and exit onto East Washington Street (Exit 52). Turn right onto VA 36 (North South Street), then turn right onto Canal Street and left onto Fleet Street. The Patton Park parking lot and trailhead for the Appomattox River Trail will be on the right.

Stone arches from the Pocahontas Mill (Battersea Mill), constructed circa 1840

The James River, viewed from a trail leading to Henricus Historical Park and Dutch Gap Conservation Area

THE 810-ACRE DUTCH GAP CONSERVATION AREA abuts Henricus Historical Park, site of an English settlement just four years younger than Jamestown. The area's present topography bears the scars of four centuries of human manipulation, beginning with the moat-building project for which it was named. Yet nature persists undaunted, and this hike, which traces a tidal inlet of the James that was formerly an oxbow bend in the river, affords you the chance to escape civilization into a marsh teeming with wildlife.

DESCRIPTION

Dutch Gap Conservation Area is undergoing a resurgence. In partnership with the City of Richmond and Henrico and Chesterfield Counties, the Henricus Foundation has spearheaded the re-creation of the 1611 Citie of Henricus within the conservation area. The area has benefited from a new visitor center, period-style buildings, and farm plots. Many visitors are quite content to tour the historical sites and gawk at the widening James River from Pocahontas Bluff, leaving the southern bulk of the conservation area to those with a few hours to spare—and some insect repellent.

Enthusiastic bird-watchers have long known about Dutch Gap's great blue heron rookery, and some of those enthusiasts might be seen, binoculars in hand, scanning the marsh on the left of Henricus Road en route to the parking area. The 4.5-mile

DISTANCE & CONFIGURATION:
5.6-mile balloon

DIFFICULTY: Easy

ELEVATION: 10' at trailhead, no significant rise

SCENERY: Tidal flats along an old channel of the James River, re-created 17th-century English settlement at adjacent park

EXPOSURE: Open, with limited shade

TRAFFIC: Low

TRAIL SURFACE: Dirt and gravel doubletrack

HIKING TIME: 2.5 hours

SEASON: Year-round, 8 a.m.–sunset

ACCESS: No fee. Fee for Henricus Historical Park is $9 adults, $7 children; the visitor center is open Tuesday–Sunday, 10 a.m.–5 p.m.

WHEELCHAIR ACCESS: No

MAPS: At Henricus Historical Park visitor center or at chesterfield.gov/parks

DRIVING DISTANCE FROM CAPITOL: 19 miles

FACILITIES: Visitor center (at Henricus Historical Park), restrooms, picnic shelters, observation blind, bird-identification trail, canoe and kayak slide

CONTACT: Chesterfield County Parks: 804-748-1624, chesterfield.gov/parks; Henricus Historical Park: 804-748-1611, henricus.org

LOCATION: 251 Henricus Park Rd., Chester

COMMENTS: The Captain John Smith Chesapeake National Historic Trail and the Lee vs. Grant 1864 Campaign Civil War trail connect to Dutch Gap Conservation Area.

Dutch Gap Trail Loop even has a 10-station ornithology trail, an Eagle Scout project. In addition to garden-variety species, such as the tufted titmouse and chickadee, the trail notes barred-owl and screech-owl habitats.

The Dutch Gap Trail journeys along a narrow spit of land that practically encircles a tidal lagoon dotted by small islands and the crumbling remains of old wooden barges. The present lagoon was formerly a sand-and-gravel quarry, and the trail crosses the channel cut to fill it on a new footbridge, installed in summer 2008. On its other, outer edge, the trail is ringed by an old channel of the James River. The antiquated nomenclature for the land underfoot, Farrar's Island, recalls the river's 18th-century route. The peninsula was once an island, if only in times of high water.

Successive efforts have sought to manipulate and truncate the river's course. It was not long after English colonists established the Citie of Henricus, named for King James's son Henry, that Sir Thomas Dale orchestrated the construction of a moat to protect the settlement. He employed a Dutch technique, and the resulting waterway was termed Dale's Dutch Gap. During the War Between the States, Union troops under the command of General Benjamin Butler began to excavate a canal across the Dutch Gap so that the Union Navy might proceed upstream out of reach of Confederate cannon fire. The canal was completed with a bang—literally—when an explosion breached the dam in 1865. The James was redirected again to its present course in the 1930s. That final extension of the canal created Hatcher's Island to the north.

Though the quarry is flooded, industry remains close as you begin this hike. As the trail heads south from the visitor center, a fence looms uphill on the right. Behind it lies a coal-ash pond, part of the adjacent Dominion Energy plant. In some stretches, the trail passes directly beside this pond and its twin to the west. And

Dutch Gap Conservation Area

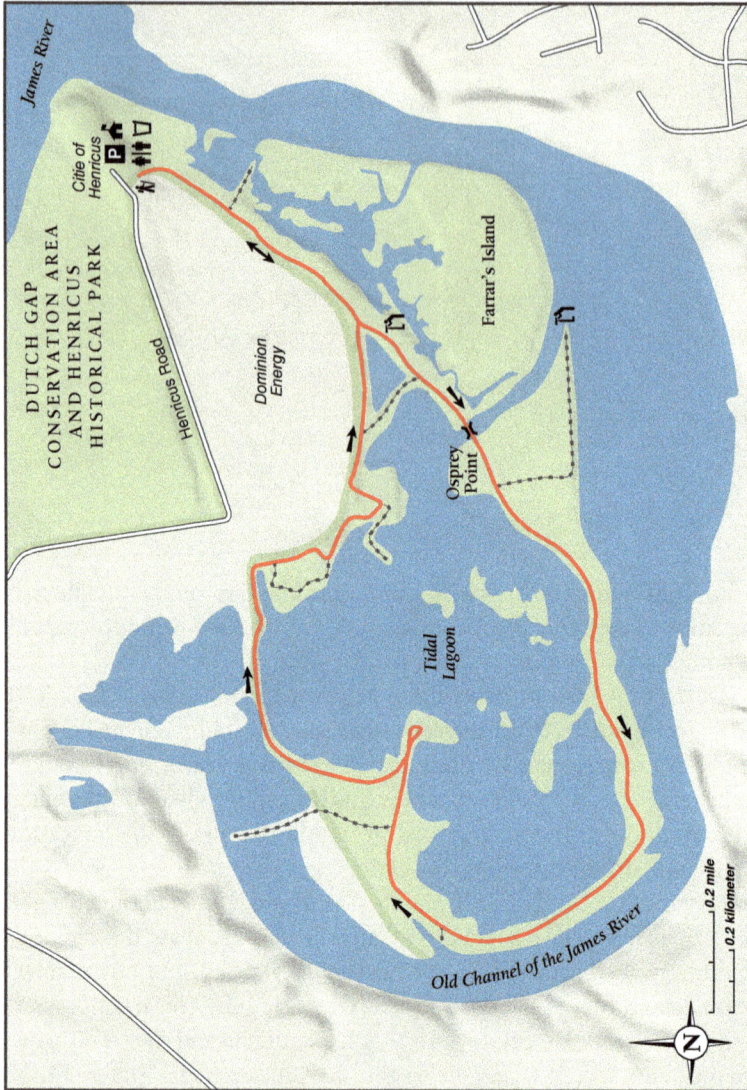

James River

Citie of Henricus

DUTCH GAP
CONSERVATION AREA
AND HENRICUS
HISTORICAL PARK

Henricus Road

Dominion Energy

Farrar's Island

Osprey Point

Tidal Lagoon

Old Channel of the James River

0.2 mile

0.2 kilometer

N

while the ponds mar about a third of the hike, it is fortuitous that they are fenced and quiet so you can focus your attention on the waterside woods.

Proceeding south on a gravel doubletrack, you will pass two spur trails on the left. The first leads to a fishing point, and the second to Twin Rock spur, a wildlife-viewing area. Beyond, at the 0.5-mile marker, the trail forks, continuing straight or veering left, away from the hillside. Take the left path onto a doubletrack under a high tree canopy. The trail will pass a small freshwater pond on the right, a remnant of a 1920s mining operation. It's speculated that miners tapped into a spring, which keeps the pit flooded to this day.

As the trail gets farther into the lagoon, your odds of spotting wildlife increase. Besides herons, you'll likely spot black cormorants (whose name was derived from the Latin word for "sea crow") bobbing on the water, distinguishable by their long, periscope-like necks. Keep your eyes peeled for long-billed kingfishers and hawklike ospreys, both of which dive underwater to grasp their prey.

About 1 mile into the hike, the trail reaches the footbridge over the lagoon channel. Installed in 2008, the bridge helped complete a loop for this trail, which used to be an out-and-back. It also increased the recreational uses for Dutch Gap, as now Chesterfield County is able to bring in more running and biking events without as many logistical and safety concerns due to the inaccessibility of the trail.

Look for fishing boats passing under the bridge as they try to locate the best spot to cast a line into the lagoon. The tidal waters contain smallmouth and largemouth bass and blue catfish, along with migratory species such as striped bass and American shad.

After the trail crosses the bridge, you may see signs of the great blue heron rookery. According to the county website, this rookery may be a replacement for one that was destroyed by storms, forcing the birds to move. Watch for a break in the treeline on your right, which is Osprey Point on the park map, and you may see several stick nests in the treetops across the narrow channel.

Farther down the trail, another optional spur to the left will take you to Dog Leg Point and provide a glimpse of the slow-moving old river channel. As the main trail continues along the southern rim of the lagoon, the next 2 miles reveal a change in the surrounding vegetative character. Sandy soil scattered with pebbles, along with slightly higher elevation, produces a small glade of twisting, scrubby oaks. There are even a few cacti trailside. We also spotted a couple of deer darting through the woods and stopped to admire the lagoon and have a snack.

The trail curls to the right and reaches a small peninsula within the lagoon, formerly the site of a hunting lodge and currently home to maintenance buildings. A whitewater kayaking class is offered at the boat launch, and there is a shelter with picnic tables if you need a rest. At the water's edge, scan the lagoon for islands that dot its eastern half. These formed through silt accumulation, which put sandy flesh on the skeletons of discarded barges. Cattails and grasses took root, expediting the accumulation of soil.

Double back on the road briefly and take the right fork to continue the loop. From this point, it is about 2 miles to the parking lot. The banks on each side of the trail are narrower here. You will soon see the old river channel on the left, and visible on the lagoon side are the remains of wooden barges, which provide a habitat for aquatic life. You may again spy anglers casting from small boats.

The trail momentarily bears right, into a wooded area, before cutting sharply left. After a few twists, the trail turns right and grazes the second coal-ash pond as it begins the final stretch back to the parking area.

NEARBY ACTIVITIES

While at Dutch Gap, visit **Henricus Historical Park** (804-748-1611, henricus.org) and its informative re-creation of the 1611 Citie of Henricus. It was here that John Rolfe crossbred Dutch tobacco with native strands, giving rise to the settlement's premier export. Ironically, the booming tobacco business, coupled with the introduction of private land ownership, served to diminish the English colony at Henricus, drawing settlers out of the city to nearby farms.

Henricus Historical Park now retells the colony's story through period-style buildings and reenactments. Mount Malady, the first English hospital in the New World, stood here, as did Rock Hall, home of Reverend Alexander Whitaker. It was Whitaker who, in 1613, converted the Powhatan princess Pocahontas, a prisoner at the time, to Christianity and taught her English; he may also have introduced her to Rolfe, her future husband. In 1622 an Indian attack halted construction on the "Colledge of Henricus," which had won support from the first Virginia Assembly three years earlier.

Currently, chickens and geese roam among the thatched-roof cottages, reenactors go about their farming chores, and craftspeople demonstrate period blacksmithing and pottery techniques. There are a few short trails to hike, but Henricus Historical Park is the main attraction.

• •

GPS TRAILHEAD COORDINATES N37° 22.383' W77° 21.785'

DIRECTIONS Coming from I-95 south of Richmond, take Exit 61A in Chester and follow VA 10 (Iron Bridge Road) east. Turn left at the first stoplight onto VA 732 (Old Stage Road). Coming from I-295 take Exit 15B and follow VA 10 west 3.5 miles before turning right onto VA 732. Head north on VA 732, and turn right upon reaching a T intersection with VA 615 (Coxendale Road). After passing Dominion Energy's Chesterfield Power Station, turn right onto Henricus Road and follow it less than 2 miles to Dutch Gap Conservation Area.

North of the parking lot is the re-created Citie of Henricus, with a precipice overlooking the James River beyond. To the east is the visitor center. Dutch Gap Trail, which this hike follows, starts behind it.

17 MID-LOTHIAN MINES PARK

The amphitheater and the reproduction of a headstock, which was once used in industrialized coal mines

THIS 44-ACRE SUBURBAN PARK features walking trails with several connector trails to adjacent neighborhoods, a pond with a 0.5-mile paved loop, ruins of former coal mining sites, and an amphitheater.

DESCRIPTION

Mid-Lothian Mines Park, part of the Richmond Coal Basin, opened in 2004 in suburban Chesterfield County, in the heart of Midlothian's coal mining past. Mining in the Midlothian area of the basin represents the first attempt at commercial coal mining in North America, according to the park's website.

In 1835 on a 404-acre tract, the heirs of William Wooldridge chartered the Mid-Lothian Coal Mining Company, issuing stock to raise funds for machinery, construction, and the sinking of shafts. The mine went on to become the largest and most successful mining syndicate in the region, with a coal seam that was approximately 36 feet thick and 700 feet deep. The Wooldridge family was among the first to undertake coal mining in the Midlothian area, although mines operated here as early as 1730. Coal from Midlothian powered arms factories during the American Revolution, and coal pits in this area supplied the cannon factory at Westham (across the James River in Henrico County) with fuel used in making shot and shells for the Continental Army.

DISTANCE & CONFIGURATION: 1.7-mile figure eight

DIFFICULTY: Easy

ELEVATION: 269' at trailhead, 244' at low point

SCENERY: Mixed forests, historic coal mining site, pond

EXPOSURE: Shaded on east side; open around pond

TRAFFIC: Moderate

TRAIL SURFACE: Paved, crushed stone

HIKING TIME: 1 hour

SEASON: Year-round during daylight hours

ACCESS: No fee

WHEELCHAIR ACCESS: Yes

MAPS: At park kiosks and chesterfield.gov/parks

DRIVING DISTANCE FROM CAPITOL: 14 miles

FACILITIES: Restrooms, portable toilets at western trailhead, stone ruins of Grove Shaft mine, pond, amphitheater

CONTACT: Chesterfield County Parks: 804-748-1624, chesterfield.gov/parks

LOCATION: 13301 N. Woolridge Rd., Midlothian

COMMENTS: There will likely be many runners and families with children, so expect to have company on the trails. Chesterfield County is continuing to improve the former mines and facilities.

The second commercial rail line laid in the United States linked Chesterfield's mines to Richmond in 1831. Midlothian coal was again an important resource during the Civil War in the 1860s, but production fell sharply during Reconstruction in the late 1800s, according to park signage. The park pays homage to this area's mining and railroad heritage.

This hike begins from the eastern parking lot. Follow the gravel yellow-blazed trail. The forest here is a mix of hardwoods and pine, with a few holly trees added in. A large wooden trestle bridge allows passage over Falling Creek. Continue to the next trail junction, with the orange-blazed trail at the Grove Shaft ruins.

At Grove Shaft, it took workmen three years to dig a distance of 625 feet. The mine employed 150 men and boys, and 25 mules stabled underground pulled coal carts on an underground railroad. An interpretive sign at the site details a violent methane explosion in 1882 that trapped 32 men in the Grove Shaft. Miners from other nearby pits braved snowy conditions to assist in several futile rescue attempts.

Veer left onto the orange-blazed trail to continue south to the Murphy Slope ruins. Park signage details the history of the stone structure (built between 1835 and 1870), which was once the mining company's main building and is the only surviving structure associated with coal mining in the Richmond Coal Basin. It housed workings such as ventilation fans, steam boilers, pumps, and hoisting equipment. A series of gas leaks and explosions caused the site to close in the 1920s.

As of my visit, a chain-link fence surrounded much of the site, but renovations are expected to continue. A spur trail connects to the Kingham subdivision farther south, and several connections from the trail will take you into the surrounding neighborhoods, many of which were developed in the late 1990s and early 2000s.

Retrace your steps, but at Grove Shaft, stay on the orange trail to the left. Another wooden footbridge crosses the creek on this straight, flat pathway. Take a left onto the

Mid–Lothian Mines Park

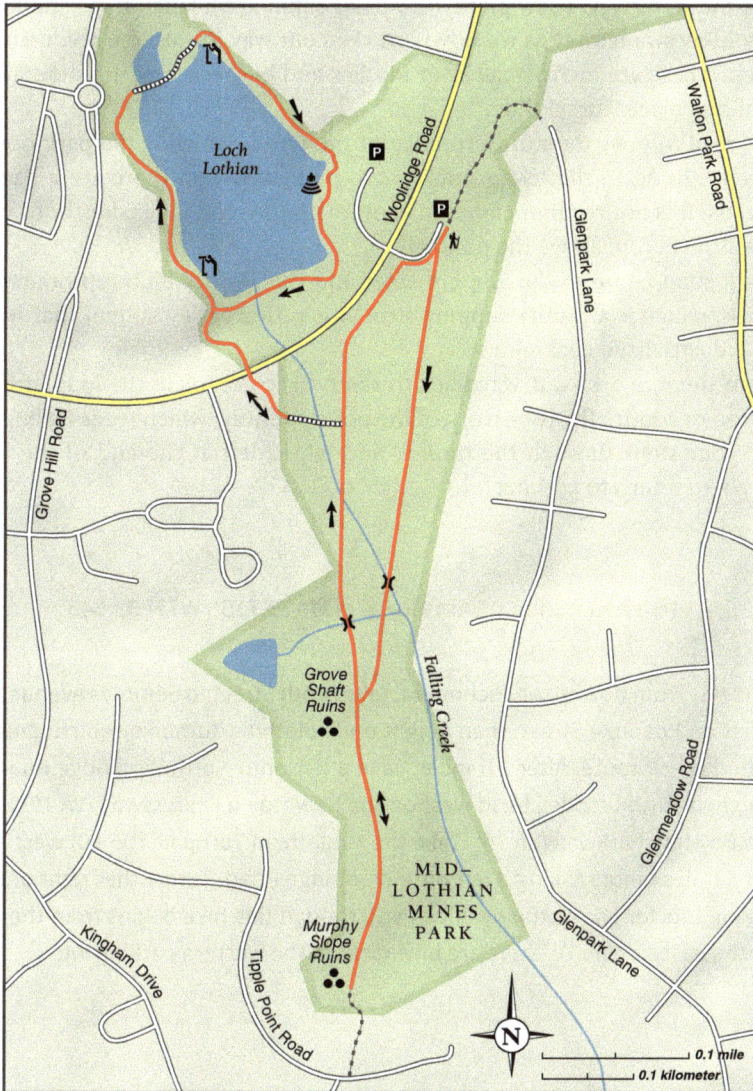

red trail, a connector that travels through a pedestrian tunnel under Woolridge Road and leads to the western portions of the park. After passing through the tunnel, you will connect with the Loop Trail around the pond (dubbed Loch Lothian on maps).

I chose to hike clockwise around the 10-foot-wide paved loop, but traffic flows both ways. As you begin the loop, there will be a large wooden observation deck to the right that provides excellent views of the pond and the park. The trail loops around to a wooden boardwalk that spans about 150 yards over the marshy western edges of the waterway. I saw plenty of turtles sunning on fallen trees and logs, and ducks politely swam away as we slowly worked our way toward the second observation deck. There are many small river birches and bushes along the shoreline, providing hiding places for wildlife.

The trail follows the northern edge of the pond, which is the park boundary. The steep hillside to the left is outside the park, although there are a handful of pirate trails. It is not recommended to venture up the eroded hillside, but I was told the view is nice from above the pond.

You'll soon come to the amphitheater and the 35-foot-high reproduction of a headstock, which is a timber support structure with a pulley system that was once used in industrialized coal mines.

From there, work your way back to the trail to complete the loop around the pond. Stop to admire the rock work of the pond spillway, which feeds Falling Creek. Retrace your steps through the tunnel, and take a left at the end of the wooden boardwalk to return to parking lot.

• •

GPS TRAILHEAD COORDINATES N37° 29.715' W77° 38.545'

DIRECTIONS From downtown Richmond, take Ninth Street to Semmes Avenue (US 60). Take a left on Roanoke Street, then a right on Midlothian Turnpike, which remains the designated US 60 route. After 9.5 miles, take a left onto North Woolridge Road. If you prefer highways (toll roads), head west on the Downtown Expressway (VA 195) and follow it to Powhite Parkway (VA 76). Take the Midlothian Turnpike (US 60) west exit and follow it 5 miles before taking a left onto Woolridge Road. Turn either right or left into the parking lots for Mid-Lothian Mines Park, though this hike begins from the parking area on the east side (left). There are bike racks in the western parking lot.

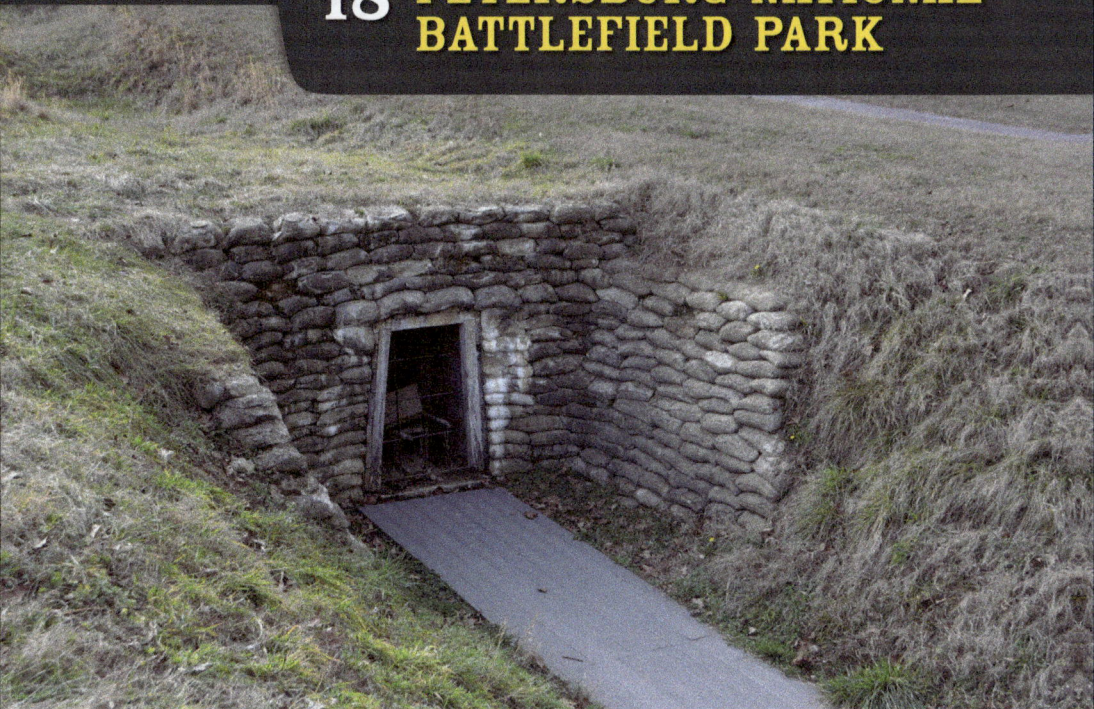

Entrance to the tunnel Union forces dug to The Crater

IN MANY WAYS, the Union siege of Petersburg was the climactic battle of the American Civil War, and the subsequent Confederate surrender was merely the denouement. Petersburg National Battlefield Park contains a plethora of earthen trenches, encampments, battlefields, and memorials, all connected by a paved roadway. Many visitors never set foot on the multiuse recreation trail that rings the park. A must-visit for residents and tourists with even a passing interest in US history, the battlefield park doubles as an outdoor escape for locals.

DESCRIPTION

The site of the longest siege in the annals of American warfare, Petersburg National Battlefield Park includes four Confederate forts northeast of the city. Here, on June 15, 1864, Federal troops commanded by General Ulysses S. Grant began their onslaught against entrenched Confederates. After more than 10 months and a combined 70,000 deaths, General Robert E. Lee's Army of Northern Virginia could no longer weather the assault. On April 2, 1865, Lee evacuated the city under cover of night. The defeat precipitated the Confederate surrender at Appomattox one week later.

This hike's route follows the park's national recreation trail system, a 7-mile loop with a 0.4-mile connector that allows you to shorten the hike to about 4 miles. Those wishing to see the park's forts and displays may use the trail instead of the

DISTANCE & CONFIGURATION: 7-mile loop, plus interpretive spurs (11.3 total trail miles in park)

DIFFICULTY: Easy

ELEVATION: 105' at trailhead, 38' at low point

SCENERY: Spurs lead to battlefield tour sights, including Civil War fortifications, a re-created Confederate fort, The Crater, and monuments

EXPOSURE: Shaded along circuit; open at tour stops

TRAFFIC: Low, except at tour stops

TRAIL SURFACE: Dirt, some gravel

HIKING TIME: 3 hours, including time spent at tour stops

SEASON: Year-round, 8 a.m.–sunset, except Thanksgiving Day, Christmas Day, and New Year's Day; museum 9 a.m.–5 p.m.; parking lot closes at 5 p.m.

ACCESS: No fee

WHEELCHAIR ACCESS: Visitor center, restrooms, and some interpretive trails

MAPS: At park and nps.gov/pete

DRIVING DISTANCE FROM CAPITOL: 26.3 miles

FACILITIES: Visitor center, museum, restrooms, driving tour

CONTACT: 804-732-3531, nps.gov/pete

LOCATION: 5001 Siege Rd., Petersburg

COMMENTS: The Lee vs. Grant 1864 Campaign Civil War driving trail connects to Petersburg National Battlefield Park. There are multiple spur trails and options to visit the park through the trail network. This hike takes you only around the perimeter of the park; consider other pathways to see more of the Civil War features.

main road. Doing so, however, makes it closer to a 10-mile hike. Those making a return visit can travel a circuit, omitting the spurs, with few reminders of the park's Civil War past—or its modern-day popularity.

Begin at the visitor center, where you can pick up both a brochure and a park map. While there, examine the artifacts and displays, which explain both the battlefield tactics and day-to-day drudgery of the 10-month siege. A film outlines the chronology of the city's defense and ultimate capture.

Dictator Trail, named for a squat, round Union mortar, departs from the visitor center. Along the interpretive path, the park has marshaled the full range of cannons employed during the battle. Made of brass or iron, these armaments range from 4 to 8 feet long. Those guarding Confederate Battery 5 just ahead retain their wheeled mounts. The trail continues beyond the fort and down a few stairs before looping back to the parking area, from which the hike itself begins.

A brief road walk leads you to the multiuse Friend Trail on the right. Be mindful of vehicles as you cross an overpass above VA 36 on the park road, and look for the earthen trail that intersects it shortly after you enter the woods. By hiking the loop counterclockwise, you save most of the optional spurs for the return trip and can explore them as you desire. After ducking into the woods, bear right along the singletrack path, switchbacking toward a tributary of Harrison Creek.

The trail heads south through a creekside plain, where maturing trees shade a thick carpet of grasses and ferns. Yellow blazes on trailside trees indicate the multiuse loop.

Shortly after the trail turns right, onto a wider path, the connector trail heads left. Accessible via the connector is a meadow dotted with cannons to mark the farthest

Petersburg National Battlefield Park

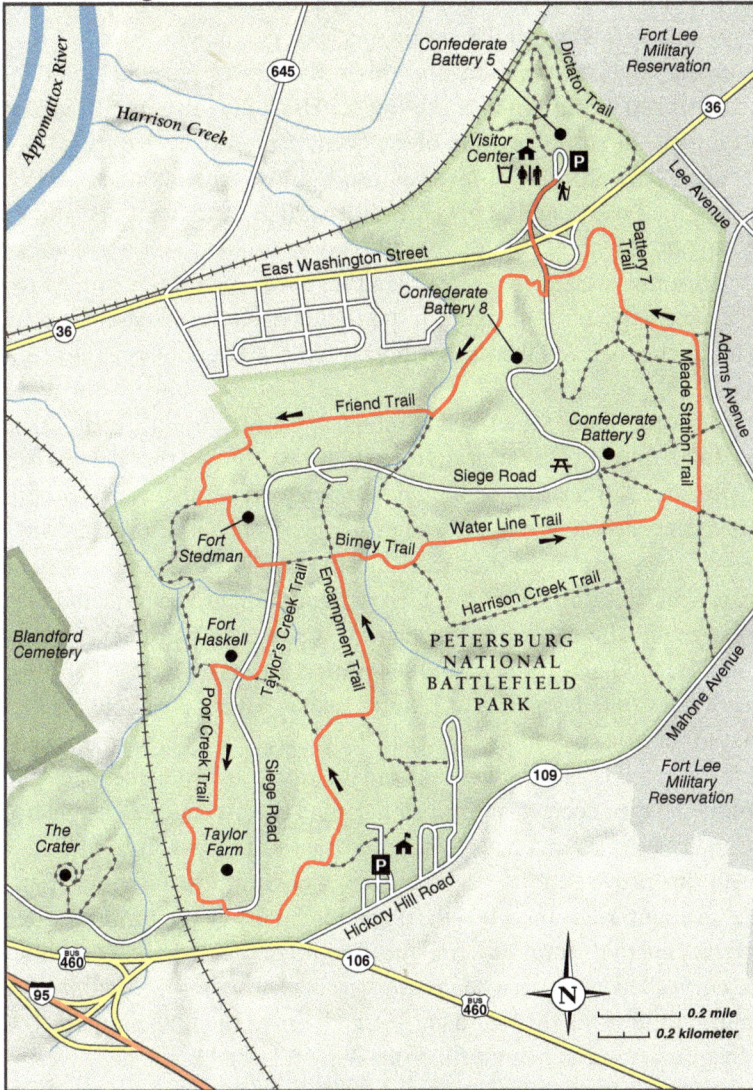

advancement of Lee's troops in their final assault, the Battle of Fort Stedman. The Confederates were halted at Harrison Creek, which you cross on a wooden bridge. From the creek, continue through a pinewood, crossing an asphalt maintenance road. Ahead, at a T intersection, bear left and then take your first right. The single-track trail crosses a clearing through which Fort Stedman is visible uphill.

At the next intersection, you may find the trail closed. In 2003, a pair of bald eagles came into the park to nest and raise their young. From mid-December to mid-July, a section of the outer loop trail was closed to provide optimal conditions for the breeding of this rare and majestic species.

Retreating from the trail closure, this route passes Fort Stedman and heads toward the park road. Continue south to Fort Haskell, which is still surrounded by a modest moat. The stopping point of the Confederate advance during the Battle of Fort Stedman, Fort Haskell was crowded so tightly with Union soldiers that most could merely load weapons and pass them forward to those stationed at the walls.

Just beyond the site, cross the paved road to connect to a wooded trail to the right along the multiuse Taylor's Creek Trail at approximately the 2-mile mark. Cross the road again at the 2.3-mile mark. If the trail is open during your visit, instead of walking along the road you'll cross a tributary of Poor Creek before the trail parallels the stream.

The route continues on a level, winding singletrack trail through thick woods. Then, as the path curves right, it draws along the meadow that descends from the Taylor Farm site. A brick foundation and chimney are all that remains of the farmstead. The trail curves left to pass through an open field below the chimney.

The trail then crosses the park road ahead. However, if you're incorporating the park's historical sites into your hike, turn right and follow the road and bridge over the railroad tracks about 0.4 mile to reach The Crater, the battlefield's most famous, and infamous, landmark. On July 30, 1864, Union troops detonated gunpowder buried beneath the Confederate fort at Elliott's salient, killing 300. Soldiers in Pennsylvania's 48th Infantry, coal miners by trade, had secretly tunneled more than 500 feet to place the explosives. The Crater is an indentation roughly 30 feet deep and 60 feet wide. Following the spectacular explosion, Union troops charged the destroyed battery, but many were so awestruck that they paused to gawk at the hole. For more than 4,000, this proved a fatal mistake. They were unprepared to meet an ensuing Confederate counter-advance, which trapped them inside the rift.

Backtracking to the multiuse trail, head south of the park road on a doubletrack trail that curves left then right to cross a seasonal stream. Veer left at an intersection uphill. Continue north along a level stretch called the Encampment Trail that is flanked by pines. You can hear traffic from Winfield Road in the distance.

Turn right on the Birney Trail, and make a quick descent to cross Harrison Creek on a wooden bridge. The trail rises to another junction, where the multiuse connector heads left and connects with the Water Line Trail, which leads forward into a shady pine forest. You will soon come to a four-way junction. For this hike as mapped, continue east along the multiuse path to connect with Meade Station Trail.

For an optional hike with a similar distance, take a left (north) at this junction, which will lead to Confederate Battery 9. Re-created wooden portions of this fort include sharpened stakes protruding from the earthen walls. The site also features a soldier's winter hut and a store that merchants established to hock canned goods and other small comforts. A Union regiment of African Americans took this position early in the siege. To the north, free blacks also captured Confederate Battery 8.

From the Water Line Trail, continue eastbound and take a right at the junction with the Prince George Courthouse Trail and expect to quickly turn left onto the Meade Station Trail, crossing two streams as you proceed northbound along the park boundary with Fort Lee. If you wish to see Battery 8, turn left at the next trail junction, and after less than 0.25 mile turn left again and eventually cross the park road. Otherwise, continue north to connect with the Battery 7 Trail. Turn left at the next T intersection to rejoin the multiuse loop, which passes a spur on the left then wends its way north near VA 36. Following the curving path south, cross two wooden bridges through gullied terrain to rejoin the park road. A right takes you back to the visitor center.

• •

GPS TRAILHEAD COORDINATES N37° 14.564' W77° 21.396'

DIRECTIONS Leave downtown Richmond heading south on I-95 and drive 22 miles to Exit 52 in Petersburg. Take Wythe Street east and merge onto VA 36 as the road curves northward. The park entrance is ahead on the right, about 2.5 miles from the interstate, and you will spot signs en route.

Ruins of Taylor Farm at Petersburg National Battlefield Park

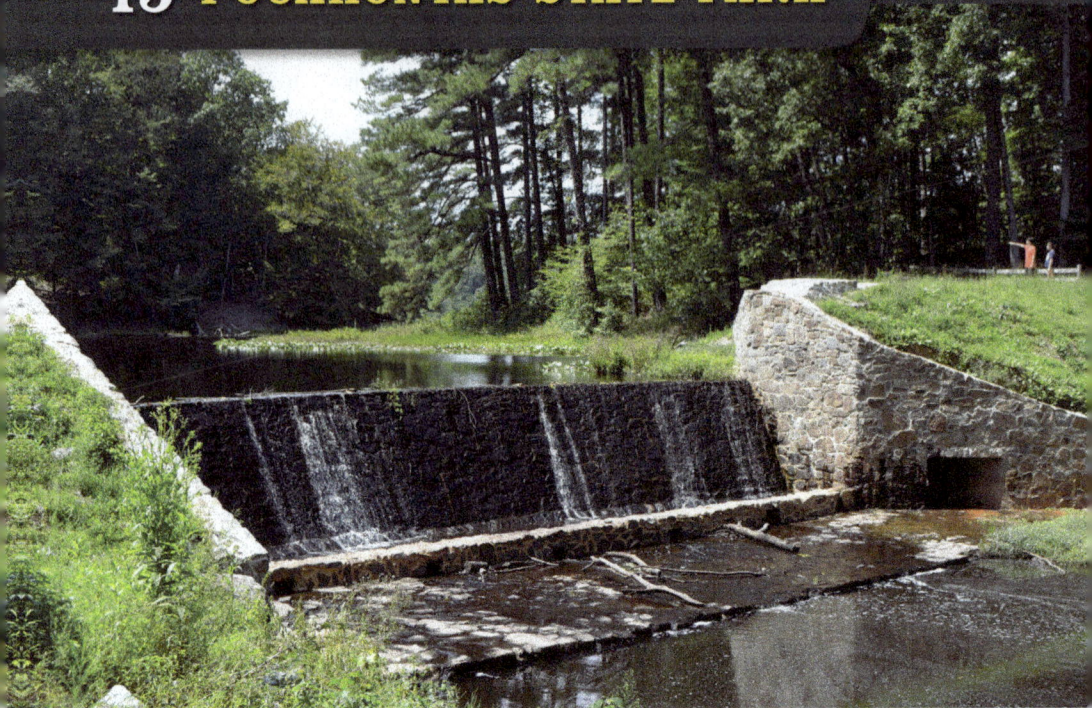

The spillway at Beaver Lake is an iconic feature of Pocahontas State Park.

THE PREMIER HIKING TRAIL at Pocahontas State Park encircles Beaver Lake. Misleadingly named, the lake was actually the work of the Civilian Conservation Corps (CCC), and this route descends from the park's CCC Museum to pass the Depression-era stone spillway before circling the lake. The Forest Exploration Trail crosses Swift Creek just where it begins to widen north of Swift Creek Lake. Though not connected (except by pavement), the two loops together highlight the park's cultural and ecological heritage.

DESCRIPTION

The first park of its kind in the Richmond environs, Pocahontas State Park was created as federally owned Swift Creek Recreational Area by the New Deal–era Civilian Conservation Corps. That legacy is today enshrined at the park's CCC Museum, which commemorates the men of CCC Company 2386, who constructed dams, cabins, and other park infrastructure. The National Park Service donated the 7,600 acres of parkland to the commonwealth in 1946.

The land was split between a state park and state forest until a 1989 planning study suggested placing the entire acreage under Department of Conservation and Recreation auspices, with a mandate to upgrade and expand Pocahontas State Park to better serve the growing population of the Richmond-Petersburg area.

DISTANCE & CONFIGURATION: 2.8-mile loop around Beaver Lake, 3-plus-mile loop on Forest Exploration Trail

DIFFICULTY: Moderate

ELEVATION: 189' at trailhead, 227' at high point

SCENERY: Pine and beech forests, stone spillway, creeks surrounding Beaver Lake, Swift Creek Lake

EXPOSURE: Shaded

TRAFFIC: Moderate

TRAIL SURFACE: Dirt, some gravel, paved at the beginning

HIKING TIME: 1 hour around Beaver Lake, 1.5 hours on Forest Exploration Trail

SEASON: Year-round, 7 a.m.–sunset

ACCESS: Parking $5 ($7 holidays and high-season weekends); swimming $6 adults ($8 weekends), $5 children ages 3–12 ($7 weekends); campsites from $30

WHEELCHAIR ACCESS: Some trails

MAPS: At park and dcr.virginia.gov/state-parks/pocahontas

DRIVING DISTANCE FROM CAPITOL: 25 miles

FACILITIES: Swimming pool, campground, equestrian trails, huge network of mountain bike trails, conference center, visitor center, museum, amphitheater

CONTACT: 804-796-4255, dcr.virginia.gov/state-parks/pocahontas

LOCATION: 10301 State Park Rd., Chesterfield

COMMENTS: The park is developing a Richmond Regional Ride Center, designed to attract and accommodate more cyclists and mountain bikers. See rvaridecenter.com for more information.

Before setting out on the trails, drop by the modest CCC Museum for a primer on the Corps' history and its work within the park in particular. Franklin Roosevelt established the CCC during the first weeks of his administration. It was open to single men between the ages of 18 and 25 who served a maximum of two years, in six-month enlistment increments. They pocketed just $5 a month, with $25 more sent home to their families. In all, more than 3 million young men passed through the Corps' ranks between 1933 and 1942. They built 40,000 bridges, created 800 state parks, and planted 2 billion trees. The pictures and stories of the men who labored here will give you a greater appreciation for their sturdy handiwork.

The densely forested Pocahontas State Park is now the largest of Virginia's state parks and has grown to more than 8,100 acres. It is a tourist attraction for the entire region, with more than 1.4 million visitors in 2016, the highest attendance figure for any park in the system. For many of those visitors, the trails are the big draw. There are more than 25 miles of directional mountain bike trails, including traditional singletrack, machine-built pump-track, flow, and hand-cycle-friendly and beginner trails. The park now has more than 125 miles of trail and gravel fire roads to hike, run, and ride.

Park planners aim to add more trails as the park develops the Richmond Regional Ride Center, a hub for cycling for the entire area. *Ride Center* is an official designation of the International Mountain Biking Association (IMBA) for "a large-scale collection of mountain bike trails that offer recreational opportunities for all skill levels, from families to expert," according to the group's website. There are only about 40 ride centers worldwide, and we have 3 in Virginia.

Pocahontas State Park

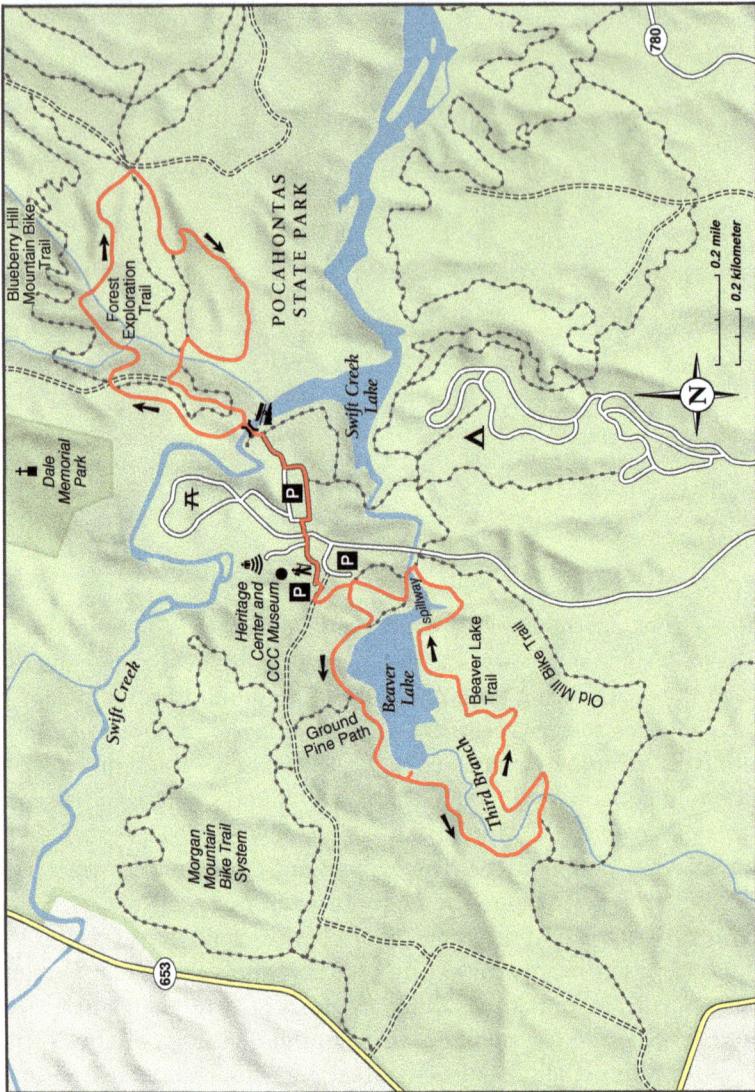

Pocahontas also offers approximately 10 miles of hiking-only trail. The Beaver Lake and Forest Exploration Trails are moderate 2.5-mile hikes through heavily wooded rolling hills. New trails on the north side of Swift Creek Lake were dedicated in January 2019. All the trails are connected by a large network of spur trails and by fire roads.

For the first half of this hike, I joined a large group on New Year's Day for a First Day Hike, an annual event that happens in most Virginia state parks. Our guided hike on the Forest Exploration Trail began from the Heritage Center. To reach the trail, we hiked northeast past the park's amphitheater, located just off the main park road. You will pass through a large parking lot, aiming for the road down to Swift Creek at the lot's northeast corner. Just downhill is a boat launch with a smaller parking area. A bridge crossing the widening creek signals the trailhead for Forest Exploration Trail.

After crossing the bridge, the trail bears left and ascends, with a meandering rivulet visible downhill on your left. Mature forest and mossy boulders lend this stretch a wilderness air. Ahead along this wide and sandy path, you'll see evidence of bygone logging operations, including stands of young pine.

The trail crosses a fire road and begins a descent toward a creekbed. As it crosses a wooden footbridge, keep an eye out for the Split Rock, a giant granite boulder that is split down the middle with a 2- to 3-inch gap in between. Park lore has it that the rock was the favorite spot of a little girl who lived nearby more than a century ago. The rock broke years later when the young woman died during childbirth.

As the trail winds up the hill, you'll pass through a thick stand of pines before reaching the junction with the Blueberry Hill Mountain Bike Trail and the Hawkins Forest Trail. Take a right onto the gravel doubletrack Hawkins Forest Trail, and walk a short distance to a small cemetery on the left. Near this site lived the Gill family in the 1800s. A sign there indicates that their daughter Fannie, the little girl associated with the Split Rock, died in childbirth in 1872, and that she and her infant daughter are buried nearby.

Take a left to follow the signs for the Forest Exploration Trail, back onto a singletrack trail. The trail will follow a creekbed and pass through a lower flat section before eventually rejoining Hawkins Forest Trail. Turn left to return to the trailhead and to the Heritage Center and CCC Museum parking lot.

The Beaver Lake Trail departs to the right of the museum as you face it, but I began from the parking lot after returning from the first hike, taking the trail counterclockwise. Begin a descent toward the water before veering right to trace above the shoreline. The earthen path undulates over small ridges and traces inlets of the lake, intermittently drawing near to water before rising away through the towering beech forest. It is inspiring to contemplate that the 100-foot-tall beech trees now shading Beaver Lake were planted as saplings by the grandfathers of modern-day visitors.

As you progress along the lake's northern shore, look for Ground Pine Path (but don't take it). On the forest floor you'll find specimens of the trail's namesake. Ground pine, a variant of club moss, resembles a tiny evergreen, growing no more than 5 inches tall. The plant spreads through lateral underground branches and favors cool, moist forest. The wee mosses are descendants of ancient species that stood 40 feet high. The Beaver Lake Trail continues, hugging the lake's western edge, which is blanketed in lily pads, and repeatedly traversing muddy stretches. A boardwalk will help keep your shoes dry.

As you reapproach the lake, another boardwalk affords dry passage through swamplike terrain. A sign describes vegetation common to this boggy landscape, including jack-in-the-pulpit and pawpaw.

You'll soon cross a babbling stream on a cement footbridge. Bear left and continue along the pebbly banks of Third Branch as it widens into a swampy delta. Beavers are in fact active in this area; you may spot one gliding through the water, but the stumps of felled trees are sufficient proof of their residence.

As the path switchbacks up the hillside, take in vistas of the lake, and admire the spillway cascade and the handiwork of the stonemasons who built it. The path curves left at the lakeshore then crosses Third Branch via a footbridge just below its reemergence from the spillway dam. Perhaps the CCC workmen who built the spillway referred to the impoundment they created as Third Branch Lake, the name it is given on some topo maps. By any name, the 24-acre lake pales in comparison to 225-acre Swift Creek Lake to the east, 0.25 mile downstream of the spillway. Follow the trail back to the parking area at the CCC Museum.

• •

GPS TRAILHEAD COORDINATES N37° 23.187' W77° 34.934'

DIRECTIONS Pocahontas State Park is in Chesterfield County, about 20 miles south of downtown Richmond. From I-95, take Exit 62, or, from the roughly parallel US 1/US 301, take VA 288 west. Exit onto Iron Bridge Road (VA 10) headed south, then turn left onto Beach Road (VA 655). The main park entrance is ahead on the right. Proceed into the park, pay your vehicle-entrance fee, and continue toward the CCC Museum and amphitheater, passing the campground on your right. Turn left then left again to park in front of the CCC Museum.

The rock foundation and chimney are all that remains of an old cabin along the Cabin Trail.

POWHATAN STATE PARK has about 12 miles of multiuse trails traversing various habitats, including field edge, upland pine forest, and mature hardwoods. The trails provide excellent opportunities for viewing wildlife. The park is also a good place to ride a horse or a mountain bike. Horse trailer parking is available just past the park office in the equestrian trailhead parking lot.

DESCRIPTION

Powhatan State Park opened in July 2013, becoming Virginia's 36th state park. Located in northwestern Powhatan County about 45 minutes from Richmond, the 1,565-acre park is nestled in a large bend of the James River and includes about 2.5 miles of shoreline and three canoe slide launches accessing the water. Powhatan also has three large picnic shelters, including one by the river.

The parkland was once inhabited by the Monacan tribe. French Protestants called Huguenots settled east of the property. According to the Powhatan State Park master plan, the land was originally part of the nearby Beaumont Juvenile Correctional Center and was transferred to the conservation department in 2003. The parkland includes about 320 acres of fields that were once farmed by prison inmates for row crops and hay. The farmlands occupy much of the well-drained uplands.

DISTANCE & CONFIGURATION: Two 6.8-mile balloon loops, plus optional spurs

DIFFICULTY: Moderate

ELEVATION: 299' at trailhead, 149' at low point

SCENERY: Hardwood and mixed forests, meadows, James River

EXPOSURE: Shaded, except segments through meadows

TRAFFIC: Low; expect mountain bikes and horses on much of the trail network

TRAIL SURFACE: Dirt, gravel

HIKING TIME: 2.5 hours

SEASON: Year-round during daylight hours

ACCESS: Parking $4, campsites from $30

WHEELCHAIR ACCESS: Some trails

MAPS: At park and dcr.virginia.gov/state-parks /powhatan

DRIVING DISTANCE FROM CAPITOL: 45 miles

FACILITIES: Restrooms, playground, picnic shelters, campground and canoe-in campground, wildlife observation areas, James River access

CONTACT: 804-598-7148, dcr.virginia.gov /state-parks/powhatan

LOCATION: 4616 Powhatan State Park Rd., Powhatan

COMMENTS: Since it opened in 2013, Powhatan State Park has continued to develop trails and facilities. Campgrounds are connected to the trail network, with more trail connections on the way. The park also offers 2 boat launches with a distance of about 2 miles between them.

The remaining acreage is in timber that has been managed in consultation with Virginia's Department of Forestry. The forests cover the slopes and ravines with less well-drained soils and range from mixed hardwood stands to loblolly pine plantations. Wooded sections include the roughly 400-acre E. Floyd Yates Conservation Area, named for a Powhatan businessman, former Virginia state delegate, and lifelong nature lover who died in 2010 at age 107. The plan is to keep that area of the park wild.

This hike begins from the gravel equestrian trailhead parking lot. The lot has a building with composting toilets but no running water as of this writing. Look for a kiosk with a park map, and the yellow-blazed Big Woods Trail should run from there straight across a field toward a stand of trees. Follow this dirt-and-grass path around the treeline at the edge of the field. Take note of the junction with the red-blazed Cabin Trail, as the route will loop back to this spot. Watch for rabbits and deer, which made appearances during my hike. Listen for a multitude of birds, including field sparrow, tufted titmouse, Carolina wren, eastern bluebird, and more.

About 0.5 mile from the start, the path crosses the main park road. Walk through the parking lot for the Big Woods Trail, and rejoin the path into the forest. Look for tulip or yellow poplar and flowering dogwood among the many hardwoods along this wide dirt singletrack surface.

The trail comes to a junction at a wooden bench. The Big Woods Trail continues to the right, but for this hike, follow the trail to the left to the white-blazed Pine Trail. This sandy trail had a few damp spots with hoof indentions and some fresh droppings, clear signs that some horseback riders were out. The trail is a rectangular loop; for this hike, I took it clockwise, so take a left at the next junction.

Powhatan State Park

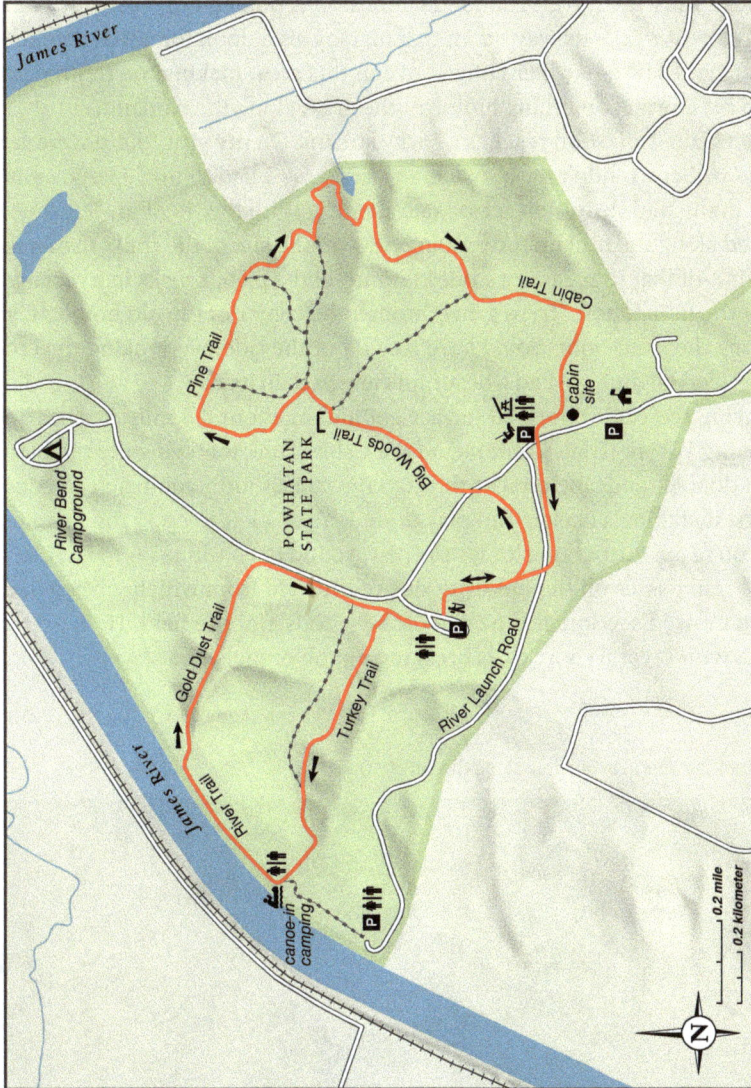

The trail follows along a doubletrack lined with many downed trees and smaller hardwoods to the outside of the trail, with a higher concentration of pine on the interior. As the trail continues and turns east, more pine needles line the trail. Watch for two shortcut spurs that cut back across this pine forest.

The Pine Trail meets the Cabin Trail, which veers off to the left. On my visit, there had been some recent cutting in the forest, and this trail was in need of repair in sections that had runoff issues. The upper portion also had large patches of deep-green moss with well-rounded white stones poking out—a lovely contrast. As the trail slowly works its way down to a marshy area, look for a wooden bench next to a clearing. I saw a hawk circling above in this area, making me think perhaps the bird had his eye on something hiding in the grass along the wetland.

The Cabin Trail soon reaches a rocky stream. On my visit, there were few crossing options that wouldn't have soaked my boots, so I had to find a large enough rock to place in the middle to step across safe and dry. With the tip of my left shoe damp, I continued along the trail up the ensuing ridge to the site of the trail's namesake, a former cabin. All that remains is a stone chimney and a pile of rocks in a rectangle shape marking the foundation. Trees grow through the center of the old home. It isn't clear which way the front door would have faced, but the side overlooking the creek from atop the ridge might have had a beautiful view back in its day.

Leaving the cabin, the trail turns right and in about 0.5 mile reaches a junction with the Big Woods Trail. Continue on the Cabin Trail, following the red blazes along a mix of double- and singletracks through the woods until you reach a series of park buildings, including a shelter and playground. Take a left to cross the main park road before you reach the parking lot for the playground to continue on the Cabin Trail.

The trail passes on the opposite side of the field from which we began the hike, tracing a mowed section at the edge of the woods and the field. High grasses cover the field, with several short trees breaking up the orangish hue.

Beautiful wildflowers in a meadow along the Turkey Trail

In less than a mile, this hike could end at 4.3 miles, as you'll be back where you started. If you still have a couple of miles in you, pass through the equestrian parking lot to the trailhead on the opposite side that leads to the Turkey Trail, which is marked with a tan blaze. Walk through a meadow that in the summer months is alive with wildflowers and bees working hard to pollinate. You have the option to walk along the treeline or down the center of the meadow on your way to the River Trail.

Descend with caution down the steep and rocky path from the upper land of the meadow through the woods to the banks of the James River. The gravel trail passes along a wetland and then winds slightly right as it passes through the canoe-in camping area to connect with the blue-blazed River Trail.

Huge sycamore, beech, and other hardwoods dominate this well-worn trail atop the banks 10 feet above the river. The well-shaded path has multiple benches and offers a great respite for a weary hiker in need of a snack or a sip of a beverage.

As the trail turns back inland, it crosses a footbridge before connecting with the Gold Dust Trail. Designated for hiking only, this dirt trail was undergoing some rerouting during my visit, but it offers an opportunity to follow the climbing ridgeline or to stay a little lower and pass what looks to be an old cabin or farm building. The trail soon emerges at the main park road and turns right to reconnect with the Turkey Trail. Retrace your steps to the equestrian parking lot to finish this journey.

• •

GPS TRAILHEAD COORDINATES N37° 40.520' W77° 55.944'

DIRECTIONS From Richmond, take I-64 west to Exit 175 (VA 288 S). Turn right onto VA 711 W (Huguenot Trail). Stay on VA 711 about 13 miles to reach US 522 (Maidens Road). Turn right and drive about 4 miles to VA 617 (Old River Trail). Turn left and go about 1.5 miles to the park entrance on the right. Follow the main park road to the large gravel equestrian parking lot.

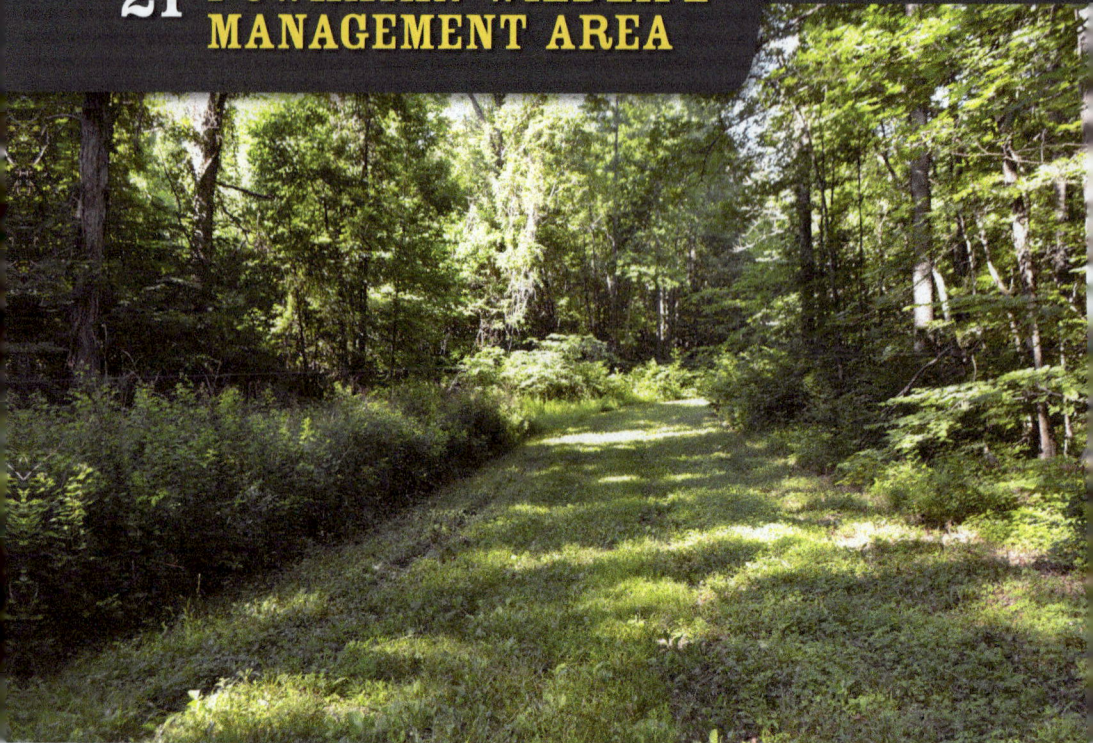

The majority of trails in Powhatan Wildlife Management Area are wide bush-hogged pathways.

JUST WEST OF ITS NAMESAKE county seat, Powhatan Wildlife Management Area offers more than a dozen trail miles. This route takes in only a portion of them, passing through low-lying wetlands, hillside hardwood forest, and fields buffered by hedgerows. As you would expect, your prospects for spotting wildlife are good, but you'll also see rusting machinery and an old cemetery, reminders of the area's past as timberland and farmland.

DESCRIPTION

Maintained by the Virginia Department of Game and Inland Fisheries, the state's wildlife management areas (WMAs) are a boon to outdoor lovers in central Virginia, where public land is in short supply. Though open for hunting in season and for fishing year-round, the WMAs also encourage hiking—and, as you'll notice at Powhatan, they are quite popular with equestrians as well.

In addition to deer hunters, Powhatan draws hunters in search of wild turkey, woodcock, dove, and quail. (Unfortunately for hikers anxious about being out with the hunters, some of these seasons coincide with fall foliage, but Powhatan is equally scenic blanketed in snow or dotted with wildflowers.) Powhatan may be most popular with anglers. Besides the twin Powhatan Lakes north of US 60, which total 58 acres,

DISTANCE & CONFIGURATION: 5-mile loop, with shorter and longer options and spurs

DIFFICULTY: Moderate

ELEVATION: 223' at trailhead, 343' at high point

SCENERY: Mostly hardwood forest, fishing lakes, creeks, fields

EXPOSURE: Open along fields; shaded on some forested trails

TRAFFIC: Low

TRAIL SURFACE: Dirt and gravel doubletrack, bush-hogged grass

HIKING TIME: 2 hours

SEASON: Year-round during daylight hours, but avoid trails during hunting seasons

ACCESS: No fee; horseback riding and mountain biking allowed; no ATVs

WHEELCHAIR ACCESS: Very limited

MAPS: At dgif.virginia.gov/wma/powhatan

DRIVING DISTANCE FROM CAPITOL: 38 miles

FACILITIES: Fishing lakes with boat launch, information boards

CONTACT: 804-370-1000

LOCATION: 2335 Ridge Rd., Powhatan

COMMENTS: The grassy trails here are mowed sporadically. If you plan to hike in summer, call to inquire about trail status. All wildlife management areas are open to hunting. Check with Virginia Department of Game & Inland Fisheries (804-370-1000, dgif.virginia.gov/hunting) for annual hunting seasons.

this WMA has four smaller lakes (2–9 acres), each named for what you might catch there: Bass, Bullhead, Sunfish, and Bream. The first three are clustered off the park's main gravel road in its western half; the last stands alone to the east.

It's worth noting that a sizable wetland in the heart of the WMA is absent from official maps, which show only Beaver Swamp on the opposite side of the CCC Trail. Also missing from those maps is mention of the washed-out bridge along the CCC Trail. Water from the unmapped marsh now streams over the fractured concrete, rendering a wet crossing inevitable. If you don't mind soggy shoes, blaze your way through the marsh near the intersection of Sallee and Salmon Creeks. Maps show Arrowhead Trail passing through this area.

Nevertheless, you have several options for longer, shorter, and drier routes, thanks in part to parking areas that dot Powhatan's perimeter. The 4,462-acre parcel includes areas of cropland that have been retained as fields, though they are now planted with wild game in mind. You'll see slender hedgerows between the fields, which host a variety of woodland mammals, such as mice and rabbits. These in turn bring such predators as foxes, owls, and snakes. A wealth of birds also nest in the hedges.

Unlike nearby Amelia WMA (see page 82), where such rolling fields abound, Powhatan also encompasses dense woods and more varied terrain. At several points the trail descends sharply to a stream crossing then promptly climbs away. Following heavy rainfall, you may find it difficult to ford these streams without getting wet, but they are generally narrow and shallow enough to cross either unaided or on rocks or logs. Near some, horse hooves have churned muddy spots in the trailbed, and you may find it easiest to stray into the woods to circumvent them. Though some are gravel, most of the trails at Powhatan are grassy passages through wide clearings.

Powhatan Wildlife Management Area

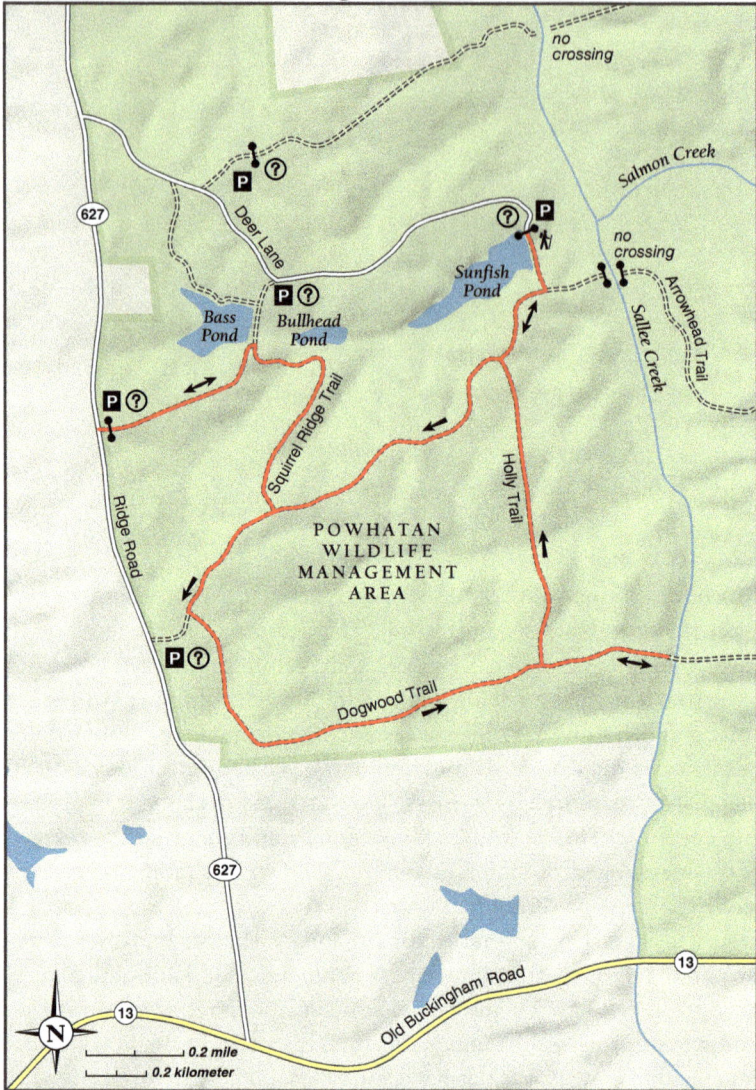

For this hike, begin from the trailhead at Sunfish Pond, which is just west and uphill from the spot where Salmon and Sallee Creeks meet. Follow the Arrowhead Trail south on a dirt-and-gravel doubletrack along the banks of the pond. On this warm June day, we found a pathway that had not been mowed in a while, which allowed for plenty of wildflowers. The path was not impassable but was slow-going at first before progressing uphill to a mowed pathway alongside a hedgerow.

Turning right along Arrowhead, the trail continued about a mile in a wide unshaded section before reaching a junction with the Squirrel Ridge Trail. This path was shaded and heavily forested, a welcome diversion from the heat. It turned out to be a 1.6-mile out-and-back spur that gave a glimpse into several open meadows and heavily wooded sections of forest. It is helpful if you are looking to add distance to your hike but not if you are trying to loop back to Sunfish Pond.

As you retrace your steps back to the Arrowhead Trail, take a right to rejoin the loop trail. The terrain offers several climbs and dips but nothing overly strenuous. At a fork, go left. The loop becomes Dogwood Trail as it veers east then continues straight 0.75 mile until it meets the Holly Trail, a north–south connector. This path will return you to Sunfish Pond, but for now continue east toward Sallee Creek.

As the road continues downhill to the creek, I caught the gaze of a deer lingering at the edge of the woods. I had the impression it knew I was there the entire time, but once I got within about 50 yards, it darted for safety into the forest. As I approached the water, the air near Sallee Creek felt about 10 degrees cooler than in the meadows and on the unshaded sections of the trail.

The return trip went back over the same path about 0.25 mile. The Holly Trail was the connection back to the parking area but ended up being a much more challenging stretch. As the trail descended along a wet path toward the wetlands and a creekbed, in the middle the overgrown weeds and wildflowers presented a difficult challenge. A machete would have been more helpful than the camera and water container I was toting. Though I could have picked ticks up anywhere in the park, I decided this section of trail is where I accumulated the majority of those I removed at the end of my hike. A word of caution when hiking in WMAs: they are not always mowed as often or as thoroughly as the typical hiker would want them to be. Perhaps a Sunday in late fall or early spring would have been a better time for a hike.

As the Holly Trail reaches the Arrowhead Trail, turn right, and then walk a short distance before descending to Sunfish Pond and the trailhead. I spotted a handful of tiny baby turtles out sunbathing on logs along the banks of the pond. They bravely stayed around long enough to keep me company while I sat on the dock removing a dozen or more ticks from my legs and feet. An interesting end to an otherwise enjoyable adventure in Powhatan County.

. . . .

GPS TRAILHEAD COORDINATES N37° 32.719' W77° 59.888'

DIRECTIONS From Richmond, travel west on US 60 (the Midlothian Turnpike) through Midlothian and on through Powhatan. One mile after US 60 narrows from four lanes to two, turn left onto VA 627 (Ridge Road). Proceed south about 1.3 miles and take a left into the WMA. The trailhead is about a mile farther, past Bass and Bullhead Ponds, in a small parking area at Sunfish Pond. Other parking areas border the WMA on all sides.

The floating boardwalk over Ashton Creek Marsh

THIS SHORT, WELL-TROD LOOP passes diverse terrain: hillsides forested in mature hardwoods, the cattail-and-cordgrass marsh along Ashton Creek, and the wide Appomattox River on its way to meet the James. Located in Chesterfield County near Hopewell, the park is as convenient to Petersburg as it is to Richmond's Southside.

DESCRIPTION

More than a quarter-century old, the trail system at 176-acre R. Garland Dodd Park at Point of Rocks (formerly Point of Rocks Park) bears the signs of wear and tear. At least one wooden footbridge is dated 1980, the year the park opened, as are a few of the many, many carvings in beech trees along the trail. These names, initials, and professions of love suggest a popular weekending spot. Yet trailside growth crowds the hard-packed singletrack surface, so the trails feel broken in but slightly past their prime, which isn't a bad thing. For instance, they haven't been "upgraded" to asphalt. Plus, if you come on a weekday, you will likely have the network to yourself, a particular incentive for bird-watchers drawn by the park's multiple habitats.

A long metal boardwalk over Ashton Creek Marsh provides excellent views of the marsh. The walkway itself floats when the tidal waters of the Appomattox push back into the marsh. Wooden overlooks on each end of the boardwalk provide

DISTANCE & CONFIGURATION: 1.7-mile loop

DIFFICULTY: Easy

ELEVATION: 92' at trailhead, 0' at low point

SCENERY: Ashton Creek Marsh, Appomattox River, bottomland forest

EXPOSURE: Well shaded; open on marsh boardwalks

TRAFFIC: Low

TRAIL SURFACE: Dirt, gravel, metal walkway over marsh

HIKING TIME: 45 minutes–1 hour

SEASON: Year-round during daylight hours

ACCESS: No fee

WHEELCHAIR ACCESS: On paved sections and some flat areas of the trail network

MAPS: On kiosk at the trailhead and at chesterfield.gov/3822/r-garland-dodd-park

DRIVING DISTANCE FROM CAPITOL: 18.6 miles

FACILITIES: Restrooms; playground; baseball, softball, soccer, and football fields; tennis and basketball courts; picnic shelters

CONTACT: Chesterfield County Parks: 804-748-1623, chesterfield.gov/parks

LOCATION: 201 Enon Church Rd., Chester

COMMENTS: The Captain John Smith Chesapeake National Historic Trail and the Lee vs. Grant 1864 Campaign Civil War driving trail connect to Dodd Park. The floating boardwalk over the tidal marsh provides an excellent place to study a wide variety of dragonflies and wetland birds, including swamp sparrows and common yellowthroats, in addition to great blue herons, egrets, and bald eagles.

additional vantage points. You'll also enjoy the chance to spot wildlife along the Appomattox River and in the bottomland forest between the marsh and the park facilities uphill.

Along with the herons, egrets, and kingfishers that attract amateur ornithologists, an array of colorful dragonflies and their daintier cousins, damselflies, make the freshwater marsh their home. Budding entomologists may identify the long-legged green darter, the eastern pondhawk, Needham's skimmer, and the eastern amberwing species. Some dragonfly species are territorial, staking small claims within a swamp, and some make long annual migrations. Though much smaller than their prehistoric ancestors, which had wingspans of up to 30 inches, these predatory members of the order Odonata still serve a valuable purpose by snacking on mosquitoes.

Begin your hike west of the ballfields, at the parking area signed for Shelters 1 and 2. It abuts a shaded field and playground on the west side of the road and near the site of a re-created homesteader's cabin. The trail begins from the corner nearest the entrance and descends wood-beam steps to a sandy trailbed. The path curves left down a heavily wooded slope, with concrete parking-lot barriers lining the downhill edge of the trail—a novel recycling scheme to prevent erosion. Look for twisting mountain laurel growing on the left beneath a mixture of oaks, then scout for a wooden footbridge that spans a trickling brook on the right.

A nondescript path veers right to cross the bridge; pause on the walkway to admire the clear-running stream and the rounded pebbles it has smoothed over time. Turn left, following signs for the marsh boardwalk and Overlook 1. (Woodthrush Trail, a spur loop through the forest, heads right.)

R. Garland Dodd Park at Point of Rocks

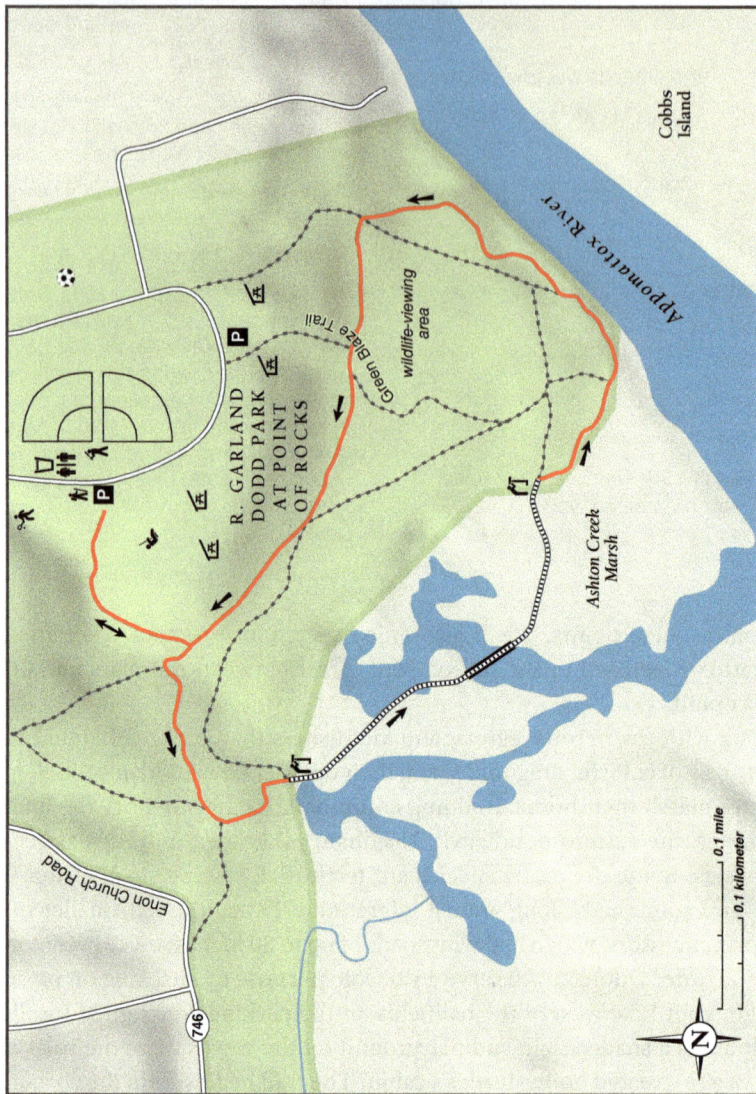

The overlook, just ahead on the right, is a small wooden platform with a bench that offers clear views of Ashton Creek Marsh, which is obscured by wetland flora for most of the hike. Wooden stairs lead to a larger wooden deck just a few feet above the marsh. This begins the 0.3-mile boardwalk that traverses the beautiful marsh. Two metal bridges span the deeper channel of the creek as it winds through the marsh. The floating structure is surrounded by cattails, swamp milkweed, and cordgrass and offers a perfect opportunity to see a variety of wild creatures up close.

A wooden staircase leads down to the floating boardwalk.

The floating boardwalk connects with a slightly longer wooden section of boardwalk that juts out over the marsh as the trail approaches the high bank and a staircase up to the second overlook. From the peninsular decking, Ashton Creek's confluence with the Appomattox River is faintly visible to your left. Continue along the trail and past a closed trail spur, now blockaded with logs, that once led onto a spit of land on the right. If you're looking for a unique vantage point, you can still avail yourself of an elevated platform that lies ahead on the left.

The main path soon turns northeast to run along the Appomattox River, with the reedy shore of Cobbs Island visible across Port Walthall Channel. The Appomattox reaches its confluence with the James at Hopewell, roughly 4 miles east. In this area, the park has been seeing some improvements, with two new wooden bridges and trail markers.

After leaving the banks of the river, the trail heads inland, abutting an open field. Brief spur trails dip down to provide access to the river's narrow, sandy shore, which is scattered with rocks, dead trees, and driftwood.

The trail continues inland, uphill along the park boundary. In the midst of a wood thick with vines and underbrush, you will pass the remains of a metal gate on the right along a path with numerous exposed roots and rocks. The trail bears left again to head west on a slow, steady climb. Resist the temptation to take the shortcut straight up the steep bank below picnic shelters 3 and 4.

After traversing a wooden bridge with chain-link sides over a seasonal-stream gully that has been lined with rock to ease erosion, a lime-green-blazed trail marked by wood-beam steps intersects your path. This well-defined spur leads left then left again in about 25 feet to reach a wildlife-viewing blind. A wide, grassy maintenance road heads east from this blind and is later visible along the main trail in a sweet-gum glade on the left. The trail then reaches a stretch of paved pathway that gently ascends to the parking area at Shelters 1 and 2. Hikers have the option to take this trail back up or continue on the main trail, which soon rises and rounds a corner back to the trailhead.

• •

GPS TRAILHEAD COORDINATES N37° 19.294' W77° 21.287'

DIRECTIONS From Richmond, take I-95 south to Exit 61A (Hopewell). Take VA 10 east and the first right onto Old Stage Road. Take the first left onto Ware Bottom Spring Road and the second right onto Ramblewood Drive. Follow Ramblewood 4 miles until it stops at VA 746 (Ruffin Mill Road). Take a left and then a quick right into R. Garland Dodd Park. The trailhead is at the re-created homestead cabin beyond the ballfields and near picnic shelters 1 and 2.

From I-295, take Exit 15A (Hopewell) onto VA 10 (East Hundred Road). Turn right onto VA 746 (Enon Church Road), which reaches the park in about 2 miles, after first passing under an I-295 overpass. The park entrance is on the left. The trailhead is at the re-created homestead cabin beyond the ballfields and near picnic shelters 1 and 2.

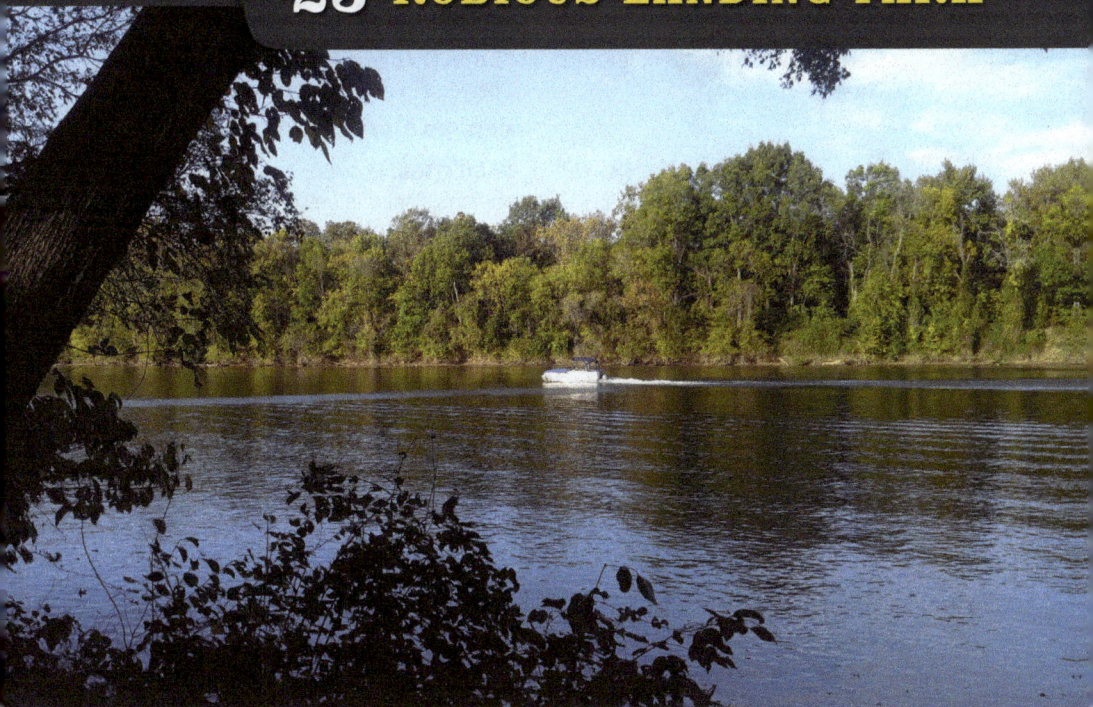

Motorboats are a common sight in the calm waters upriver of the falls of the James.

THE 102-ACRE ROBIOUS LANDING PARK abuts the James River and is a popular destination for anglers and trail runners alike. With a playground, picnic tables, and fishing piers, it makes for a great family outing in northwestern Chesterfield County. The level, mostly gravel trail traverses the stream-laced terrain on a series of footbridges. A predominantly hardwood forest of sycamore, white oak, and pawpaw keeps the trail well shaded in the summer.

DESCRIPTION

Upstream of the rocky fall line, the James River is not tidal but remains wide and flat. Trees line the banks on both shores. In the woodlands south of the river, the white-blazed gravel loop and yellow-blazed, mostly dirt trail in this park combine for an easy, pleasant hike. You may come upon a few perplexing intersections, mostly at junctions with spur trails from adjoining neighborhoods, but the park borders are well signed, and if you follow the white blazes, you can't get turned around for long on this compact trail network.

There are two parking lots at Robious Landing. The official trailhead is at the western lot near a large playground, but the main Loop Trail is just as easily accessed from the eastern lot near the boat launch and fishing pier. On busy weekends, stick

DISTANCE & CONFIGURATION: 1.8-mile loop, with optional balloon

DIFFICULTY: Easy

ELEVATION: 122' at trailhead, 155' at high point

SCENERY: Stream-laced hardwood forest along the James River

EXPOSURE: Mostly shaded

TRAFFIC: Moderate

TRAIL SURFACE: Dirt and gravel singletrack

HIKING TIME: 45 minutes

SEASON: Year-round during daylight hours

ACCESS: No fee

WHEELCHAIR ACCESS: On the paved sections

MAPS: On sign at trailhead and at chesterfield.gov/3823/robious-landing-park

DRIVING DISTANCE FROM CAPITOL: 16.3 miles

FACILITIES: Restrooms, picnic tables and shelters, fishing piers, playground, volleyball court, boat slide (nonmotorized craft)

CONTACT: Chesterfield County Parks: 804-748-1623, chesterfield.gov/parks

LOCATION: 3800 James River Rd., Midlothian

COMMENTS: Robious Landing Park is adjacent to James River High School. The park is home to the Virginia Boat Club's scull house, and you can sometimes catch rowers out on the flat waters of the James River.

with the official trailhead lot—turn left before passing the hilltop restrooms—to avoid congestion at the boat launch. You'll be strolling beside the lazy river in no time.

Visitors may encounter nesting woodland songbirds, including flycatchers, woodpeckers, and vireos, according to the Virginia Department of Game and Inland Fisheries. In this bottomland forest you may also find eastern bluebirds, common yellowthroats, waterthrushes, wood thrushes, warblers, red-bellied woodpeckers, redheaded woodpeckers, and more.

Robious Landing also has a tree identification trail that lists the names and details of 27 tree types found in the park. This hardwood forest includes sycamore, pine, sweet gum, tulip poplar, bladdernut, pawpaw, winged elm, and seven types of oak. The trail is less than a mile and appears to be wheelchair friendly (I saw one person using an electric wheelchair on it during my visit). It follows along the Loop Trail until it reaches a fork near the park's main road, where it veers right to circle back to the beginning.

This hike travels clockwise along the white-blazed Loop Trail. Begin at the trailhead just east of the main takeout, a paved path that briefly passes near the banks of the James River before dipping into the woods beyond Shelter 1 and the Virginia Boat Club's scull house. The trail becomes a mix of sand, dirt, and rock; it is quite compact and hardened through this section, though there are rutted and eroded portions as well. Watch for roots if you are with small children or running the trail.

You will pass a narrow, winding stream before the trail crosses a creek on a wooden footbridge before it curves right toward the interior of the park. Keep an eye out for white blazes, as there are a few blue-blazed access trails leading to the adjacent neighborhoods and James River High School. Cross the main park road, and continue on the white-blazed loop.

Robious Landing Park

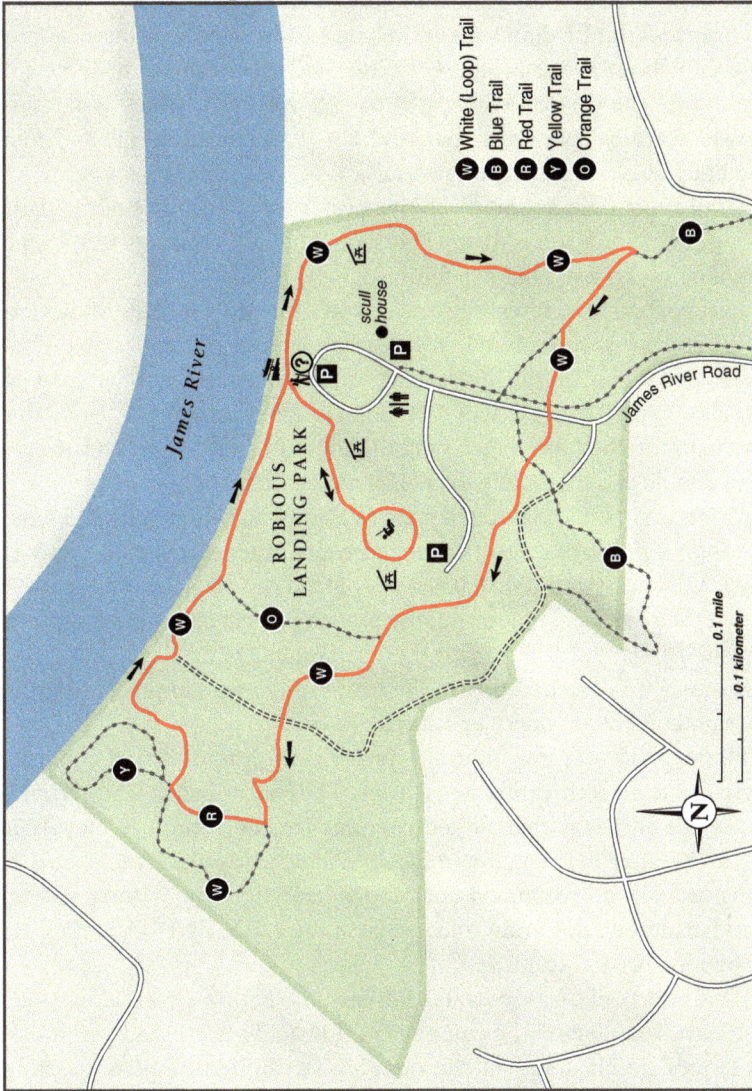

White (Loop) Trail
Blue Trail
Red Trail
Yellow Trail
Orange Trail

scull house

James River

James River Road

ROBIOUS LANDING PARK

0.1 mile

0.1 kilometer

On a nice day, you'll likely hear children on the playground through the woods on the right. An orange-blazed trail intersects the main loop, offering a shortcut to the river, but continue straight. You will cross a gravel doubletrack trail that accesses the emergency boat ramp. Closed to the public, this ramp is used only for rescue and law-enforcement boats.

In this corner of the park, on a separate visit on an early spring morning, I encountered what I've always believed to be a barred owl. I was walking along the path and not paying attention. The bird's brown-and-white feathers blended in with the tree branches, and I didn't see it. Maybe I even startled it because the owl let me get within about 30 yards before it screeched loudly and quickly flew off. I felt the breeze from the raptor's wings as it passed overhead, which was intimidating. Barred owls typically have a wingspan of about 45 inches and weigh 2–3 pounds, but I jumped like it was five times that size.

The trail veers right as you reach the westernmost portions of the park. You're now hiking toward the James River. This segment passes through fern-carpeted forest and again crosses a stream on a footbridge.

Alongside the river, interpretive signs tell the story of the Monacan Indians who fished along this shore four centuries ago. The Monacan people, who spoke a Siouxan dialect, inhabited the forests of central Virginia and were often at odds with the Powhatan Indians living east of Richmond in the coastal plain. "Upon the head of the Powhatans are the Monacans," wrote John Smith, whose own relations with the Powhatan people and their namesake chief were often strained.

The Monacan natives migrated west as European settlers claimed large swaths of land along Virginia's rivers to grow tobacco and other crops. In the early 18th century, King William III granted 10,000 acres of land to a group of Huguenot refugees. Having fled their Catholic homeland, the French Protestants evoked sympathy from the English. The Huguenots named their settlement Manakintown in reference to the Monacans who preceded them. The name still lingers in present-day Manakin-Sabot, located nearby on the river's north shore.

South of the river a few miles lies present-day Midlothian, a community that traces its roots to an 18th-century coal mine. The coal mined in Chesterfield County helped fire the furnaces that forged cannons for the American Revolution. The industry arose after a Huguenot refugee inadvertently discovered coal deposits. According to a legend recounted at Robious Landing, he slid down a riverbank in pursuit of his hunting dog and noticed coal in the earth. By 1730, several Huguenot families operated coal pits nearby.

As the Loop Trail turns to head back east, the pathway runs alongside a meandering stream. You'll enjoy the company of this sandy-bottomed perennial stream; smooth stones lie clustered in the bending streambeds, and ferns cling to the mossy banks.

Continuing along the riverbank, you will again cross the boat-ramp access and reenter woodlands along the path. Views of the river flash through the pawpaw trees. On warm days, the hum of motorboats and the chatter of tubing youth rise from the river. The James is slow here, as the falls of the James are nearly 4 miles east from Robious Landing, beginning at Bosher's Dam.

You will cross two more wooden bridges over streams on your way back to the trailhead and parking area.

For this hike, I added a 0.4-mile spur past Shelters 2 and 3 to the playground, which also has a paved loop—good for parents who want to push a stroller for some short laps while the older children play nearby on the playground equipment. When you are ready to return, retrace your steps back to the trailhead and parking area.

• •

GPS TRAILHEAD COORDINATES N37° 33.541' W77° 38.845'

DIRECTIONS Take Chippenham Parkway (VA 150) east to the US 60 W/Midlothian Turnpike exit. Proceed west on Midlothian Turnpike 4.3 miles, then turn right on Robious Road. Continue 5.2 miles and follow the signs for Bettie Woodson Weaver Elementary School and James River High School. Turn right on James River Road and proceed 0.5 mile, passing both schools before entering the park. Alternately, from I-64 west of Richmond, take US 288 south across the James River, then exit eastbound on Huguenot Trail (VA 711, which becomes Robious Road to the east). Continue about a mile and look for park signs telling you to turn left on James River Road.

Lush tree canopy shades the majority of the crushed-stone walking path.

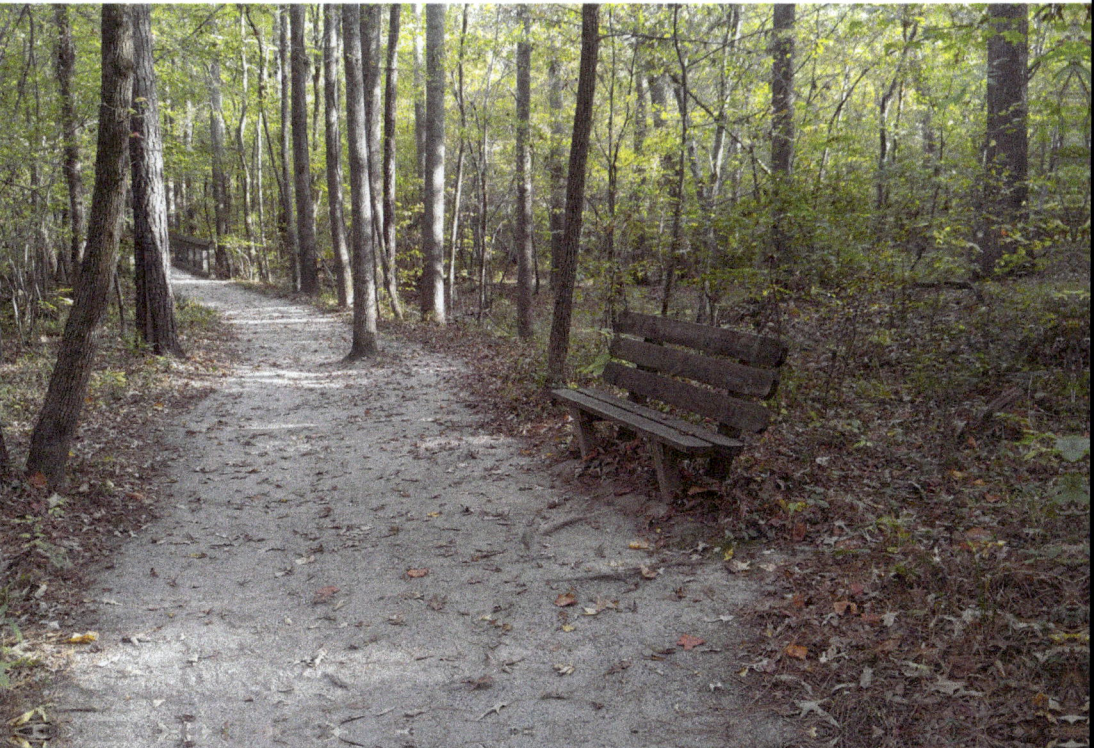

24 ROCKWOOD PARK

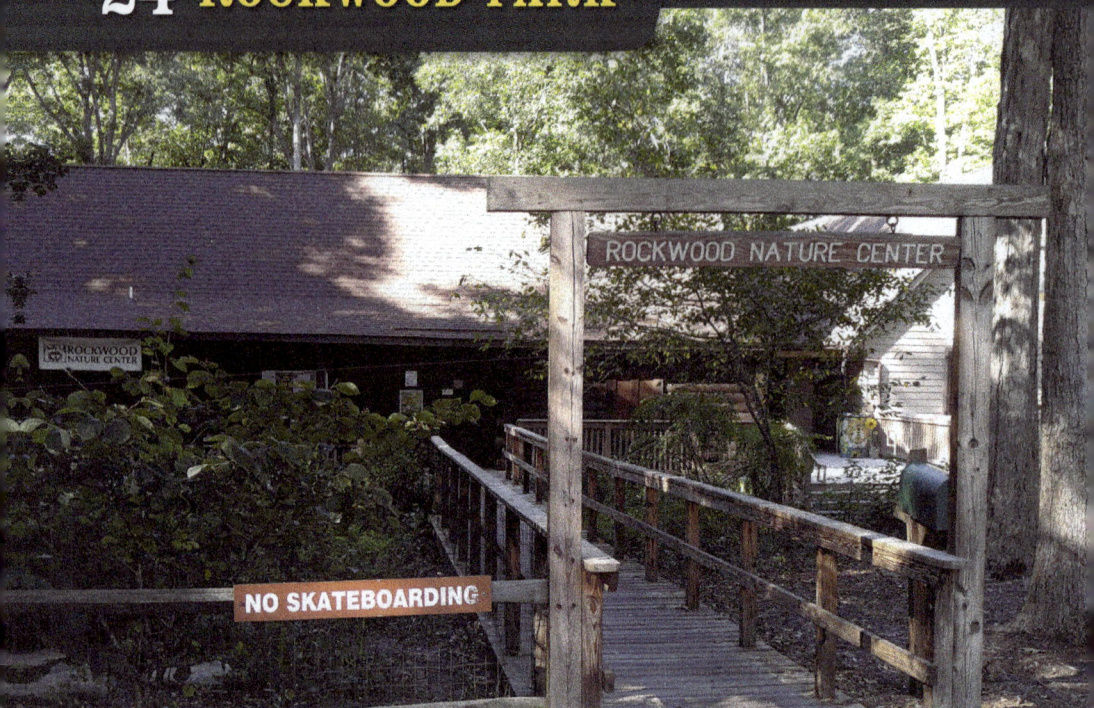

The nature center at Rockwood Park offers wilderness classes and animal interactions.

INDULGE YOUR INNER CHILD with an afternoon visit to Rockwood. Hike the paved trails, or run if you prefer, but don't miss your chance to wander—in this case, along the beaten paths. The paved balloon at Rockwood Park is popular with Southsiders out for a walk or run, but the park's web of dirt paths—some of which are maintained and mapped—is surprisingly extensive. Trails trace the park's border with Gregory's Pond and crisscross its woodland interior. There's even a boardwalk for wetland-wildlife viewing.

DESCRIPTION

Chesterfield County does a thorough job of maintaining this 161-acre gem. The county's oldest park, opened in 1975, Rockwood has something for everyone, including community garden plots. If you're primarily interested in the park's web of dirt trails, you may choose to begin at the nature center, where a paved trail departs from behind the building to connect to the Purple, Red, Orange, and Yellow Trails. If you're lucky, you'll find an interpretive pamphlet in a mailbox near the start.

The system of colored blazes has improved, though watch for a few unmarked intersections and unofficial shortcuts, which make it surprisingly easy to inadvertently walk in a circle. But as long as you have time to spare, you can wander with little fear of getting lost because the park's woods are hemmed in by Gregory's

DISTANCE & CONFIGURATION: 2.1-mile balloon, interwoven with numerous dirt trails

DIFFICULTY: Easy

ELEVATION: 222' at trailhead, 167' at low point

SCENERY: Suburban woods, pond

EXPOSURE: Mostly shaded

TRAFFIC: Moderate

TRAIL SURFACE: Paved, dirt

HIKING TIME: 1 hour

SEASON: Year-round during daylight hours

ACCESS: No fee; fishing not permitted in adjacent pond

WHEELCHAIR ACCESS: On the paved sections

MAPS: On kiosks at trailhead, at nature center, and at chesterfield.gov/3824/rockwood-park

DRIVING DISTANCE FROM CAPITOL: 13.5 miles

FACILITIES: Restrooms, picnic tables, grills, group shelters, concession stand, playground, ballfields, tennis and basketball courts, archery range, arboretum, nature center, dog park

CONTACT: Chesterfield County Parks: 804-748-1623, chesterfield.gov/parks

LOCATION: 3401 Courthouse Rd., North Chesterfield

COMMENTS: Rockwood Park offers a broad range of trails, from a paved loop with fitness stations to root- and rock-strewn singletracks.

Pond (a private, no-fishing pond) and the creek that feeds it, as well as by the park's numerous sports fields.

For this hike, park near Shelter 4 and begin by heading north on the Blue Trail. You will traverse the park's paved trails as a balloon. The counterclockwise route is a good first go-round and will give you the lay of the land. Note that Rockwood has shapes in addition to colors for its trails. The Blue Trail has a rectangle shape.

Follow the path past the archery range. An interesting sign at the range gives a little information about the history of archery. "Native Americans usually used turkey feathers as fletching for their arrows. They would cut the feathers to size, trim them, and attach them to the shaft with a sinew. The arrow shaft was made from a straight sapling of a birch or willow tree."

Continue straight through an intersection with the Orange Trail (circle). Take a right onto a dirt trail that descends slightly toward Gregory's Pond along the shore. (Watch for a sign warning of a potential beehive nearby.) If you prefer, you may also sidetrack onto the asphalt fitness loop.

Numerous earthen trails may tempt you to head up the hill to the left away from the lake, but instead follow the eroded and rooted shoreline about 0.3 mile. After a sharp left at the northernmost stretch of the loop, the trail bends away from the lake and follows a wetland habitat beside the park's primarily hardwood forest. We saw two great blue herons scanning the landscape during our visit.

A park sign flanked by two benches nestled into a small clearing provides more information about the Powhatan tribe: "The Powhatan were located in Eastern Virginia around the Tidewater Region. The main Powhatan tribe was located in what is now Henrico County. The Powhatan Confederacy was spread out all around Virginia and some parts of Maryland and consisted of 31 tribes. These tribes were either allied with or conquered by Powhatan."

Rockwood Park

ROCKWOOD PARK

Gregory's Pond

Nature Center

Courthouse Road

Hull Street Road

360

653

653

N

0.1 mile
0.1 kilometer

O Orange Trail
W White Trail
B Blue Trail
Y Yellow Trail
P Purple Trail
G Green Trail
R Red Trail

Follow the Orange Trail as it continues west, crossing over a wide creek on a wooden bridge with a railing. The trail winds through a hardwood forest with heavy understory in this next section before crossing another wetland on a wooden bridge with no railing. The trail then begins a slight ascent of a hill.

Continue following this outermost dirt loop over an old but markedly sturdy wood-and-metal bridge. You may notice a few houses opposite the creek that feeds the pond and forms the park's northwest boundary. Such reminders of Rockwood's suburban locale are not infrequent, but the park retains a pleasantly rustic feel, particularly in summer, when these woods—full of white oak, sweet gum, beech, and river birch—are flush with verdant summer foliage. Even along the stream, mossy banks and lichen-blotched boulders, not to mention a path rough with roots, contrast with the nearby toy-strewn backyards. It's a lucky youngster who can rock-hop to the park from his or her back door.

Look for a large birch tree with an extremely wide and exposed root system. It would provide a good opportunity to teach children about how roots support and feed trees. As the trail continues, watch for a few large boulders covered in lichens that could make for a brief climb for young and old.

The trail slowly veers left and begins a southeastern trek toward the nature center. Continue straight along the Orange Trail at the junction with the paved White Trail. Several spur trails crisscross the pathway for more options. Ballfields come into view as the trail follows along the clearing for the large power lines that cut through the heart of Rockwood Park.

The trail passes through the junction of many trails just down from the nature center. Continue along the Orange Trail until you meet up with the Blue Trail, then retrace your steps to the parking lot from which the hike began.

• •

GPS TRAILHEAD COORDINATES N37° 26.919' W77° 34.819'

DIRECTIONS Rockwood Park lies near the intersection of Courthouse Road (Huguenot Road farther north) and Hull Street Road (US 360), with entrances on both (although you can only exit the park from Courthouse Road).

From Chippenham Parkway, exit onto Hull Street Road going southwest. Look for a wooden sign on the right. From Midlothian Turnpike (US 60) or the Powhite Parkway (VA 76), exit right onto Courthouse Road, heading south; signs indicate the approaching entrance, on the left. After you enter the park from Courthouse Road, pass the nature center and the official trailhead on your left, and continue past another lot to the parking area for Shelter 4 and the archery range. If you enter from Hull Street Road, bear right past the arboretum, and park in the lot on the right.

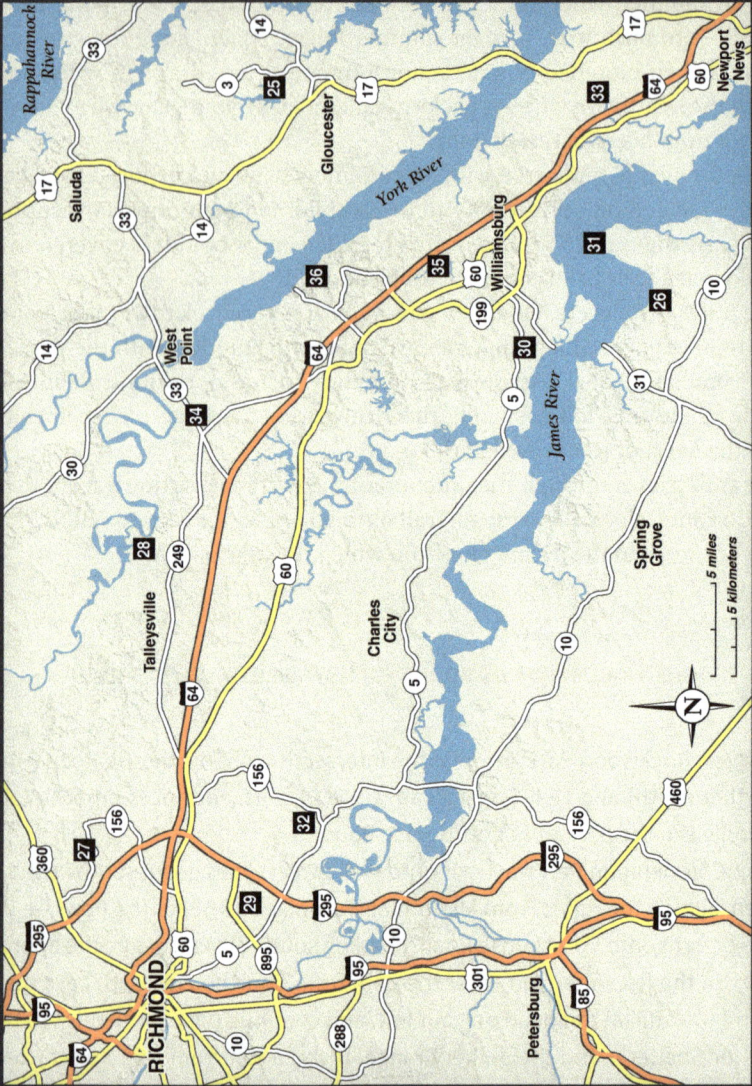

EAST TO WILLIAMSBURG AND TIDEWATER

The trail at Beaverdam Park provides many beautiful views of Beaverdam Lake.

THIS ROUTE BEGINS on Beaverdam Park's hiking-only path to trace the southeastern arm of Beaverdam Reservoir, bisecting numerous stream-fed marshes along the way. A return leg across forested hills on the park's multiuse trail completes the loop. Watch for mountain bikes and horses on the multiuse trail.

DESCRIPTION

Were it solely the work of tree-felling semiaquatic mammals, Beaverdam Reservoir would be quite a feat. But in fact the 635-acre lake is the product of a human-made dam. Before its 1990 inundation, the submerged area was a tangle of creeks and wooded beaver ponds known as Beaverdam Swamp. Today, the beavers are relegated to the lake's many marshy inlets, and the reservoir is home to 20 fish species. Consequently, the lake is a popular destination with anglers, who vie for largemouth bass, bluegill, and several varieties of sunfish but could inadvertently land an American eel.

The adjacent park is also popular with mountain bikers and equestrians, who enjoy more than a dozen miles of multiuse trails. Nevertheless, thanks to the area's relative isolation, the trails are rarely crowded. Moreover, many visitors linger near the playground, picnic shelters, and fitness trail just south of the boat docks rather than head north on the nature, hiking, or multiuse trail. The starting point of all

DISTANCE & CONFIGURATION: 5.9-mile horseshoe loop, plus optional 9.5-mile multiuse trail with loops

DIFFICULTY: Moderate

ELEVATION: 58' at trailhead, no significant rise

SCENERY: Beaverdam Reservoir, marshes, hardwood forest

EXPOSURE: Mostly shaded, open on Backbone Trail and along river

TRAFFIC: Low, except near boat launch; busier with horses and mountain bikes along multiuse trail

TRAIL SURFACE: Dirt, gravel, boardwalks

HIKING TIME: 2.5 hours

SEASON: Year-round during daylight hours

ACCESS: No fee

WHEELCHAIR ACCESS: Wheelchairs not recommended on trails

MAPS: At park office, trailheads, and gloucesterva.info/523/park-trails

DRIVING DISTANCE FROM CAPITOL: 60 miles

FACILITIES: Restrooms, picnic tables and shelters, playground, fitness trail, boat rental and ramp, fishing pier, group camp, meeting lodge, amphitheater

CONTACT: Gloucester County Parks, Recreation, and Tourism: 804-693-2107, gloucesterva .info/497/beaverdam-park

LOCATION: 8687 Roaring Springs Rd., Gloucester

COMMENTS: The multiuse trail along the shoreline of Beaverdam Reservoir totals 9.5 miles one-way.

three trails is just downhill from the outdoor classroom, with the multiuse trailhead farthest from the lake and the hiking trailhead in the middle. To begin this hike, pick up a trail guide at the trailhead and head straight onto the hiking-only trail.

(If you prefer, take a left at the starting junction to hike the 0.33-mile Lake's Edge Interpretive Trail. The trail guide details 20 stations along that trail, each denoted by a numbered signpost. Outlining many familiar aspects of Virginia's ecology, such as common tree species, riparian reptiles and amphibians, and migratory waterfowl, Lake's Edge serves as an informative primer for your hike. Look closely and you'll easily find all the plants identified by the booklet, as well as some of the animals, as you traipse along the shore of Beaverdam Reservoir. After crossing a small inlet on a sturdy wooden bridge, turn left to stay on Lake's Edge Interpretive Trail; straight ahead is one of several connectors to the hiking path.)

The green-blazed hiking trail curves slightly away from the water's edge to terminate at a T intersection opposite an attractive three-tiered wood. Sweet gum and yellow poplar trees shade a glade of shorter dogwoods, which themselves stretch above thickets of pawpaw. Turn left onto the footpath, which you will follow around a lengthy arm of the lake, as well as around and through many smaller, marshy inlets. The first of these swampy sloughs soon appears through a narrow screen of trees on your left. Fallen logs and truncated tree trunks project from the water amid reeds and grasses. Turtles are commonly found sunning on dry logs but slip into the water at the sound of approaching footsteps.

This is the first of several inlet crossings that vary in scale but are similar in design. The hiking path traverses an earthen levee, with the lake visible on the left and a small pond on the right. Above that pond is another earthen dam along

137

Beaverdam Park

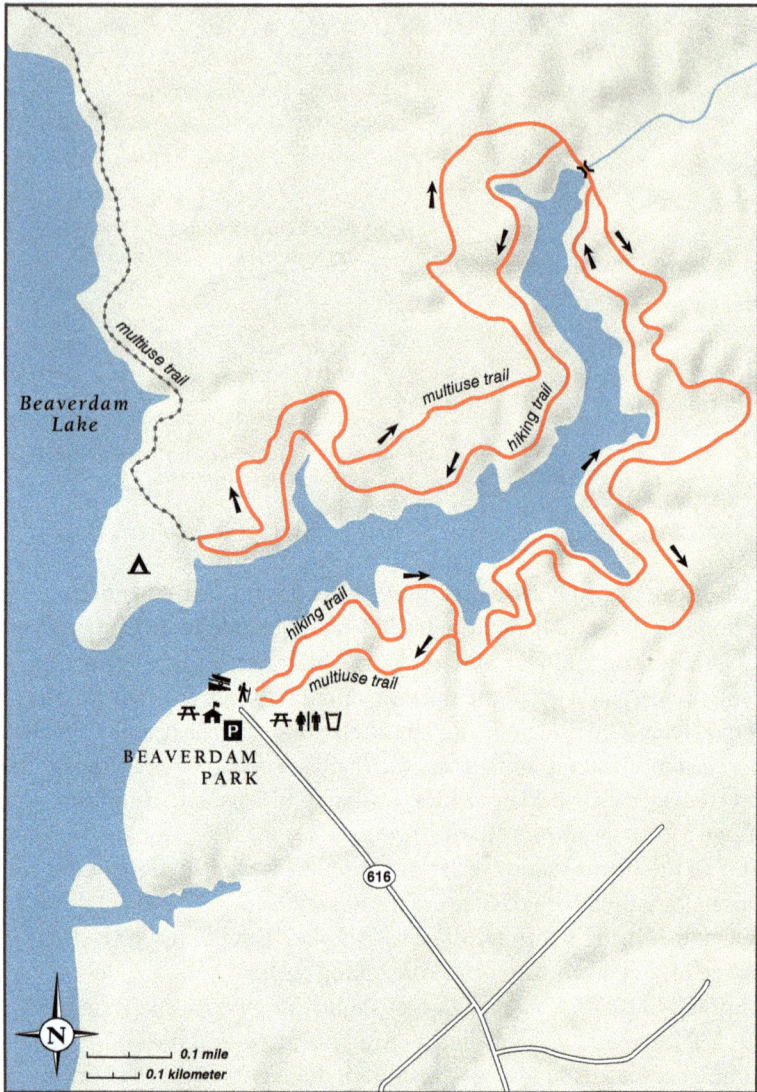

Beaverdam Lake

multiuse trail

multiuse trail

hiking trail

hiking trail

multiuse trail

BEAVERDAM PARK

616

N

0.1 mile
0.1 kilometer

which the multiuse trail passes. The modest streams that feed these marshy inlets are routed through the earthen dams via metal pipes. In summer, clusters of pinkish swamp milkweed and orange jewelweed grow alongside the trail, while pale lotus blossoms dot the still water. Approach the lake's sloughs with a watchful eye, and you will likely spot a great blue heron or snowy egret stalking prey amid the marsh grass and cattails.

Once across, the hiking path turns left then veers inland, bypassing a closed trail section, through a forest of beech, white oak, scarlet oak, and Virginia pine filled out by American holly and younger ironwood. Stay with the green blazes, and the trail is easy to follow as it continues along the edge of Beaverdam Reservoir's southeastern arm. After the second inlet crossing, ignore any arrows you find spray-painted on the trail, telling you to leave the main path and veer right. These directions, accompanied by the letters *XC,* are intended for local high school cross-country runners.

The two paths share the narrow wooden boardwalk of Morgan Bridge to cross the reservoir and the marshy farther reaches of the lake's southeastern arm. Once across, the hiking path begins to tack south and west, mirroring itself across the water to complete the horseshoe out-and-back. If you wish to cut this hike roughly in half, use the bridge as your turnaround point. The clearly marked multiuse trail climbs uphill on either end of the bridge, so it's possible to hike a smaller loop—or, for that matter, to convert this hike into a figure eight.

To continue the hike as mapped, stay on the trail as the sycamores and red maples growing at the lake's edge give way to beeches, chestnut oaks, and tulip poplars. Follow the green blazes as an older trail segment runs nearer the lake and a connector takes the multiuse trail to the right. A black snake calmly slithered his way across the path as we hiked along. Unlike most snakes, this one showed little anxiety in our presence, and we granted it the time it needed to progress toward the lakeshore. The trail continues over the undulating, root-studded path, which repeatedly approaches the water in marshy inlets then bears inland. The boathouse comes into view across the lake, signaling the hiking path's impending terminus at the multiuse trail.

As it heads north from this well-marked junction, the multiuse trail crosses an old doubletrack near a spur trail leading west to the peninsular group camp. Five miles and four bridges on, the multiuse trail reaches its trailhead at the park's Farys Mill Road entrance. The prescribed route here, however, doubles back eastbound on the multiuse trail, which runs uphill from and roughly parallel to the hiking path. Blue iconic blazes, indicating hiker, cyclist, and equestrian use, dot the route, which is sometimes muddier than its pedestrian-only counterpart.

Though these are upland woods that drain toward the lake, the sandy soil remains damp enough to sprout numerous ferns along the path. You'll also notice more frequent elevation changes, particularly when the trail dips to cross lake sloughs south of Morgan Bridge.

After recrossing the bridge, the trail rises steeply to enter a fragrant pine-dominated wood where needles carpet the trail. Ahead the path dips to a break in the woods with three sturdy benches. A streamlet runs beneath the trail here. The end of this hike is a pair of piney knolls and one more lake inlet away.

NEARBY ACTIVITIES

While in Virginia's Middle Peninsula, consider visiting the charming community of **Gloucester Courthouse.** A square in the center of town hosts regular events and markets. Visit gloucestercalendar.org for an updated calendar.

Gloucester Museum of History (804-693-1234, gloucesterva.info/820/museum-of -history), located south of the county seat at the junction of VA 616 and VA 614, is housed in a circa 1770 brick tavern on Main Street named for the Colonial governor Lord Botetourt. It's also the birthplace of Walter Reed, who, as an army physician in the Spanish-American War, helped eradicate yellow fever after discovering its transmission by mosquitoes.

• •

GPS TRAILHEAD COORDINATES N37° 26.902' W76° 32.034'

DIRECTIONS From Richmond, take I-64 east to Exit 220. Exit onto VA 33, heading northeast. Proceed through West Point and turn right onto VA 14 after 14 miles. Heading east, you will intersect US 17 after 6 more miles. Veer right and continue another 8 miles southeast on US 17 to Gloucester. Turn left onto US 17 Business (Main Street), then take the first left onto VA 616 (Roaring Springs Road). The park's main entrance is at the road's terminus, 2.4 miles ahead. The park's secondary entrance—the multiuse trail's optional trailhead—is off VA 606 (Farys Mill Road), which intersects US 17 2.4 miles northwest of US 17 Business. To use this entrance, take VA 606 north 2.6 miles to the entrance on your right.

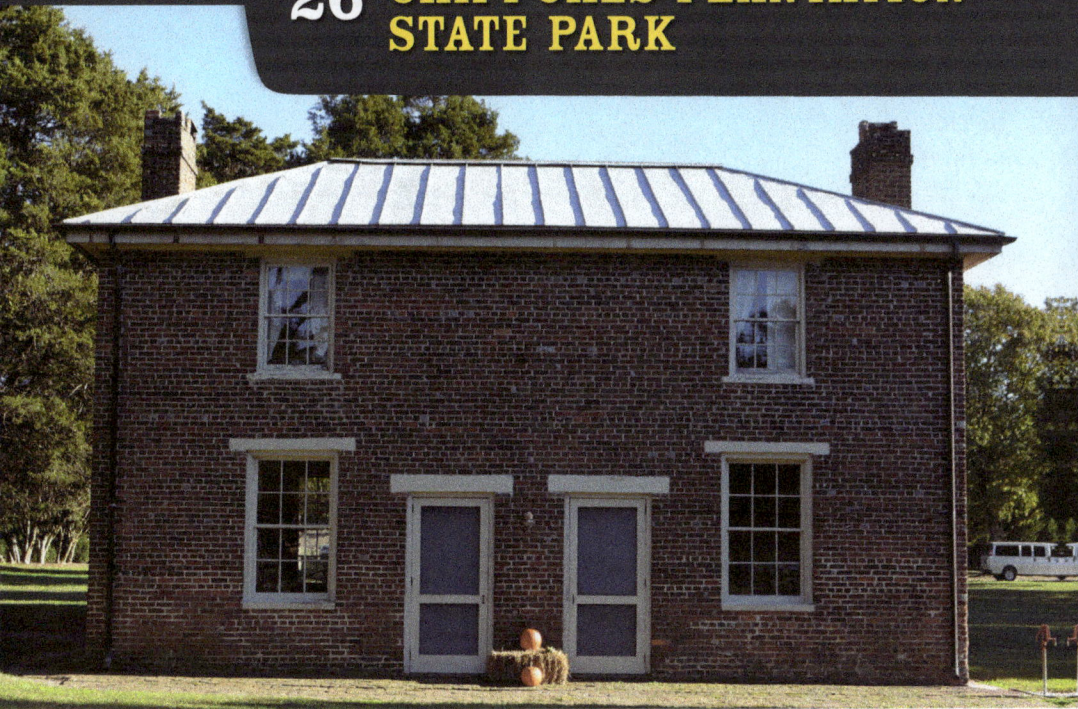

Chippokes Mansion at Chippokes Plantation State Park

THE PASTORAL ENVIRONS of this park are positively evocative. It's easy to imagine Native Americans paddling a canoe through the lush wetlands where Chippokes Creek meets the James River or to imagine early settlers tending the nearby fields of corn and wheat.

DESCRIPTION

A wealth of history awaits at Chippokes Plantation State Park. Nearby Colonial- and American-history landmarks at Williamsburg, Jamestown, and Yorktown draw more than a million visitors annually. But here, just across the 5-mile-wide James River, the pace is slower and the setting bucolic. And in addition to its human past, Chippokes highlights the region's natural history, including a fossil record that reaches back eons. To appreciate the park's diverse offerings, begin your trek at the visitor center, where centuries-old farming tools; fossils, shells, and bird nests; and a diorama detailing the plantation's early history all vie for attention. Peruse the brochure rack for maps and leaflets to augment your hike.

After exiting the visitor center, head east on the paved College Run Trail, which promptly descends to a cypress swamp on the right. Frogs chirp among the cypress knees. Note the short path on the left, which leads to the James River; it will later provide your return from the beach. You may also note the buzz, and possibly bite, of

DISTANCE & CONFIGURATION: 5.3-mile triangular balloon with out-and-back spur

DIFFICULTY: Easy

ELEVATION: 45' at trailhead, no significant rise

SCENERY: Cobham Bay beach along the James River, 19th-century plantation home, Chippokes Creek

EXPOSURE: Open, with limited shade

TRAFFIC: Moderate

TRAIL SURFACE: Paved, dirt

HIKING TIME: 2.5 hours

SEASON: Year-round during daylight hours; tours of Jones-Stewart Mansion available April–October, Friday–Monday; Chippokes Farm and Forestry Museum open for self-guided tours the first Friday in March–the first Monday in December, daily, 9 a.m.–5 p.m.

ACCESS: Parking $5

WHEELCHAIR ACCESS: Some trails and at most facilities; no access to mansion

MAPS: At park and dcr.virginia.gov/state-parks/chippokes-plantation

DRIVING DISTANCE FROM CAPITOL: 58.5 miles

FACILITIES: Restrooms, showers, picnic area, campground, cabins, swimming pool, beach, visitor center, museum

CONTACT: 757-294-3728, dcr.virginia.gov/state-parks/chippokes-plantation; Jones-Stewart Mansion and Chippokes Farm and Forestry Museum: 757-294-3439

LOCATION: 695 Chippokes Park Rd., Surry

COMMENTS: A water trail of the Captain John Smith Chesapeake National Historic Trail connects to Chippokes. Wear shoes with sturdy soles for the 1-mile trudge down a shell-covered beach.

deerflies (or mayflies), which, depending on the time of your visit, may accompany you from this point on should you fail to use insect repellent. Cross a wooden bridge just ahead, and look for wild yellow iris blooming in the spring.

Lucas's Landing, the wide, sandy shoal where College Run meets the James, served as early as 1626 as a loading point for tobacco and other crops bound for England. The surrounding property had been granted to Captain William Powell in 1619. His plantation and Chippokes Creek, which borders it on the east, were named for an Algonquian chieftain who befriended Colonial settlers. In 1646, Colonel Henry Bishop, having acquired the plantation, expanded it from 550 to 1,403 acres, an area slightly smaller than that of present-day Chippokes Plantation State Park.

The plantation's fields are among the oldest continuously cultivated cropland in North America, and demonstration fields of corn and wheat still surround the historic plantation structures. It is fitting that the park is home to Chippokes Farm and Forestry Museum, which showcases the agricultural implements of four centuries, including a Depression-era sawmill.

The path soon veers away from the James and uphill to pass the River House, the park's oldest structure, on the left. The Farm and Forestry Museum is visible across the road that parallels the trail on your right. Buildings along Quarter Lane, now part of College Run Trail, are fronted by interpretive signs illuminating the workings of a 19th-century farm, including the hard labor done by slaves and sharecroppers. The lane was named for the slave and tenant quarters that dot the route. It also passes barns that were rebuilt in the 1930s.

Chippokes Plantation State Park

On opposite ends of the lane stand the park's most notable structures: the Colonial-style clapboard River House, built in 1830, and the stately brick Chippokes Mansion, also known as the Jones-Stewart Mansion. The latter was constructed in 1854 under the direction of Albert Jones, who had purchased the farm in 1837 and promptly enlarged the River House. The plantation prospered under Jones's ownership, and here operated one of the few legal distilleries in Virginia. Legend holds that Chippokes Mansion and Plantation were spared the torch during the Civil War because Jones sold peach and apple brandy to both the North and the South.

The Stewart name now associated with the mansion recognizes Victor Stewart and his wife, who capped a succession of owners when they obtained sole ownership of the plantation in 1925 for a sum total of $52,000. The couple devoted time and resources to restoring the mansion (including purchasing the rare portable sawmill now displayed at the museum), and in 1967 Mrs. Stewart donated it to the people of Virginia as a memorial to her husband. Today visitors can tour the mansion, stocked with antiques, for a small fee and stroll its Paradise Garden for free. Be sure to pick up a garden-guide leaflet at the visitor center beforehand.

You may incorporate the mansion and garden (and even the museum) into your hike or return by car afterward. To continue the hike, head northeast on the double-track path in front of the mansion. The path will fork just beyond the grounds, with a pasture on the left and corn and wheat fields to the right. Turn right onto Lower Chippokes Creek Trail—there's a field to your left and a band of trees to your right. You can forgo this approximately 2-mile out-and-back if you're short on time, but the creekside dock at its terminus is an excellent spot for wildlife-watching. Brilliant green foliage surrounds the meandering channel, herons fish among the shallows, and crabs scurry along the shore. An outdoor classroom used for scheduled programs overlooks the dock.

Cypress trees line the sandy shoreline.

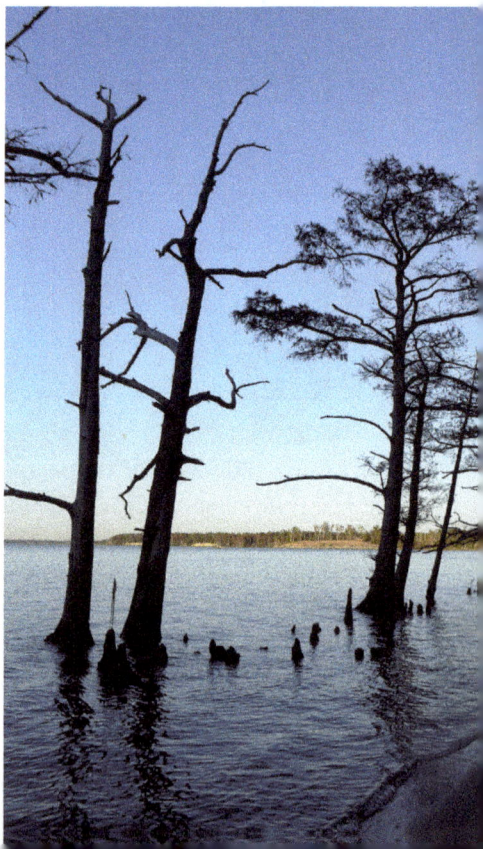

From the creek, retrace your steps along the field, then turn right onto James River Trail. With a field on your right and forest on your left, you hike about 0.7 mile before entering the woods to descend to the James River. You can elect to return by backtracking on the James River and College Run Trails, but indulge your sense of adventure instead and return along the beach for about a mile. For my family, the beach was the highlight of this hike. You may have to scramble over a few deadfalls from the slowly eroding reddish sand cliffs, but the scene is practically tropical. The sandy beach of Cobham Bay sweeps across the horizon.

The same slow erosion that created the bay and beach has littered the shore with fossils. And the tide washes new shells ashore, its gentle lapping ever so slowly grinding them to sand. Be sure to grab a brochure from the visitor center that explains the various fossil types, generously including unaltered remains, such as shells and bones. It also cites some of the fossils and shells commonly found along the beach. Visitors are asked not to dig any fossils from the bluff and are not permitted to keep the fossils they find.

You will know you are approaching the end of your walk along the beach when you come to College Run. The creek fans out in a small delta with fingers too wide to leap. Plan to wade through the cool, clear shallows. The trail passes through several stands of cypress growing along the shoreline and into the James. We even found an osage orange tree that was full of ripe lime-green horse apples (not edible). They smelled so sweet. Next look for the short, narrow path on the left that returns you to College Run Trail and to the trailhead. (You could trek farther down the beach to pick up the beach-access trail that leads back to the visitor-center parking lot, but the trail is closed in winter.)

• •

GPS TRAILHEAD COORDINATES N37° 08.704' W76° 44.338'

DIRECTIONS From Richmond, take I-95 south to Exit 61A (Hopewell) or I-295 south to Exit 15A (Hopewell) and head east on VA 10. Continue about 40 miles to the hamlet of Surry. Turn left at the intersection with VA 31, then turn right at the blinking light, remaining on VA 10 all the while. (If you're coming south from Williamsburg via VA 31 and the Jamestown–Scotland Ferry, turn left onto VA 10 here.) Turn left at VA 634 (Alliance Road) and follow it 4 miles to the park on the left. Drive through the park past the pool and campgrounds to park beside the visitor center at the road's end. College Run Trail heads east out of a small roundabout in front of the visitor center.

27 COLD HARBOR BATTLEFIELD, RICHMOND NATIONAL BATTLEFIELD PARK

A cannon near the visitor center marks the beginning of the hiking trail.

DUG IN AT COLD HARBOR, Confederate forces repelled the Union advance toward Richmond in a protracted engagement that left 16,000 men dead. The victory amounted to a stay of execution for the besieged Confederate capital and later prompted General Ulysses S. Grant to confess, "I have always regretted that the last assault at Cold Harbor was ever made . . . No advantage was gained to compensate for the heavy loss." Today those somber words are emblazoned on the battlefield's visitor center. Earthen fortifications still wend their way through the now silent woods, and an interpretive trail explains the grim reality of what in 1864 was a new phenomenon: trench warfare.

DESCRIPTION

Richmond National Battlefield Park encompasses 10 units, a central visitor center at the Tredegar Iron Works, and the Chimborazo Medical Museum. The park's most notable trail, however, is here at tiny Cold Harbor, northeast of Richmond. A mere crossroads, Cold Harbor erupted in violence on May 31, 1864. General Robert E. Lee's Confederate troops made a decisive stand in order to protect their capital 9 miles to the south.

The initial Union assault was disastrous, claiming 6,000 troops from the Federal ranks in a single day, June 3, 1864. The Union matched the entrenched Confederates

DISTANCE & CONFIGURATION: 3.3-mile loop

DIFFICULTY: Easy

ELEVATION: 172' at trailhead, 116' at low point

SCENERY: Open field, woods, eroded Civil War earthworks

EXPOSURE: Well shaded; open in fields near visitor center

TRAFFIC: Light

TRAIL SURFACE: Dirt and gravel singletrack

HIKING TIME: 1.5 hours

SEASON: Year-round during daylight hours

ACCESS: No fee

WHEELCHAIR ACCESS: Only along paved main road and at visitor center

MAPS: At visitor center and nps.gov/rich

DRIVING DISTANCE FROM CAPITOL: 10 miles

FACILITIES: Restrooms, water fountains, visitor center

CONTACT: 804-226-1981, nps.gov/rich

LOCATION: 5515 Anderson-Wright Dr., Mechanicsville

COMMENTS: The Lee vs. Grant 1864 Campaign Civil War driving trail connects to Cold Harbor. Metal detecting, picnicking, and walking on earthworks are prohibited. The brief paved route through the park passes some fortifications not visible from the trail. Just east of the battlefield is Cold Harbor National Cemetery, where 2,000 Union soldiers, 1,300 of them unknown, lie entombed. The nearby Watt House and Gaines Mill Battlefield offer another 0.3-mile trail.

by constructing earthworks along the battle lines, but the subsequent fighting saw little Union progress. On June 12, General Grant, who had assumed command of all Federal units only three months earlier, ordered a retreat, ending the battle. It would be Lee's last major victory. Lessons learned at Cold Harbor would shape not only Grant's subsequent, successful assault on Richmond from the south but also military tactics through the Great War.

Today, Cold Harbor Battlefield is an inauspicious park, one of many along the Virginia Civil War Trail driving tour route. Drive the park's loop road to see territory not covered by the footpath. En route you will spy a granite memorial to Connecticut soldiers, testimony to the ongoing remembrance the battlefield inspires. Moss now carpets the earthen berms behind which soldiers once crouched, and trees, notably red oak and loblolly pine, tower overhead. There is a solemnity to the place that cannot be fully appreciated from your car. Take the opportunity to view the extensive earthworks up close and read trail signage that illuminates both the importance of the battle and the miserable lot of the Civil War foot soldier.

Begin your hike at the visitor center with a primer on the battle. Walk beneath two mammoth oaks and a stand of pines, canopies on the side of the center nearest VA 156 (Cold Harbor Road). The trailhead is marked with two cannons and an aging monument placed by the Confederate Memorial Literary Society. The society, whose all-female membership included the wives and daughters of Confederate veterans, was chartered in 1890, with Belle Bryan (who deeded Joseph Bryan Park to the City of Richmond in her husband's honor) serving as president for its first 20 years. Besides erecting numerous historical markers, the society established the Museum of the Confederacy in Richmond.

Cold Harbor Battlefield, Richmond NBP

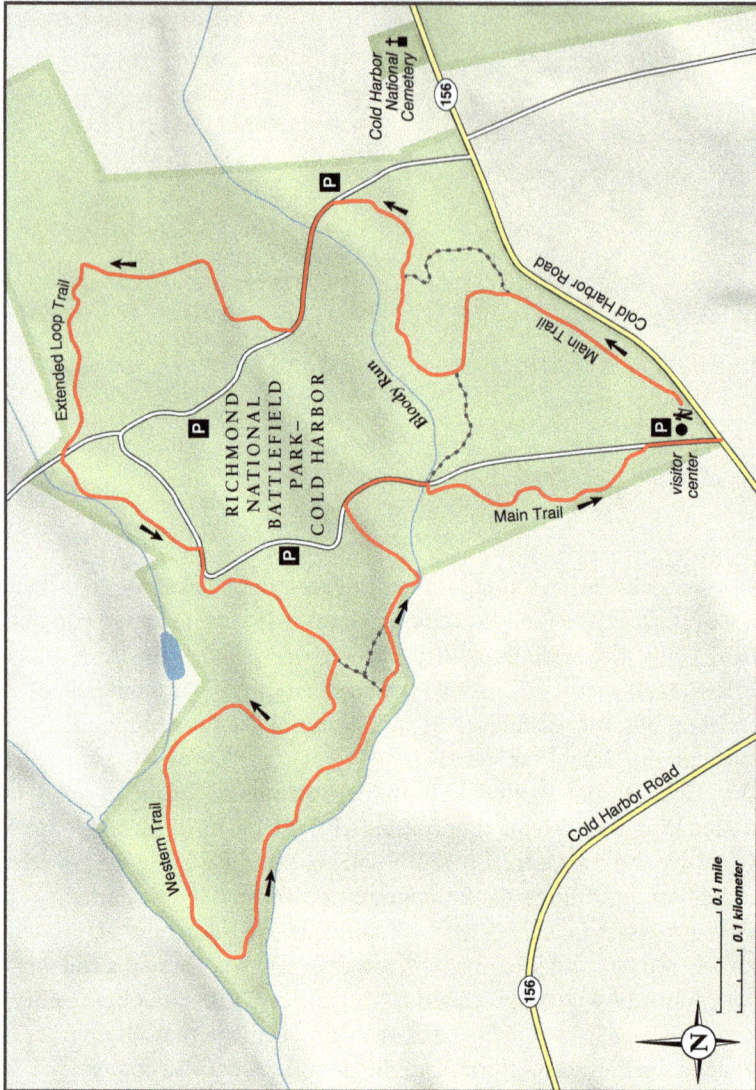

Also near the trailhead, a sign explains that the battlefield encompassed thousands of acres, far beyond what is visible along the path. In fact, the opposing battle lines extended almost 7 miles. The present battlefield park is located in about the center of the line of battle. This hike will be a counterclockwise loop and begins on the wide, well-worn Main Trail heading east from the visitor center through a grassy field that parallels Cold Harbor Road some 20 yards away. The decidedly pastoral scene visitors find today—a gently rolling meadow bounded by thick forest—is in marked contrast to the bloody scene recounted on park signs and in the literature.

The trail veers right to enter the woods and presents hikers with their first up-close view of an entrenchment. In this case it's a Union zigzag, dug to provide passage between two trench lines. As the battle wore on, intense fighting gave way to stalemate, and most casualties came at the hands of trained sharpshooters. Despised by the infantrymen on both sides, these snipers imposed a lethal penalty upon any troops who dared leave the confines of the trenches. According to park signage, one infantryman said crawling through the trenches carrying rations and ammunition made him feel like "some unholy cross between a pack mule and a snake." Another lamented, "A man's life is often exacted as the price of a cup of water from the spring."

The trail crosses a string of earthworks on an elevated bridge that protects them from wear. The trenches and berms visitors see today are significantly weathered and would have afforded greater protection at their original size. Constructing such earthen fortifications was no easy task, done as it was under the threat of enemy fire, using bayonets and bare hands in lieu of shovels.

The blue-blazed Main Trail soon meets the white-blazed Extended Loop Trail. Take a right and continue, crossing a gurgling brook known as Bloody Run, named in memory of the violent hand-to-hand combat that occurred here. Meandering through the woods, you will find that downed trees, holly thickets, and other brush intermittently disguise the earthworks, but the path remains obvious. The trail makes the most of the limited woodland area, winding beneath white oaks before passing numerous fire-scarred tree trunks.

About two-thirds of a mile into the hike, the trail passes a granite monument to the 2nd Connecticut Volunteer Heavy Artillery. Cross the park road and resume on the Extended Loop Trail into the woods. You will find a series of Union fortifications, built between June 1 and 3, 1864. The trenches form a battlefield map of sorts, with the Union trenches representing the Federal army's farthest point of advancement. Unable to break through enemy lines, Union soldiers dug in under cover of night and remained for two grueling weeks. A park sign indicating a Union rifle pit notes that its Confederate likeness is a mere 50 yards away. In between is the gulf that would be dubbed no-man's-land. The trail passes along the earthworks lines about 0.25 mile and emerges at a gravel road and a pond. Continue across the road, and reenter the woods along the path.

For the soldiers confined for days to squalid trenches, the brief truce of June 7 must have seemed surreal. During the three days following the Union's first unsuccessful charge, Generals Lee and Grant, in a precursor to their meeting at Appomattox, negotiated a 2-hour cease-fire, which afforded Union medics the opportunity to attend to soldiers who lay wounded from the initial failed advance. Along one stretch of the battle line, a Union work party recovered 244 dead and only 3 survivors. A New Jersey soldier recalled, "During the truce the enemies were talking to each other and exchanging newspapers. The works were lined with unarmed men, all gazing upon the solemn scene. The 2 hours soon passed. The signal was given. The men rushed to their arms and the rattle of musketry was again commenced along the line."

The trail emerges along the paved park road loop, which would have been in between the Confederate and Union fortifications, according to a park sign. The lines were separated by about 200 yards in this section of the earthworks. Follow the white blazes and trail markers to continue along the Extended Loop Trail. At a trail junction, take a right to follow the yellow-blazed 0.9-mile Western Trail. If you prefer a shorter hike, continue straight along the white-blazed trail.

The Western Trail has signs explaining Confederate mortar positions. This portion of the battlefield site is much more of a nature walk, with chances to walk along Bloody Run again. A private home on the right signals the path's impending end. Soon the trail emerges from the woods in view of the parking lot.

• •

GPS TRAILHEAD COORDINATES N37° 35.108' W77° 17.245'

DIRECTIONS From downtown, take I-64 west to Exit 192 for Mechanicsville Turnpike (US 360), following it about 4.5 miles. Turn right onto Cold Harbor Road (VA 156). Drive about 2.2 miles and then turn right to continue on Cold Harbor Road another 3.2 miles to the battlefield on the left.

From I-295, take Exit 34A to follow Creighton Road (VA 615) northeast. Turn right onto Cold Harbor Road (VA 156) and drive 2.5 miles. The battlefield is on your left, and the visitor center and two cannons are visible from the road. Plenty of signs from the interstate will direct your route.

The trail at Cumberland Marsh Natural Area Preserve offers occasional views of Holts Creek.

IN 1993 THE NATURE CONSERVANCY purchased the 1,193 acres of uplands, agricultural fields, and marsh that make up this preserve. The blufftop trail at Cumberland Marsh is a bird-watcher's delight. The grassy islands and still waters of Holts Creek are a valuable stopover for migratory waterfowl traveling the Atlantic flyway and are a year-round home for herons, egrets, and raptors. The network of trails is maintained by volunteers and traverses a recovering forest.

DESCRIPTION

Cumberland Marsh is home to the world's largest population of a rare plant called sensitive joint vetch and is one of only two preserves set aside for the plant (the other is in Cumberland County, New Jersey). Also known as Virginia joint vetch because its shrinking range now lies primarily within the commonwealth, the annual legume grows to 6 feet and in the summer produces small, red-veined yellow flowers. Its name derives from its reflexive fernlike leaves, which fold slightly when touched.

Vetch favors the periphery of brackish tidal marshes where the soil is inundated twice daily. Invasive reeds can overrun stands of the plant, but muskrats—like the one we saw swimming beside the pier at Cumberland Marsh during our visit—often clear the way for sensitive joint vetch by consuming perennial vegetation.

DISTANCE & CONFIGURATION: 4.1-mile out-and-back with balloon

DIFFICULTY: Easy

ELEVATION: 20' at trailhead, no significant rise

SCENERY: Bluffs overlooking marshy Holts Creek (a waterfowl haven), laurel-flanked ponds, mixed forest

EXPOSURE: Mostly shaded

TRAFFIC: Low

TRAIL SURFACE: Dirt

HIKING TIME: 2 hours

SEASON: Year-round during daylight hours

ACCESS: No fee; bicycles and pets not allowed

WHEELCHAIR ACCESS: Wheelchairs not recommended on trail

MAPS: On signboard at trailhead

DRIVING DISTANCE FROM CAPITOL: 31.5 miles

FACILITIES: Parking area with kiosk, metal dock into Holts Creek

CONTACT: Virginia Department of Conservation and Recreation Natural Heritage Program: 804-786-7951, dcr.virginia.gov/natural-heritage /natural-area-preserves

LOCATION: 9407 Cumberland Rd., New Kent, next to Cumberland Hospital for Children and Adolescents

COMMENTS: Cumberland Marsh is owned by The Nature Conservancy and accessed through a private farm. Be respectful of rules established by these landowners. You may reach the Virginia Office of The Nature Conservancy at 434-295-6106 or at nature.org.

Other wildlife you can expect to find in the preserve includes ospreys, bald eagles, herons, egrets, wild turkeys, salamanders, beavers, river otters, turtles, and deer, just to name a few. Dominant trees include American beech, sweet gum, black and red oak, hickory, pawpaw, loblolly pine, and more.

For a close-up glimpse of the other species thriving in this protected marsh, begin your hike with a brief out-and-back along the L-shaped boardwalk and pier northeast of the trailhead. Approach quietly to avoid startling the songbirds flitting among the buffer vegetation and the waterfowl bobbing about on Holts Creek. Big Creek runs beyond the flat, wooded peninsula visible before you, with Lilly Point Marsh beyond that. Holts Creek flows northeast, disappearing around a bend before its confluence with the Pamunkey River at Cumberland Thorofare, once an important shortcut for merchant vessels hauling goods downstream to the much wider York River.

Patient visitors, armed with binoculars, can spot wintering populations of canvasbacks, wood ducks, mallards, and of course chatty Canada geese. Springtime visitors will also find flowering mountain laurel overhanging the preserve's pond and crowding the interior doubletrack.

Begin your hike by heading southwest from the trailhead, passing a crop field to reach the singletrack. Volunteers have taken the time to ensure the trails are well-marked throughout the preserve. The crop field remains close at hand on your left as the path works its way through a buffer of forest overlooking the marsh below. Though rustic, the trail remains level atop the bluff. Vines and thorn bushes thicken the surrounding forest—a collage of trees, including northern red oak, hackberry, loblolly pine, river birch, and yellow poplar.

Cumberland Marsh Natural Area Preserve

The trail may offer glimpses of the marshy area to the right, the remains of the two ponds that were once part of the preserve. Originally the preserve contained two earthen embankment dams that provided water for irrigation and livestock, but The Nature Conservancy removed them in 2010, restoring more than 1,700 linear feet of stream and nearly 8 acres of wetlands to their natural state.

The trail comes to a junction for the loop around the western portion of the preserve. To follow the mapped route for this approximately 2-mile, counterclockwise hike, take a right to head north, following the red blazes. Lofty poplars shade young beeches and holly, with ferns sprouting amid the roots nearer the marsh as the trail approaches Holts Creek. Look for signs of beaver activity.

After the initial stretch of winding, narrow trail, you'll come upon a small bluff populated by chestnut oak and mountain laurel, with the marsh to the right. Just a little farther on, the trail will continue to the left (southwest) to follow along the heavily wooded banks of Holts Creek.

Enjoy occasional views of the marsh below, keeping an eye out for a wooden sign on a tree that says VIEW to indicate a short trail and overlook that affords a better and clearer view of the watershed. This mossy promontory is graced with an ancient white oak, and a bench awaits just downhill. Holts Creek widens before you, with geese dotting its placid waters. From this vantage, I spotted a northern harrier, or marsh hawk, flying low above the grassy islands. Distinguishable by the white spot on its back, the only harrier native to North America has an owl-like face and a keen sense of hearing that enables it to hunt by flying near the ground.

When you're ready to continue, backtrack a few paces and look for the single-track that heads south (right) along an inlet of the marsh to rejoin our counterclockwise hike. The trail soon widens and continues into the interior forest. Loblolly and Virginia pines shade younger hardwoods in the thicker forest ahead. Veer slightly left as you pass through a small clearing flanked by cedars, following the blazes as the path rounds its westernmost corner. Here, young laurel has sprung up in the center of the old dirt road, its forebears pressing the doubletrack on either side.

This rabbit lingered long enough to get his photo taken before hopping into the tall grass.

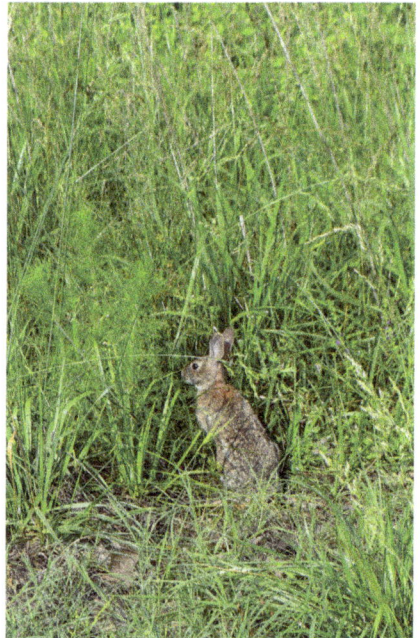

The phenomenon recurs ahead, as the trail winds on to draw alongside a more open, forested hill on the right. You'll soon reach a sign indicating that the path ahead is closed, and the trail makes a left onto another doubletrack. Follow this stretch through a more open forest, passing several sinewy hornbeams, to draw alongside another hill on the right. Yet another trail closure lies ahead, and the trail makes a second sharp left, this time onto a winding singletrack. A smattering of laurel persists among the holly in this young forest; fallen logs outline the twisting, narrow path. If you are hiking in mid- to late spring, you may still catch a few blooms on the laurel.

The loop will soon return to the junction with the trail from the parking area; it was marked by a wooden sign on our visit to the preserve. Take a right to begin the return path toward the trailhead.

Shortly after this junction on our hike, we found a large snapping turtle resting in the center of the trail. He noticed us right away but paid little mind. After a few minutes watching him slowly trudge along with his wide, clawed feet raking the topsoil as he progressed, we tiptoed around to continue our hike.

As the trail exits the wooded path along the marsh, the trail will continue to the left between the crop field and the trees. Retrace your steps along the path back to the trailhead.

• •

GPS TRAILHEAD COORDINATES N37° 32.639' W76° 59.175'

DIRECTIONS From Richmond, take I-64 east to Exit 214, and head north onto VA 155 (North Courthouse Road) 2 miles. Turn right, onto VA 249 (New Kent Highway), and continue 2.25 miles, passing through the hamlet of New Kent before turning left onto VA 637 (Cumberland Road; look for signs for Cumberland Hospital for Children). Follow the road more than 2 miles, passing the signed end of state maintenance. Shortly beyond a white wooden fence on the right and with the hospital coming into view ahead, turn left onto a gravel road. A 20-foot cedar shades a sign for Cumberland Marsh Natural Area Preserve at this turn. Parking is available at the road's end near the trailhead signboard.

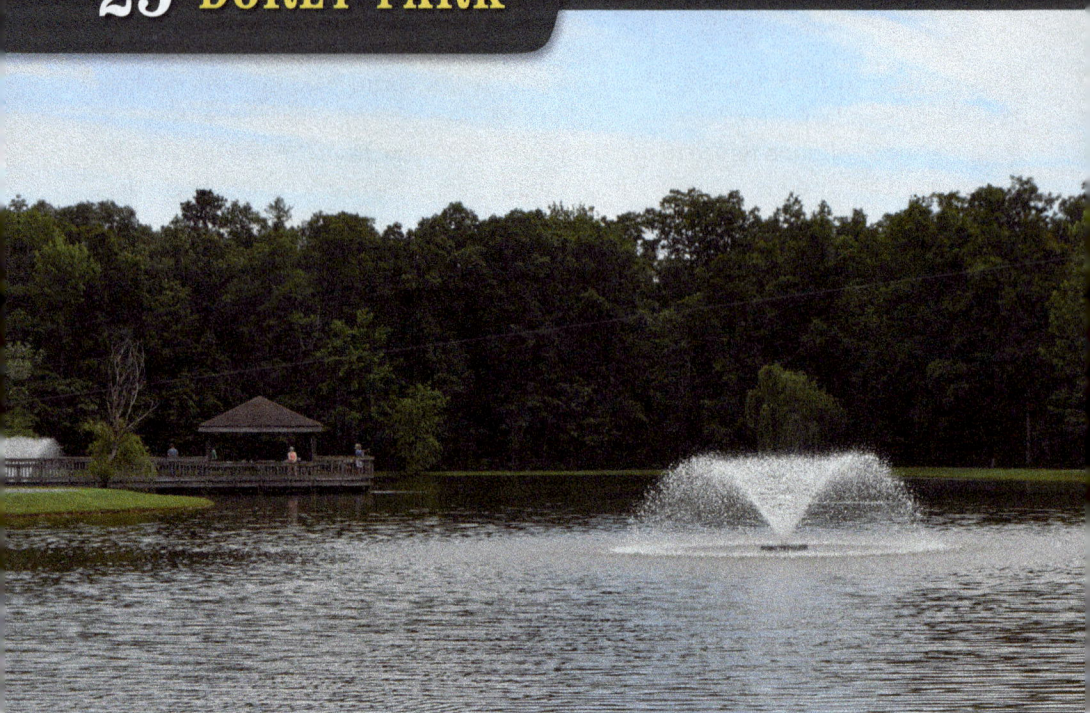

A paved walking path encircles the pond at Dorey Park.

JUST SOUTH OF RICHMOND INTERNATIONAL AIRPORT, 400-acre Dorey Park is a model county park. The well-maintained facilities, from ballfields to equestrian trails, cater to a range of interests. By combining a stroll around the pond, a brief jaunt into the woods, and a loop of the exercise trail, you can easily to string together a couple of miles on wide gravel paths. Elongate your hike by venturing onto the singletrack in the southern reaches of the park, near the disc golf course, or out on the Virginia Capital Trail (see page 75).

DESCRIPTION

Dorey Park offers the citizens of eastern Henrico County a wide variety of recreational activities. Besides numerous sports, including tennis and disc golf, the park accommodates equestrians and mountain bikers. There is plenty of wind and open space for kite flying. You may even spot people fishing around the park's 5-acre pond as you head out. Though no more than 10 feet deep, the pond has been part of the Virginia Department of Game and Inland Fisheries (VDGIF) Urban Program since its inception in 1993. The VDGIF now stocks the pond with catfish, although some anglers are lucky enough to land largemouth bass, bluegill, and redear sunfish.

Starting in the parking lot at the playground, follow the paved path past picnic shelters situated along the pond's northern edge. Two fountains located within

DISTANCE & CONFIGURATION: 2.1-mile loop with spur, plus optional 2.6-mile mountain bike trail

DIFFICULTY: Easy

ELEVATION: 137' at trailhead, no significant rise

SCENERY: Woods, duck pond

EXPOSURE: Mostly shaded, open around pond

TRAFFIC: Moderate, higher near pond

TRAIL SURFACE: Paved, gravel

HIKING TIME: 1 hour

SEASON: Year-round during daylight hours

ACCESS: No fee

WHEELCHAIR ACCESS: On paved loop around the pond

MAPS: At henrico.us/rec/places/dorey

DRIVING DISTANCE FROM CAPITOL: 11 miles

FACILITIES: Restrooms, fitness trail, equestrian trails, picnic shelter, disc golf course, soccer fields, baseball and softball fields, tennis courts, playground, pond (fishing allowed), recreation center, access to the Virginia Capital Trail (see page 75)

CONTACT: Henrico County Recreation and Parks: 804-501-7275, henrico.us/rec

LOCATION: 7200 Dorey Park Dr., Henrico

COMMENTS: More than 2.6 miles of mountain bike trails make the most of limited space at Dorey Park. These are suitable for hiking except on crowded weekends. Equestrian trails on the opposite (eastern) half of the park exceed 3 miles.

the pond enhance the parklike atmosphere. This section of the trail around the pond attracts the most walkers. You'll pass a wooden deck, complete with gazebo, jutting out over the water. Many park visitors cast fishing lines from this relaxing spot. Pass beneath a weeping willow, under which park benches invite you to relax and toss crumbs to the resident geese. Soon turn left onto a gravel trail, heading southwest into the woods.

The park's designated hiking trail is not easy to find, and as of this writing, there are no signs or maps posted near the trail detailing the path. The trail abuts the disc golf course on the left. Along its length you will find trees such as sweet gum, pignut hickory, white oak, and red maple. In wintertime, spindly holly and shaggy red cedar lend color to the forest understory. An abundance of labeled species renders this an informative outing for the budding naturalist.

The wide, level hiking loop is free of obstacles and conducive to both leisurely strolls and running. Follow it behind the restrooms and picnic shelters near the playground. The gravel path winds in and out of the woods closer to the ballfields. At this point, the majority of the sounds come from planes taking off and landing at the airport, loud pings from softball bats, and chatter from picnic shelters. If you are out for exercise, the park's fitness trail connects on your left. You can augment your walk or run with pull-ups, sit-ups, and the like.

Once you reach the clearing for the pipeline easement, bear right, and then continue to the left to walk along the wooded nature trail on a short ridge below a creek bottom. The switchbacks visible downhill to the right host occasional mountain bikers. On our visit, we rustled up a few deer bedded down in the woods farther down the hill from the trail. Continue along this trail to the disc golf course.

Dorey Park

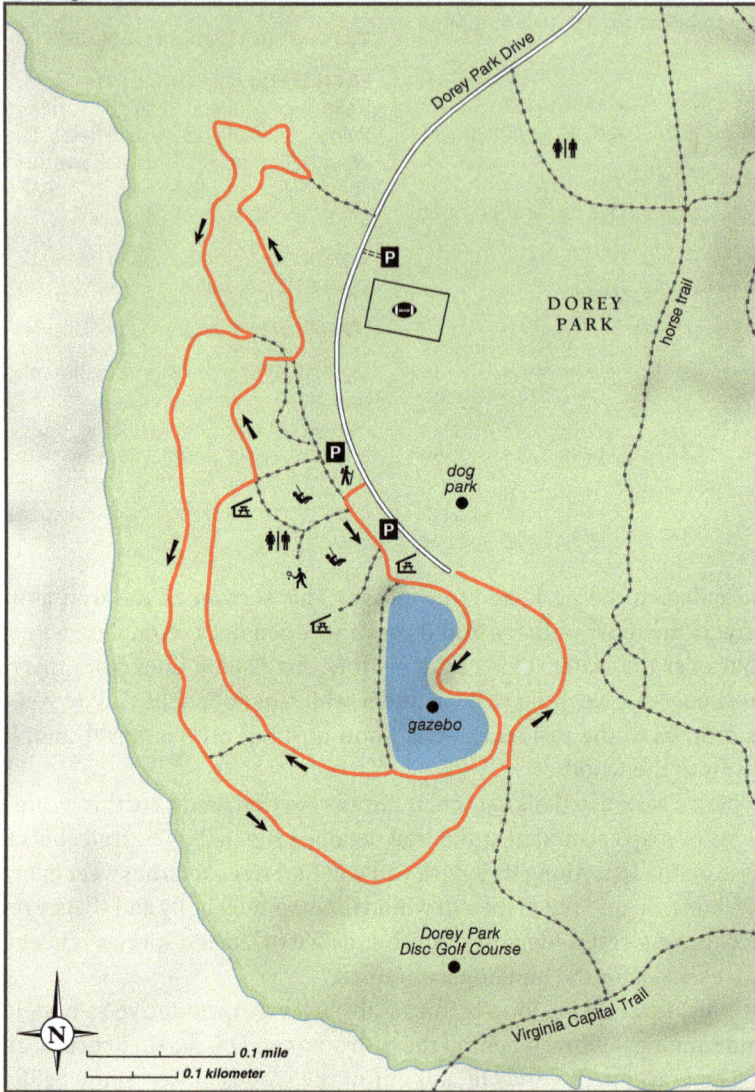

Once you reach the disc golf course, turn left to traverse the remaining portion of the hiking loop, which reemerges along the pond. Turn right again to pick up a brief section of Dorey Park's paved connector trail to the Virginia Capital Trail before you reenter the parking lot at the playground.

NEARBY ACTIVITIES

If you have more time, explore a section of the **Virginia Capital Trail** (virginiacapital trail.org), a 10-foot-wide paved path that accommodates all modes of nonmotorized transportation. It connects Jamestown and Richmond along the scenic VA 5 corridor. The trail traverses approximately 52 miles, four jurisdictions, and more than 400 years of history along one of the first inland routes in North America. From Dorey Park, a left onto the trail provides a 4-mile out-and-back connection to Henrico's Four Mile Creek trailhead. Visit the website above for trail maps and more information.

• •

GPS TRAILHEAD COORDINATES N37° 27.649' W77° 20.424'

DIRECTIONS From Richmond, take I-64 to Exit 195 (Laburnum Avenue) and travel south to Darbytown Road. Turn left; the park entrance will be on your right after you pass under VA 895 (Pocahontas Parkway). An open field and a Virginia Civil War Trail marker signal the upcoming turn.

From I-295, take Exit 22B onto VA 5 (New Market Road), heading northwest, and make the third right onto Doran Road. Proceed north until the road terminates at Darbytown Road. Turn left; the park entrance will soon be visible on your left.

Once inside the park, follow the main road, passing soccer fields on the right and the Dorey Park Recreation Center, in a converted barn, on the left. Continue through a gate, passing ballfields and the equestrian center, and park in a lot on the right at the road's end. The lot fronts a large playground and picnic shelters. The pond is visible a short distance to the south.

Most of the trails at Dorey Park are well shaded.

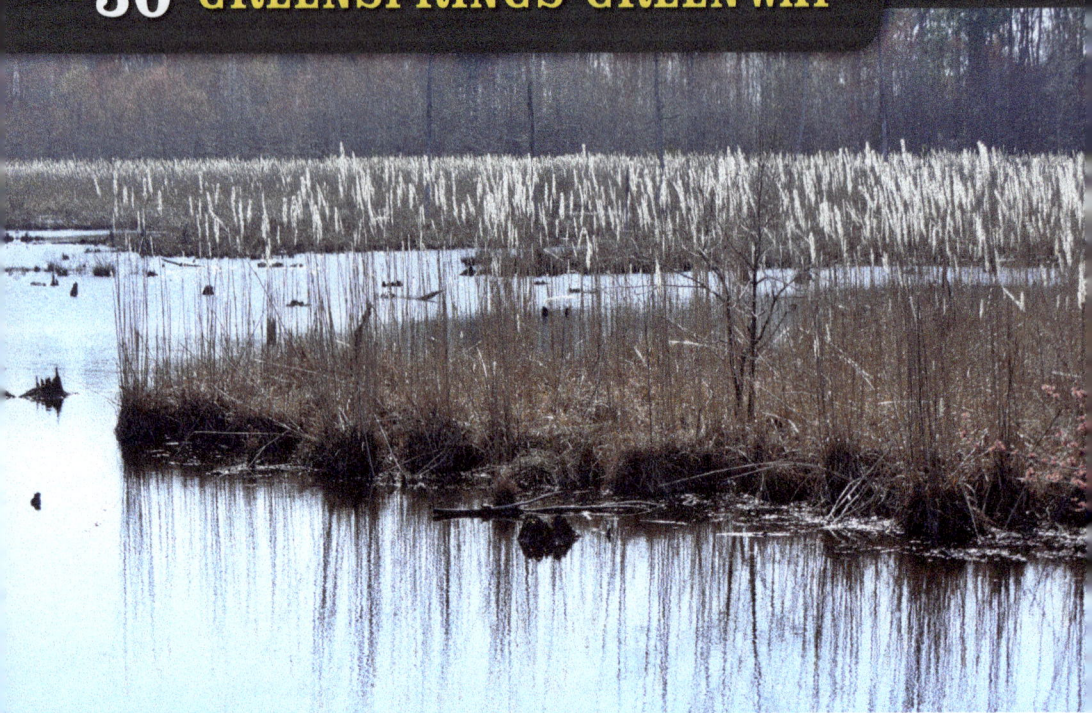

Look for great blue herons and turtles in the marsh at Greensprings Greenway.

POPULAR WITH RESIDENTS of the surrounding neighborhoods, Greensprings Greenway is equally inviting to after-work runners, dog walkers, and out-of-town history buffs. Interpretive signs highlight the ecosystem that English colonists found here and the centuries of agrarian heritage they established, as well as the Revolutionary War Battle of Green Spring. The wide, paved Virginia Capital Trail intersects the greenway—sharing the same path for a stretch—and this hike briefly follows it. The woodland character of this shaded hike, however, differs from that of the mostly open and completely paved Virginia Capital Trail.

DESCRIPTION

The suburban surroundings of Greensprings Greenway belie the area's historical significance. The trail encircles a beaver pond where snowy egrets and redheaded woodpeckers nest. Turtles sun on fallen logs in the marshes. Virginia's earliest English colonists might have happened upon similar sights when first venturing beyond their haven at Jamestown Island, less than 5 miles south. In exploring the woodlands north of the James River, the colonists had agrarian ambitions foremost in mind. Their charge was to produce crops for export (they soon settled on tobacco). Bordering the trail to the south is Mainland Farm, which has been under cultivation as long as or longer than any farm in the nation.

DISTANCE & CONFIGURATION: 3.3-mile figure eight

DIFFICULTY: Easy

ELEVATION: 34' at trailhead, no significant rise

SCENERY: Swampland, historic cropland, mostly hardwood forest, long boardwalk, access to the Virginia Capital Trail

EXPOSURE: Well shaded, except on boardwalk and near parking area

TRAFFIC: Moderate

TRAIL SURFACE: Mostly dirt and gravel, boardwalk, paved segment

HIKING TIME: 1.5 hours

SEASON: Year-round during daylight hours

ACCESS: No fee

WHEELCHAIR ACCESS: Yes, especially on the paved and boardwalk portions

MAPS: At trailhead and tinyurl.com /greenspringsinterpretivetrail

DRIVING DISTANCE FROM CAPITOL: 48.5 miles

FACILITIES: Restrooms, signboard with maps, multiple interpretive signs en route

CONTACT: James City County Parks: 757-259-5360, jccalert.org

LOCATION: 3751 John Tyler Hwy., Williamsburg (entrance is at the end of Eagle Way, past Jamestown High School)

COMMENTS: The trailhead is located beyond Jamestown High School and borders the school's athletic fields. A portion of this hike traverses the Virginia Capital Trail, which is profiled on page 75. The park is about 2 miles from the eastern trailhead at Jamestown by way of the Virginia Capital Trail (5 miles driving).

The greenway begins inconspicuously, marked only by a green sign that directs you south. Pass between a piney wood on the left and the school's practice fields and track on the right. Bear left when you come upon a drainage pond to reach the trailhead signboard. Although a spur leads right, follow the path that bends left into the woods if you plan to read all of the informational signs that line the main loop in their intended order.

As you enter the woods along a slight descent, willow oak, swamp chestnut oak, holly, and loblolly pine—the tallest of the lot—greet you. A granite marker commemorates Earth Day volunteers who helped develop the trail system. Nearby, the first interpretive signs recount the familiar story of the English arrival at Jamestown in 1607 and describe the ecology they encountered. Turn right at a T intersection and continue straight.

Shortly beyond a sign devoted to the Powhatan Creek watershed, you'll pass the first of several modest boardwalks. A sign explaining the role of streams within the water cycle is nearby. You'll note ferns thriving in this lush environment. A path soon veers right, but the main, signed loop turns left across one of two major boardwalks with railings. This one traverses the swamp. Approach quietly so as not to spook the herons, turtles, and songbirds frequently seen here. Alongside the boardwalk to the north, young sweet gums cling to purplish leaves; to the south, the limbless trunks of their drowned predecessors tower precipitously above the water.

Resuming the pea-gravel trail, you'll soon arrive at a junction with the Virginia Capital Trail, which boasts its own imposing two-lane boardwalk. Take a right

161

Greensprings Greenway

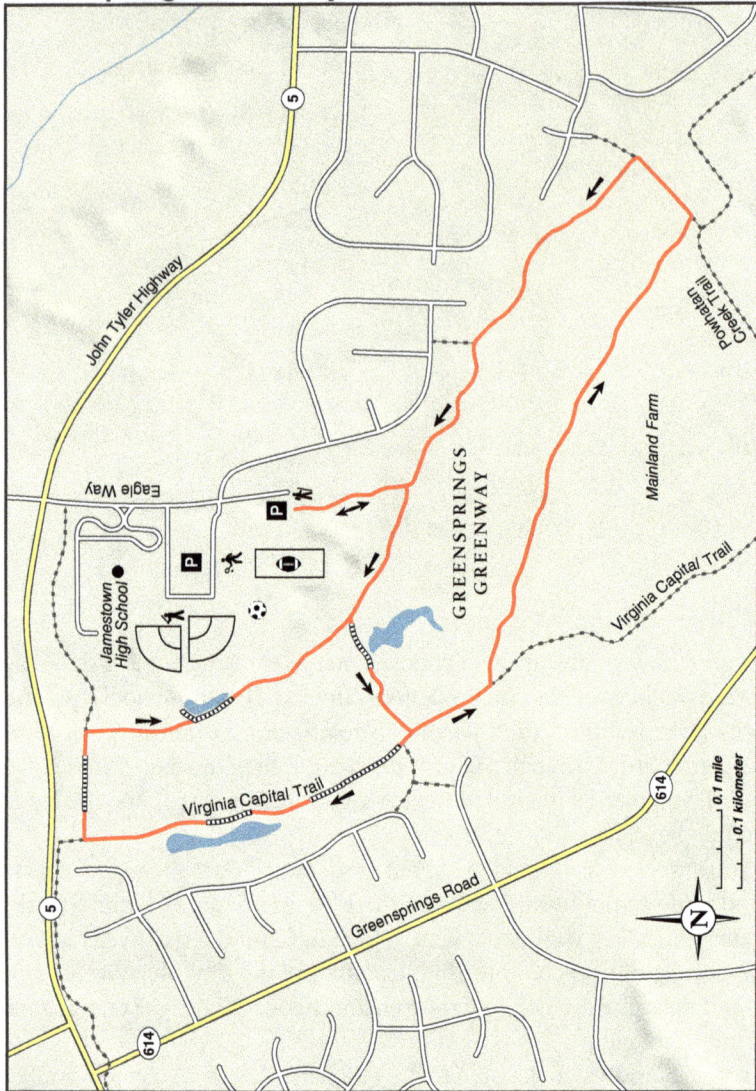

onto the trail, and follow it northwest along the boardwalk and paved trail 0.5 mile before taking another right to loop back over the marsh. Take another right into the wooded trail to continue the upper half of this figure-eight hike. Take another right for a second trip over the boardwalks, and get ready for the lower loop.

Turn left to follow the main loop along the Virginia Capital Trail south about 0.1 mile before veering left again to pass beneath several maples. The loop soon reaches another boardwalk, which traverses a peripheral, thickly vegetated area of the wetland. In the summer, look for cardinal flower blooming below.

The trail draws along Mainland Farm in an area where the trees, including several white oaks, are visibly more mature. Dogwoods fill out the forest beneath them. Eastbound, the trail passes several interpretive signs devoted to the land's agricultural heritage. Beyond a pine grove, an abandoned relic of early mechanized farming lies rusting on the left.

Just ahead, an interpretive sign recounts the Revolutionary War Battle of Green Spring, in which British general George Cornwallis nearly ensnared 800 Revolutionary troops under the command of Frenchman Marquis de Lafayette and American general "Mad" Anthony Wayne. Near the Main (of Mainland Farm), an American expeditionary force unexpectedly engaged the bulk of Cornwallis's army, which was preparing to cross the James in a move toward Portsmouth. Drastically outmanned, Wayne nevertheless ordered a defiant charge. Though the Revolutionaries suffered 140 casualties, twice those of their enemy, the counteroffensive stalled the advancing Royalists long enough for Wayne to orchestrate a successful retreat.

Aided by gathering darkness and marshy terrain such as you just traversed, the Americans were able to evade capture and rejoin their compatriots. The British subsequently crossed the James, meeting ships in Portsmouth that carried them on to Yorktown, and promptly set about constructing the batteries and redoubts in which they would weather a combined American–French siege until Cornwallis's famous surrender on October 19, 1871. That climactic event may have played out elsewhere, or differently, had Commander-in-Chief George Washington not received word that French reinforcements, led by Count de Grasse, were en route from Haiti to Virginia. Upon hearing the news, the first president cleverly maneuvered south from New York to assume command of the combined forces at Yorktown.

As you continue on the trail, you'll encounter a sign devoted to another kind of revolution, an agricultural one. Though inefficient by modern standards, the then-new fertilizers and horse-drawn plows of the 19th century allowed each farmer to produce more crops.

Along this southernmost stretch, the trail spans multiple seasonal streamlets on small boardwalks and passes beneath a grove of tall tulip poplars and beside a maple with a partially horizontal trunk. If it has been raining, you will be forced to navigate around some muddy stretches after the raised pea-gravel trailbed gives way to dirt. Upon reaching a T intersection, turn left to head northeast through open, drier forest, passing an enigmatic concrete cylinder beside the trail. Tall grasses replace ferns along this forest floor, giving the odd appearance of a prairie sprung up in a wood.

Turning left at the next intersection keeps you on the main trail, which parallels a culvert on the right. Following another fork to the left, the main loop employs additional boardwalks in traversing a boggy area. As you again approach the spur that links the trailhead and main loop, additional signs highlight the larger oaks and gnarled holly trees along the trail—loggers spared the former to delineate property boundaries and the latter because their wood was undesirable. Turn right at this trail junction to return to the trailhead.

NEARBY ACTIVITIES

For another good hike located just 6 miles north off Centerville Road (VA 614), consider **Freedom Park** (757-259-4022, tinyurl.com/freedomparkva), which offers 3 miles of multiuse doubletrack, plus at least 15 miles of excellent mountain bike singletrack, created by volunteers. The routes are signed well. If you hike them, please be mindful of cyclists.

Also, drive just a couple of miles south to tour **Colonial National Historic Park's Jamestown unit** (757-898-3400, nps.gov/colo), which recounts the arrival of English colonists in Virginia. The National Park Service's **Colonial Parkway** links the Jamestown unit to Williamsburg and Yorktown.

• •

GPS TRAILHEAD COORDINATES N37° 14.946' W76° 47.239'

DIRECTIONS For the scenic route from Richmond, take VA 5 (John Tyler Highway). Turn right onto Eagle Way at a stoplight signed for Jamestown High School.

For a faster route, take I-64 east to Exit 234. Follow VA 199 south about 8 miles to VA 5, then turn left and continue 3 miles. Turn left onto Eagle Way at the stoplight signed for Jamestown High School. You will pass the school on your right. Parking spaces are available straight ahead at the road's terminus at a trailhead. A mailbox here contains trail maps.

The sandy shores of the James River at Hog Island Wildlife Management Area

TO REACH THE MAIN TRACT of Hog Island Wildlife Management Area (WMA), you must first pass through a perfunctory security screening at Dominion Energy's Surry Nuclear Power Station. But once inside, you're surrounded by tidewater marsh teeming with wildlife, and the civilized world seems miles and miles away.

DESCRIPTION

The Virginia Department of Game and Inland Fisheries (VDGIF) manages Hog Island WMA primarily for the benefit of migratory waterfowl, though a host of other birds and animals also benefit from the managed habitat and resultant hunting restrictions. Even fishing is limited to the James River along the western shore of the peninsula. That's correct: Hog Island is an island no more. Construction of earthen levees (atop which you will enter and hike through the WMA) linked Hog Island to the peninsula known as Gravel Neck. No longer truly tidal, the marshes within the WMA are now filled and drained through dikes. This allows the VDGIF staff to create optimum conditions for specific species.

During the Colonial era, Hog Island was separated from the mainland, at least in high water, as it is scarcely above sea level. Its name harks back to the bygone farming practice of allowing swine to wander and forage freely on islands.

DISTANCE & CONFIGURATION: 3.8-mile loop, plus options

DIFFICULTY: Easy

ELEVATION: 10' at trailhead, no significant rise

SCENERY: James River, tidewater marsh, pine forest, waterfowl

EXPOSURE: Open, with little shade

TRAFFIC: Low

TRAIL SURFACE: Gravel doubletrack

HIKING TIME: 1.5 hours

SEASON: Year-round during daylight hours, but best avoided during hunting seasons

ACCESS: No fee, but identification is required; mountain biking allowed; no ATVs

WHEELCHAIR ACCESS: Limited due to gravel surface

MAPS: At trailhead and at dgif.virginia.gov /wma/hog-island

DRIVING DISTANCE FROM CAPITOL: 68 miles

FACILITIES: Office, two wildlife-viewing towers, designated fishing area, boat launch on noncontiguous Carlisle Track

CONTACT: 757-357-5224, dgif.virginia.gov/wma /hog-island; for hunting and fishing, Virginia Department of Game and Inland Fisheries: 804-367-1000, dgif.virginia.gov/hunting

LOCATION: 7938 Hog Island Rd., Surry

COMMENTS: A water trail of the Captain John Smith Chesapeake National Historic Trail connects to Hog Island. Admission to the WMA requires passage through the Surry Nuclear Power Station, where security guards will need to see identification for all adults and inspect your vehicle (no exceptions; my wife was not allowed entrance because she did not have her ID). All WMAs are open to hunting or fishing, but much of Hog Island is closed to both.

You won't find any wild boars on modern-day Hog Island, but a great diversity of wildlife remains. In a single morning I spotted two herds of deer, numerous white herons, nesting ospreys, bald eagles, cormorants, a wide variety of butterflies, a pair of foxes, and paw prints in the mud of a raccoon—some very large. I also spied commonplace songbirds, raptors, and the seemingly ubiquitous flocks of Canada geese. It's no wonder bird-watchers are among the repeat visitors at this off-the-beaten-path WMA.

Anglers, too, frequent the area's western shore, but aside from those you pass on the way in, you won't find any on this route. In fact, apart from the gravel double-track underfoot, the only sign of civilization I saw in the area's eastern half were ships plying the James River, which is 3 miles wide east of Hog Island and passable by oceangoing vessels.

Begin your hike along the James, heading southeast from the park office at the entrance road's terminus along the doubletrack road that follows the shoreline. The James River is between 2 and 3 miles wide in this stretch, with Williamsburg visible on the other side. First scan the field, brilliant green in the springtime, stretching northwest of the office to northernmost Hog Point. Look for grazing deer and for raptors nesting in the still-standing skeletons of dead trees that border the cultivated field. Proceed past the maintenance shed and two residences on the right to draw along a sandy beach on the James River.

Hog Island Wildlife Management Area

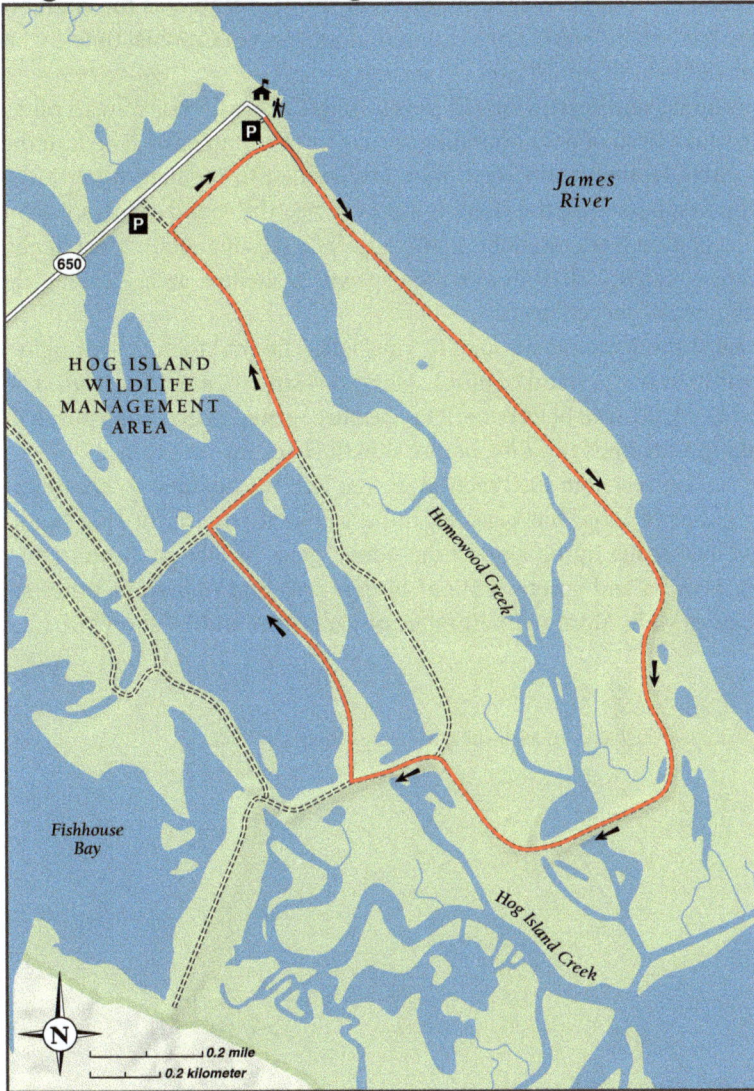

You may be lucky enough to spy an eagle swooping down to snatch a fish from the water. White-chested ospreys, or fish hawks, also nest on Hog Island; unlike eagles, these birds catch fish by diving underwater. According to the *National Audubon Society Field Guide* for the eastern United States, in places where the two species coexist, "eagles obtain much of their food by stealing it from the smaller fish hawk." This is not exactly model behavior for a national symbol, but Americans can take pride in conservation measures that have produced a resurgence in both species since pesticides decimated their numbers in the 1960s. But, as the Audubon guide notes, the bald eagle "is still not as numerous as it was in Colonial times, when it was a familiar sight along almost every coastline."

Continuing southeast, you will pass through an area forested with pines, where you may spot a herd of deer bounding through the underbrush. The trail then bears right to circle Homewood Creek, now impounded to regulate water levels in the marsh you first passed on the right. It was here that the sound of fish splashing about the trunks of pine trees lured me to the edge of a seasonal pool. Most likely the fish were carp, which splash about as they spawn in shallow areas, leaving their eggs among the marshy vegetation.

Views of the James soon open to your left. The trail then curves right again to head northwest past a stand of pines. Along this stretch, a red fox trotted out of the grass and along the trail before me. The creature turned to give me a puzzled look, as if rethinking its famous timidity, before slinking back into the brush.

You'll soon reach an intersection on the left. It's possible to continue straight here for a shorter loop, but bear left to pass a northern arm of Hog Island Creek, where white herons tiptoe among the marsh grass in vibrant contrast to the surrounding browns and greens. Patient birders will find numerous other species in abundance as well. More than 30 types of waterfowl and 35 shorebirds have been

The marshlands and high grasses are inviting to a wide variety of wildlife.

identified within this WMA, prompting its inclusion on the state birding trail. You may wish to walk beyond the next turn to better approach the creek.

In this area, look out in the James beyond the tall grasses in the creek for a series of large military ships in the water. These are known as the Ghost Fleet and are part of the National Defense Reserve Fleet. The numbers of these mothballed ships have been slowly reduced over the years. They seem out of place in this beautiful natural setting.

To follow the mapped route, however, make the next right, which leads to a narrow spit of land bordered by marsh-ringed ponds. Along this strip you can scan the water on both sides. When the path reaches a T intersection, turn right to continue along another narrow earthen ridge overlooking a wetland expanse to the east. You will soon encounter a second T intersection. Bear left this time, and head northwest through a low-lying plain where Canada geese often forage. Depending on the time of year, there may be old corncobs strewn about the dirt road, likely by foraging wildlife.

The staff residences and maintenance shed you passed earlier are visible on the horizon. Rather than returning to the main park road, turn right at your next opportunity, then go left to pass the maintenance building and return to your car. You may find yourself not yet ready to head home, though. There is, after all, negligible elevation gain or loss on this hike, and as long as you're wearing insect repellent, Hog Island Wildlife Management Area is a fascinating place. The vibrant ecosystem teems with life, so you will never make the same hike twice.

. . . .

GPS TRAILHEAD COORDINATES N37° 11.529' W76° 40.940'

DIRECTIONS From Richmond, take I-95 south to Exit 61, or I-295 south to Exit 15, and head east on VA 10. Continue about 40 miles to the hamlet of Surry. Turn left at the intersection with VA 31, then turn right at the blinking light, remaining on VA 10 all the while. (If you're coming south from Williamsburg via VA 31 and the Jamestown–Scotland Ferry, you'll turn left onto VA 10 here.) Head east on VA 10 another 6.5 miles before turning left (east) onto VA 617 at Bacon's Castle. In 1.5 miles, the road reaches a T intersection with VA 650 (Hog Island Road, which also intersects VA 10, to the south). Turn left (north) onto VA 650 to reach Hog Island in less than 5 miles, passing through the power-plant security check en route.

Chimneys are all that remains of the Parsonage site at Malvern Hill Battlefield.

MALVERN HILL WAS THE SITE of the final, bloody clash between Union and Confederate troops during the Seven Days Battles in 1862. Unlike other preserved Civil War sites in the Richmond area, at 953-acre Malvern Hill there are very few encroachments to the battlefield itself. The lines of sight are essentially what they were during the battles. This hike takes visitors around the perimeter and behind the lines for both sides.

DESCRIPTION

The Seven Days Battles ended at Malvern Hill on July 1, 1862. The Union and Confederate armies collided for the final time that week on ground that gave an immense advantage to the defenders, which in this case was Union General George B. McClellan's Army of the Potomac. Confident in their support from naval warships behind them about 2.5 miles away on the James River, McClellan elected to stop and invite battle, according to the Civil War Trust and Richmond National Battlefield Park.

Confederate General Robert E. Lee recognized the power of Malvern Hill. Working with General James Longstreet, Lee devised a plan whereby Confederate artillery would attempt to seize control of the battlefield by suppressing the Union cannon there. Lee suspected his infantry could assault and take the position if they did not have to contend with the Union batteries.

DISTANCE & CONFIGURATION: 3-mile loop, plus optional spurs

DIFFICULTY: Easy

ELEVATION: 125' at trailhead, 70' at low point

SCENERY: Battlefields, mixed forest, open fields and farmland

EXPOSURE: Mostly open, except a wooded stretch in the middle

TRAFFIC: Low

TRAIL SURFACE: Dirt, gravel doubletrack, brief sections on paved road

HIKING TIME: 1.5 hours

SEASON: Year-round during daylight hours

ACCESS: No fee

WHEELCHAIR ACCESS: Wheelchairs not recommended on trails

MAPS: At parking lot shelter kiosk and nps.gov/rich

DRIVING DISTANCE FROM CAPITOL: 15.6 miles

FACILITIES: Shelter with benches and interpretive recordings; no restrooms

CONTACT: 804-226-1981, nps.gov/rich

LOCATION: 9175 Willis Church Rd., Henrico; Glendale/Malvern Hill Battlefields Visitor Center: 8301 Willis Church Rd., inside the Glendale National Cemetery

COMMENTS: The Lee vs. Grant 1864 Campaign Civil War driving trail connects to Malvern Hill. Metal detecting is prohibited. Stop by the nearby Glendale/Malvern Hill Battlefields Visitor Center (8301 Willis Church Rd., 804-226-1981, nps.gov /rich), inside the Glendale National Cemetery, to see its interpretive displays.

Gently sloping open fields lay in front of the Union position, forcing Confederate attacks against the hill to travel across barren ground. McClellan unlimbered as much artillery as he could at the crest, facing in three directions. Nearly 70,000 infantry lay in support, most of them crowded in reserve behind the hill.

Malvern Hill's trail system enables visitors to see almost every position of the battlefield. This battle took place before earthworks became a focal part of battlefield strategy. Interpretive signage along the trails, along with park maps and recordings, details the events of the Seven Days Battle and what happened at Malvern Hill. The White Trail is 1.5 miles long and has almost no shade. It can be accessed from the trailhead parking lot on Carters Mill Road. Interpretive signage along the way helps explain the events of the Malvern Hill battle. The Blue Trail connects with the White Trail and is also 1.5 miles long. It begins just west of the Parsonage and reconnects with the White Trail at the location of the Confederate artillery. Much of this loop is shaded, passing through woods and along streams where Confederate soldiers traveled and gathered to await orders to attack Union troops at Malvern Hill.

For this hike, park at the main trailhead on Carters Mill Road. From the trailhead, look for cannons positioned across the open fields to see the Confederate lines. You're standing along Union battle positions. Follow the White Trail in a counterclockwise loop, walking along the road briefly before crossing and continuing along the field edge.

To the right of the trail, you'll see the Thomas J. West house, which stood as a prominent part of the battlefield scene—a goal for attacking Confederates and a landmark along the Union line. Most of the fresh Federal troops marching from the

Malvern Hill Battlefield, Richmond NBP

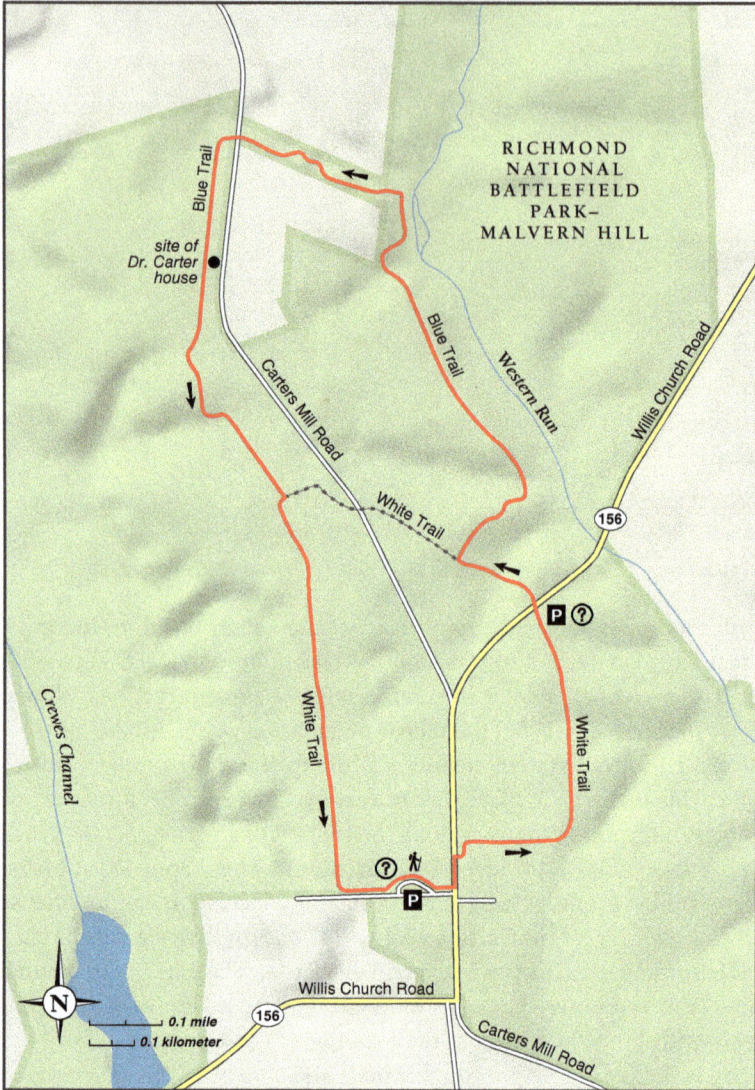

James River to the front on July 1 moved past the house, coming under direct fire for the first time here.

The Union army had nearly 200 cannons at its disposal. When the Confederate artillery appeared on the opposite fields, the Union cannons blasted them into silence. Gunners then attacked the Confederate infantrymen, firing into unprotected masses charging up Malvern Hill's gentle slope. The trail continues along the field's edge. During our late-June hike, corn was growing in the fields and mulberries were ripe for the picking along the edge of the forest. The trail soon meets the parking lot opposite the Parsonage on Willis Church Road. Stop to read about the infantrymen on both sides and their positioning during the battle.

The two chimneys at the edge of the treeline are all that's left of the Parsonage, which was an important landmark during the battle. Before the attacks, Confederate division commander D. H. Hill met with his officers near the house. Colonel W. Gaston Meares of North Carolina was killed by a shell in the yard. Confederate artillery attempted to take position in nearby fields as Lee watched from a blacksmith shop across the road. The Parsonage was destroyed by fire in 1988.

From here, pick up the trail as it enters the woods. Cross over a small footbridge and follow the rooted and worn path to a junction with the Blue Trail. For a shorter hike, continue along the White Trail. For this mapped route, turn right onto the Blue Trail and walk deeper into the forest.

On the afternoon of July 1, 1862, much of the Confederate division led by General D. H. Hill crowded into this forest, which offered cover from the Union artillery. Hill believed there would be no attack at Malvern Hill, but it quickly became evident that an attack had begun. Hill's division formed lines of battle in these woods, considered "exceedingly rough" terrain.

As you hike, the mixed hardwood forest is characterized by American beech, red and white oak, and tulip poplar. American holly and flowering dogwood are common in the understory, and the ground layer is characteristically sparse, with a variety of ferns, sedges, and vines. This type of forest is valuable, as it creates needed habitat for birds, many of which are rare and endangered. Known inhabitants include the Acadian flycatcher, Carolina wren, Carolina chickadee, red-eyed vireo, tufted titmouse, and red-bellied woodpecker.

As the trail crosses a muddy creek, signs of horseback riders are evident. Frogs quietly peep, birds sing, and the wind slowly moves through the trees. The trail emerges from the woods at Carters Mill Road. Carefully cross the road and follow the signs to take a left and walk along the edge of a field. This trail passes the former home of Dr. Carter, which stood on a knoll in this field in July 1862. The original Carters Mill Road also passed through the field during the battle. Although the trees farther along the trail blocked the view of Malvern Hill, it did not prevent Union batteries there from regularly dropping shells into this field.

Enter the woods briefly before reemerging in another open field. This is the Confederate position visible from the trailhead, which should now be easy to see as you reach the cannons. This is also where the path rejoins the White Trail loop.

For a moment, ignore the historical aspect of Civil War sites and consider the value of battlefields preserved as green space. The grassland provides an abundant natural ecosystem, and these fields are ideal for bird and wildlife observation. Grasslands of warm-season native grass species were much more common during and just after

Colonial settlement, when they existed as pasture and fallow agricultural fields. Now, in many areas suburban growth threatens wildlife, and native grasslands have declined due to human development and conversion of pasture to cool-season grasses. This has precipitated the decline of the bird and pollinator species that nest and forage in this habitat. By maintaining Civil War battlefield lands in native warm-season grasses—rather than in crops, lawn grass, or cool-season hay—the park can portray the historical appearance of a fallow field while providing critical habitat for grassland wildlife.

Continue on the White Trail to the right of the cannon positions, and trace it back to the trailhead. The trail follows an old farm road. At the time of the Malvern Hill battle, soldiers likely found cover in the well-worn roadbed, situated below the fields.

As of this writing, the nonprofit Capital Region Land Conservancy had reached a deal to purchase the adjacent 900-acre Poindexter Farm, a heavily forested property in Henrico and Charles City Counties that includes a portion of the Malvern Hill battlefield. Much of Poindexter Farm is on the other side of Western Run Creek, farther east of the West House and the Parsonage.

NEARBY ACTIVITIES

Not far from Malvern Hill is **Glendale/Malvern Hill Battlefields Visitor Center** (804-226-1981, nps.gov/rich). The adjacent cemetery holds nearly 1,200 graves, many of them Union soldiers who died in the battles of June 30 and July 1, 1862. At present there is no developed access to the park's property at Glendale.

While in eastern Henrico, Civil War buffs may also want to visit the Fort Harrison unit of **Richmond National Battlefield Park** (804-226-1981, nps.gov/rich), to the southwest. To reach it, follow Willis Church Road south back to VA 5 (New Market Road) and take a right. Drive about 10 miles, then turn left onto Battlefield Park Road, which takes you through several properties of the battlefield.

• •

GPS TRAILHEAD COORDINATES N37° 24.787' W77° 15.045'

DIRECTIONS From Richmond, take I-64 to I-295 heading south. Take Exit 22A and VA 5 (New Market Road) southeast. Travel 4.5 miles and take a left onto Willis Church Road (VA 156). Take a left at a T intersection to stay on Willis Church Road. The entrance for the park will be on the left.

You can also take VA 5 from downtown Richmond. Drive 15 miles east on East Main Street, which becomes VA 5 (New Market Road) after crossing into Henrico County. Follow the directions above to Willis Church Road.

The long boardwalk over the Lee Hall Reservoir is a highlight of the hike at Newport News Park.

AT 8,000-PLUS ACRES, Newport News Park is the largest municipal park east of the Mississippi, though large swaths are essentially untrammeled. The loop described here takes in both historical and ecological landmarks. It works well as an introduction for campers—or anyone else—looking to explore the outlying trail network.

DESCRIPTION

Before setting out, take a moment to visit the park's Discovery Center, where you will find aquariums, terrariums, and related displays on park wildlife. In addition to maps, you can pick up a trail guide that corresponds to numbered posts along the way. Then begin the hike outside the center beside a historical marker noting the role the now-submerged Warwick River played in the Civil War. The first trail of this loop, the Twin Forts Loop, tells that story in detail.

A short wooded stint and a small bridge follow before you cross the park road to reach the Dam #1 Bridge. The long wooden boardwalk across Lee Hall Reservoir is named for the first of three dams hastily erected here during the Civil War. At the eastern end of the bridge, beside a granite monument, is the first of several interpretive signs devoted to the 1862 Peninsula Campaign.

DISTANCE & CONFIGURATION: 4.2-mile loop, with optional spurs

DIFFICULTY: Easy

ELEVATION: 23' at trailhead, no significant rise

SCENERY: Lee Hall Reservoir, reforested Civil War trenches, marshy Beaverdam Creek

EXPOSURE: Well shaded, except on boardwalks and bridges

TRAFFIC: Moderate; high in summer

TRAIL SURFACE: Dirt, wooden bridge over lake

HIKING TIME: 2 hours

SEASON: Year-round during daylight hours

ACCESS: No fee; campsites from $31.50

WHEELCHAIR ACCESS: Restrooms, snack bar, some campsites; trails not accessible

MAPS: On signboard and at visitor center, Discovery Center, and nnparks.com

DRIVING DISTANCE FROM CAPITOL: 62 miles

FACILITIES: Restrooms, picnic tables, grills, campground (188 sites), playground, 5-mile Bikeway loop, approximately 8-mile mountain bike singletrack at the Richneck Road Trails, fishing area, boat rental and launch, visitor center, Discovery Center

CONTACT: 757- 886-7912, nnparks.com

LOCATION: 13560 Jefferson Ave., Newport News

COMMENTS: The 1862 Peninsula Campaign Civil War driving trail connects to Newport News Park. This hike is a singletrack loop, but old fire roads increase your options.

That spring, Confederate general John Bankhead Magruder determined to dam the Warwick River at the present location of Lee Hall Reservoir. The resulting water obstacles initially deterred Union soldiers from advancing against Confederate positions. Finally, on April 16, members of the Vermont Infantry, known as the Green Mountain Boys, stormed the entrenched Southerners. They met with initial success but, pinned down and soaked, could not endure the reprisal by a Georgia brigade.

The standoff ultimately proved anticlimactic. The Union Army spent 17 more days arraying cannons in preparation for an assault. They stormed the line only to find that the Confederates had fled two days earlier to prepare Richmond for an impending siege. The remains of an extensive network of Confederate trenches and a few Union rifle pits—some of the best-preserved Civil War earthworks anywhere— are visible at numerous points along this hike.

After crossing the reservoir, bear left with the Twin Forts Loop (0.7 mile), forestalling your walk along the White Oak Trail, which departs to the right. Along the lakeshore grow water tupelo trees, whose trunks are swollen at the base like their bald cypress neighbors. Earthworks are visible on your right, shaded by a forest of white oak, red maple, holly, and loblolly pine.

Beyond a sign marking the Green Mountain Boys' initial attack, veer right, away from the lake, to bisect a trench line. The trail turns left to cross a streamlet on a footbridge. It then intersects a doubletrack and makes two successive right turns, first onto the Long Meadow Trail then back into the woods to continue on the Twin Forts Loop.

This hike recrosses the aforementioned rivulet to encircle the wall of Confederate earthworks here. After rounding the defenses, the path passes a sign devoted to their original appearance, explaining that they were braced by logs and supported

Newport News Park

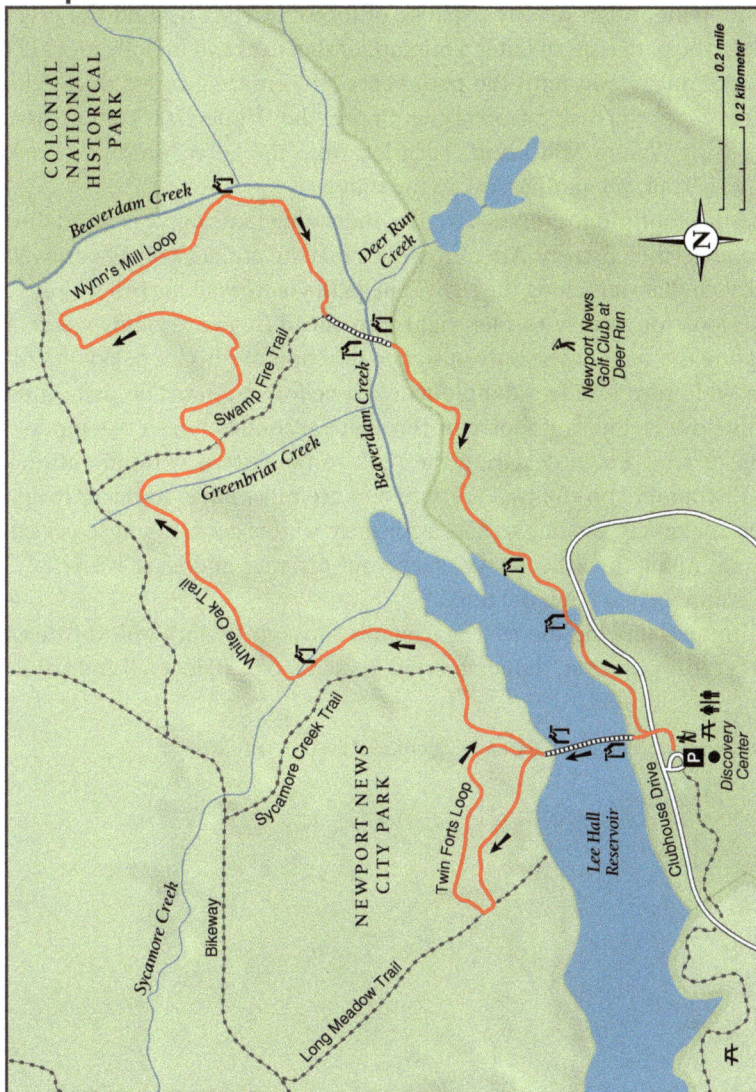

cannons trained on the opposite shore. This completes the loop, and the reservoir bridge should be visible just ahead. Turn left onto the White Oak Trail.

A marshy stretch of lakeshore borders the trail on its right as you head north across a stream toward a junction with Sycamore Creek Trail, another connector to the Bikeway. Remain on the well-trod White Oak Trail. Holly grows more thickly beneath the forest canopy as the trail curves left. An inlet of the lake fed by Sycamore Creek stretches inland on the right. A wooden overlook allows you to scan the swamp, which is dotted with yellow poplars.

A low-lying, often-muddy expanse of forest extends beyond the creek to the right; then the path rises to enter a mixture of shortleaf and loblolly pines. The evergreens accompany you until the path veers left, entering forest thick with young beech trees. After crossing Greenbriar Creek, the White Oak Trail approaches its junction with Wynn's Mill Loop. Turn left onto the latter, promptly crossing the Swamp Fire Trail, yet another link to the Bikeway.

Ahead, a footbridge crosses a trench, indicating that you've entered the remains of a second earthen battery. After crossing a marshy drainage on a boardwalk, you'll note a trench that runs along the right. The path you're walking briefly joins an older roadbed; look for an easy-to-miss right turn ahead (if you reach Beaverdam Creek, you've gone too far). At the only unsigned junction on this loop, Wynn's Mill Loop makes a wide turn beside a double-trunked yellow poplar. The path immediately bisects one trench line and soon cuts through a second between two pines.

Stop to read a sign declaring the park to be eastern cottonmouth habitat. It reads: "Encounters on the trail are rare and are most likely to occur in spring and fall when snakes are moving to and from their winter dens. If you see or encounter a cottonmouth or any other snake, keep your distance and leave it alone." The best advice given was to stay on the trail.

Continue following the trail as it winds through Wynn's Mill fortification and barracks earthworks that, though eroded, remain up to 10 feet tall and are arrayed in

A boardwalk crosses the marsh in the eastern portion of the Lee Hall Reservoir.

complex formations rather than straight lines. A pier on your left also affords you a view of the cattail marsh along Beaverdam Creek, which feeds the reservoir. As you round the earthworks on the right, the swamp is visible to your left, just beyond the gnawed tree trunks that prove the creek's name was no accident.

Turn left to cross the lengthy wooden Swamp Bridge boardwalk, also part of the White Oak Trail, which arrives from the opposite direction. An elevated observation deck built into the bridge invites you to pause and scan the marsh northeast of Lee Hall Reservoir for tundra swans or resident mallards. Once across, turn right onto a narrow singletrack against a mossy bank.

The city's Deer Run golf course is visible uphill and through the mature hardwoods on your left. As it proceeds along the widening lake, your path repeatedly approaches the course. The path curves slightly inland to cross Deer Run Creek on a bridge with sycamore and beech growing nearby. Then it runs along the lake to reach its final boardwalk, a zigzagging affair that deposits you within a short walk of the Dam #1 Bridge and the Discovery Center.

· ·

GPS TRAILHEAD COORDINATES N37° 10.913' W76° 32.250'

DIRECTIONS From Richmond, take I-64 east to Exit 250B. Take a left off the exit ramp onto VA 105 (Fort Eustis Boulevard) 0.35 mile northeast, then turn left to take VA 143 (Jefferson Avenue) roughly the same distance northwest. Turn right to enter the park.

From I-64, Exit 247 is also a good option. Turn left from the exit onto VA 143 (Jefferson Avenue) and drive 3.5 miles to take a left into the entrance of the park (passing fire roads and the campgrounds entrance).

From the park entrance, pass the visitor information building on your left, and proceed 0.85 mile to park at the Discovery Center on your right. The trail departs just north of the center near a historical marker.

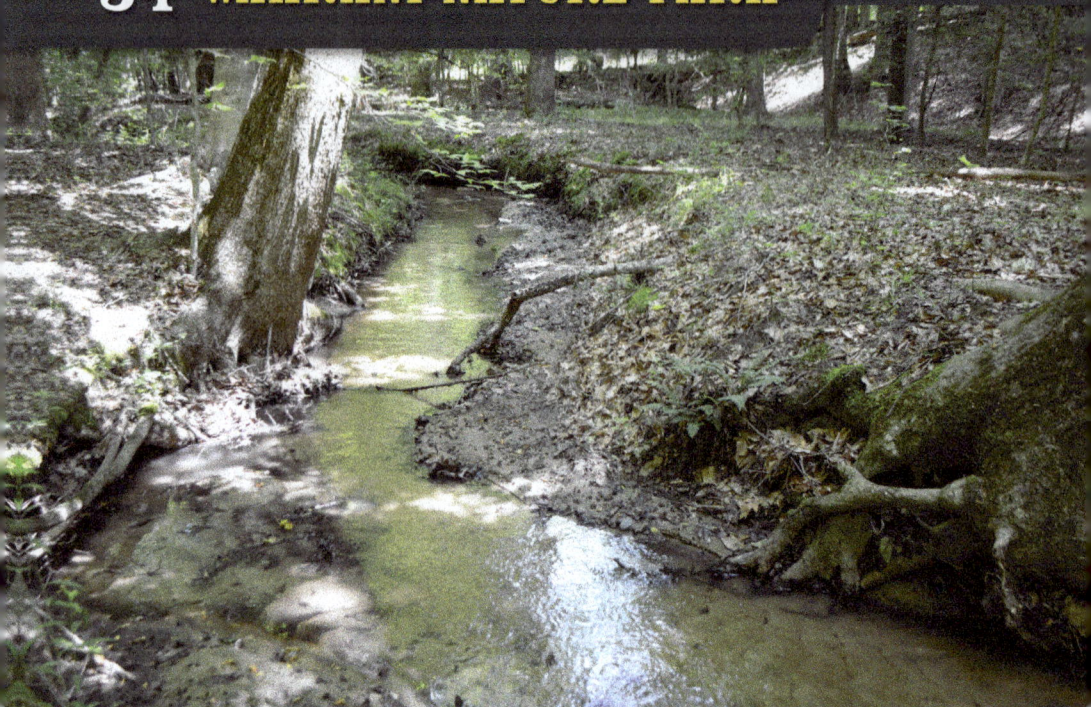

The northern portion of the hike follows along banks of a meandering sandy creek.

THE HILLS AND FOREST FLOOR of Wahrani Nature Park are blanketed with ferns and decaying fallen trees. Despite the park's location in the coastal plain, there are many distinct elevation changes along this route, which takes hikers to a sweeping overlook over a couple of meandering streams and a pair of Colonial graves.

DESCRIPTION

In 2001, New Kent County assumed jurisdiction over the 138-acre parcel encompassing this long-standing nature trail, making it the first holding of the county's fledgling parks department. Until recently, this route was alternately referred to as Chesapeake Nature Trail, because Chesapeake Forest Products Company owned the land, or Warreneye Nature Trail, in honor of the 18th-century Warreneye Church that once stood here. In 2003, New Kent renamed the area Wahrani Nature Park to reflect the word's Native American origins. That same spelling is now applied to a swamp south of the park. In their efforts to anglicize the indigenous term, colonists also came up with Warrenigh, Warreny, and Warren I.

New Kent was settled more than a century before the American Revolution and was inhabited by tribes of the Powhatan Confederacy prior to that. It was in New Kent that George Washington wed Martha Dandridge Custis. Located on the

DISTANCE & CONFIGURATION: 3.6-mile loop, plus optional spur and 1.5 miles of trail

DIFFICULTY: Moderate

ELEVATION: 39' at trailhead, 133' at high point

SCENERY: Steep hillsides in mature hardwood forest, ridgetop pinewoods, numerous rivulets, 18th-century gravestones

EXPOSURE: Well shaded

TRAFFIC: Low

TRAIL SURFACE: Dirt

HIKING TIME: 1.5 hours

SEASON: Year-round during daylight hours

ACCESS: No fee

WHEELCHAIR ACCESS: Wheelchairs not recommended

MAPS: On kiosks along the trail and at co.new-kent.va.us

DRIVING DISTANCE FROM CAPITOL: 35 miles

FACILITIES: Parking area, trail kiosks, picnic pavilion, playground, composting toilet, trash cans

CONTACT: New Kent County Parks: 804-966-8502, co.new-kent.va.us

LOCATION: 17485 Eltham Rd., Lanexa

COMMENTS: After acquiring the park from Chesapeake Forest Products Company in 1973, New Kent County opened the trails in 2007 to mountain bikers, walkers, and runners, making all these trails multiuse.

Pamunkey River a couple of miles northwest of this park, Eltham Plantation was among the finest of its era and was home to Washington's brother-in-law, Burwell Bassett. The first president recalled visits to Eltham in his diary, and the Washingtons frequently joined the Bassetts for Sunday worship at Warreneye Church.

Also known as the Upper Church of Blisland Parish, Warreneye Church was built in 1703. It was already in disrepair when soldiers of the Richmond Militia camped there during the War of 1812. One, Samuel Mordecai, wrote: "The church was set on a high elevation overlooking the junction of the Pamunkey and Mattaponi Rivers at the formation of the York. It was by the old road, the Colonial highway, that ran from Eltham to Williamsburg. In 1814, only the walls and a part of the roof remained."

The route mapped here takes you to the site of Warreneye Church, though all that remains today are two flat gravestones, easily spotted thanks to a much newer white picket fence. Dated 1736 and 1745, the gravestones display varying degrees of erosion. The better-preserved stone includes an ornate circular crest. Families can make an educational adventure of this hike, teaching children about history and archaeology by making rubbings of the stones with crayon and butcher paper.

Setting out from the parking area, the trailhead is distinguishable by the first of four map signboards along the network. This hike traverses a counterclockwise loop with a second smaller loop halfway through. The park has been organized into four singletrack trail loops, but they can be connected to form larger loops.

The path forks almost immediately. Head right, following a low-level sign for the main trail. This small marker, like the numbered posts along the trail, is a vestige of the privately built nature trail. The county added new diamond-shaped blazes to distinguish the four trail loops by color: green (A), yellow (B), red (C), and blue (D). These colors should correspond to the painted blazes along the trail network.

Wahrani Nature Park

As you begin this trek on the green A trail, notice several signs naming and detailing the many varieties of trees found within the park. You may also spy bright-green club moss growing on the forest floor amid a mixture of pines and young hardwoods. Watch for turtles and frogs crossing the trail. Water runoff often clears the sandy trail of leaves, and sometimes puddles remain. The trail divides to offer a hiking-only path, away from the A trail but reconnecting with it in about 0.25 mile. Continue on the A trail.

You'll soon pass a triple-trunked tulip poplar—also known as yellow poplar—on your left. Many more of these grow on the hillside ahead. First, however, the trail curves left to squeeze between two steep-sided knolls. Ferns grow on these wet banks, and exposed tree roots protrude from them. Short wooden boardwalks guide you over muddy seeps before the trail emerges onto a hillside that slopes steeply away.

Tulip poplars give way to pines, their needles blanketing the trail, before the trail makes a sharp left downhill. The old grade you've just followed continues along the hill, but a log blockade serves to deter anyone dismissive of the blazes. As the trail descends into a small valley, the path veers right, leaving the A trail briefly. Follow the arrow directing you to parking briefly, then veer left to meet a sandy-bottomed stream. A wooden footbridge spans the rivulet in a lush fern garden. Just ahead, follow the trail markers for trail B, heading right, crossing another footbridge over a seasonal stream before rising uphill.

As you ascend along a mossy trail studded with roots, a network of small streams is visible behind and below you. Beech trees prevail in this damp wood. The trail begins a wide curve to the left and continues climbing. Though ferns still dot the ground, the forest makeup shifts slightly as you gain elevation, with an increased presence of white and chestnut oaks as well as broad-leaved shagbark hickories. The climb now behind you, the trail undulates and winds gracefully, maintaining its elevation as the hillside drops steeply away on the left.

Another trail kiosk marks the junction between B and C trails. Take the path to the right on trail C, which will run about 0.8 mile to the next trail junction. However, trailside vegetation, thriving in the abundant sunlight left by downed trees, now crowds the path. If the trail is passable, interested hikers can take a spur to see an eroding cliff about halfway down the path. The cliff and the boulders that have broken away from it are studded with seashells, testimony to an ancient sea that once covered this region.

The fauna presently inhabiting this mature hardwood forest and the parcels of younger woods that lie ahead include white-tailed deer and wild turkeys, both of which can be spotted here.

Beyond the spur, the path descends to a seasonal stream then rises again to another hillside. It soon crests then descends just as quickly, passing through a pine-wood before reaching a power-line clearing. Cross the clearing, looking for songbirds in the brush. Zigzag right then left upon entering the woods opposite. The path should be marked by red blazes.

After crossing two streams on wooden footbridges, you'll spot another trail kiosk and a sign for the trail D (blue) loop. Take the right fork in the trail and go 0.25 mile to reach the site where Warreneye Church once stood. The location includes a white picket fence around the 18th-century gravestones and an information kiosk with details about the history of the church.

Trail D continues along a ridgeline to a small overlook, revealing a vista of the Mattaponi and Pamunkey River valleys. The rivers join to form the York 3 miles northeast. After the loop returns to the trail D kiosk, turn right to travel back over the two footbridges and follow a return route to the parking lot, which is about 0.75 mile from this junction. Recross the power-line clearing to continue along the red-blazed trail, first passing through mixed forest and paralleling a creek on the right. Bear right at a junction where the trail heads in both directions. You will soon connect to the trail B loop, which continues alongside a streambed. Turn right onto trail A at the next trail junction, relishing the wild character of this park for another 0.25 mile as you return to the trailhead.

• •

GPS TRAILHEAD COORDINATES N37° 30.367' W76° 51.583'

DIRECTIONS From Richmond, take I-64 east to Exit 220 and onto VA 33 heading northeast. From Williamsburg or Newport News, head west on I-64 to Exit 220 and onto VA 33 heading northeast. The entrance to the park is on your right after 3.8 miles. The trailhead's small gravel lot is just before the turn.

Gravestones dating back to the 18th century at the site where Warreneye Church once stood

This observation deck provides a beautiful view of the reservoir at Waller Mill Park.

WALLER MILL PARK makes a fine addition to a tourist itinerary that includes nearby attractions at Jamestown, Williamsburg, and Yorktown. An afternoon at the lake can have restorative effects on young children whose appetite for historical sites doesn't match that of their parents or siblings. Consider pairing this hike with a picnic or paddle: the flat water at Waller Mill Reservoir makes it a good place to try out canoeing or kayaking for the first time.

DESCRIPTION

The first Virginians never saw Waller Mill Reservoir—it was constructed in 1942—but colonists and speculators representing the Virginia Company of London no doubt explored the area. They would have seen the present shore as hilltops overlooking the now-flooded valley of Queen's Creek, which still drains east from the reservoir to the York River. However, in light of one intriguing historical account, it's possible that those English colonists were not the first Europeans to attempt settlement here. According to the story, it was along Queen's Creek that ill-fated Spanish Jesuits attempted to establish a mission in 1570 (though some suggest that New Kent County's Diascund Creek was the more likely locale).

Led by Friar Juan Bautista Segura, the expedition numbered fewer than a dozen, and only two survived: their teenaged assistant, Alonso de Olmos, and an

DISTANCE & CONFIGURATION: 4.2-mile figure eight, including the 2.7-mile Lookout Tower Trail and 1.5-mile Bayberry Nature Trail, which can be walked separately

DIFFICULTY: Easy on Bayberry; moderate on Lookout Tower

ELEVATION: 52' at trailhead, no significant rise

SCENERY: Turtles, waterfowl, and paddlers on Waller Mill Reservoir; mixed forest

EXPOSURE: Mostly shaded, open at lake's edge and along railroad grade

TRAFFIC: Moderate; high near park office

TRAIL SURFACE: Sand and dirt on nature trail; paved along railroad grade

HIKING TIME: 2.5 hours

SEASON: Generally year-round during daylight hours, but hours vary with seasons

ACCESS: $2 per vehicle

WHEELCHAIR ACCESS: On paved trail; wheelchairs not recommended on sand or dirt trails

MAPS: At park office and williamsburgva.gov

DRIVING DISTANCE FROM CAPITOL: 50.5 miles

FACILITIES: Restrooms, playground, picnic tables and shelters, grills, dog park, disc golf course, volleyball nets, playing fields, fishing docks, boat launch, boat rentals, boathouse store

CONTACT: 757-259-3778, williamsburgva.gov

LOCATION: 901 Airport Rd., Williamsburg

COMMENTS: Waller Mill Park has enough amenities to rival a day-use state park. Choose from paddling, picnicking, and fishing for post-hike relaxation. The 1.5-acre off-leash dog park has two fenced areas for dogs to run, one for dogs weighing up to 30 pounds and the other for all dogs.

Algonquian native christened Don Luis. Don Luis had been taken from Ajacan, as the Spanish called Virginia, by an expedition sent to explore the Bahia de Madre de Díos, now the Chesapeake Bay, in 1560. Educated in Mexico, he was to serve as the Jesuits' interpreter and to help lead his native tribe toward his adopted faith.

The apparent advantage of an Algonquian guide convinced Segura that Spanish troops need not accompany the expedition. As it happened, Don Luis was quickly reabsorbed into his native tribe. The Spaniards were thus left defenseless and unable to communicate with the Indians. Celebrating Mass in a crude hut, the mission persisted for some five months. However, in February 1571 Don Luis murdered three priests sent to beckon him back to the mission. He then led a band of tribesmen to the mission, where they stealthily killed the remaining Jesuits.

That was the account of the teenage de Olmos, who was spared and later escaped to be rescued by a Spanish resupply ship in 1572. Sent to avenge the murders, Spanish troops hung eight native Indians accused of participating in the raid, although Don Luis was never found. An improbable legend holds that he survived to instigate a 1622 raid on the Jamestown settlement in which 347 colonists perished.

That colony, of course, persisted, and plantations were established along Queen's Creek in the 1640s. Its waters also served to power gristmills for the first plantations and those several centuries thereafter. Today, a millstone some 4 feet in diameter welcomes visitors outside the Waller Mill Park office. It was found in the lake during a 1963 dam upgrade and may have been part of the park's namesake mill, which was swallowed in 1942 by the rising waters. Also nearby is a historical marker commemorating Oak Grove School, which was just outside the park. Established in 1911 during

Waller Mill Park

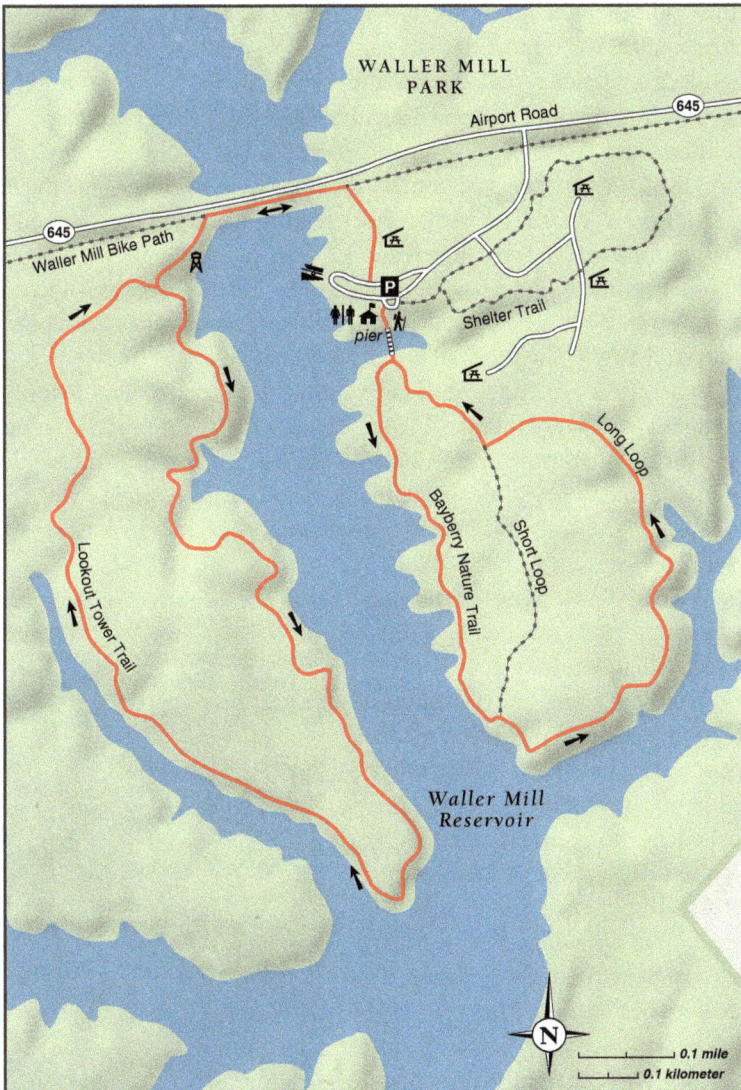

WALLER MILL PARK

Airport Road · 645

645
Waller Mill Bike Path

Shelter Trail

Long Loop

Bayberry Nature Trail

Short Loop

Lookout Tower Trail

pier

Waller Mill
Reservoir

N

0.1 mile
0.1 kilometer

an era of entrenched racial segregation, the school provided education to area African Americans until 1940, when a lightning strike set the two-story schoolhouse ablaze.

Constructed by the federal government to provide water to World War II naval recruits training at Camp Peary to the north, Waller Mill Reservoir was sold to the City of Williamsburg in 1945 and still provides drinking water for much of the area. The 2,400-acre park along the shore was not established until 1972. Since then, it has become a favorite sunny-day destination for Williamsburg residents, with amenities to match. Picnic shelters and grills host family gatherings; fishing piers and row-boats afford anglers the opportunity to land carp, striped and largemouth bass, and foot-long black crappie; rental canoes and kayaks invite paddlers to explore the shoreline; and trails invite everyone—seniors, joggers, cyclists, and nature lovers—to stretch their legs.

For this hike, the park's two main trails, the Lookout Tower Trail and the Bayberry Nature Trail, have been paired with a short section of the recently paved railroad grade paralleling Airport Road to create 4.2-mile figure eight, but you have the option of hiking either loop on its own (the paved trail still serves as a necessary link to Lookout Tower Trail). The park also offers a 2-mile paved bike path along Airport Road and the 0.75-mile Shelter Trail.

The Bayberry Nature Trail begins just south of the park office on a wooden foot-bridge that spans an inlet of the lake. Pause here to survey your rental-boat options at the dock. Bear right after the bridge, passing Shelter 1, and follow the sandy, worn, root-laced path south. You'll recognize many of southeast Virginia's most common hardwoods along the trail—white oak, sweet gum, beech, and hickory—shading equally familiar thickets of holly. Watch for the nearly two dozen signs identifying trees and giving details on their qualities and characteristics.

Moss lines the path among the hardwoods on the Lookout Tower Trail.

After winding along the lakeshore, the path soon reaches a memorial meditation bench overlooking a small inlet. A second bench awaits farther down the path, backed by holly and shaded by a mammoth red oak. The trail then circles northward and uphill to pass through an open wood. The abundance of downed trees here has made room for opportunistic overgrowth beside the path.

As you continue, small inlets of the lake are visible on your right. After crossing the upper reaches of a drainage that feeds a finger of the lake below, the reservoir fades from view. The path bears left to pass first a shelter then the playground on the right as you reapproach the bridge that leads back to the park office. Turn right to pass beside the office and then traverse the parking area.

Continue north past picnic tables through a beech glade. You will reach the paved bike/walk trail on a former railroad grade. It leads right (east) about 0.5 mile, passing the park entrance. Turn instead to the left. The trail continues 1.5 miles before reaching a turnaround, but to reach Lookout Tower Trail, continue across the bridge over the lake, with Airport Road running parallel on your right. Ahead, a sign directs you left, off the path, and uphill to the observation tower, which is braced against the steep hillside above the lake. After a few moments watching the boats below, head south along the bluff above the lake.

The Lookout Tower Trail is more challenging than the Bayberry trail, with several switchbacks and steeper climbs over undulating ridges. It traces the shore south through mixed forest and tends to stay above the lake but dips through several creek drainages. Moss clings to shaded sections of compacted clay and decaying fallen trees. Rounding the southern tip of a peninsula, the trail bears right (north). A narrow finger of the lake stretches along the path, and the trail soon dips to the water's edge. Climb back onto the hillside above the lake, and continue north as it recedes behind you. Enjoy this final woodland stretch as the trail begins to wind generally east.

Upon intersecting with the trail again above the lake, simply retrace your steps to the parking area, or turn left and head back downhill to explore the paved trail. Farther west along the paved trail, red maples and tulip poplars shade relaxation benches, and some fields border the path, offering promising butterfly- and bird-watching.

· ·

GPS TRAILHEAD COORDINATES N37° 18.961' W76° 42.134'

DIRECTIONS From Richmond, take I-64 east to Exit 238 and onto VA 143 (Capitol Landing Road). Take an immediate right onto East Rochambeau Drive. Then take a left onto Airport Road. The entrance to the park will be on your left. Ample parking is available near the park office at the restrooms, trailheads, and boat launch.

Wooden footbridge over a marsh at York River State Park

AT 2,531 ACRES, York River State Park encompasses a great diversity of terrain and ecosystems. Visitors likewise enjoy numerous options for exploring the park's estuarine marshes, the sandy shoreline of the tidal York, and the wooded ridges overlooking both. This balloon hike can be extended to the east or west.

DESCRIPTION

Prior to English colonization, Mattaponi and Pamunkey Indians inhabited the York River shoreline. As settlers converted former hunting grounds to crop fields, the tribes withdrew inland and upriver along their namesake tributaries, which converge to form the York 10 miles northwest of the park. Tobacco grown for export was the Virginia farmer's lifeblood, and Taskinas Creek was a point of departure for tobacco headed downriver to Yorktown, then on to Bristol or Birmingham.

Today all that remains of the Taskinas Plantation tobacco warehouse are the wooden "corduroy" roads visible along the muddy creek bank at low tide. The park visitor center displays Native American artifacts unearthed on the property. Far-reaching, if not encyclopedic, the center examines the many lives of the York River. Aquariums simulate tidewater habitats, 20,000-year-old fossils tell of an ancient sea, and modern fishing gear testifies to the commercial importance of the Chesapeake Bay.

DISTANCE & CONFIGURATION: Two 6.4-mile balloons, plus 5.6 miles of optional trails (mostly out-and-backs)

DIFFICULTY: Moderate

ELEVATION: 40' at trailhead, 116' at high point

SCENERY: Upland woods, creek-fed marshland, York River beach

EXPOSURE: Mostly shaded, open on Backbone Trail and along the river

TRAFFIC: Low; higher near visitor center

TRAIL SURFACE: Dirt, gravel

HIKING TIME: 3 hours

SEASON: Year-round, 8 a.m.–sunset

ACCESS: Parking $4

WHEELCHAIR ACCESS: At visitor center

MAPS: At the park and dcr.virginia.gov /state_parks/york-river

DRIVING DISTANCE FROM CAPITOL: 46 miles

FACILITIES: Restrooms; picnic tables and shelters; playground; boat rental and pier; fishing pier; in-season bicycle, canoe, and kayak rentals; visitor center; gift shop; vending machines; amphitheater

CONTACT: 757-566-3036, dcr.virginia.gov /state_parks/york-river

LOCATION: 9801 York River Park Rd., Croaker

COMMENTS: A water trail of the Captain John Smith Chesapeake National Historic Trail connects to York River State Park. The park includes more than 20 miles of mountain bike trails. It also allows horseback riding on its main trails.

Descending the bluff west of the visitor center, a short, switchbacking paved trail leads through a garden of native vegetation. The labeled flowers and shrubs make an excellent prehike primer on Virginia botany of the sort often overlooked. At the base of the hillside, the park's fleet of canoes and kayaks stands marshaled. Step out onto the small dock jutting into Taskinas Creek and scan the cattails opposite for great blue herons, great and snowy egrets, and long-billed Virginia rails. The Taskinas Creek Trail runs along the southern reaches of this marsh, leaving from the parking area. Consider tacking this 1.7-mile loop onto the beginning or end of your hike; it features several wooden boardwalks and puts you at eye level with the dragonflies darting about this national estuarine-research reserve.

From the parking area, follow the Woodstock Pond Trail to connect with the park's gravel Backbone Trail. Turn right at a fork to join the Backbone Trail. Note the junction, as you'll take the Mattaponi Trail from here on the return trip.

Proceed southwest along the wide gravel path, passing an entrance to the Laurel Glen mountain bike trail on your left. The Backbone then makes a distinct curve eastward, with the park's entrance road visible on your right. The two soon part ways. Accompanied by a power line, the Backbone now progresses southeast, with the Black Bear Run and Marl Ravine mountain bike trails visible on the left and the equestrian Meh-Te-Kos Trail running parallel on the right.

After passing through a wooden cattle gate that blocks horses from the northern reaches of the park, continue south, with forest on your left and fields veiled by a thin barrier of pines to the right. Just as I was questioning this wide, exposed path, a pair of quail darted across the trail before me and into the field. At the first left beyond the wooden gate, the Pamunkey Trail departs. Follow it into the woods, a blend of

191

York River State Park

Trail Legend

- **BA** Backbone Trail
- **BE** Beaver Trail
- **DL** Dogwood Lane Trail
- **MO** Majestic Oak Trail
- **MA** Mattaponi Trail
- **PA** Pamunkey Trail
- **PF** Powhatan Forks Trail
- **PE** Powhatan Forks Trail East Fork
- **PN** Powhatan Forks Trail North Fork
- **RT** Riverview Trail
- **ST** Spur Trail
- **TC** Taskinas Creek Trail
- **WT** Whitetail Trail
- **WP** Woodstock Pond Trail

yellow poplar, Virginia pine, white oak, and holly. Just a short walk ahead, the aptly named Spur Trail heads right. Follow the Spur to hike the route mapped here, but consider hiking the entire 0.77-mile Pamunkey as an out-and-back if you wish. It follows a finger of land bordered by marshy creeks to an overlook of the York.

Hike the Spur past an area carpeted with ferns and another opened to the sky by downed pines, then turn left onto the Majestic Oak Trail. Make a gradual but steady descent from 100 feet in elevation to almost sea level. The land falls away steeply on either side of this pebble-studded trail so that the crowns of tall trees are visible at eye level. You'll find Majestic Oak Trail's namesake hard to miss as you approach the York. Atop a bluff, just before the path curves right and downhill to a boardwalk, it passes a huge fallen white oak, which was unquestionably one of the oldest in the park, with a trunk at least 8 feet in diameter. A nearby sign indicates it was at least 250 years old.

Pause at the bench overlooking the river ahead, or dangle your feet from the boardwalk and take in the view. Pass through a triangular walk-in fence (to block horseback riders) before traversing the boardwalk across a reedy marsh. Wend your way up a set of wooden-beam stairs to pass through a stand of Virginia pines on a sandy path. Now on the north fork of the Powhatan Forks Trail, you must regain the elevation lost en route to the water's edge. Unlike the preceding ridge path, this trail climbs a wider hill through mixed woods. Once you've gained the hilltop, the east fork of the Powhatan Fork Trail tempts you back to the river. This 0.47-mile spur option departs left at an intersection marked by a seven-trunked yellow poplar.

Continuing west, back toward the Backbone, you will traverse an area dotted with clearings left by storm-downed trees. The 1.5-mile Riverview Trail meets your path twice on the left. The Riverview Trail also intersects the Backbone to the west. As its name suggests, the out-and-back optional spur follows a ridge to another marshy creek junction with the York.

Still more options await just a bit farther east (left when you regain the Backbone Trail). The Whitetail and Dogwood Lane Trails, each 0.75 mile, leave left just before the Backbone's terminus. These spurs access some of the more remote and scenic reaches of the park and offer good wildlife-watching and photography prospects. Bring plenty of water and some snacks, and you can easily spend the day exploring York River State Park.

To stick with the more modest 6.4-mile loop, simply return along the Backbone Trail. Bear right when it forks to follow the Mattaponi Trail toward Woodstock Pond. Across the boardwalk, the trail continues beneath diminutive Virginia pines and water oaks, discernible by their scarcely lobed leaves. Ascend a hillside braced by wooden beams to reach the bluff's top, Powhatan Overlook. The York is slowly eroding this band of ancient sedimentation even as mud and silt deposits accumulate on the river bottom. Be cautious when approaching the edge—trees now scattered along the shore 30 feet below toppled when this bluff gave way. A bench affords you the chance to rest and look out across the York.

A beach-access trail soon heads right. Follow this short spur through a culvert to the water's edge. Swimming is prohibited, and downed trees complicate a lengthy beach walk, but look among the flotsam for seashells, and scan the crumbling bank for fossils. You'll almost certainly spot clamshells, but whale teeth are a real coup.

Returning to the trail, descend briefly to reach a boardwalk through a marsh at least 50 feet wide that is fed by a meandering streamlet only a few feet across at low tide. Cattails and marsh grasses grow waist-high along the boardwalk, but peer through their stalks to the mud below, and you will see 1- to 2-inch fiddler crabs scuttling about. As many as 200,000 fiddler crabs can inhabit a single acre of marsh. Nevertheless, males, distinguished by a single large claw, are aggressively territorial, often battling other males who invade the vicinity of their burrows.

Pass between the cattail-lined pond and the York River before bearing inland and uphill. Woodstock Pond comes into view as the trail descends a small hill. The freshwater pond was created as a water source when the surrounding territory was farmland. In the 1950s it was stocked with largemouth bass and bluegills; a small fishing pier juts out over the water on the right. Take the Woodstock Pond Trail back up a long hillside to the parking lot and visitor center, passing sand volleyball courts, a playground, and a shelter along the way.

• •

GPS TRAILHEAD COORDINATES N37° 24.797' W76° 42.873'

DIRECTIONS From Richmond, head east on I-64 about 37 miles; from Williamsburg, head west on I-64 about 8 miles. Take Exit 231B and drive north 1 mile on VA 607 (Croaker Road). Turn right onto VA 606 (Riverview Road) and continue 2 miles to the signed park entrance road (VA 696) on the left. Follow the road 2 more miles to the entrance station, and after paying your parking fee, park in the main parking area near the visitor center. Croaker Landing boat launch, a noncontiguous portion of the state park, lies farther north along VA 607 and requires a (signed) right turn onto VA 605.

The trails at York River State Park offer several vantage points from bluffs high above the river's wide tidal waters.

NORTH TO FREDERICKSBURG AND THE NORTHERN NECK

A vibrant red barn near the camp store at Belle Isle State Park

SURROUNDED BY WATER on three sides, Belle Isle State Park is a boon for anyone looking to cast off or cast a line into the Rappahannock River and its tributaries. However, at 892 acres, the park is also rich with agrarian history and ecological diversity and is easily accessible via wide, level trails.

DESCRIPTION

Belle Isle State Park, on the northern shore of the Rappahannock River, is not to be confused with the Belle Isle of downtown Richmond, though, like the latter, it was once home to a Powhatan fishing village. Specifically, the Moraughtacund tribe inhabited the area concurrent with the earliest English colonization. The name Belle Isle is telling because it nods to one of the peninsula's first European-born landholders, Huguenot John Bertrand, who acquired the property in 1692. Often persecuted at home, French Calvinists arrived in Virginia with a wave of mostly Protestant Europeans—Germans, Scotch-Irish, Dutch, Swiss, and Swedes—whom the Anglican gentry admitted to settle vast tracts of land and provide a buffer against native tribes pushed westward by war.

Belle Isle is misleadingly named, however, in that, like Hog Island on the James, it is now contiguous with the mainland. Bertrand likely found the peninsula's westernmost spit of land inaccessible, enveloped by Mulberry Creek to the north,

DISTANCE & CONFIGURATION: 5.2-mile out-and-back with 3 arms

DIFFICULTY: Easy

ELEVATION: 6' at trailhead, no significant rise

SCENERY: Estuarine creeks, Rappahannock River, wetlands, woodlands, fields

EXPOSURE: Mostly open

TRAFFIC: Moderate

TRAIL SURFACE: Dirt and gravel doubletrack

HIKING TIME: 2 hours

SEASON: Year-round during daylight hours

ACCESS: Parking $4, campsites from $30, paddle-in primitive campsites from $11

WHEELCHAIR ACCESS: At restrooms, picnic shelters, and a short trail

MAPS: At park and dcr.virginia.gov/state-parks/belle-isle

DRIVING DISTANCE FROM CAPITOL: 73 miles

FACILITIES: Restrooms; picnic shelters; playground; in-season bicycle, canoe, paddleboard, and kayak rentals; boat launches; observation blinds; amphitheater; campgrounds; Bel Air House and Bel Air Guest House available for overnight stays

CONTACT: 804-462-5030, dcr.virginia.gov/state-parks/belle-isle

LOCATION: 1632 Belle Isle Rd., Lancaster

COMMENTS: The Captain John Smith Chesapeake National Historic Trail and Civil War trails connect to Belle Isle. To reserve the Bel Air Mansion, call the park office.

the Rappahannock to the west, Deep Creek to the south, and swampland to the east. Yet at 10 feet above sea level, the land was arable. Subsequent plantation owners built levees and roadways through the swamp to enlarge their cropland. The trail to the mouth of Mulberry Creek passes over a raised roadbed then threads between cultivated cornfields. Crops still blanket much of the park's interior, and you will pass an old barn opposite the office en route to the trailhead.

The fields now model sustainable agricultural practices intended to mitigate tainted runoff into the Chesapeake Bay. The health of the wetlands buffering the park is evidenced by the breadth and abundance of wildlife: noisy migratory waterfowl favor the shallow, protected waters between the Mud Creek and Neck Fields Trails, while bald eagles, ospreys, and hawks hunt just offshore near Brewer's Point, which is this hike's northwestern turnaround.

Begin your hike with a loop along the trail that leaves from the trailhead to the right of the parking lot. A short gravel spur leads to a boat launch on Mulberry Creek and the wooden Mulberry Creek Boardwalk, which passes alongside a marshfringed inlet. Here you may find anglers tempting rockfish, flounder, croaker, and other species tolerant of these brackish waters. Venture out onto the pier for farreaching views of the estuary before following the boardwalk to begin the Mud Creek Trail. The path turns to dirt as it heads southeast through a sweet gum grove, the narrowing inlet still visible to the west.

The trail passes beneath pine and ash trees before curving right to emerge alongside the forest. There is a cultivated field on the left, the expanse of which may be obscured by tall cornstalks, depending on the season. The Mud Creek Trail soon

Belle Isle State Park

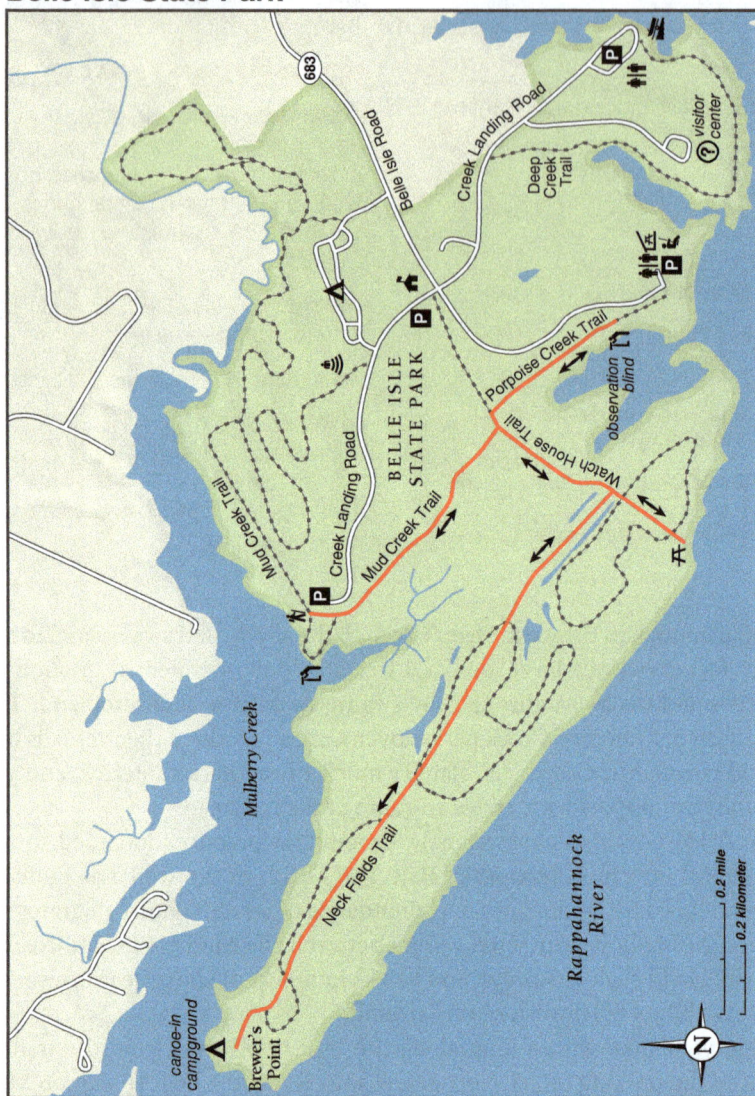

dead-ends at the Watch House Trail. Belle Isle proper lies to the right, but turn left first to follow the Porpoise Creek Trail as a spur. You will walk a short segment of the Watch House Trail before turning right, into the woods. The Porpoise Creek Trail weaves through the trees as an earthen path before emerging as a grassy corridor alongside a cornfield.

At the corner of the cornfield lies a short access trail to the observation blind on the right. Straight ahead, across a small meadow, are a playground and picnic area with restrooms and vending machines. This area overlooks Deep Creek's confluence with the Rappahannock and can serve as an alternate trailhead—perhaps a more convenient one for families looking to spend a day at the park. The observation blind doesn't face the river but does offer a view of a wide, still inlet linked to the Rappahannock by a narrow channel. Almost landlocked and ringed with pines, the placid water recalls a pond rather than an estuary. Patient wintertime hikers enjoy good prospects for spotting tundra swans and snow geese through the short, wide windows of the blind.

Backtrack to the Watch House Trail, and head southwest (left) toward the Rappahannock. On your left you will pass fingers of the calm inlet you recently scanned from the observation blind. On your right, a wall of cedars rises to a stand of pines before yielding to marsh grasses as the trail approaches the state park's namesake former island. As you pass along this narrow stretch of trail, the croaks and chirps of frogs give way to splashes as they retreat from your oncoming footsteps into the shallow waters.

Continue beyond an intersection with the Neck Fields Trail, which departs to the right, to reach a small clearing on the shore of the Rappahannock. Wild persimmons grow alongside the trail, and a picnic table nearby invites hikers to pause for a moment's respite. Deer also frequent this part of Belle Isle, and you may spot a few bounding away should you disturb their grazing. A 1-mile Watch House Trail loop from here takes hikers around marshy fields of wildflowers that might bring joy to bird-watchers.

Return to the junction with the Neck Fields Trail, and head northwest (left) toward Brewer's Point, about 1.2 miles away along a straight, flat doubletrack gravel road. The park map shows several subloops in this area, but these are merely the grassy corridors that ring cornfields or travel along forest edges around meadows. Explore them if you like. The Neck Fields Trail emerges from a stand of pines to squeeze between crop fields. Sycamores also abut the fields, thriving in the moist soil. On your right a swampy pond shelters geese more often heard than seen through the screen of trees.

Ultimately the fields give way to reforesting meadows edged by locust and mulberry trees. A smattering of wildflowers vie for sunlight amid the dense, vine-clad shrubs. Watch closely and you may find bald eagles perched on standing dead trees or ospreys looking for their next meal. At Brewer's Point, discover the primitive paddle-in campsites set in a pine forest along the banks of the Rappahannock.

After enjoying the view during a snack break at a picnic table, we backtracked along the Neck Fields, Watch House, and Mud Creek Trails to the parking lot trailhead.

NEARBY ACTIVITIES

If you're looking to pair history and ecology on your visit to the Northern Neck, stop by the **Kilmarnock Museum** (76 N. Main St., Kilmarnock; 804-436-9100), which focuses on the maritime heritage of Northumberland and Lancaster Counties. Farther northeast, the **Reedville Fishermen's Museum** (804-453-6529, rfmuseum.org) is a beacon to avid anglers. It chronicles the evolution of Chesapeake Bay fishing and aquaculture, beginning with the region's Native American tribes.

• •

GPS TRAILHEAD COORDINATES N37° 46.950' W76° 36.170'

DIRECTIONS From Richmond, follow US 360 northeast across the Rappahannock River to the small town of Warsaw (about 45 miles beyond I-295). From Fredericksburg, take US 17 for 47 miles to Tappahannock, then US 360 another 7 miles to Warsaw. From Warsaw, turn right onto VA 3, and proceed 14 miles southeast before turning right again onto VA 354. Continue 3.1 miles, then make another right onto VA 683. A kiosk collecting vehicle-entry fees is less than a mile ahead. Take a final right at the park's office and camp store following within another 0.5 mile. At that road's northwest terminus, Creek Landing Road, you'll find the trailheads for the Mud Creek Trail in the southwestern corner of the parking area.

We spotted egrets and herons in the marshlands on our hike at Belle Isle State Park.

The Boyd's Hole Trail leads to an overlook above the Potomac River.

A NATIONAL NATURAL LANDMARK known for its old-growth forest and a summer home to many American bald eagles, Caledon attracts many bird-watchers. Trails, including the central Boyd's Hole Trail, which leads to the Potomac River, are open year-round. This loop descends through oaks to wind along a riparian floodplain and then makes an undulating return over beech-studded hillsides. It offers a more challenging hike in the western portions, as the trail climbs and descends a series of ridges.

DESCRIPTION

Provided it's open, start your visit to Caledon with a walk through the visitor center, where you'll find exhibits on the property's history and the bald eagles that roost along its stretch of Potomac shoreline. The exhibits are housed in the white-clapboard Colonial that Lewis Smoot built in 1910, shortly after inheriting the property. He lived there until his death in 1962, along with his wife, Ann Hopewell Smoot, who donated the property to Virginia in 1974. It was designated Caledon Natural Area in 1984. In 2012, Caledon was reclassified as a state park rather than a natural area.

The Smoots' home replaced a burned two-story manor erected in 1759 by descendants of John Alexander, who had established Caledon Plantation exactly a century before. A Scottish immigrant, Alexander named his farmstead after the

DISTANCE & CONFIGURATION: 4-mile loop, with connectors for shorter options

DIFFICULTY: Moderate

ELEVATION: 162' at trailhead, 20' at low point

SCENERY: Hardwood-forested hillsides and creek drainages

EXPOSURE: Well shaded

TRAFFIC: Low

TRAIL SURFACE: Dirt singletrack

HIKING TIME: 2 hours

SEASON: Year-round, 8 a.m.–sunset (visitor center hours vary with seasons)

ACCESS: Parking $4, campsites from $11

WHEELCHAIR ACCESS: Visitor center, some picnic tables; wheelchairs not recommended on trails

MAPS: At park office and dcr.virginia.gov /state-parks/caledon

DRIVING DISTANCE FROM CAPITOL: 72 miles

FACILITIES: Park office, visitor center, restrooms, picnic shelters, grills, playground, small amphi-theater. Interpretive programs, including an eagle-viewing outing, are available by reservation (fees apply).

CONTACT: 540-663-3861, dcr.virginia.gov /state-parks/caledon

LOCATION: 11617 Caledon Rd., King George

COMMENTS: A water trail of the Captain John Smith Chesapeake National Historic Trail connects to Caledon State Park. The park has 6 paddle-in and hike-in primitive campsites available for rent year-round, but there are no cabins or drive-to campsites.

sweeping forest of Caledonia. Like many Virginia farmers of the Colonial era, Alexander and his sons grew tobacco. And it was tobacco that took him upriver to the city that would eventually bear his name, Alexandria.

In 1669 Alexander traded 6,000 pounds of tobacco for as many acres north along the Potomac from Hunting Creek to Little Falls. Virginia governor William Berkeley had awarded the territory to English ship captain Robert Howsing less than a month before. The seaman hauled his tobacco to market in London, while Alexander set about clearing the land. By 1749, the profitable crop blanketed northern Virginia, and farmers successfully petitioned Virginia's General Assembly to establish a town named in honor of the land's first real owner.

The intrepid settlers who transformed the forests of then-western Virginia into rolling fields were among the first wave of America's agrarian entrepreneurs. Their spiritual descendants would push west across the continent, but none did so without consequence. In Virginia, the proliferation first of farms along the Potomac and then of suburbs all but decimated the indigenous bald eagle population. By 1977, only 33 pairs of eagles nested within the commonwealth. The population has rebounded thanks to a resurgent appreciation for our national symbol and growing support for wildlife conservation. Today the number of nesting pairs in the Old Dominion approaches 500, and up to 60 eagles roost in Caledon alone during the summer months. But to ensure that the shy eagles remain, many of Caledon's 2,587 acres are restricted, as is the adjacent 1,108-acre Chotank Creek State Natural Area Preserve.

Your best bet for eagle-watching is to join one of the park's guided tours along the Potomac. This trail, which has the distinct advantage of being open year-round, winds through forest a mile south of the shore. Eagles rarely venture so far inland,

Caledon State Park and Natural Area

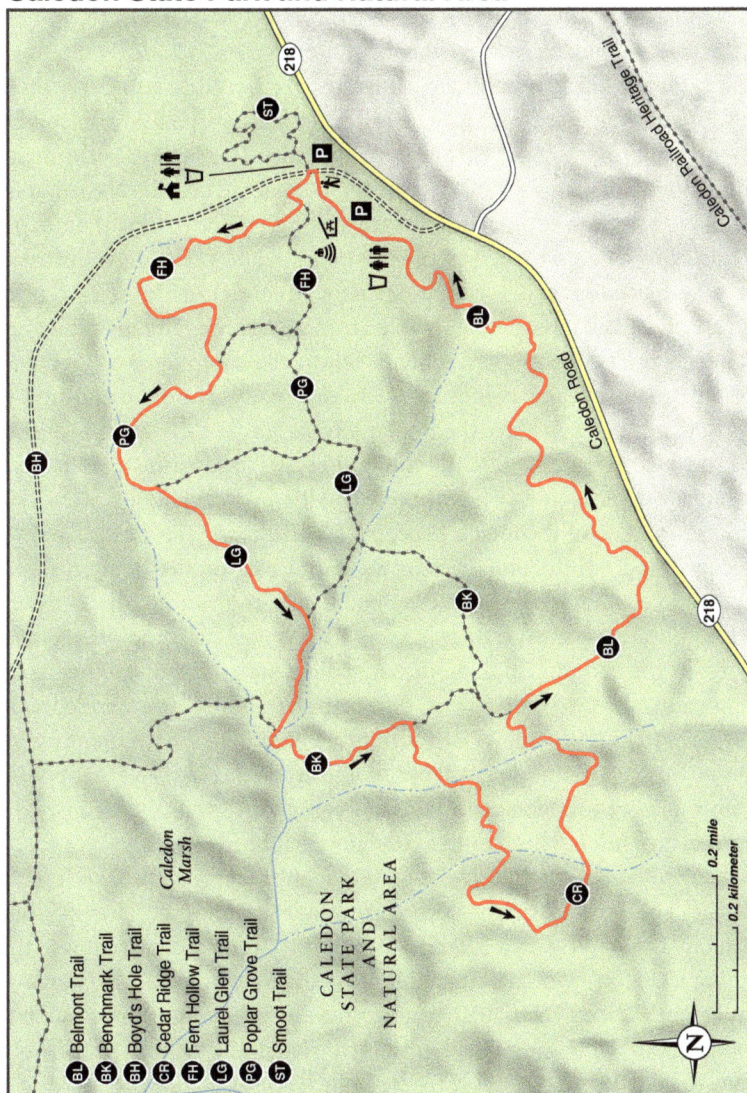

but you stand good odds of spotting pileated and red-bellied woodpeckers, as well as numerous songbirds.

Set out from the parking area near the visitor center on the roomy singletrack outlined by fallen limbs, and enter a glade of tall yellow poplars. Veer right when the Fern Hollow Trail forks. The red-blazed loop is the first of five interwoven loops that make up Caledon's hiking trail network. Curve left to a slight rise, and pass an area of deadfall pines before making a 90-degree left to cross a rivulet on a footbridge. Climb through a collage of oaks: southern red, northern red, scarlet, white, and chestnut. True to the trail's name, ferns make the forest floor green in warmer months.

Briefly double back, then make a distinct right to descend from the modest ridgeline. Even as you work your way steadily downhill to creekside bottomland, you establish a familiar pattern for this undulating loop. The hike dips through several draws, first along the winnowing ridges near an unnamed creek and then uphill, near the headwaters of its feeder branches. Before making a 90-degree right onto the Poplar Grove Trail, cross a culvert with steep, mossy banks, and veer briefly upstream.

The blue-blazed loop descends to cross a streamlet just upstream of its junction with another. The mossy, root-crossed trail then runs along that unnamed creek through beech and yellow poplar. It bends left to cross two deep-gullied feeder rivulets just upstream of their confluence. Crossing the second stream on a wooden bridge with handrails, you leave the Poplar Grove Trail for the Laurel Glen Trail.

This southwest-bound stretch of the trail begins its rise on wooden-beam steps then bisects a ridgeline in a grove of holly shaded by beech and white oak. Ample yellow blazes guide you through a depression and across a second ridgeline before the trail curves left. Mountain laurel grows abundantly on the western slope as you descend toward a stream valley and the Benchmark Trail.

Take the orange-blazed trail to the right, keeping the sandy-bottomed brook on your left as you round a knoll on the right. The eroded banks of the brook, up to 10 feet high and laced with tree roots, diminish as the valley floor widens. Cross the brook on a wooden footbridge just south of its confluence with the growing creek you first saw upstream. Briefly stroll beside the creek through a verdant bottomland forest. After passing a sign showing the footprints of various animals that reside in these woods, turn left to climb onto a ridgeline that heads south.

Move inland and uphill along the laurel-laden ridgetop. Where it intersects the Cedar Ridge Trail, a sharp right takes you down the hillside. The trail bends left before finally descending to a footbridge. Mature beech trees dominate the forest surrounding Caledon's westernmost and most challenging trail. The narrow single-track underfoot indicates that many visitors never traverse the entire trail network.

Following the Cedar Ridge Trail through the wide valley, you'll next cross another steep ridge to take the westernmost feeder branch of this hike. Crossing it on a bridge with handrails, follow the zigzagging trail downstream a short distance before it doubles back. Climb southwest through open forest before making a left at a bench. Now headed east, your path descends to recross the rivulet, noticeably shallower upstream.

Though the prongs and branches of this drainage are generally narrower on your return trip, its ridges are noticeably steeper. Take the opportunity to view these woods from a new perspective, looking north toward the low-lying forest you recently traveled. After the first of four successive climbs, descend to cross a rivulet, and then keep it to your left as you work your way downstream.

A winding ascent over the next ridgeline takes you through numerous holly trees. Farther ahead, the path dips to rejoin the Benchmark Trail (east) for an optional hike to return to the parking lot. This route would also connect along the southern portions of the Laurel Glen, Poplar Grove, and Fern Hollow Trails. Watch for the signs directing you up the ravine back to the trailhead.

For this mapped hike, however, turn right (southeast) onto the dark-green-blazed Belmont Trail. From this point, it will be approximately 2 miles of hiking back to the parking area. Follow a relatively long and level stint uphill as you cross this wide knoll. The trail's sharp descent leads you across another feeder branch; the path then rises up the opposite hillside. During our visit, many trees had been cut and the trail network had some areas of rework but should by now be well reestablished. Hardwoods are gradually reclaiming the surrounding forest.

As the trail gets closer to the top of undulating ridgelines along this portion of the hike, you can hear the occasional sounds of passing vehicles on Caledon Road (VA 218). Clusters of occasional cedar then Virginia pine can be spotted closer to the roadway. The trail exits the forest, and we walked across the driveway of what appeared to be a residence for the park. Continue into a wide field near the park's main entrance. Before completing the loop, pass the amphitheater, picnic shelter, and playground. After cresting a small hill, you will see the trailhead just ahead.

• •

GPS TRAILHEAD COORDINATES N38° 20.040' W77° 08.558'

DIRECTIONS From Richmond, head north on I-95 to Exit 104. Follow VA 207 almost 12 miles to the town of Bowling Green, where it merges with US 301. Continue northeast on US 301 through Fort A. P. Hill and across the Rappahannock River. Drive 25 miles, then turn left onto VA 218 (Windsor Drive). After 0.25 mile, a second left keeps you on VA 218 (Dahlgren Road), now running west, parallel to VA 206. Follow the right fork when the two roads separate after 2.2 miles, and you'll find the park just over 1 mile ahead on the right.

From Fredericksburg, simply follow VA 218 east from its junction with VA 3 (Kings Highway). Upon entering the park, continue past a parking lot on your left to the visitor center lot. The trailhead, marked by a signboard, is in the northwestern corner of the lot.

The Heritage Trail provides many fine views from bluffs above the Rappahannock River as it flows through Fredericksburg.

POPULAR WITH AREA WALKERS, runners, and cyclists, this paved loop traces an important remnant of Fredericksburg's commercial past. The Canal Path and Rappahannock River Heritage Trail were connected to form a 3.1-mile loop with connections to Old Mill Park in 2012. Wetland parcels en route, home to swans and herons, are a welcome counterbalance to the concrete underbelly of US 1. The northwest portion of the trail along a high bluff above the Rappahannock provides beautiful views of the river and heavily forested Laucks Island.

DESCRIPTION

Constructed over two decades beginning in 1829, the Rappahannock River canal system once stretched 50 miles upstream to Fauquier County. The notion of using canals to promote trade and industry along the river was originally endorsed by Virginia legislators in 1811. Early proponents of canal navigation, including George Washington, had envisioned a system of controlled waterways lacing the commonwealth, ferrying goods to market and supplies upriver to farmers and settlers. That vision was never realized, as most commerce moved from canals to railroads. Nevertheless, canals were an integral component of commerce in Fall Line cities such as Fredericksburg and Richmond, where they helped transfer cargo around waterfalls and rapids.

DISTANCE & CONFIGURATION: 3.1-mile loop

DIFFICULTY: Easy

ELEVATION: 18' at trailhead, 62' at high point

SCENERY: Rappahannock River, canal, pockets of wetlands amid suburban homes, parcels of floral landscaping

EXPOSURE: Mostly open

TRAFFIC: Moderate

TRAIL SURFACE: Paved

HIKING TIME: 1.5 hours

SEASON: Year-round

ACCESS: No fee

WHEELCHAIR ACCESS: Yes

MAPS: On kiosks along trail

DRIVING DISTANCE FROM CAPITOL: 61.4 miles

FACILITIES: Playing fields, picnic tables, and restrooms at Old Mill Park. Trail loop connects through neighborhoods and has a few options for finding beverages or snacks along the way.

CONTACT: City of Fredericksburg Parks: 540-372-1086, fredericksburgva.gov

LOCATION: Old Mill Park, 2201 Caroline St., Fredericksburg

COMMENTS: Old Mill Park and Quarry Trails connect to this loop trail, which took more than a decade to create. The trail provides a safe nonmotorized-vehicle space to get around on foot or 2 wheels.

The private Rappahannock Navigation Company mustered sufficient capital to undertake construction of a canal stretching west from Fredericksburg in 1829. Fifteen years later, when the cash-strapped company folded, the project remained incomplete; however, a short-lived gold-mining boom upriver hardened the city's resolve, and Fredericksburg assumed control of the project with state backing. The canal route was completed in 1849. But as its turbulent creation presaged, the canal's heyday was fleeting. In 1852, railroad lines reached the upper Rappahannock Valley, and traffic along the canal network dwindled.

The enterprise was never sufficiently profitable to maintain its 47 locks and 20 dams. Enter entrepreneurship. Just six years after the network's completion, the Fredericksburg Water Power Company purchased the stretch of canal along which the city's Canal Path now runs. The channel proved far more profitable as a millrace, turning the turbines of flour, wool, and electricity mills, the remains of which lie just beyond the trail's terminus near Old Mill Park. In fact the conduit is often referred to as the VEPCO Canal, after the acronym for Virginia Electric and Power Company, which maintained the 1910 Embrey Dam on the canal's west end and the Embrey Power Plant on its east end through the 1960s.

Begin this hike from Old Mill Park, which has a path from the parking lot to connect up a sloping hill to the Canal Path/Rappahannock River Heritage Trail loop as it runs along Caroline Street. Take a left onto the trail to follow a clockwise loop. The path follows the river side of the street two blocks before crossing Caroline at a crosswalk on Germania Street.

Follow the path about 0.3 mile until it turns right onto a winding path through the former site of the Germania Mill, which was built in 1866. The upper canal powered this business, and Germania Family Brand Flour was shipped all over the East

Canal Path/Rappahannock River Heritage Trail

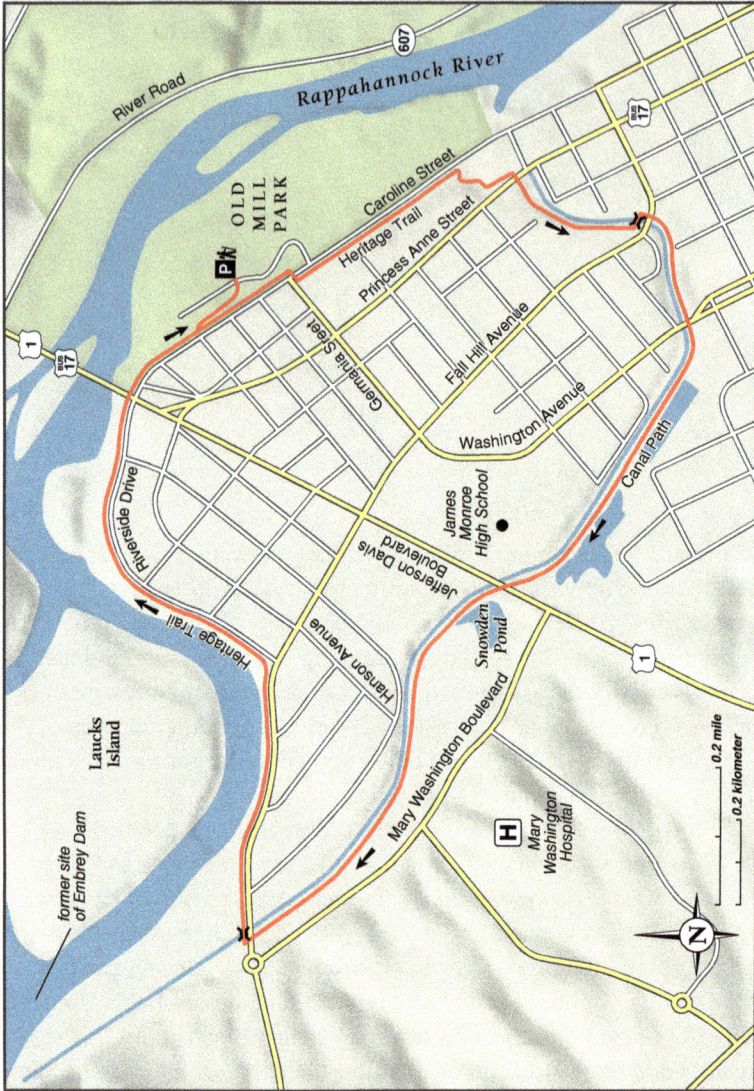

Coast. Production at this facility stalled in the mid-20th century, and the site burned in 1980. It was finally demolished in 2010 and became part of the Canal Path. Before continuing, note that the site of the former hydroelectric-power-generating Embrey Power Plant is just one block farther south on Caroline Street. The Army Corps of Engineers dismantled the dam in 2006.

As the trail crosses Princess Anne Street, note a kiosk with a map and benches. The sign contains plenty of useful information about the canal's history and how the canal shaped the development of Fredericksburg. The canal soon comes into view, a trickle of its former self. When it served to float barges towed by horses treading the same path we now hike, the water level was kept higher, as evidenced by the sturdy stone walls that rise on both sides of the 20-foot-wide channel. The trail continues along a trail then passes through a grassy field before reaching a metal footbridge over the canal and crossing at Fall Hill Avenue.

A small landscaped park graces this intersection with blooming coneflowers and black-eyed Susans. Visible on your left up the street as you cross Washington Avenue is the Mary Washington Monument, a worthwhile detour to the gravesite of George Washington's mother. She was interred beside Meditation Rock, said to be one of her favorite spots, near her daughter's home. An 1833 effort by President Andrew Jackson to have a shrine erected on the spot foundered, but 60 years later Grover Cleveland commissioned the present obelisk. As you continue along the canal on the paved path, the Fredericksburg Dog Park and Old Cossey Holding Pond lie ahead on the left. The pond is a rectangular impoundment built for an adjacent water-treatment facility.

As the Canal Path continues northwest, it passes alongside Gayles Pond and College Marsh. Trail signage indicates this marsh is a nontidal wetland, characterized by plants that have adapted to growing in wet areas. A few leafless trees, some with trunks smoothed like driftwood by the wind and rain, remain standing at the periphery of the marsh. Here you may find great blue herons hunting for small fish.

Next, the trail's urban character is hard to ignore when it passes beneath busy US 1. The cavernous walkway beneath the overpass is scarcely inviting, but taking it is safer and more expedient than crossing the street above. Your imagination may conjure visions of bats, but rest assured those are barn swallows darting about in the dim passage. Ahead is Snowden Pond, where a sign aids novice bird-watchers in identifying the waterfowl and songbirds that reside here. Shrouded by a wall of vine-draped ash trees, the shallow pond fringed with mallow and rush feels surprisingly serene.

Power lines run concurrent with the path. A field on the left gives way to a buffer of trees, most notably river birch, red maple, sweet gum, and yellow poplar. Suburban back lawns are visible across the canal, and soon you come to a bridge that leads left to access the neighborhood.

About 2.2 miles into this hike, the trail passes under Fall Hill Avenue. The bridge connection here was the final piece to completing the trail loop. The Virginia Outdoor Center and the trailhead for the Fredericksburg Quarry Trail System are both accessible after crossing a metal bridge over the canal.

From here, the Rappahannock River Heritage Trail begins. Take a moment along the banks of the river to admire the view. The paved 10-foot-wide path follows Fall Hill Avenue about 0.3 mile before veering left along Riverside Drive. Most of the trail is exposed with little shade through this section. The views of the river as it bends around heavily wooded Laucks Island from the vantage point atop this high bluff are a highlight of the hike.

Watch for a quick stop to see the Indian Punch Bowl, a giant granite boulder with a bowl shape carved out. Several other interpretive signs along the way detail the Native American, Colonial, and industrial history of the Rappahannock. As the trail travels again under US 1, retrace the path to Old Mill Park and the parking area.

NEARBY ACTIVITIES

Want more? This one might take a while. The **Fredericksburg Quarry Trail System** (fredtrails.org/trails/fredericksburg-quarry) connects to this hike at the Fall Hill Avenue bridge. Set into the hillsides above the Rappahannock River and bisected by I-95, the trails offer excellent river scenery on mostly shaded pathways. The nearly 14 miles of trails are popular with mountain bikers, especially in the upper sections. Hikers tend to stay on the shoreline along the Scout, USGS, and Beach Trails. See a trail map and more at fambe.org.

The area's biggest attraction, of course, is **Fredericksburg and Spotsylvania National Military Park** (540-693-3200, nps.gov/frsp). Civil War history buffs can tour four battlefields (five if you count a tiny allotment on the site of the Battle of Salem Church), though the park's premier hiking trail, a 7-mile loop, is located at the Spotsylvania Court House Battlefield.

• •

GPS TRAILHEAD COORDINATES N38° 19.012' W77° 28.096'

DIRECTIONS From Richmond, head north on I-95 to Exit 133. Travel east on VA 17 about a mile, then turn right onto US 1. Continue 1.5 miles south, then turn left onto Princess Anne Street. Turn left again on Amaret Street and right onto Caroline Street. A left turn into Old Mill Park will be less than 0.5 mile away. The trail begins from the parking lot and loops around in either direction.

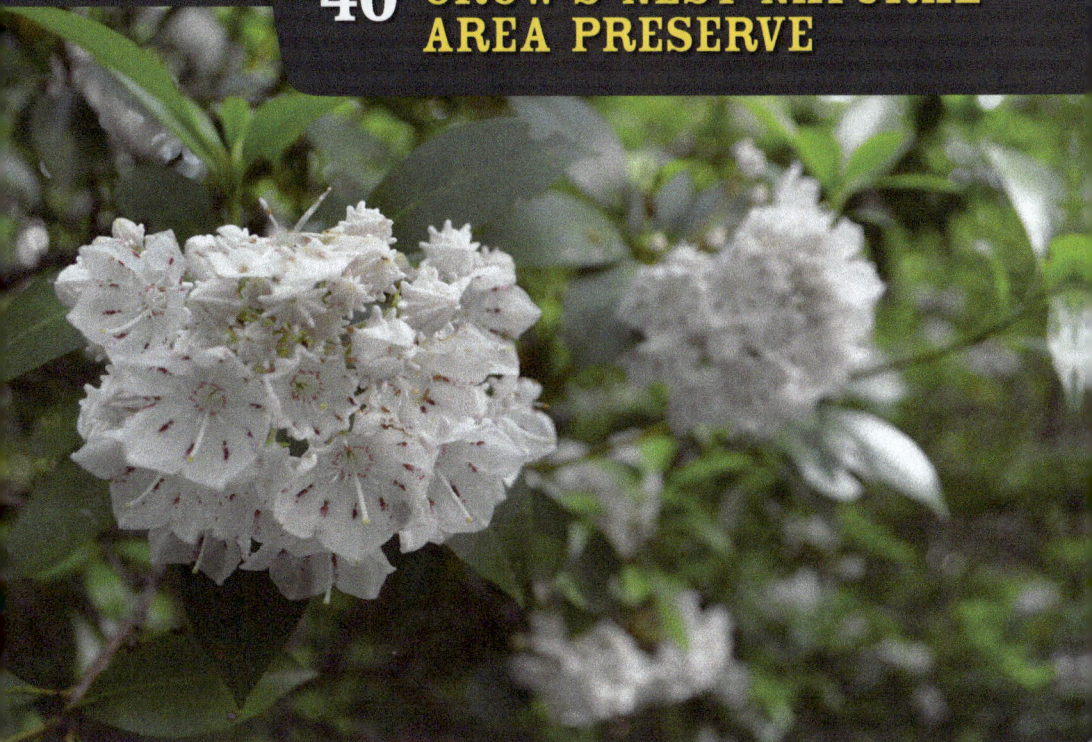

At the beginning of the hike, you'll see mountain laurel, whose white and light-pink flowers bloom in May.

40 CROW'S NEST NATURAL AREA PRESERVE

THE 14 MILES OF HIKING TRAILS at Crow's Nest Natural Area Preserve, opened in April 2017, provide a unique perspective on the natural and cultural history of Virginia. The preserve is a habitat for nesting bald eagles, short-nose sturgeon, a variety of fish and mussel species, and migratory waterfowl, and more than 60 songbird species are known to breed here.

DESCRIPTION

Officially open since April 2017, Crow's Nest is touted by the Virginia Department of Conservation and Recreation (DCR) as "one of Virginia's highest land conservation achievements." The Stafford County preserve became a reality in 2008 with the first parcel acquisition; then in 2009, the DCR and Stafford County added 1,110 acres, bringing the total area of Virginia's 54th state natural area preserve to 2,872 acres at a cost of more than $34 million.

Named after a merchant sailing ship that once docked in the Potomac Creek during the 1700s, the more than 4,000-acre peninsula is home to a number of rare, threatened, and endangered species of plants, fish, and animals, including significant migratory bird populations, according to the DCR. The preserve is considered one of the most pristine areas in the lower Potomac River. The high, narrow peninsula

DISTANCE & CONFIGURATION: 5.5-mile loop with out-and-back spur

DIFFICULTY: Moderate

ELEVATION: 175' at trailhead, 4' at low point

SCENERY: Steep hillsides in mature hardwood forest, Potomac River, marshes, numerous rivulets

EXPOSURE: Well shaded

TRAFFIC: Low

TRAIL SURFACE: Dirt, gravel

HIKING TIME: 2.5 hours

SEASON: Generally year-round during daylight hours (hours vary with seasons). Raven Road Access Point is open Thursday–Sunday only.

ACCESS: No fee

WHEELCHAIR ACCESS: Wheelchairs not recommended

MAPS: On kiosks at trailhead and at dcr.virginia .gov/natural-heritage/document/cnnap -trailmap.pdf

DRIVING DISTANCE FROM CAPITOL: 71.5 miles

FACILITIES: Parking area, portable toilet, kiosk, trash cans, canoe/kayak launch from Brooke Road access

CONTACT: Northern Region Steward: 540-658-8960; Virginia Department of Conservation and Recreation: 540-658-8690, dcr.virginia.gov

LOCATION: 81 Raven Rd., Stafford

COMMENTS: Dogs must be leashed at all times. Camping, fires, and relic hunting are prohibited. Hunting and general discharging of firearms is prohibited unless permitted as part of a managed hunt program. There is an ADA–compliant canoe/kayak launch with a 20-space parking lot on Brooke Road. The John Smith water trail connects to Crow's Nest. Raven Road access and hiking trails are open Thursday–Sunday. Brooke Road access and water trail are open 7 days a week. The water trail is an 8-mile round-trip between the Brooke Road access and Boykin's Landing on the southern tip of the preserve.

contains 750 acres of tidal and nontidal wetlands, which account for 60% of all the marshes in Stafford County. It also includes 2,200 acres of mature hardwood forest.

The topography of Crow's Nest is varied, with the high, narrow ridgeline rising 160 feet above the tidal Potomac and Accokeek Creeks. Park signage indicates the peninsula is divided by a "series of deep ravines cutting into ancient coastal plain marine sediments and feeding tidal marshes along the bordering creeks."

With 21 miles of stream, riparian, and wetland buffer, the preserve's diverse plant communities provide important habitat for breeding birds, neotropical migrants, and overwintering waterfowl. Bird diversity peaks during fall and spring migrations, when waves of birds pass through the mid-Atlantic region. A checklist available on the DCR website identifies more than 160 bird species that have been seen within the preserve or from the shoreline.

The DCR conducts managed waterfowl hunts (by lottery) each year at Crow's Nest. Hunting is restricted to one day per week. Fishing in the public waters surrounding the preserve is open to anglers in boats, though there are no fishing piers or docks here and the preserve offers few places to fish from the shoreline. Fishing is not permitted from the Brooke Road–access canoe/kayak launch platform on Accokeek Creek. Managed deer hunts may be conducted as needed.

Visitors can ride bicycles and licensed motorcycles on the entrance road and to access the preserve parking areas designed for automobile access. However,

Crow's Nest Natural Area Preserve

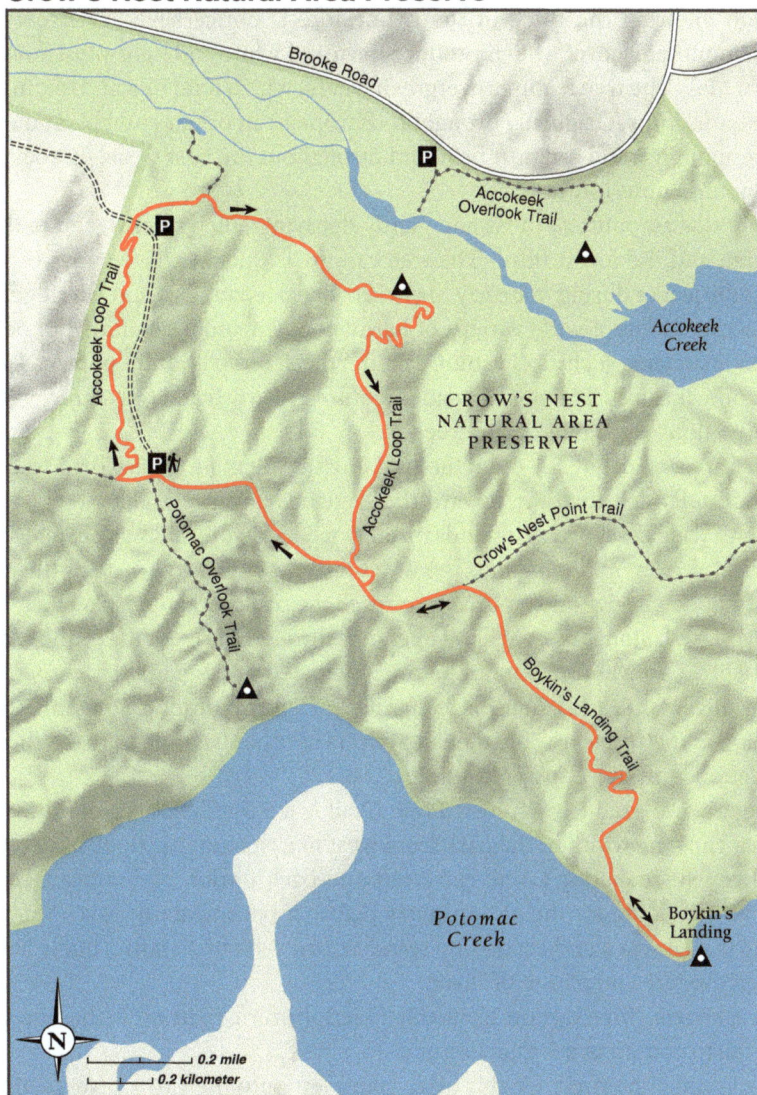

bicycles, motorized vehicles, and horses are prohibited on the trails within the preserve, to protect from soil disturbance, which leads to increased erosion and the spread of invasive plants.

To begin this hike, look to the west side of the Raven Road parking area for Accokeek Loop Trail. The name comes from Accokeek Creek, which this trail leads down to after about a 1-mile hike. Note that the trail markers are of the same high quality found at Virginia state parks. This is consistent throughout Crow's Nest, so don't fear getting lost.

Upon entering the thick of the ravine forest, notice several narrow tunnels through mountain laurel, which produce beautiful white and light-pink flowers that bloom in May. The tree features evergreen leaves, which tend to stand out in late-fall and winter months. Originally brought to Europe as an ornamental plant during the 1700s, mountain laurel can now be found throughout the East Coast on rocky slopes and in mountainous forest areas.

Generous amounts of moss and gently decaying fallen trees decorate the sides of the trail and the forest floor. The tree canopy is thick, with few rays of sunlight piercing the leaves during our early May visit. The deep ravines and tall ridges within the preserve feature a wide variety of hardwoods, including chinquapin oak, with common associates such as chestnut oak, northern red oak, tulip poplar, American beech, and white ash. The tidal wetlands feature green ash and red maple, with a few sycamores along the banks of the creek.

After approximately 0.7 mile, the trail crosses the main access road to continue down a doubletrack roadway toward the wetlands and Accokeek Creek. Note the muddy and wide creekbed as it winds through tall hardwoods. Frogs peeped loudly as we passed by, many plopping into the water for safety. The trail crosses the creek by way of a wooden bridge and continues to reach the banks of the Accokeek.

As you walk along, there will be openings through the trees to see the creek. We spotted a great blue heron, but not before it detected us first and flew away. The trail bends briefly inland, and a blue blaze directs you left to continue along the Accokeek Trail Loop as it rises nearly 140 feet and covers another 0.6 mile to reach the central trail junction with the Crow's Nest Point Trail.

The green-blazed Crow's Nest Point Trail is a 5.5-mile gravel and dirt double-track that runs the width of the park from west to east to an overlook at Crow's Nest Point. It might make for a fine extra out-and-back option and appears to be the former vehicle route for the old property before it became a preserve. Much of the roadway is well worn and eroded by weather and vehicular traffic, but it has excellent tree coverage and plenty of shade.

For a shorter hike option from this junction, turn right onto the Crow's Nest Point Trail to complete a 3-mile journey.

To continue the route for this hike, take a left onto the Crow's Nest Point Trail, and walk about 0.3 mile to a fork. Turn right onto the red-blazed Boykin's Landing Trail, a 2-mile out-and-back that finishes along the sandy banks and high bluffs of Potomac Creek. This descent toward the creek includes several switchbacks and damp brooks through a thick hardwood forest before reaching a stand of pine protecting the high shoreline. Low-lying marshlands reveal wildflowers that attract a plethora of butterflies and songbirds.

We stopped at a bench on a bluff overlook at Boykin's Landing for a moment to enjoy the view and a quick snack. According to park signage, archaeological evidence has shown that this peninsula has been used by humans for the past 11,000 years. We pondered how many different ways the land had been used and altered during that time frame.

Take the same Boykin's Landing Trail back, rising more than 150 feet along the way. Turn left at the trail junction with the Crow's Nest Point Trail for an approximately 1-mile return trip to the parking area.

NEARBY ACTIVITIES

For additional vantage points of Accokeek Creek, consider arriving via the Brooke Road access and taking the 1-mile out-and-back **Accokeek Overlook Trail,** which connects to a large wooden boardwalk and canoe/kayak launch. On our visit, we saw signs of a large beaver dam and a multitude of colorful songbirds (including what we think was a red-winged blackbird) hiding in the high grasses of the tidal waterway. An 8-mile round-trip water trail travels around the peninsula between the Brooke Road access and Boykin's Landing on the southern tip of the preserve.

• •

GPS TRAILHEAD COORDINATES N38° 21.749' W77° 20.532'

DIRECTIONS From Richmond, take I-95 north to Exit 140 (Stafford). Take VA 630 (Courthouse Road) 1 mile east to Stafford (intersection of VA 630 and US 1). Cross US 1 and continue east on VA 630 about 2.5 miles. Turn right onto VA 629 (Andrew Chapel Road) and continue 0.9 mile. After passing under the railroad overpass at the community of Brooke, turn left onto VA 608 (Brooke Road). Continue 1.4 miles, then turn right onto gravel VA 609 (Raven Road). Cross the one-lane bridge over Accokeek Creek and continue 0.2 mile. The Raven Road Access gate will be on the left.

The Railroad Ford Trail at Lake Anna State Park

ESCAPE THE CROWDS along the shore of Lake Anna, the park's main draw, by following this loop through mostly hardwood forest, past scenic rivulets, and alongside an inlet of the lake. Most are multiuse, so expect the occasional manure pile or wet spots scarred by horse hooves. Exhibits trace the county's gold mining history and highlight the park's natural features. Nature and gold panning programs are popular, and guided tours of the Goodwin Gold Mine are available.

DESCRIPTION

The gold rush on the land that is today Lake Anna State Park preceded its famous California counterpart by 20 years. Mining continued in the area, known as Gold Hill, through the 1940s, although prospecting peaked some 60 years earlier. The last gold found was discovered in a zinc mine.

The foundation of the Goodwin Gold Mine now crumbles within the state park, opened in 1983. Lake Anna itself was formed in 1971 to provide cooling water for the North Anna Nuclear Power Station, located about 4.5 miles away, as the crow flies. A sign at the park entrance reminds visitors of the facility's proximity, but fortunately, traces of industry are scarce within the park's 3,127 acres. Instead, a sandy beach helps kids while away sunny, school-free days. On summer weekends, throngs

DISTANCE & CONFIGURATION: 7-mile loop, with balloon offshoot and more than 15 miles of optional trails

DIFFICULTY: Moderate

ELEVATION: 356' at trailhead, 248' at low point

SCENERY: Mostly hardwood forest, fingers of Lake Anna, creeks in the park's interior

EXPOSURE: Mostly shaded

TRAFFIC: Low; higher in summer

TRAIL SURFACE: Dirt

HIKING TIME: 3 hours

SEASON: Year-round during daylight hours; high season Memorial Day–Labor Day

ACCESS: Parking $5 low season, $7 holidays

and high-season weekends, out-of-state vehicles add $2; campsites from $24

WHEELCHAIR ACCESS: Visitor center, restrooms, picnic areas, fishing pier

MAPS: At the park and dcr.virginia.gov /state-parks/lake-anna

DRIVING DISTANCE FROM CAPITOL: 65.2 miles

FACILITIES: Restrooms, showers, picnic shelters, grills, campground, cabins, playground, swimming beach, boat launch, fishing pier, visitor center

CONTACT: 540-854-5503, dcr.virginia.gov /state-parks/lake-anna

LOCATION: 6800 Lawyers Rd., Spotsylvania Courthouse

COMMENTS: Horseback riding is popular at Lake Anna, and almost all of the trails are designed for horseback riding, cycling, and hiking.

of youngsters frolic on the beach, parents tend their barbecue grills, and motorboats roar across the lake. The park has 10 miles of lake frontage.

On a chilly late-fall day, however, a profound silence enshrouds Lake Anna. The breeze passes through trees hastily ejecting their leaves, and the waves dare not lap at the shore. Overlooking the swimming beach are showers, restrooms, a concession stand, and a playground. Downhill to the east stands the visitor center, behind which the fishing pond is startlingly modest relative to its 13,000-acre neighbor a few yards away. A former landowner dammed a stream to create the pond, and the park subsequently encircled it with Old Pond Trail. A leaflet highlights the plants and animals visible from nine stations along the route. Although brief, the path is an informative primer for a more serious hike at Lake Anna State Park.

West of the beach are the boat launch, picnic tables, and a fishing pier. The Fisherman's Trail, a brief lakeside stroll, leaves from this area. Those opting to cast a line in Lake Anna can hope to catch walleye, channel catfish, sunfish, and striped bass. East of the beach are the Railroad Ford Trail and the park's campground.

To reach the trailhead for the route mapped here, turn left off the main road after passing the park office. Behind the office is a parking lot for horse trailers, which was full during my visit. Just a bit farther down the road, find a five-car trailhead parking lot on the right. Even farther down this road, past the trailhead for this hike, are the park's rental cabins.

To begin your venture, briefly walk along the right side of the road past the trailhead parking lot before ducking to the right into the woods on Turkey Run Trail, heading southeast. After an open field, pass through a predominantly oak forest, in which deep-green American holly is particularly evident.

Lake Anna State Park

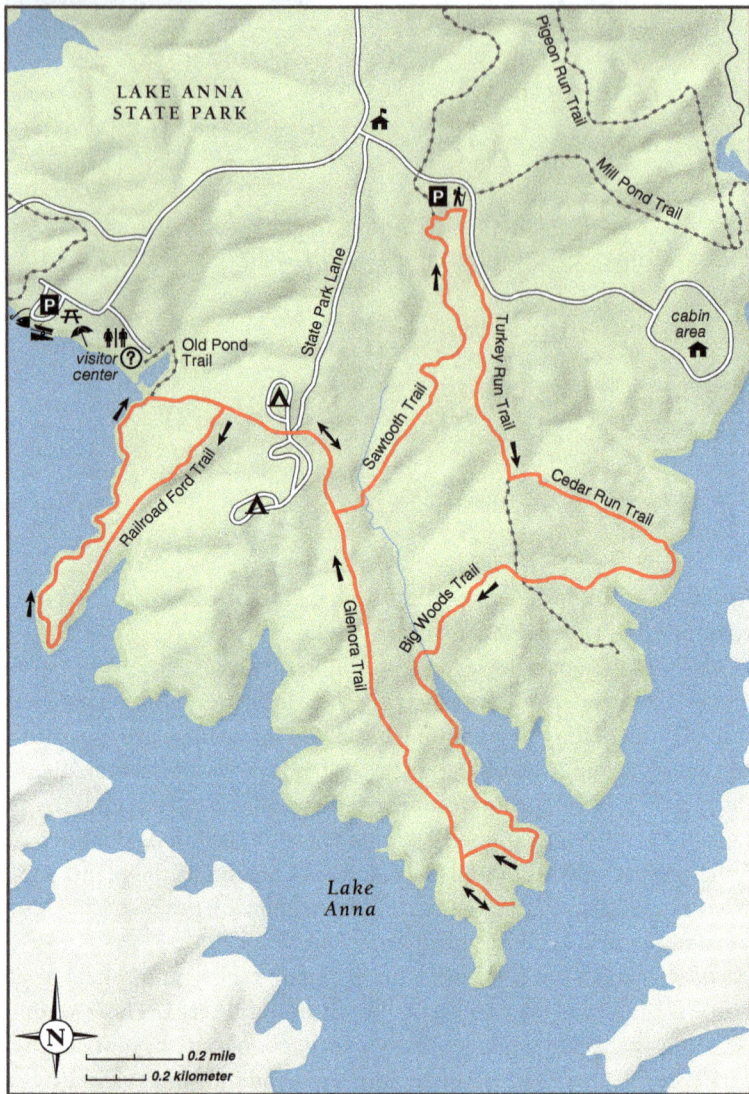

You'll soon arrive at a fork in the mostly level trail; the fork is marked by an unusual white oak with a secondary trunk jutting first horizontally then vertically. Veer left on the 0.8-mile Cedar Run Trail, which approaches the lake before rejoining Turkey Run. This route periodically traces a finger of the lake where Pigeon Run once descended to meet the North Anna River. Just beyond the junction where the Cedar Run Trail rejoins the Turkey Run Trail, the trail veers left again onto the Big Woods Trail. Descend through a young forest thick with pines and cedars. The forest is recovering from logging done in the 1950s. The entire area was selectively logged during the first half of the 20th century; hence it was dubbed Big Woods.

It was in this area that the sound of my hiking boots shuffling through the thick layers of fallen leaves must have rustled up a few deer bedded down just off the trail. I looked quickly into the woods to see several white tails bouncing over the next ridge.

Cross a wooden footbridge over a small stream winding its way to Lake Anna. Nearby a streamside boulder beckons picnickers. On most sections of trail in the park, horseback riders are diverted from the trail to ford rivulets, but the two paths quickly rejoin. In general, the wet earth nearer the lake is more easily scarred by equine passage.

A thoughtfully placed bench, courtesy of the Friends of Lake Anna State Park, affords hikers a place to rest and gaze across the lake. The woods grow thick with vines, and red cedars begin to replace holly in the understory before the Big Woods Trail intersects the Glenora Trail, which bears right. At this point, consider a short spur to the left (toward the lake) to see the smokehouse that was once part of the Pigeon Plantation.

Moving upland on the Glenora Trail, the surface turns briefly to red clay, recalling the hills of Georgia. You'll pass a section of trail where bricks were used in vain to riprap the path; they are now scarcely visible in the worn soil.

Next, the Sawtooth Trail meets the Glenora Trail at a T. Remember this intersection for later, but continue straight as mapped, and pass through the campground to hike the 1.6-mile Railroad Ford Trail. This balloon path offers an undulating tour of another lake peninsula and is mercifully off-limits to all but pedestrians. The trail follows a 1916 railroad grade built to transport lead and zinc for ammunition production during the Great War. The waters of Lake Anna subsequently submerged a short but nevertheless vital stretch of track.

A portion of the trail is paved as it passes through the campground and descends to the beach. There are tree identification signs along the path, so take a few minutes to bone up on your arboreal knowledge. The Railroad Ford Trail is an easy hike but offers the best and most satisfying views of Lake Anna and the rocky shoreline. Several spur trails to the shore beckon hikers to stop and admire the view. The trail loops back near the park's beach before beginning a steep climb back to the campground by way of a paved trail. Note the outdoor classroom and excellent amenities for playing in the park, especially if you are visiting with young ones.

Retrace your steps along the Glenora Trail back to the T intersection with the Sawtooth Trail. As you head north, the abandoned railroad grade is visible on the left. You will ultimately reach the sawmill site, which offers a short spur trail that links to the trailhead.

If you're not too tired and want more, continue straight instead, and cross the park road. The Sawtooth Trail formerly paralleled the park's main road for a significant stretch; it was mercifully rerouted to traverse the upland forest.

The path eventually veers right alongside asphalt for a short stretch before it cuts a sharp right to become the 1.5-mile Pigeon Run Trail. Ahead, the Gold Hill Trail balloon departs from the left. If you're feeling frisky, you can add another 3.1 miles to your total by taking this trail, which passes the remains of a 19th-century gold mine. However, note that the trail relies for half its length on a power-line right-of-way. Though the power lines detract somewhat from the woodland experience, the relatively wide clearing provides an excellent vantage for bird-watching.

The Pigeon Run Trail fords not its namesake (according to my topo map) but a scenic feeder stream. The stream sparkles with quartzite and fills the glade with its gurgling before ascending a steep hill cloaked in mountain laurel. In the late 1800s, Hailey's Mill, a gristmill, operated on hydraulic power from Pigeon Run. As the park brochure notes, the dam broke in an 1889 storm. Also gone now are the passenger pigeons from which the stream took its name.

The Pigeon Run Trail veers right for a hill-and-vale stretch on the aforementioned right-of-way before turning right onto the 0.9-mile Mill Pond Trail. After the junction you'll pass through an area of recently cut pines. A rivulet again meanders along the footpath. As you pass under mature forest, a pine beam in the trail signals your impending completion of the loop. Emerging onto the road, the parking area should be just to the left across the road.

• •

GPS TRAILHEAD COORDINATES N38° 07.053' W77° 49.113'

DIRECTIONS From I-95, take Exit 118 and head west on VA 606 (Mudd Tavern Road/ Morris Road), which turns left to merge with VA 208 (Courthouse Road). After approximately 8 miles, turn right onto VA 601 (Lawyers Road), then left into the park after 3 miles. The necessary turns are marked with brown signs from the interstate. The park is about a 20-minute drive from the interstate through rolling hills and rural farms.

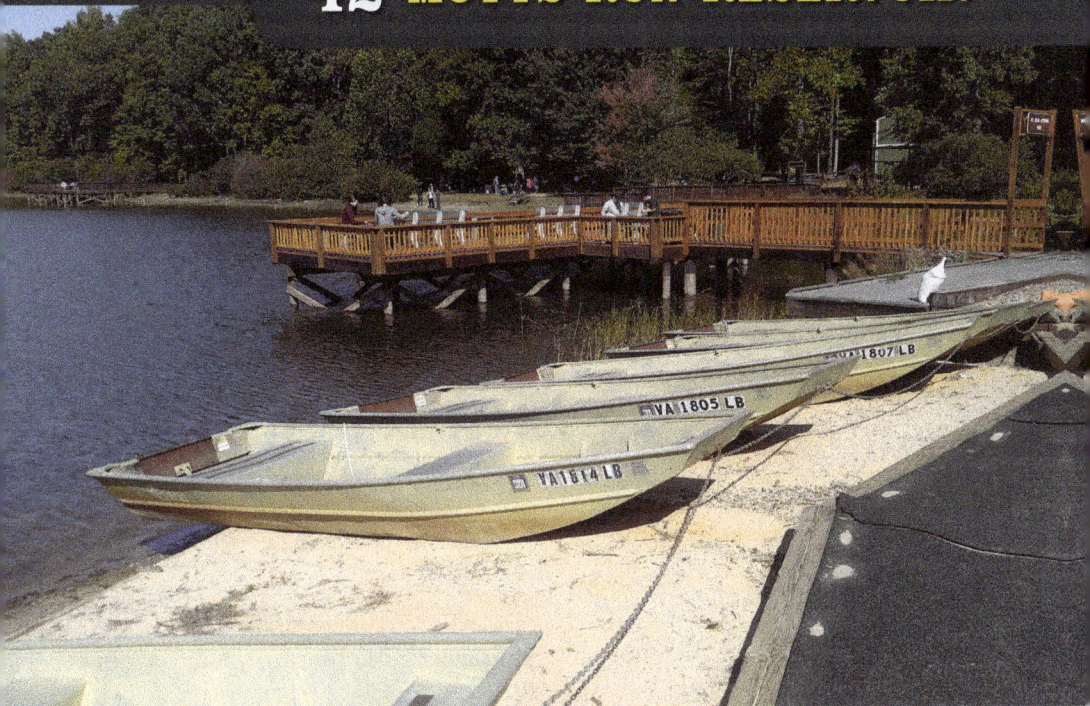

Fishing is popular on Motts Run Reservoir.

NORTH OF MOTTS RUN RESERVOIR, trails lace the heavily wooded hillside, looking out across the lake. Undulating terrain and towering forest belie the tight-knit nature of the trail system, which can be customized to different lengths.

DESCRIPTION

The trail network at Motts Run Reservoir serves the threefold aim of this 860-acre city park, which fuses outdoor recreation with environmental education and habitat preservation. In a scenario familiar to Virginia hikers (see Ragged Mountain Natural Area, Beaverdam Park, and Walnut Creek Park in this book), the City of Fredericksburg elected to open a nature park on the shores of its recently completed reservoir in 1974. The park's initial appeal was lake fishing, which remains a significant draw. However, the nature center is a testament to the park's focus on education.

Though cool weather banishes first the throngs of picnickers, then the anglers, and finally the park's seasonal staff, the nature center remains open to school and civic groups for scheduled programs. Also during the off-season, local Scout troops help maintain the trailbed and bridges. An Eagle Scout even helped develop the park's new orienteering course. Armed with a compass and instructions obtained from the office or nature center, would-be trailblazers can crisscross the park on one

DISTANCE & CONFIGURATION: 2.2-mile figure eight, with optional spurs

DIFFICULTY: Moderate

ELEVATION: 100' at trailhead, 263' at high point

SCENERY: Hardwood-forested hillsides overlooking Motts Run Reservoir, mountain laurel thickets above rocky streams

EXPOSURE: Well shaded, except along the lake

TRAFFIC: Low; higher in summer

TRAIL SURFACE: Dirt singletrack

HIKING TIME: 1 hour

SEASON: April 1–October 31, Thursday–Monday, 7 a.m.–7 p.m.; Nature Center open weekends, noon–5 p.m.

ACCESS: No fee

WHEELCHAIR ACCESS: On fishing pier; wheelchairs not recommended on trails

MAPS: At park office and trailhead, and at fredericksburgva.gov/documentcenter/view/7304

DRIVING DISTANCE FROM CAPITOL: 60.5 miles

FACILITIES: Restrooms, picnic shelter and tables, grills, concessions, nature center, boat launch, canoe and kayak rentals, 3 fishing piers

CONTACT: City of Fredericksburg Parks: 540-786-8989, fredericksburgva.gov

LOCATION: 6600 River Rd., Fredericksburg

COMMENTS: Trails are for hiking only. Mountain biking allowed only on designated trails. No swimming, horseback riding, or ATVs permitted.

of eight routes that vary in difficulty and distance. Numbered posts at key points along the course help keep hikers on track.

A relatively mature forest and open understory help make off-trail orienteering feasible at Motts Run, though navigating around a thicket of mountain laurel or stand of beech saplings is no doubt occasionally required. Those abundant species share the forest with holly, white oak, northern red oak, and dogwood, among others. Trails wind beneath them in two parcels of land separated by the park's entrance road. The route outlined here makes a figure eight, using both halves of the network but not all the trails. To shorten your hike, simply choose one of this route's two loops; to elongate it, follow the bypassed spur trails.

Beginning from the lower, lakeside parking lot, head east, opposite the park office, on the signed Hidden Creek Trail. After you make a brief stride along the lake, blue blazes guide you upland and northeast along a hillside above an inlet, with the stream that feeds it visible just ahead. Upon reaching a fork in the trail, turn right and descend to cross the rivulet on a wooden footbridge just above a mossy rockslide.

The path rises steeply away, promptly gaining 60 feet in elevation. As it levels, look for a T intersection ahead. Here the Osprey Point Trail heads right. Follow this balloon for views of the lake beyond the waterside foliage. The trail rises slightly then drops dramatically to approach the shore. Fallen limbs and logs outline the path as benches invite you to relax and enjoy the vista. Upon completing the loop, proceed north along a finger ridgeline.

An intersection lies just beyond a tree with a rotund burl protruding from its trunk, as noted on the park map. Head right with the proper Hidden Creek Trail, bypassing a cutoff trail that veers left. Descending southeast through maturing

Motts Run Reservoir

hardwood forest dotted with laurels and cedars, the path again nears the water as it rounds a point. A steady climb follows as the trail curves left, away from the lake-shore and along an inlet on the right.

A parcel of young trees crowns the hilltop, having sprung up after strong winds toppled the shallow-rooted conifers that preceded them. The cutoff trail rejoins the main loop here as the main loop bends right, off the hilltop, to pass a spur, the Old Silo Trail, on the right. This brief out-and-back leads to the remains of an old granary.

Beyond it, the Hidden Creek Trail widens as it approaches River Road, screened by the woods to your right.

Making a distinct left beside a mossy mound, however, the path retreats from the noise of traffic and down a draw. The stream you previously crossed emerges from a small spring on your left, growing to a steady trickle as it descends. The path runs along the stream gully, twice crossing feeder-runoff channels on wooden footbridges. Mountain laurel proliferates on either side of the stream but particularly on the steep bank opposite.

The lake comes into view shortly before the trail rejoins the access path to the parking lot, the first bridge of your hike now visible on the left. Briefly retrace your steps across the bridge to the Hidden Creek trailhead, and then continue through the parking lot and past the office toward the picnic area. Beyond a parcel of landscaping, begin following the lake's edge near a cluster of picnic tables shaded by cedars and yellow poplars. The nature center and a storage shed stand inland on your right.

Just beyond here, the yellow-blazed Turkey Ridge Trail heads uphill for this hike. Sweet gums mingle with the preponderance of oaks in the surrounding wood. You'll pass the white-blazed Possum Path loop as the trail curves slightly west as it climbs north. The trail enters younger forest on the reaches of drier upland bluff. Lichens grow on low banks beside the trail.

A bench provides a pleasant spot to admire the view of the reservoir.

As the Turkey Ridge Trail loops right, note the junction for the red-blazed Mine Run Trail, which is a 2.6-mile out-and-back from this spot. Continue along Turkey Ridge. In autumn, scattered scarlet oaks brighten this stretch with their purplish leaves. Enjoy level walking before the path veers closer to River Road, visible through a screen of trees on your left. The trail steers away from the road to head briefly south back to the main parking area.

If you prefer a longer hike, instead of taking the Turkey Ridge Trail loop, continue through the picnic area along the lake. This well-worn waterside singletrack also serves for bank fishing. Beyond the picnic tables, a pipeline clearing perpendicular to the trail precedes a footbridge over a small rivulet. The green-blazed Lakeview Trail (0.5 mile) and the aptly named, purple-blazed Laurel Trail (0.4 mile) connect farther west and can be looped back to the parking area by way of the Mine Run Trail, which also includes the aforementioned out-and-back option.

Following the route as mapped, however, take the Turkey Ridge Trail downhill through increasingly numerous beeches, hornbeams, and red maples. The trail completes its loop with a steep ascent behind the nature center through enclaves of running cedars, club moss, and Virginia pines. To complete the figure eight, veer left, away from the Turkey Ridge Trail, and return through the picnic area to your starting point.

• •

GPS TRAILHEAD COORDINATES N38° 19.002' W77° 33.459'

DIRECTIONS From Richmond, head north on I-95 to Exit 130B. Head west on VA 3 (Plank Road) less than a mile, then turn right onto VA 639 (Bragg Road). After driving north almost a mile, turn left onto VA 618 (River Road). The park entrance is on the left, 2.4 miles ahead.

From Fredericksburg, it's possible to arrive from the east on VA 639 (Fall Hill Avenue north of VA 618) then turn right onto VA 618.

A footbridge crosses a creek in densely wooded North Anna Battlefield Park.

THE SITE OF A CIVIL WAR BATTLE between May 23 and 26, 1864, this park retains well-preserved earthworks. Ten interpretive signs along the Gray Trail, which was once Ox Road, recount the battle from the Confederate side. The 13 signs along the Blue Trail detail the Union positions. Under the command of General Robert E. Lee, who was ill during the battle, Confederate troops halted the Union advance but failed to give chase, thereby allowing the Union to regroup and move toward Richmond.

DESCRIPTION

The Battle of Ox Ford unfolds as you hike through this Hanover County park. Interpretive signs describe the events in chronological order, highlighting the personalities, tactical strategies, and logistical constraints that shaped the conflagration. In many ways, this hike serves as a precursor to Cold Harbor Battlefield (see page 146) because the Confederate Army's successful use of earthen defenses along the North Anna River informed the subsequent strategy of entrenchment.

Rarely crowded, the park stimulates contemplation. The soft rustling of wind in the trees overhead is in marked contrast to the shouts and explosions of battle evoked en route. Yet the pleasant woodland setting alone is worth the trip (or a repeat visit). A few tables and a trash can at the gravel trailhead parking lot invite a picnic, and numerous benches invite you to relax along the way.

DISTANCE & CONFIGURATION: 4.8-mile out-and-back, with multiple spurs

DIFFICULTY: Easy on Gray Trail; moderate on Blue Trail

ELEVATION: 193' at trailhead, 234' at high point

SCENERY: Hardwood forest, North Anna River, Civil War earthworks, interpretive signs

EXPOSURE: Well shaded

TRAFFIC: Low; higher in summer

TRAIL SURFACE: Crushed stone, dirt

HIKING TIME: 2 hours (if stopping to read interpretive signs)

SEASON: Year-round during daylight hours

ACCESS: No fee

WHEELCHAIR ACCESS: Wheelchairs not recommended

MAPS: The map included here is sufficient to keep you on the 2 clearly marked trails. A map of the battlefield can be found at battlefields.org /learn/maps/battle-north-anna.

DRIVING DISTANCE FROM CAPITOL: 28.3 miles

FACILITIES: Portable toilets at trailhead, picnic tables, trash cans, interpretive signage, overlooks, access to North Anna River

CONTACT: Hanover County Parks and Recreation: 804-365-7150, hanovercounty.gov

LOCATION: 11576 Verdon Rd., Doswell

COMMENTS: The Lee vs. Grant 1864 Civil War driving trail connects to North Anna Battlefield Park. Keep an eye on children near the North Anna River overlook.

A covered stone-and-wood signboard at the edge of the parking lot marks the trailhead. Along with a painting depicting the 57th Massachusetts Infantry rallying before their initial, ill-fated charge is a brief explanation of events that preceded the battle of Ox Ford, including Confederate stands at Wilderness and Spotsylvania Court House. On May 21, Ulysses S. Grant ordered his Army of the Potomac south to nearby Hanover Junction (present-day Doswell), which held strategic value as the intersection of the Richmond, Fredericksburg, and Potomac Railroad and the Virginia Central Railroad. Subsequent interpretive signs pick up the saga, explaining the battle as it played out. Next to the trailhead sign, a granite memorial honors the fallen.

From the parking area, head northwest through primarily diminutive Virginia pines, characterized by small 1.5- to 2.5-inch cones and 1- to 3-inch needles, interspersed among loblolly pines that are easily twice as large. The well-maintained gravel trail, on average 5 feet wide, traces the route of Ox Ford Road, which formed one side of Lee's much-vaunted "hog snout line," also known as the inverted V. The hike illuminates the strength of this formation.

The Doswell quarry property, about 50 yards to your left, is visible intermittently along the hike on the park's western border. The first remnant of earthworks soon appears on your right; then the path descends a series of steps made of wooden beams with a wooden rail. Atop the stairs is the first of several benches.

At the bottom of the stairs, the trail draws parallel to a rivulet then crosses it on a wooden footbridge. This wet lowland is dotted with birch trees and ferns; the latter were unfurling new fronds during my springtime visit. Though many trees had yet to leaf, monarch butterflies floated sporadically across the trail before me. The surrounding forest includes white oak, holly, and pignut hickory.

North Anna Battlefield Park

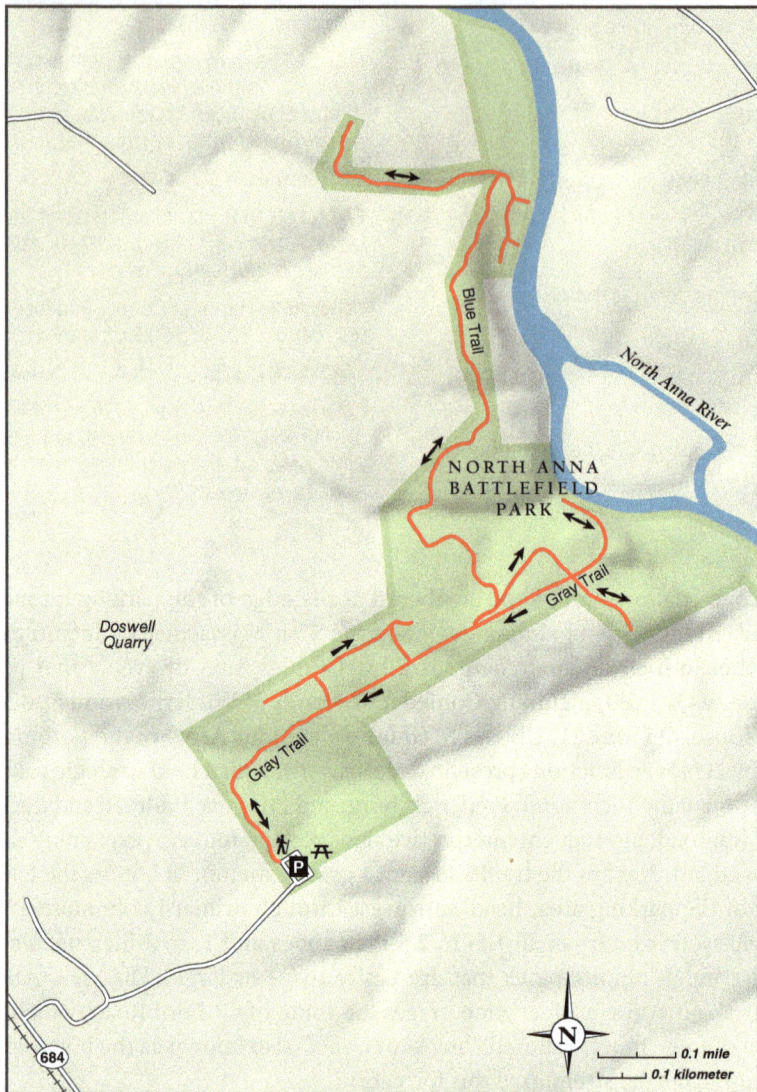

Ascend to approach the first interpretive sign for the Gray Trail, which describes the events that transpired between 11 a.m. and 8 p.m. on May 23, 1864—primarily the positioning of Confederate cannons along Ox Ford Road in the wake of a Confederate retreat from the Telegraph Road bridge upstream. Pass a large, double-trunked white oak on your right before approaching the first fork in the trail.

Up the trail, the next interpretive sign explains that Virginians under the command of Colonel David A. Weisiger began construction of earthen trenches here on

May 24, following orders from Lieutenant General A. P. Hill. Turn left to trace a short spur for a close-up examination of the earthworks. Note that the hillside visible to the north through the trees is a product of modern industry; the entrenched rebels surveyed very different terrain in search of a Union advance.

Confederate earthen defenses remain clearly visible throughout this portion of the park, despite being more than 150 years old. Many are cloaked in moss, and trees have risen up through them. Yet the eroded trench lines remain, with ditches averaging 3 feet deep, and berms up to 4 feet high.

Continue northwest to the third sign on the Gray Trail, which notes that Grant, having misjudged the Confederates, ordered his men to rout any remaining rebels and continue to Richmond. He instructed Major General Ambrose Burnside to cross the North Anna River at Ox Ford, but Burnside found it too well defended. The next sign describes the initial Union advance by Brigadier General James H. Ledlie's brigade, forthrightly denouncing Ledlie as one of the Union's least-qualified generals. Having commanded the Massachusetts infantrymen for merely a week, the drunken general ordered a foolhardy charge. His troops were exposed to the fire of entrenched Confederates led by Brigadier General William H. Mahone, and a bloodbath ensued.

A mossy stretch of trail with a rivulet flowing beneath it precedes the fifth sign, found beside a cul-de-sac in the trail. It details the deployment of Confederate brigades from Mississippi and Alabama that fought in the trenches visible here. Descend past another mossy patch in the trail to rejoin the main path and continue northeast. A small rivulet has eroded a sizable gully on your right.

Turn left at the next intersection to reach Stop 6, which recounts the repulse of Ledlie's charge, ordered in defiance of his division commander, on the evening of May 24. A quote from Captain John Anderson of the 57th Massachusetts Infantry recounts the scene: "It was just a wild tumultuous rush where the more reckless were far to the front and the cautious scattered along the back but still coming on. Many of the Confederate soldiers stood upon their breastworks and called out in a tantalizing manner, 'Come on, Yank. Come on to Richmond.'"

At this point the Blue Trail begins. With spurs and opportunities for exploring along the banks of North Anna River, our hike was nearly 2.5 miles. There are 13 stops along this route, detailing Union positions, trenches, and actions during the fight for Ox Ford. The Blue Trail is a little more challenging than the Gray Trail, as it descends and climbs a couple of ravines, including a steep section on the path down to the clear, serene waters of the river, which is certainly worth a close look. There is no official access to the river from the bluffs along the Gray Trail.

As the Blue Trail begins winding through the woods, the trail approaches a wooden deck worthy of a suburban backyard, by Stop 1 of the Blue Trail, where the marker describes the countercharge made by the 12th Mississippi Infantry, from which the Federals beat a hasty retreat. Perhaps the lone Union hero to emerge from the battle, in stark contrast to Ledlie, was Lieutenant Colonel Charles Chandler. He valiantly rallied the 57th, but the infantry fell back when he was struck down.

A portion of the hike walks along a gravel doubletrack road nearly 0.5 mile, likely a shared access for the neighboring quarry property. The park signage is well placed; follow the markers and you won't get lost. A large wooden deck is the end of the Blue Trail, with signs 12 and 13 positioned along the railings. From here, retrace your steps to return to the Gray Trail.

Back to the Gray Trail, Stop 7 details the importance of the terrain. Had Union generals appreciated the strength of General Lee's position, they might have reshaped their tactics (it's been suggested that want of a topographic map cost Grant the battle). Stop 8, approached by way of a small out-and-back spur, marks the tip of Lee's so-called inverted V. Perhaps an A better represents the Confederate position, with the crossbar representing the easy exchange of men and material between flanks. Union forces, on the other hand, had to break ranks to assault the rebel positions. Gazing downhill through the trees, one appreciates the literal uphill battle Grant's men faced.

Continuing along the Gray Trail, turn left. After passing another gulch on the right, the trail veers left. Juniper bushes dot both sides of the trail as you approach another sizable wooden deck, from which the North Anna River is visible below. A steep descent separates you from the river, and there is no approved trail down. The Stop 9 marker explains that on the night of May 24, 1864, when Grant's scattered army was most vulnerable, the sickly Lee "lay in his tent repeating over and over again, 'We must strike them a blow. We must never let them pass us again. We must strike them a blow.'" Failure to do so, however, allowed the Union army to dig in. A two-day siege followed, costing each side 2,000 lives and merely forestalling Grant's approach to Richmond.

The final Gray Trail marker, Stop 10, which designates the trench line of the 10th Georgia Battalion, notes the extensive use of heavy artillery during the battle. To reach the trench line, retrace your steps from Stop 9 to an out-and-back spur on the left near the junction with the path coming from Stop 8. To complete your hike, return to the main path, and follow it back to the trailhead.

• •

GPS TRAILHEAD COORDINATES N37° 52.870' W77° 29.935'

DIRECTIONS From I-95 take Exit 98 (Doswell), and go west on VA 30 (Kings Dominion Boulevard) 0.7 mile to US 1 (Washington Road). Turn right, drive 1.5 miles, and turn left onto VA 684 (Vernon Road). Continue 2.5 miles along a railroad track and a string of power lines on your left. A small brown park sign and a VIRGINIA CIVIL WAR TRAILS sign indicate the entrance on your right. Enter along a gravel road, promptly passing a historical marker, and follow the road to the trailhead.

Stagg Creek runs along the western border of Poor Farm Park.

RENOWNED AMONG MOUNTAIN BIKERS, the dirt trails of Poor Farm Park are also great for hiking and technical trail running. There are very few directional markers, and the trail network can be confusing to new visitors, but this alluring park draws people from around the Richmond region.

DESCRIPTION

In the early 1900s, this land was part of a philanthropic farm, located about 4 miles west of Ashland, that offered housing and food to families in need in exchange for labor, according to a park brochure. Another angle is that the rocky ground may have made a poor farmstead. No doubt plowing the steep terrain that rises east from the creek would have been difficult, especially using traditional methods.

These days, the 254 acres along Stagg Creek make a fine Hanover County park. The hillside is ideal for the amphitheater nestled into the surrounding hardwood forest, and bikers and trail runners have carved a web of singletrack trails in the woods.

Entering the park, you'll pass level sports fields. The road veers right to reach the playground and popular picnic shelters, with horseshoe pits, a volleyball court, and an open playing field adjacent. It's easy to see why area residents flock to this park for family gatherings, church picnics, and the like. The trail network lies beyond the fields, in the wooded northwest reaches of the park, and the official trailhead is

DISTANCE & CONFIGURATION: 2.3-mile loop, plus numerous additional options

DIFFICULTY: Moderate

ELEVATION: 223' at trailhead, 117' at low point

SCENERY: Hardwood forest, Stagg Creek

EXPOSURE: Well shaded

TRAFFIC: Moderate

TRAIL SURFACE: Dirt

HIKING TIME: 1 hour

SEASON: Year-round during daylight hours

ACCESS: No fee

WHEELCHAIR ACCESS: Wheelchairs not recommended

MAPS: At parking lot kiosk

DRIVING DISTANCE FROM CAPITOL: 23.4 miles

FACILITIES: Portable toilets; picnic shelters; amphitheater; baseball, softball, football, and soccer fields; sand volleyball courts; horseshoe pits

CONTACT: 804-365-7150, hanovercounty.gov

LOCATION: 13400 Liberty School Rd., Ashland

COMMENTS: Occasional NO TRESPASSING signs separate the park from adjacent private land, but there is no fence, and some trails freely cross the boundary. Avoid crossing Stagg Creek and you'll stay within the park.

to the right of the horseshoe pits as you face the field. The gravel road off to the left and just past the playground serves as a secondary trailhead; the route mapped here returns from that direction to make a loop.

The park's own maps are lacking, and the trail network is simply too extensive and too compact to render completely, even with the aid of a GPS unit. But precisely because the trails are packed into a relatively small area, your risk of getting lost—at least for long—is minimized. In summer, vegetation fills the woods, providing a sense of serenity but obscuring landmarks and nearby trails. Make the loop described here first to grasp the lay of the land, then take another pass, giving yourself leave to wander onto the numerous side trails. Think twice about fording Stagg Creek, though. It's not that the meandering stream poses a threat, but the park boundary lies just beyond it. (Some users have blazed trails on the adjacent land, but it is well marked as private; do not trespass.)

This hike travels counterclockwise along the perimeter of the trail network. Many spur trails and connections cross into the heart of the offerings, but this path will attempt to keep you along the edges. Keep in mind that Poor Farm is popular with mountain bikers, so keep your ears and eyes on the trail, and be prepared to share the singletrack pathways.

Leaving from the primary trailhead at the picnic shelter, enter along a narrow path into the woods. The trail descends to a wooden footbridge to cross a wide ravine. Take a right after crossing the bridge, and continue along the banks of the ravine. As the trail approaches a clearing beyond the woods, take a left to continue along the perimeter.

The trail will traverse a ridge and begin another slight descent. You will come upon a stand of young pine trees. At the time of this hike, the network of pines (covering about an acre) was very thick. It had two spur trails that crisscrossed through the

Poor Farm Park

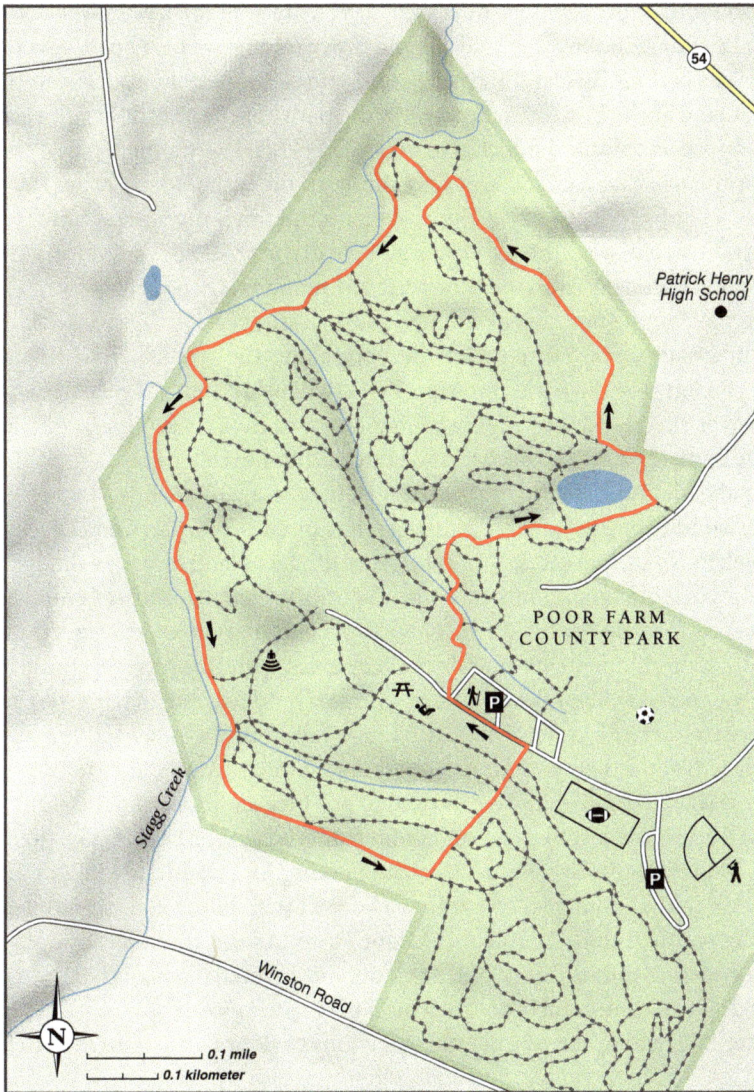

southern portion and made for a unique diversion, almost like a maze. The pathway through the pines does connect with the trail network on the other side, or you can retrace your steps to the perimeter trail to continue this hike.

As the trail approaches the back side of Patrick Henry High School, it veers left, around the stand of pines. In a short distance, take a right, and continue along a heavily wooded section dotted with a few downed trees that act as log jumps for mountain bikers. Hikers get to just step over them.

As the trail approaches another ravine, you are walking along the park's northwestern boundary. Follow the trail left and down a steep pathway over several rutted and eroded sections. Be careful of tree roots and slipping if the trail is damp. As you reach flat land at the bottom, take a left as the path heads toward Stagg Creek.

The portions along the banks of Stagg Creek can be the best part of a hike in Poor Farm Park. Stagg Creek flows northeast to meet the South Anna River about 1.5 miles from Poor Farm Park. Depending on the time of year and how recent the last period of rain was, the creek gurgles over rocky shoals, some of which may remind you of scenery from the Blue Ridge Mountains when viewed from above.

The path undulates as it continues southwest, occasionally overlooking Stagg Creek on small bluffs, but stick to the path along the waterway when side trails beckon you left into the park's interior. There will be a couple of small wooden footbridges over tiny trickles of water seeping down to the creek. The trail follows low along the banks heading upstream, and benches offer excellent vantage points. If you planned ahead, find a spot to hop in the water and play for a while.

The woods along the creek are home to river birches, pawpaws, and beeches, while holly thickets, oaks, hickories, and some pines fill the upland forest. In the springtime, white dogwood blossoms dot the woods, and brilliant red maples catch your eye in the autumn. You may also notice the preponderance of mayapple growing on the forest floor. The foot-tall plants have umbrellalike leaves with five to seven prongs. Those with only one leaf will not flower; those with two produce a small white flower, growing where the stem forks, in or around May. A yellow berry follows in the summer. A known laxative, this berry was once incorporated into folk remedies for digestive ailments and warts, and even today it is used to produce anticancer medication.

You'll approach a trail junction not far from the amphitheater. The doubletrack path to the left leads directly back to the parking lot. Continue straight along the creek-bank trail and up a steep incline. The trail will follow a chain-link fence that marks the southwestern boundary of Poor Farm. As the trail reaches a gate in the fence, turn left to follow this doubletrack trail back north through the woods toward the parking lot from which you began. There are more trail options within this perimeter hike and in the southeastern portions of Poor Farm, known as the flats.

· ·

GPS TRAILHEAD COORDINATES N37° 46.862' W77° 32.425'

DIRECTIONS From Richmond, follow I-95 north to Exit 92, and take VA 54 (England Street) west. Drive through Ashland (VA 54 becomes West Patrick Henry Road) and in about 5 miles turn left onto VA 810 (Liberty School Road). There is a sign for the park at this intersection. Drive past Liberty Middle School to enter Poor Farm Park. Continue on the entry road, veering right, and park in a gravel lot on the right at the road's end.

A cannon overlooks the battlefield at Bloody Angle.

WEAVING ITS WAY through Spotsylvania Court House Battlefield, this national recreation trail intermittently runs along park auto-tour roads before ducking back into woods. The circuit passes numerous earthen trenches, as well as the Bloody Angle, scene of a 20-hour, rain-soaked battle, and the ruins of three period homes and Robert E. Lee's battlefield headquarters.

DESCRIPTION

Fredericksburg and Spotsylvania National Military Park encompasses four Civil War battlefields—Fredericksburg, Chancellorsville, Wilderness, and Spotsylvania Court House—where more than 100,000 soldiers perished. For a year and a half, Fredericksburg and farms to the west served as a linchpin in the defense of the Confederate capital of Richmond.

Union soldiers first attempted to cross the Rappahannock at Fredericksburg late in 1862 but were repulsed. A second crossing attempt upstream in Chancellorsville was thwarted the following spring. A year later, Federal soldiers crossed still farther upriver and met Confederate resistance at the Battle of the Wilderness. Indecisive struggles there and at Spotsylvania Court House to the south amounted to a Union victory: Grant's troops had made it across the Rappahannock and would press on to Richmond.

DISTANCE & CONFIGURATION: 5.4-mile loop

DIFFICULTY: Easy

ELEVATION: 334' at trailhead, 270' at low point

SCENERY: Recovering hardwood forest, Civil War earthworks, monuments

EXPOSURE: Some sun, some shade

TRAFFIC: Moderate; higher along roads

TRAIL SURFACE: Dirt, grass, some paved and rubber surfaces

HIKING TIME: 2.5 hours, plus time spent at tour stops

SEASON: Year-round during daylight hours; visitor center 9 a.m.–5 p.m. except Thanksgiving Day, Christmas Day, and New Year's Day

ACCESS: No fee

WHEELCHAIR ACCESS: Some of the interpretive trails

MAPS: At exhibit shelter and nps.gov/frsp /planyourvisit/trails-brochures.htm

DRIVING DISTANCE FROM CAPITOL: 56.6 miles

FACILITIES: Exhibit shelter with restrooms, audio driving tour through all 4 battlefields

CONTACT: Fredericksburg Battlefield Visitor Center: 540-693-3200, nps.gov/frsp

LOCATION: 9550 Grant Dr., Spotsylvania Courthouse

COMMENTS: The Lee vs. Grant 1864 Campaign Civil War driving trail connects to Spotsylvania Court House Battlefield. Notable on my visit, there were as many road and trail runners in the park as hikers and motorists. The park is about a dozen miles from Fredericksburg, and the well-maintained trail network and low-traffic paved roads appear to be a big draw.

Today most visitors tour the park's 7,600 acres by car. Short walking tours serve as leg stretchers along the route. Noteworthy among these is the 2-mile Gordon Flank Attack Trail at the Wilderness Battlefield Exhibit Shelter. The Spotsylvania History Trail—your route for this hike—is different, though. Rather than supplementing the park auto tour with up-close views, it lets you explore the entire battlefield on foot.

Begin your trek with an overview of the battle at the exhibit shelter near the trailhead. An illustrated aerial view of the area during the May 8–21, 1864, battle depicts the positions held by each side. Pick up a trail guide and follow the trail clockwise around the park so that you approach the tour stops in their intended order. This hike passes six of the seven recommended battlefield tour stops. The seventh could be visited on the way out if you exit via Burnside Drive.

Ignore a small sign indicating that the trail begins southbound toward VA 613 and instead head north from the parking area at the exhibit shelter to pick up the roadside singletrack just beyond a group of picnic tables on the right. Across the road runs a line of Union earthworks. Tall oaks now dominate the surrounding wood. During the Civil War, most of the battlefield was cropland. Many of the fields you see within the park were cleared by the National Park Service so as to present the land as soldiers found it.

Follow the blue blazes painted on roadside trees along the road as it dips to cross a tributary of the Ni River then curves to the east. Upton's Road will be on the right (about 0.5 mile from the trailhead). Cross the pavement to follow it southeast onto a dirt singletrack. Named for Union colonel Emory Upton, this wide path was used by his troops to assault the Georgia brigade ensconced in earthworks at Dole's Salient.

Spotsylvania Court House Battlefield

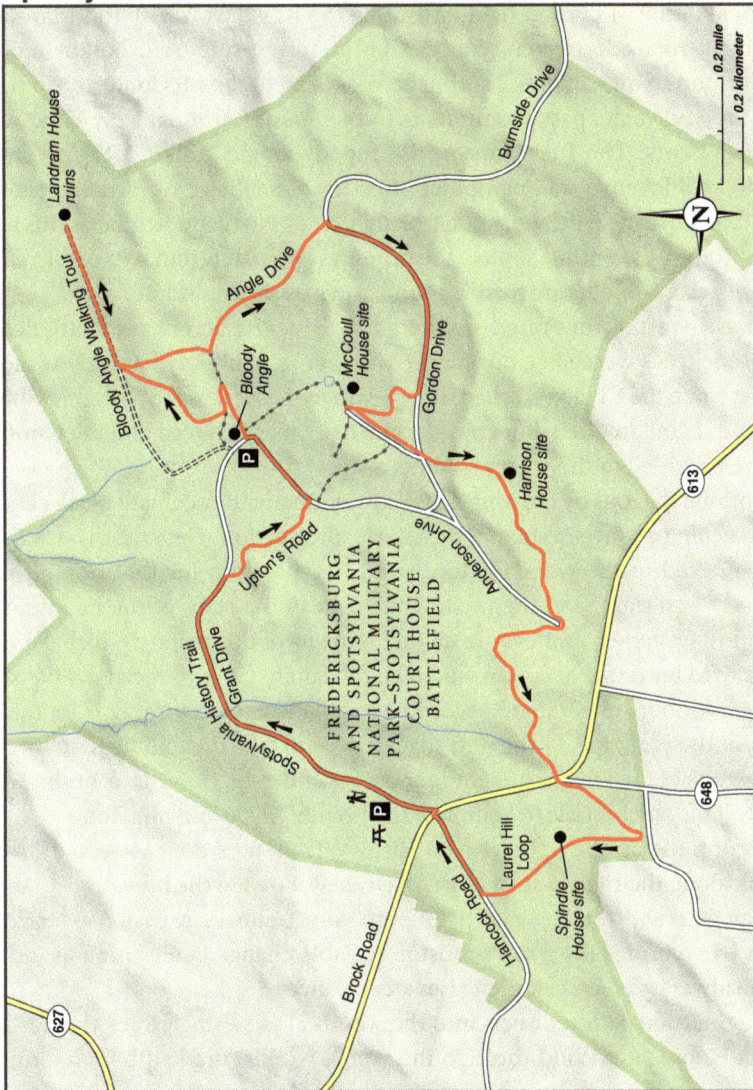

The surprise attack allowed the Federal soldiers to take 1,000 prisoners before losing an equal number of their own men in a counterattack.

The path emerges in a field at a stout granite obelisk, a monument to the Sixth Corps soldiers who fought in Upton's charge. You will bisect Dole's Salient just before reaching Anderson Drive ahead. Turn left to follow the road, crossing to the right side as you approach the epicenter of the fighting at Spotsylvania Court House, the Bloody Angle. Continue beyond the parking area, noting a side trail leaving right at the lot's southeast corner. If, after touring the Angle, you wish to forgo the loop's easternmost roadside stretch, you can backtrack to this trail. Following it south through woods, you will pass a spring before rising to the McCoull House ruins.

At Bloody Angle, pass monuments to the South Carolina, New York, and New Jersey regiments. The first stop on the Bloody Angle Walking Tour fronts these monuments. Pick up a trail pamphlet, then head northeast toward Burnside Drive. Turn left to cross the earthworks on a bridge. A solitary cannon guards this junction, and a reproduced painting depicts the gruesome conflagration that occurred here at the apex of the Confederate fortification known as the Muleshoe.

It was here that my mind wandered as I looked across the battlefield. How many of the trees were alive during the two weeks of bloody battles? At more than 150 years since the Civil War, there may be no witness trees left. In surveying the lay of the land, I couldn't help but consider the trees that survived and the comfort they may have provided to the weary soldiers.

Continue the tour by crossing a meadow dotted with cedar and black cherry trees before reaching a gravel road at a three-way intersection. General Ulysses S. Grant's troops amassed in the woods before you in preparation for their assault on Lee's Muleshoe. Turn right, and then follow the path to the ruins of the Landram House. Two opposing stone chimneys are all that remains of this manor, which survived the battle only to burn in 1905. "It would take the family years to reclaim a life shattered by just a few hours of combat," according to a park sign. Returning from the ruin, at the fork in the road, follow the sign suggestion and take the middle path through the meadow to pass the Ohio regiment monument and get a closer look at the New York and New Jersey memorials to complete the Bloody Angle Walking Tour.

To continue on the Spotsylvania History Trail, pass the east face of the salient and walk along the right side of Gordon Drive, following the blue blazes. Across the road, Confederate trenches run parallel to your trailbed. A roadside stretch along Gordon Drive brings the route's most noticeable change in elevation as it descends to the headwaters of a creek then rises steeply away.

The roadside path redirects into the woods along a singletrack that leads to the McCoull House site. Wind through the young woods, marked by numerous deadfalls, to emerge in an evergreen-dotted meadow facing the McCoull House site. Proceed to the foundation, bypassing a hard left in the History Trail. The stone rectangle is all that remains of the family home. They survived the battle by hiding in the basement. Downhill to the north is the aforementioned shortcut to the Bloody Angle.

From the McCoull House, follow the History Trail as it runs along a paved access road back to Gordon Drive. Cross the road and climb a gentle grassy slope to the stone-and-earth remains of the Harrison House. The home served as Confederate general Richard Ewell's headquarters, where Robert E. Lee pitched his tent on the lawn.

On this part of my hike, five deer could be seen munching quietly on grass. It was interesting for me to see them so relaxed because I had been hearing gunshots in the distance throughout the hike. Apparently hunters were finding deer elsewhere that day.

Follow the trail southwest to enter a forest of mixed oak, Virginia pine, and holly. The path emerges at the terminus of Anderson Drive. On your left are reconstructed earthworks. Logs brace the short stretch of trench. Soldiers propped their muskets atop those wooden walls to fire then crouched behind them to reload. The surrounding trenches of Lee's Last Line were built by General Martin Smith, who also oversaw the fortification of Confederate positions at Vicksburg and New Orleans.

After examining the re-created earthworks, proceed west on the trail, with the original trench line on your left. Cross a wooden footbridge to weave through a dense wood. A second footbridge crosses the headwaters of another creek just ahead. Leaving the western trench of Lee's Last Line, the path emerges from the pines near Brock Road.

Carefully cross the road, and bear left on a path that runs along a wide field punctuated by a large double-trunk sycamore. Briefly enter the adjacent forest of Virginia pines and red oaks to approach a turn-of-the-20th-century monument. Placed by a judge wounded in the fighting, it honors the Maryland regiment defending Spotsylvania Court House that opened the battle with a charge across the field at Laurel Hill.

Emerging from the woods, head north across the field, bisecting an old farm road. Ahead, the trail runs beside a band of trees then enters woods to cross a streamlet on a footbridge. After a short, winding ascent across a Union trench line, turn right on Hancock Road and look for a sign with information about Warren's Line. Recross Brock Road and stop to read about Union general John Sedgwick, who was honored with a monument at the park entrance. Another park sign details the Laurel Hill Trail, most of which was accomplished on this hike but can be done on its own as a 1-mile loop. From here, the History Trail runs along Grant Drive a short distance back to the trailhead at the exhibit shelter.

• •

GPS TRAILHEAD COORDINATES N38° 13' 07.2912" W77° 36' 53.9672"

DIRECTIONS From Richmond, head north on I-95 to Exit 118. Head west on VA 606 (Mudd Tavern/Morris Road) 5.1 miles, then turn right onto VA 208 (Old Block House Lane/Lake Anna Parkway). Continue 3.9 miles north before turning left onto VA 608 (Robert East Lee Drive). Shortly after, turn right, onto VA 648 (Old Block House Lane). Turn left onto VA 613 (Brock Road). Look for Grant Drive shortly ahead on the right. Bear right, then park in the lot on your left at the Spotsylvania Battlefield Exhibit Shelter.

46 WESTMORELAND STATE PARK

Horsehead Cliffs overlook the tidal waters of the Potomac River at Westmoreland State Park.

LEAVING FROM ITS TRAILHEAD along the park road, the Turkey Neck Trail heads southeast then forks to create a loop. Hiked counterclockwise, the loop descends a ridge to trace Big Meadow Run through a swampy valley. Follow a lengthy boardwalk to the sandy Potomac River shore for views of Horsehead Cliffs before turning around to complete the loop. Optional trailheads let you interchange the strings on this balloon hike.

DESCRIPTION

One of the commonwealth's first state parks, 1,321-acre Westmoreland was constructed by the New Deal–era Civilian Conservation Corps (CCC) and opened in 1936. With shovels and wheelbarrows, young men left jobless by the Depression were put to work building roads and trails. The trees they felled served to build the conference center, with its rough-hewn log beams and flooring. Stationed atop the 150-foot Horsehead Cliffs, the center overlooks the wide Potomac River.

Shale-dolomite cliffs run along much of the park's almost 2-mile shoreline. Gradually eroding, the whitish cliffs are crowned with wind-shaped pines. Visitors often take to rented kayaks or canoes to approach the striated rock face and scan it for fossils, reminders of the ancient sea that once covered the Chesapeake Bay basin.

DISTANCE & CONFIGURATION: 3.3-mile loop, with a few spurs and optional additional trails

DIFFICULTY: Moderate

ELEVATION: 133' at trailhead, 8' at lowest point

SCENERY: Hardwood forest, marshy creek valley, Potomac Beach

EXPOSURE: Shaded in forest, exposed on boardwalk and at the shore

TRAFFIC: Moderate

TRAIL SURFACE: Dirt, 1 extensive boardwalk, sandy along beach

HIKING TIME: 2 hours

SEASON: Year-round during daylight hours, cabins year-round, campground March 1–first Monday in December, pool Memorial Day–Labor Day

ACCESS: Parking weekdays $5, weekends $7, campsites from $20

WHEELCHAIR ACCESS: Restrooms, visitor center, campground, pool; wheelchairs not recommended on most trails

MAPS: At visitor center, trailhead, and dcr.virginia.gov/state-parks/westmoreland

DRIVING DISTANCE FROM CAPITOL: 72 miles

FACILITIES: Restrooms, visitor center, meeting facility, campground, cabins, coin laundry, riverside picnic area, swimming pool, boat launch, boat rentals

CONTACT: 804-493-8821, dcr.virginia.gov/state-parks/westmoreland

LOCATION: 145 Cliff Rd., Montross

COMMENTS: A water trail of the Captain John Smith Chesapeake National Historic Trail connects to Westmoreland State Park. The park gets very crowded on the weekends, especially along the Potomac River. Campgrounds often fill up early as well; consider planning ahead with reservations.

The visitor center displays a collection of shark teeth recovered from the cliffs, one of several exhibits on Chesapeake ecology.

Speaking of shark teeth, on a previous trip to Westmoreland, we made the discovery of a lifetime while paddling along the shoreline below Horsehead Cliffs. We found what is likely the tooth of a *Carcharodon megalodon*, a prehistoric shark that is estimated to have been three times the size of a great white shark. Megalodon went extinct at least 2.6 million years ago. The triangular tooth is the size of an adult palm, roughly 5 inches point to point. We found it just sitting on the shoreline in an area that showed a fair amount of erosion. We later compared it to hundreds of other teeth on display in the visitor center, and ours was the biggest. Quite a find.

Anglers with modern marine life in mind can rent boats near the Potomac River boat launch. Nearby, at the western base of the cliffs, swimmers and sunbathers enjoy an Olympic-size pool, and picnickers fill the tables along the sandy shoreline, an area often packed with visitors enjoying the Potomac. The river is almost 6 miles wide in this area. Keep in mind that as soon as you touch the water, you're in Maryland.

This northwestern corner also offers an alternate trailhead to elongate the hike outlined here. The Laurel Point Trail departs from the boat launch just west of the parking lot. Getting off to a steep start, it then climbs moderately, skirting a cluster of cabins. The path then descends to cross a streamlet running beside Rock Spring Pond. Bound by Westmoreland's tall bluffs, the pond drains west as Potter's Branch. After feeding into Canal Swamp, itself a tributary of Pope's Creek, the water meets the Potomac near the site of George Washington's birth. The Laurel Point Trail,

243

Westmoreland State Park

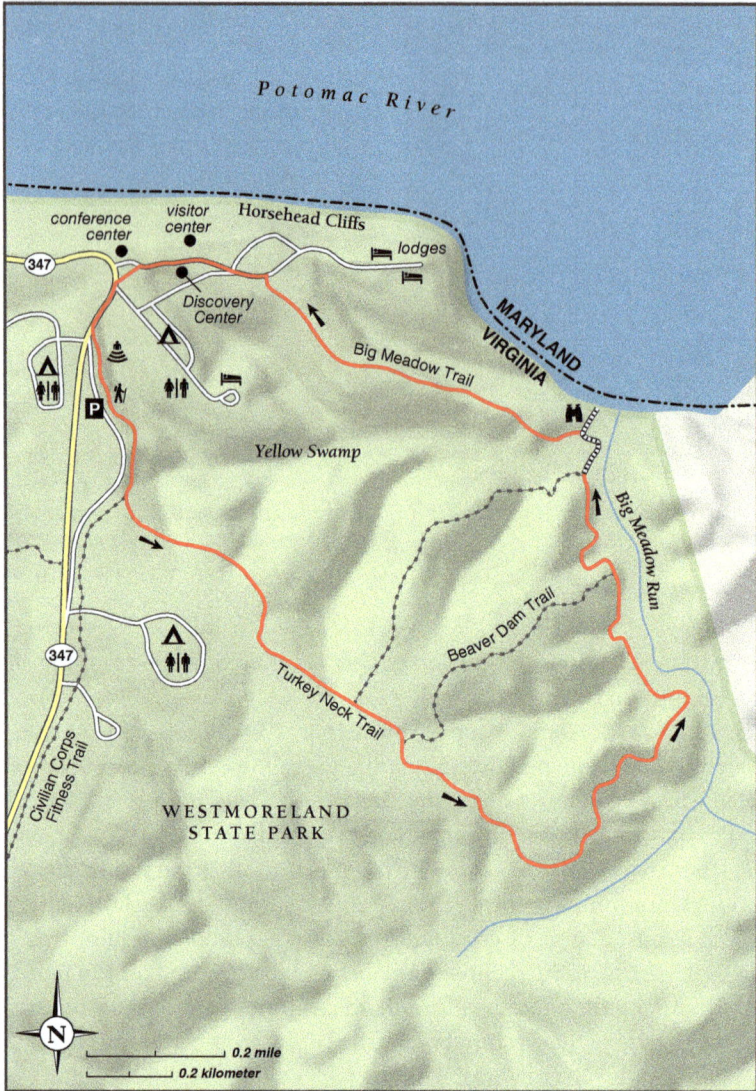

Potomac River

conference center

visitor center

Horsehead Cliffs

lodges

347

Discovery Center

MARYLAND

VIRGINIA

Big Meadow Trail

P

Yellow Swamp

Big Meadow Run

347

Beaver Dam Trail

Turkey Neck Trail

Civilian Corps Fitness Trail

WESTMORELAND STATE PARK

N

0.2 mile

0.2 kilometer

however, bends eastward to scale a hillside forested with towering beech trees. After crossing the park road, pass through Campground C to reach the loop portion of the Turkey Neck Trail via a short spur. Turn right and continue as follows. This longer option totals 5.5 miles.

The proper start to the balloon-shaped Turkey Neck Trail is on the east side of the park road, just south of the camp store and Campground A. Curving left shortly away from the park road, the path veers steadily deeper into the forest. If you want to add 3.2 miles, follow the red-blazed Conservation Corps Fitness Trail, which is a paved and gravel out-and-back that has trailside fitness equipment.

To continue our hike, follow the blue-blazed path through a parcel of mixed forest along a wide doubletrack trail where Virginia pines and mountain laurel green the woods. Your wide, sandy path dips twice then curves right behind Campground C to undulate once more before reaching a trail junction. The Turkey Neck Trail heads in two directions here; follow it to the right.

Ahead, bypass the Beaver Dam Trail when it branches off to the left. (You can use the Beaver Dam Trail to make a figure eight if you wish, adding a mile to your total, or use it to cut off the northwestern segment of the Turkey Neck balloon, reducing your hike by about 0.5 mile.) The wide Turkey Neck Trail continues along a broad, level hilltop that abounds with white and southern red oak. The path extends east onto a ridge, and inlets of Yellow Swamp on Big Meadow Run are visible below.

Descend from the ridge to the valley floor on wooden steps as a view of the creek-fed swamp opens before you. Approach quietly, and you may well find a heron stalking prey or a woodpecker hammering at the still-standing trunk of a downed tree. Work your way along the base of the hillside, green with patches of ferns and club moss. The trail here is narrowed singletrack and laced with exposed roots. A boardwalk aids your passage north beneath the bluffs, but watch for a muddy stretch that follows before the trail climbs just slightly onto the hillside.

To your right, water-tolerant red maples, also fittingly called swamp maples, dot the grassy marsh. Stands of poplar rise across the marsh-grass expanse. An early-autumn visit will find Yellow Swamp ablaze in color. The trail descends a flight of wooden steps, opening to a vista of the Potomac ahead. Beech trees shade the final stretch of trail before you reach a boardwalk (where we spotted a curious skink) before the Beaver Dam Trail descends to enter on your left. The trail follows along the tidal marsh before another lengthy boardwalk that connects with a 15-foot observation platform constructed at its center.

As you follow the L-shaped boardwalk out across the marsh, look for small crabs scuttling about in the muck below. Perched on the observation platform, patient visitors can see beavers and muskrats gliding through the marsh, ospreys and hawks circling overhead, and turtles coming out to sun themselves on fallen trees. At the boardwalk's terminus, Big Meadow Trail heads left, but follow a spur to the right to visit the beach.

Strewn with driftwood, clamshells, and flotsam, the narrow, rustic beach runs west beneath rising cliffs. Fallen trees evidence the ongoing erosion. Natural-history buffs can scramble over them and walk a short distance along the beach to scan the cliff face for fossils. If you're staying in one of the lodges, consider taking Big Meadow Trail to this spot early in the morning, when the rising sun illuminates the east-facing cliff wall.

To complete this hike, retrace your steps across the boardwalk, and turn right. The Turkey Neck Trail traces the periphery of a blackwater swamp on the right then becomes Big Meadow Trail, which traverse a short boardwalk before rising out of the bottomland and onto a narrow ridge. Initially, mountain laurel crowds the path, with holly displacing it as the ridge widens. A few tall specimens of Virginia pine grow amid the oaks and beeches. Watch for educational signs along the path that identify at least 10 tree species found along Big Meadow Trail, including pawpaw, mockernut hickory, black cherry, and dogwood. The winding path soon regains the hilltop junction at the park's visitor center, which sits atop Horsehead Cliffs. The view of the Potomac from here is spectacular. Follow the park road and look for a trail that connects back to the camp store, your starting point.

NEARBY ACTIVITIES

Virginia's Potomac shoreline is rich with history, and **Westmoreland State Park** (804-493-8821, dcr.virginia.gov) makes a good base camp for anyone looking to couple outdoor recreation with excursions to nearby historical sites. Bordering the park on the west is **Stratford Hall** (804-493-8038, stratfordhall.org), birthplace of Robert E. Lee. The plantation manor and grounds are open for tours. Just west of Stratford Hall is **George Washington Birthplace National Monument** (804-224-1732, nps.gov/gewa), which has a short hike of its own.

• •

GPS TRAILHEAD COORDINATES N38° 10.054' W76° 52.081'

DIRECTIONS From Richmond, take US 360 E. Turn left onto US 360/VA 17 and head north through Tappahannock. At the second light, past Lowery's Restaurant, turn right to continue on US 360 E. At the third stoplight, turn left onto VA 3 W (Kings Highway). Stay on this road until about 6 miles past Montross, then turn right into the park's entrance on VA 347 (State Park Road).

The Mattaponi River meanders slowly around the shoreline of Zoar State Forest.

DIVIDED INTO TWO NONCONTIGUOUS PARCELS, Zoar State Forest has two separate hikes, each with its own character. The Main Trail passes the Pollard family farmstead and highlights forestry practices en route. The Nature Trail traces the scenic Mattaponi River and its tributary Herring Creek.

DESCRIPTION

The town of Aylett was named for William Aylett, whose Colonial estate was located here. In 1782, Robert Pollard purchased the land north of town that would become his family's farmstead. According to forest literature, Aylett was, at the time, a cross-roads of such ill repute that Pollard named his home Mount Zoar in reference to the biblical city where Lot took refuge after fleeing Gomorrah. Flames engulfed the manse in 1885. The present structure was erected in 1890. It remained in the family until 1987, when it was donated to the state by Pollard's great-great-grandson. The white hilltop house now serves as the forest office.

Like all of Virginia's state forests, the 378-acre Zoar is self-sustaining. Unlike most, it includes crop fields still under cultivation, along with forestry-demonstration areas and hunting by permit. Fishing is also allowed. The forest maintains a canoe put-in on Herring Creek, allowing paddlers to make a 4-mile oxbow trip to the Virginia Department of Game and Inland Fisheries boat landing at US 360.

DISTANCE & CONFIGURATION: Main Trail: 1.8-mile balloon; Nature Trail: 2 loops totaling 1.4 miles

DIFFICULTY: Easy

ELEVATION: 72' at trailhead, 7' at low point

SCENERY: Hardwood-forested bluffs, boggy bottomland, Mattaponi River, pine plantation, wetland pond, old farmhouse

EXPOSURE: Limited shade on Main Trail; well shaded on Nature Trail

TRAFFIC: Low

TRAIL SURFACE: Dirt, some gravel doubletrack on Main Trail

HIKING TIME: 2 hours

SEASON: Year-round during daylight hours

ACCESS: No fee; no ATVs

WHEELCHAIR ACCESS: Wheelchairs not recommended

MAPS: On signboards in the parking area and at trailheads, and at dof.virginia.gov/stateforest/list/zoar.htm

DRIVING DISTANCE FROM CAPITOL: 27.3 miles

FACILITIES: Parking, boat launch in northern section; no restrooms

CONTACT: 804-769-2962, dof.virginia.gov/stateforest/list/zoar.htm

LOCATION: 4445 Upshaw Rd., Aylett

COMMENTS: The Nature Trail is divided into the Mattaponi Bluffs and Herring Creek loops. Guides detailing the stops along each are available online. Mountain biking allowed only on the Main Trail.

The forest's two trails total 3.2 miles. Though they can't be combined—unless you want to take a 2-mile road walk—both can be hiked in a single visit.

MAIN TRAIL

A booklet detailing Zoar's Main Trail is available from a signboard in the parking area. With a focus on forestry education, it lists the sights and environments along the route. Begin by heading up the gravel doubletrack that leads to the old Pollard home, which is shaded by a broad beech and numerous cedars. The road passes below the home on the east then curves up between it and the family cemetery. In addition to the brick-walled graveyard, several outbuildings surround the house. When the gravel ends, follow a mowed path behind (west of) the graveyard. The path borders a cultivated field on the left and a barn on the right before it turns right. Downhill, turn left upon intersecting another mowed path that is a continuation of the entrance road. An open-sided metal maintenance shelter stands to your left.

The Main Trail now proceeds between two fields. In each, native shrubs and grasses serve as both cover and a food source for rabbits, quails, and songbirds. Another mowed path enters on the right. This out-and-back detour leads to a field planted with warm-season grasses designed to attract young quail. Along the loop, the cultivated field reappears on your left as the shrubbery on your right rises to a hardwood forest.

The trail then veers right to enter the woods on a wide path. The Main Trail continues beneath tall willow oaks and alongside sassafras and cedar saplings before the tree population shifts to include more Virginia pines. After crossing a small creek on a rudimentary bridge, turn right upon reaching a T intersection. A left would

Zoar State Forest

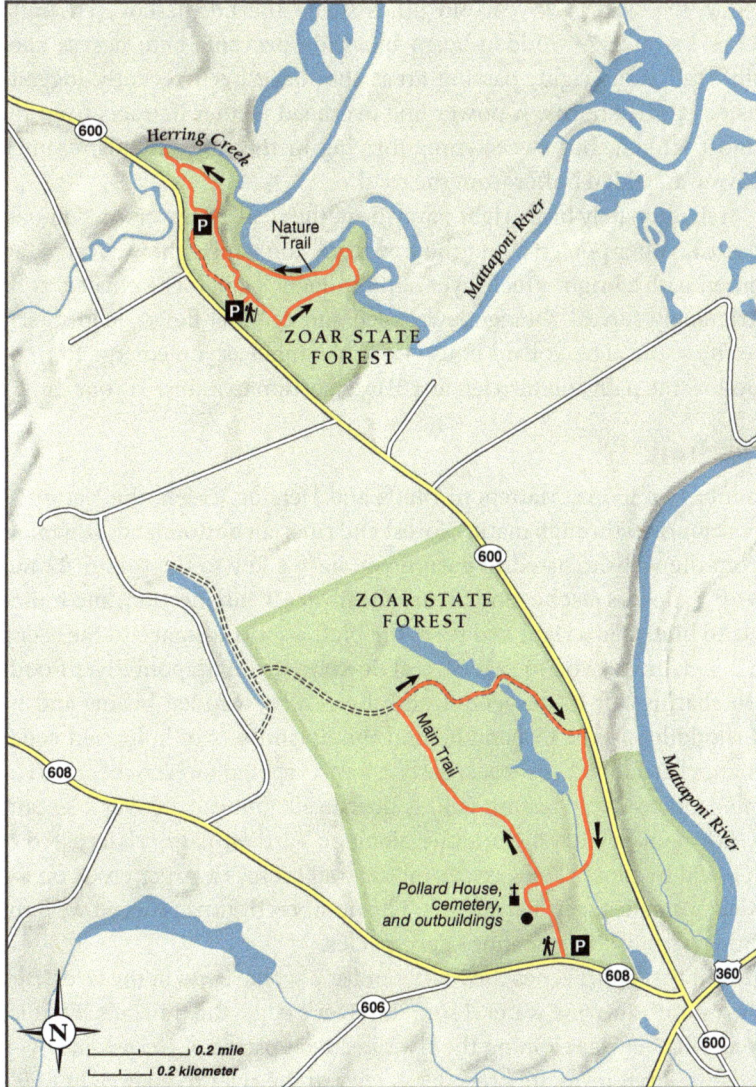

take you on an out-and-back spur to four demonstration plots that are also planted with pines but in different densities.

The creek you just crossed feeds a swampy wood ahead on your right, shaded by river birch and red maple. The creek then drains into a wetland pond visible on both sides of the raised trail. A small wooden dock on the left provides views across the marsh. Rotting tree trunks protrude from the shallow impoundment, and grasses fringe the pond.

Beyond the water, 20-year-old pines shade the needle-covered trail until it approaches VA 600. A wooden-beam blockade prevents auto access ahead, and the Main Trail turns right, passing areas that have been recently logged and/or have hosted control burns. A power line overhead further detracts from the loop's easternmost stretch, but sweet gums thriving in the now-abundant sunlight will soon provide an added buffer from the road.

The trail ultimately bears right, away from the road, to traverse a demonstration-wetland road. Water pooled about the tree trunks on your right is covered, at least in the summer, with a bright-green layer of tiny aquatic plants. The effect is at first eerie then intriguingly surreal. Orange jewelweed and cardinal flower lend their brilliant colors to the scene. The Pollard house is visible uphill as you emerge from the trees. Simply follow the path and turn left at a T intersection to return to your car.

NATURE TRAIL

Divided into two loops, Mattaponi Bluffs and Herring Creek, the Nature Trail is a singletrack journey through mature forest and riparian bottomland. Download a trail guide from the website listed to ensure you have a key to the route's 22 numbered stops. Stop 1 appears just beyond the trailhead, at a T intersection, and indicates this is an upland bluff. Turn right and trace the bluff a short distance to the second stop, where a bench invites you to gaze 50 feet down to the Mattaponi River floodplain.

Turn sharply left to descend a path braced by wooden beams and bordered by wild rhododendrons. Leaving behind the upland mix of holly, red cedar, white oak, and mockernut hickory trees, enter a fern-carpeted forest of beech, river birch, red maple, and swamp chestnut oak. A boardwalk guides you over a streamlet that scarcely flows on dry days. Continue along an earthen path crisscrossed by roots and blanketed by moss. The easy-to-follow trail crosses a larger creek on a wooden bridge then a smaller seasonal stream. The numbered stops proceed with the route, highlighting various forest features and species.

The trail first approaches the Mattaponi at a scenic bend in the river. Birch trees shade the smooth-flowing water. From the river's edge, the trail cuts left, bisecting a small peninsula before rejoining the river headed upstream. Occasional overgrowth crowds the trail but invariably recedes. Views of the river to your right reward your persistence. Look for turtles sunning on rocks and beavers that have gnawed trees along the trail. The path traverses additional culverts on wooden bridges, periodically venturing inland to more open glades, including a mature stand of holly.

Approaching its halfway point, the trail turns inland (left) to cross an old river channel on a boardwalk. Sedimentation and erosion have rerouted the river, but this low-lying area still holds water and is routinely drenched by the surging river. Gazes to each side of the boardwalk show fallen trees with wide, exposed, and upturned root balls. Across the boardwalk, ascend a steep flight of wooden steps to regain the bluff.

Turn right and continue, descending gradually then steeply, to emerge in a gravel parking area. Along the way, look for a granite marker with the inscription: "Capt. John Smith. To the cross hath bin discoverd. A.D. 1607." The misspellings, I assume, were accurate to historical writing.

At the base of the bluff in the parking area, two paths head north and uphill on stairs from the lot. Take the one on the right. Approaching it, you'll see a third spur that departs eastbound to the canoe put-in and views of Herring Creek's confluence with the Mattaponi. Herring Creek was named for the fish that spawn here in the spring. *River herring* refers to either of two difficult-to-distinguish species: alewife and blueback herring. River herring have drawn fishers since Colonial times, but modern anglers are more likely after striped bass that forage for herring hatchlings.

The Nature Trail rises from the lot to the bluff above Herring Creek. After curving westward through open forest above the creek, the trail reaches a T intersection. Turn right for an out-and-back visit to the 20-foot-wide creek. Relax for a moment on the sandy shore before returning uphill and continuing straight through the intersection. The trail briefly comes within sight of VA 600 before curving away to the left, with traffic audible through the trees. The trail guide highlights a beech tree perforated by small cavities—one almost expects a pair of owl eyes to glare back— and an oak with a goiterlike growth on its trunk.

The Nature Trail's northernmost loop is soon completed, as you descend back to the canoe put-in parking lot. Continue, ascending back to the bluff-top trail on which you arrived. You'll pass the wooden stairs on your left, then wind slightly through an abundance of rhododendrons and laurel before reaching an intersection. A right takes you back to the trailhead lot.

• •

GPS TRAILHEAD COORDINATES
N37° 47.251' W77° 06.567' (Main Trail)
N37° 48.344' W77° 7.286' (Nature Trail)

DIRECTIONS From Richmond, follow US 360 northeast to the hamlet of Aylett (about 20 miles beyond I-295). In Aylett, turn left onto VA 600 (West River Road). To reach the Pollard homestead—now the forest office—make an immediate left onto VA 606 (Upshaw Road). There is a sign indicating this turn. The trailhead for the Main Trail is 0.2 mile ahead on the right. The forest office/farmhouse is up the hill. A trailhead kiosk advises visitors to park in a small lot outside the often-locked gate. To reach the Nature Trail, continue straight on VA 600 for 1.7 miles, then turn right at a forest sign. The trailhead is in the northern corner of the first parking lot, to the right of the gravel road. A second lot down the road accesses the canoe put-in at Herring Creek.

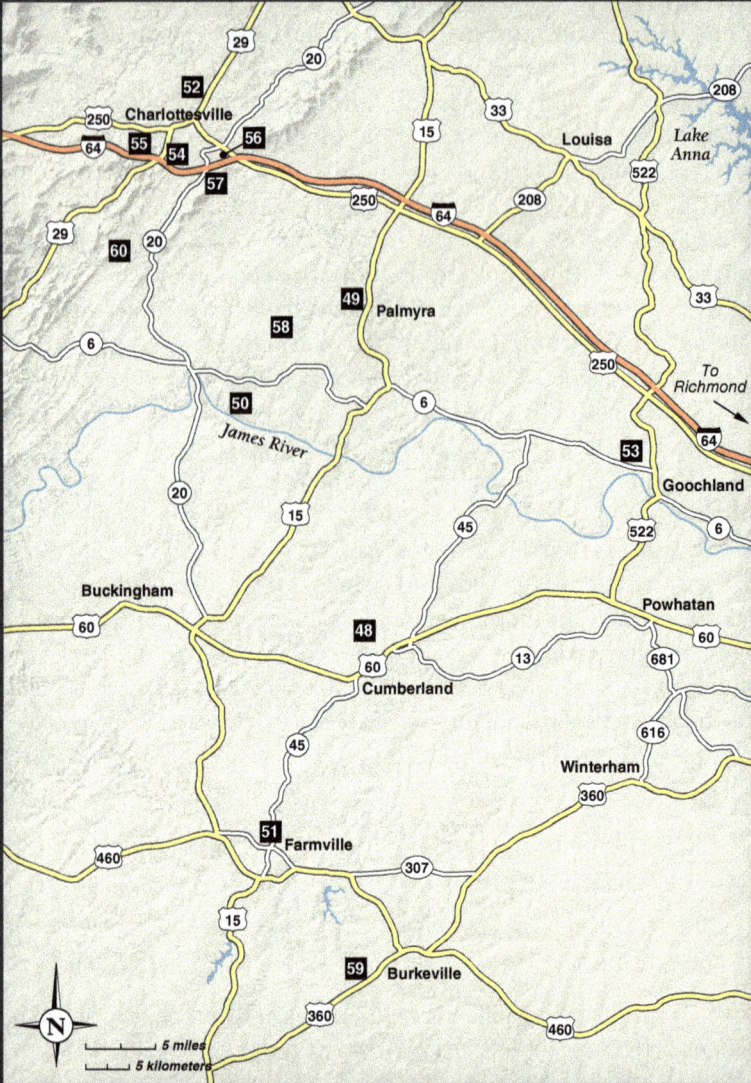

WEST TO CHARLOTTESVILLE AND CENTRAL VIRGINIA

Ducks enjoy the calm waters of Bear Creek Lake.

THIS COMPACT JAUNT showcases the natural beauty of the park's woodlands. Birds linger on the marshy periphery of Bear Creek Lake. The Lost Barr Loop on the west side of the lake was completed in 2007. You can add 2 miles to this hike by taking the Channel Cat Loop Trail on the eastern side of the lake; the loop circles the campgrounds on that side and offers ample informational signage and educational interpretation.

DESCRIPTION

Just 329 acres, Bear Creek Lake State Park is engulfed by the 16,000-acre Cumberland State Forest. But the park has the larger lake (at 40 acres) and all the amenities to make it a popular weekend-camping destination. On crowded days, the surrounding forest makes it easy to escape the throngs for either hiking or fishing. But you may find that, with everyone lounging on the beach, this hike is surprisingly serene. It skirts the eastern shore of Bear Creek Lake, crossing Little Bear Creek then tracing the western shoreline, which offers enticing views of the beach, campgrounds, and open waters of the placid lake.

It's hard to believe, threading beneath tall oaks along the creek, that this land was farmed as early as the 1740s. Though most of that former cropland has been reforested, evidence of its agrarian past remains. A monument on VA 663 marks the

DISTANCE & CONFIGURATION: 5-mile out-and-back with balloon, plus optional spurs and loops

DIFFICULTY: Moderate

ELEVATION: 302' at trailhead, 357' at high point

SCENERY: Hardwood and mixed forests, small streams, Bear Creek Lake

EXPOSURE: Shaded, except segments along the lakeshore

TRAFFIC: Moderate

TRAIL SURFACE: Dirt singletrack

HIKING TIME: 2.5 hours

SEASON: Year-round, 8 a.m.–sunset

ACCESS: Parking $4, campsites from $30 with hookups or $20 without hookups, cabins from $119

WHEELCHAIR ACCESS: At restrooms, snack bar, some campsites; no trail access

MAPS: At park and dcr.virginia.gov/state-parks/bear-creek-lake

DRIVING DISTANCE FROM CAPITOL: 54 miles

FACILITIES: Restrooms; picnic shelters; grills; campground; cabins; showers; snack bar; playground; archery range; swimming beach; boat launch; canoe, kayak, and rowboat rentals Memorial Day–Labor Day; meeting facility

CONTACT: 804-492-4410, dcr.virginia.gov/state-parks/bear-creek-lake

LOCATION: 22 Bear Creek Lake Rd., Cumberland

COMMENTS: Visitors can also enjoy the adjoining 16,000-acre Cumberland State Forest, including the 14-mile Cumberland Multiuse Trail, which is available for hiking, biking, and horseback riding. There is limited cell phone service in Bear Creek Lake State Park. They offer emergency phones in the Acorn Loop campground and outside the linen building in the cabin area. I did not have trouble tracking the hike by GPS.

homestead of Jesse Thomas, a Revolutionary War colonel who famously warned Baron von Steuben of Cornwallis's impending attack. On a rainy June 2, 1781, Thomas rode his horse Fearnaught as far north as the James then swam the river to the Continental camp. Also in Cumberland State Forest is the Charles Irving Thornton tombstone, a registered landmark bearing an inscription written by Charles Dickens. Found in the small Oak Hill Cemetery off VA 629, the tombstone marks the infant's grave with an original 31-line epitaph.

The US government purchased most of the surrounding land from struggling farmers under President Franklin Roosevelt's New Deal then leased it to the commonwealth. Some 100 farmers and laborers left jobless by the Depression found work with the Virginia Department of Agriculture, damming Bear Creek and erecting this park's first pavilions and grills. You can still identify their handiwork near the park's beach: shelters made with rough-hewn logs and freestanding stone hearths. In 1940, the park was one of six original parks deeded to the nascent state-park system. It was operated as a day-use recreation area until 1962, when campgrounds were added.

This hike begins at the northeast parking area for the lake and beach, which also offers a snack bar and picnic area. A singletrack trail descends from the lot to a creekbed and over a wooden bridge. Take a right onto the orange-blazed Lakeside Trail to approach the lakeshore.

Look for yellow poplar, red maple, and hornbeam as you near the lake, then follow the shoreline southeast. The trail bends inland alongside slow-flowing Little Bear Creek, and birch trees shade a spit of land opposite. Ascending just slightly,

Bear Creek Lake State Park

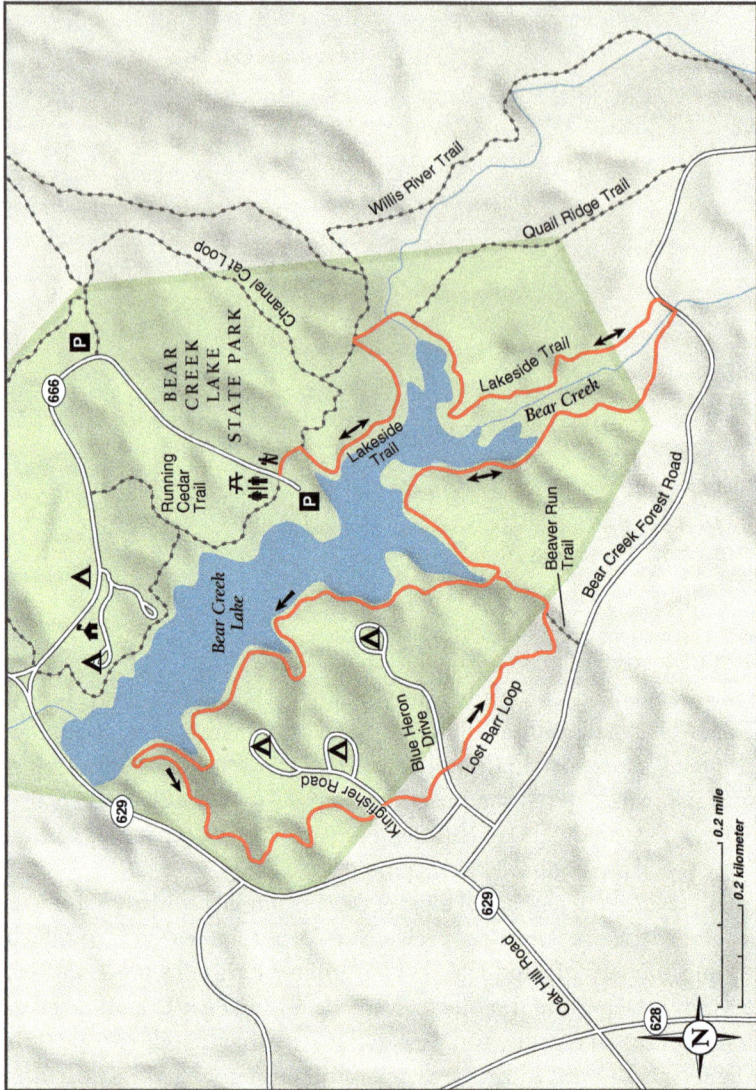

you reach a trail junction. Straight ahead is a spur trail to Willis River Trail, but turn right to stay with Lakeside Trail as it rounds the easternmost finger of the lake on a lengthy boardwalk. Beaver-gnawed stumps spike the flat where smaller streamlets convene and flow into the lake. Look for salamanders in the pools that dot the flood-plain. On your right, the lake extends beside the aforementioned birch trees.

Across the boardwalk, step over a small streamlet to reach another junction. Here Quail Ridge Trail leads toward the Cumberland Multiuse Trail, but bypass it to continue through northern red and white oaks. Rounding a peninsula in the lake, look for waterfowl and songbirds amid the shrubs and sycamores on the small islands below. Trace a finger of the lake south as it narrows to the point where Bear Creek empties into its namesake. Birches arc from another spit of land here and shade the creek as the path turns to follow it.

Sandy banks flank the water on your right; a chorus of frogs is audible in all but the coolest months. Look for beaver dams and raccoon tracks along the sandy shores of the creek before the trail veers left to wind between younger mixed forest and riparian bottomland. White blazes indicate that you're now on the Lakeside Trail, which takes you beyond the park boundary to Bear Creek Forest Road. You can extend the hike mapped here by turning right onto the forest road then right again back into the woods (still on the Lakeside Trail). Follow the path north along a finger of the lake, and after crossing a brook over a small rock garden, you'll reach a junction with the 1.7-mile Lost Barr Loop.

Our hike followed the Lost Barr Loop counterclockwise. The trail follows pine woodlands above the lake and traces marshes along the water's edge before looping back behind the cabins to this trail junction with the Lakeside Trail.

The mixed forest extends along the shoreline. Southern red oak, white oak, beech, and shagbark hickory overtake occasional stands of pine and cedar. We stopped for a snack at a picnic table overlook, which offered a nice view of the beach and fishing pier, located just across the lake. We listened as a mother instructed her young son how to paddle and keep a canoe straight in open water before they stopped to cast their fishing lines.

Continuing along the purple-blazed Lost Barr Loop, on a path of mostly crushed stone, you will pass below the park's upscale cabins, which offer two- and three-bedroom options. All provide connections to the trail and the shoreline.

At about the 2.5-mile mark of this hike, the trail takes a sharp left into the woods, away from the shoreline. Oak Hill Road and the dam for Bear Creek Lake may be visible from here, depending on the tree canopy during your visit. This portion of the hike traverses several small ridges and is mostly in shade. The trail exits Bear Creek Lake for about 0.5 mile as it approaches Kingfisher Road (which accesses cabins). Cross that paved road and Blue Heron Drive before completing Lost Barr and reconnecting with the Lakeside Trail. Retrace your steps back to the parking area, about 1.5 miles.

NEARBY ACTIVITIES

If you have the time and energy, try the trails at **Cumberland State Forest** (804-492-4121, dof.virginia.gov/stateforest/list/cumberland.htm), which envelops the park. The Willis River Trail is a 16-mile point-to-point, and the Cumberland State Forest Multiuse Trail is an 8.4-mile loop with optional extensions. Both intersect the state park's trail network at multiple points and afford numerous route permutations.

While camping is allowed only within the state park, there are four lakes, each smaller than Bear Creek Lake, where you can generally fish in solitude. Bonbrook, Arrowhead, Oak Hill, and Winston Lakes have boat launches and are stocked with largemouth bass, sunfish, and channel catfish. The forest also operates a wheelchair-accessible sporting-clay range. Also, consider hiking an out-and-back stint on the Willis River Trail, which offers views from atop a rocky bluff, tracing the rocky Little Bear Creek through open, mature hardwoods. The trail is popular with horseback riders and mountain bikers.

• •

GPS TRAILHEAD COORDINATES N37° 31.728' W78° 16.211'

DIRECTIONS From Richmond, travel west on US 60 (Midlothian Turnpike). Continue through Midlothian and Powhatan to Cumberland, seat of its eponymous county (about 40 miles west of Chippenham Parkway). East of town you will pass VA 622 (Trent's Mill Road) on the right, which is signed for Bear Creek Lake State Park. Follow the road 3.3 miles north, then turn left onto VA 629 at Bear Creek Market. Veer left again after 0.8 mile to pass the park office and entrance-fee station. The trailhead is on the left 0.4 mile ahead, beyond the campgrounds and at the snack shop and beach area.

A couple of hikers on the Lost Barr Loop

49 FLUVANNA HERITAGE TRAIL

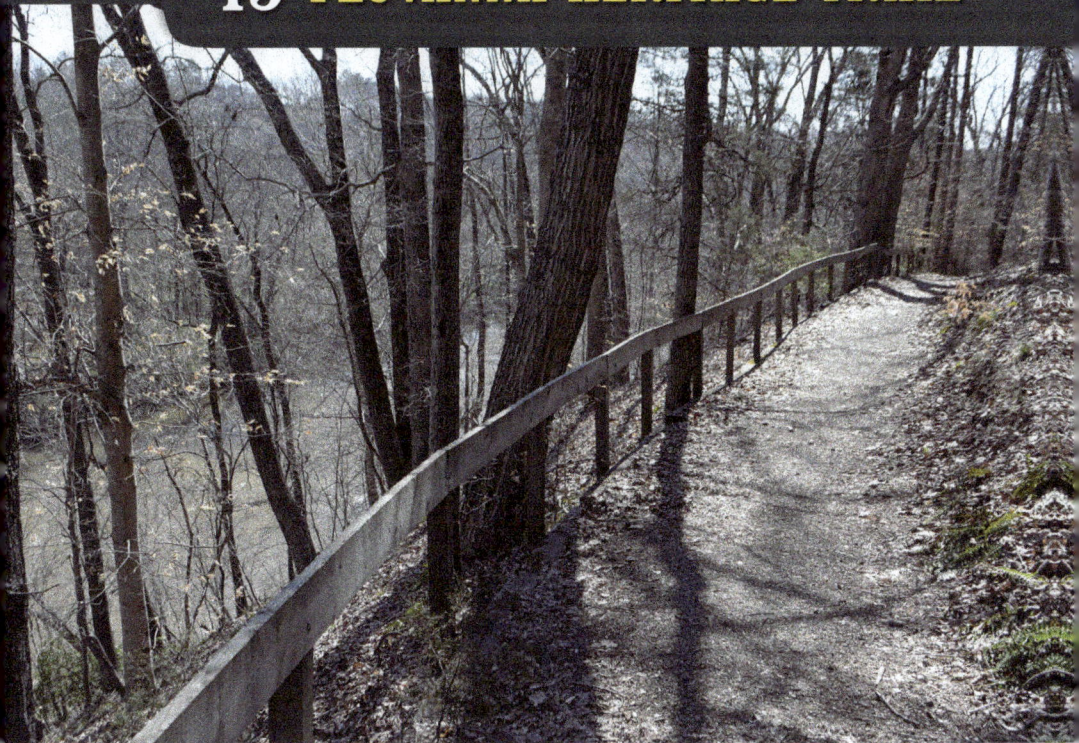

A railing along a high bluff overlooking the Rivanna River on the Heritage Trail

A DESCENT FROM THE EASTERN TRAILHEAD to a pebbled shoal on the Rivanna River affords hikers an up-close encounter with the waterway they will only glimpse through the trees for most of this hike. After running along hilly bluffs between recovering forest and a riparian floodplain, the route ventures to a second overlook at Burke Creek then uphill to the former Haden farmstead. A return trip loops through meadows and mixed forests farther up the same ravines from the first half of the hike.

DESCRIPTION

Fluvanna's history is inseparable from that of the Rivanna River, which bisects the county and meets the James on the county's eastern border. Besides providing water to farms, the river powered mills and carried crops to market. The Fluvanna Heritage Trail traces the river's western shore, opposite the hamlet of Palmyra, itself a tribute to the area's rich past.

The names Fluvanna and Rivanna are both vestiges of the reign of Queen Anne, for whom English colonists also named the North and South Anna Rivers. The name Fluvanna—the Latin equivalent of Rivanna—was applied to the James west of its confluence with the Rivanna River, though its usage was later abandoned.

DISTANCE & CONFIGURATION: 6.7-mile figure eight, with many optional spurs

DIFFICULTY: Moderate

ELEVATION: 297' at trailhead, 382' at high point

SCENERY: Hillside forest and bottomland along Rivanna River

EXPOSURE: Mostly shaded along river; more open near trailheads; open field through Quail Meadow bird-watching area

TRAFFIC: Low

TRAIL SURFACE: Dirt, rocks, grass

HIKING TIME: 3 hours

SEASON: Year-round during daylight hours (museum and visitor center hours vary with the seasons)

ACCESS: No fee

WHEELCHAIR ACCESS: First 0.5 mile follows accessible gravel trail to riverside; wheelchairs not recommended on full route

MAPS: On signboard at hilltop eastern trailhead near dog park and restrooms, and at fluvanna county.org/parksrec/page/trails-pleasant-grove

DRIVING DISTANCE FROM CAPITOL: 58 miles

FACILITIES: Restrooms; picnic shelters and dog park at eastern trailhead; picnic tables and museum at western trailhead

CONTACT: Pleasant Grove House Museum and Welcome Center (near western trailhead): 431-589-2016; Fluvanna County Parks: 431-842-3150, fluvannacounty.org

LOCATION: 271 Pleasant Grove Dr., Palmyra

COMMENTS: The park allows horseback riding and mountain biking along most of the extensive network of trails. Pleasant Grove Park has a museum, ballfields, gardens, a playground, and more.

Fluvanna County was founded in 1777, in the midst of the Revolutionary War. Yet the fledgling county's population more than tripled, to 3,300, in its first five years. In 1824, Fluvanna's multidenominational Brick Meetinghouse (present-day Brick Union Baptist) was built under the supervision of prominent landowner General John Hartwell Cocke, who, like his friend Thomas Jefferson, was a Renaissance yeoman. The citizenry found occasion to erect a jail in 1829, today the Old Stone Jail Museum. The brick courthouse, with a classical stone portico, remains a fixture of quaint Palmyra. Cocke was also the catalyst behind construction of the courthouse two years later. The original courthouse is an architectural gem, largely because it never suffered the indignity of addition or modernization. The 1813 gristmill (later a woolen factory), just south of town along the Rivanna, wasn't so lucky: Union troops burned Palmyra Mills in 1865.

Rebuilt, the mill remained in use through the Depression and is now surrounded by a small park. It is linked by footpath from the Rail Trail, off Main Street in Palmyra, and is a pleasant stroll (1.2 miles out-and-back) on the opposite bank of the Rivanna River from this hike. It is worth a side trip.

For this hike, starting from the eastern trailhead, set out on the ADA-accessible Sandy Beach Trail, a gravel path that leads west and will quickly connect with the network's backbone path, the Heritage Trail. You will pass mile marker 0—you will spy these markers frequently along the Heritage Trail.

For a glimpse of the Rivanna River, follow the Sandy Beach Trail along the gravel switchbacks through a sloping meadow, where young cedars have pushed their way

Fluvanna Heritage Trail

through a tangle of thorns and vines. Before reaching the riverside, the path curves through a sycamore-dominated wood to reach another junction. You will return here to access River Bluff Trail, but first follow the Sandy Beach Trail through a meadow brightened by goldenrod and orange jewelweed in the summer. The gravel terminates at two benches, but a sandy path leads downhill to the water's edge.

On the Heritage Trail, passing through a lush flat where vine-draped birches, sweet gums, yellow poplars, and bitternut hickories grow, the mowed path quickly gives way to earthen singletrack. After crossing the first of many rivulets—some spanned by wooden walkways—the trail makes a sharp left, ascending from the floodplain.

Turn right upon meeting another mowed path to remain on the dirt Heritage Trail. Along this hillside, you will pass through the first of many Virginia pine thickets. Characterized by scaly bark, short needles, and small cones, this small but sturdy tree can survive in poor soils. Pine thickets promote soil accumulation and provide nutrients as their needles and fallen limbs decay.

Bold yellow blazes with a dragonfly logo mark the trail, and scattered markers point to alternate equestrian paths. The hiking trail makes a sharp right after heading uphill then curves left, following the river before regaining elevation along a finger ridge.

One of my favorite educational displays to find along hiking trails is a group of tree identification signs. Girl Scout Troop 883 posted at least a dozen along the Heritage Trail between the Beech Grove and Deep Creek Trails. They include the Latin name for each tree species and even give tidbits of knowledge about each tree type. The scouts identified white oak, eastern black oak, red maple, American beech, American hornbeam, American elm, American sycamore, box elder, black locust, redbud, river birch, and shortleaf pine. On a 7-mile hike, it never hurts to have some good reading material along the way.

A distinct right precedes the 0.8-mile marker. An area of older hardwoods with a brighter, open understory follows. A short descent then takes you across a wooden bridge over a marshy creek, where bottomland species thrive. The trail briefly follows this creek east, passing the 1-mile marker, before a left brings the Rivanna into view on your right from atop a bluff high above the river.

As it progresses, the trail undulates with the terrain, dipping into a sizable drainage before cresting a knoll and descending to a second valley. Shortly after mile marker 1.8, the trail bears inland before curving north to cross a sturdy wooden bridge. The path then bears right, running parallel to the stream you just crossed as it passes the 2-mile point. A steady ascent then leads to a hillside, where the trailbed turns to gravel.

At about the 2.8-mile mark, just after the trail junction with the Reds Trail, the Heritage Trail crosses a wooden footbridge and then takes a sharp left uphill. Additional spur trails and a loop are accessible on the other side of Burke Creek, if you desire. Stones are placed strategically to help you cross the water without getting wet.

From this point on my hike, I found the trail markings on this western portion of the trail to be less frequent, and it was somewhat harder to be sure I was on the right path. Best to stay with the singletrack, ignoring spurs to an equestrian area on your left. A steady descent takes you to a narrow streamlet before intersecting a mowed path. Continue forward, passing a NO HORSES sign. After traversing a beech grove, the trail turns left, running along a creek on the right.

Finally, you will emerge into a meadow. Continue to the western trailhead, enjoying the vista of rolling fields on your left before passing a chimney. Just ahead are the Pole Barns, open-sided shelters named for the tree-trunk poles that serve as support columns. A signboard trail map, a water spigot, a portable toilet, and picnic tables are located here. The path continues west as a gravel doubletrack. Beyond a gate, visitors can tour the Pleasant Grove House Museum and Welcome Center. In the 1854 home, browse the exhibit galleries or visit the reading room to learn more about Fluvanna's history. Beyond the historical site is Pleasant Grove Park, home to multiple sports fields and ample parking.

For the return loop, birders may elect to follow the Birding Trail, a 1-mile series of connecting mowed loops through a meadow west of the Pleasant Grove House Museum. Follow the lime-green blazes for the Rock Brook Trail from the roadside kiosk to pass through Quail Meadow and complete the hike back to the eastern trailhead. That path passes through a wide variety of trees, from thick stands of pine and cedar to hardwoods with high canopies and wide-open forest floors. It follows long flat sections of a creek and offers multiple other connections back to many of the same trails offered along the first half of the hike.

· ·

GPS TRAILHEAD COORDINATES N37° 51.640' W78° 16.247'

DIRECTIONS From Richmond, follow I-64 northwest to Exit 136. Take VA 15 south about 9 miles to Palmyra. Just beyond the small town and across the Rivanna River, make a right onto VA 53 (Thomas Jefferson Parkway). For a more scenic drive, take VA 6 (Patterson Avenue). In Dixie, turn right onto VA 15 and head north about 6.5 miles. Take a left onto VA 53. The turn for the eastern trailhead is 0.3 mile from VA 15 on the right. It is marked by a small sign, and there is a gravel parking area uphill. To reach the western trailhead, continue 1.5 miles on VA 53, then turn right. Parking is available at the Pleasant Grove athletic fields, on the right 0.75 mile ahead. A sign beneath a large oak signals the trail, reached via the gravel doubletrack past the old Haden family farmhouse and Pole Barns picnic shelter. Charlottesville residents can reach the trail by following VA 53 southeast 15 miles from its junction with VA 20.

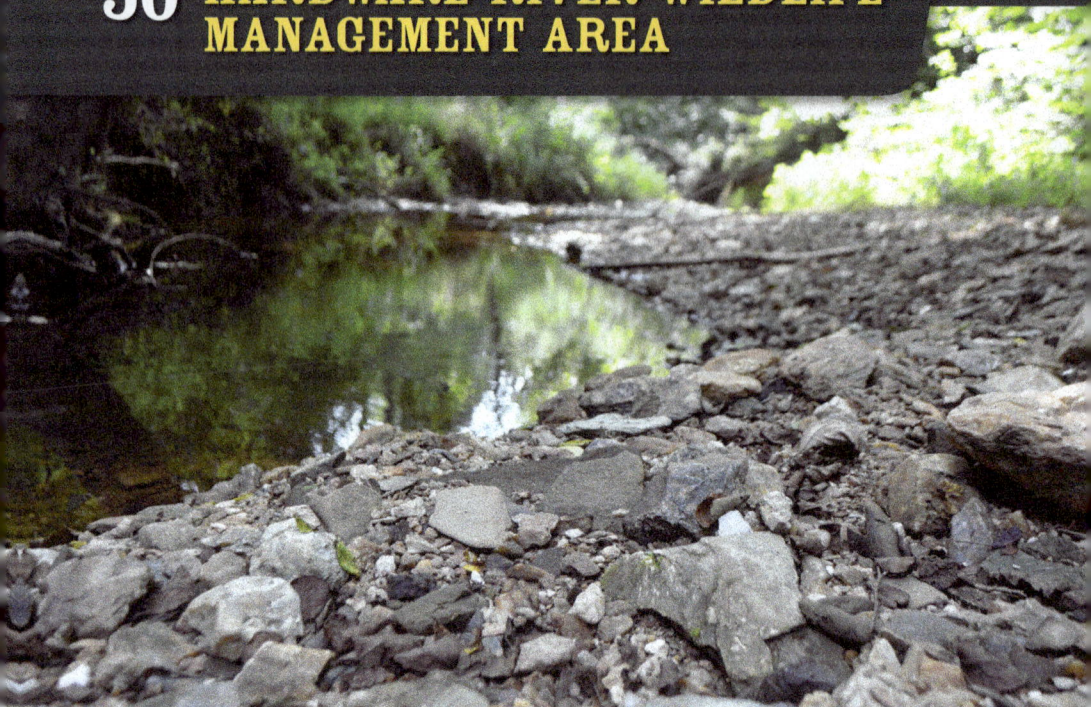

The clear and serene waters of Hardware River and Dobby Creek were highlights of our hike.

THE 1,034-ACRE Hardware River Wildlife Management Area (WMA) is located in the southwestern portion of Fluvanna County along the northern banks of the James River, about 5.5 miles east of Scottsville and 14 miles west of Fork Union. The WMA is wild, natural, quiet, and situated far from any large roadways or man-made noises. It offers small-boat access to the James River, and the Hardware River and Dobby Creek provide water and drainage.

DESCRIPTION

Named for the river that winds along its boundary and through the center, Hardware River Wildlife Management Area offers hunting, fishing, wildlife, wildflowers, and plenty of trees. The majority of the WMA is forested, primarily with hardwoods, according to the Virginia Department of Game and Inland Fisheries (VDGIF). Among them are oak, maple, hickory, and gum. Some pure pine stands are found at the highest elevations. Most of these stands occupy former farmland abandoned during the early 1930s. The terrain in the park traverses many ridges and ravines. Except for the low ground along the James and Hardware Rivers, this is an area of low ridges and gentle slopes.

The VDGIF professes that hunters should find ample opportunities to pursue deer and turkey, especially along forest edges throughout the area. Populations are stable, and hunters should find a diversity of habitat types to hunt. During most

DISTANCE & CONFIGURATION: 2.3-mile out-and-back

DIFFICULTY: Easy

ELEVATION: 402' at trailhead, 253' at low point

SCENERY: Hardware River, Dobby Creek

EXPOSURE: Mostly open except along riverbank

TRAFFIC: Low

TRAIL SURFACE: Gravel and dirt doubletrack, bush-hogged grass

HIKING TIME: 1.5 hours

SEASON: Year-round during daylight hours

ACCESS: No fee

WHEELCHAIR ACCESS: No

MAPS: On-site or at dgif.virginia.gov/wma /hardware-river

DRIVING DISTANCE FROM CAPITOL: 67 miles

FACILITIES: Information kiosk, boat ramp; no restrooms

CONTACT: 540-899-4169, dgif.virginia.gov/wma /hardware-river; Virginia Department of Game and Inland Fisheries (for hunting): 804-367-1000, dgif.virginia.gov/hunting

LOCATION: Kidds Mill Lane off VA 611, Scottsville

COMMENTS: The grassy trails here are mowed sporadically. If you plan to hike in summer, call to inquire about trail status. All wildlife management areas are open to hunting.

years, hunters searching the uplands for squirrels and woodcocks may find exciting results along the James and Hardware Rivers. Small game hunting for quail and rabbits occurs along the bottomland and timber harvest sites in the WMA. Easy access to the James provides good opportunities to hunt waterfowl and fish.

Anglers can cast for largemouth bass, smallmouth bass, channel catfish, and a variety of sunfish from the banks of both rivers. The James moves fast as it flows past the WMA, and smallmouth bass and redbreast sunfish are common. A concrete boat ramp provides small-boat and canoe access to the James just upstream from the mouth of the Hardware (at the end of VA 646 after the road crosses the railroad tracks). There is ample room for parking near the boat ramp, and other parking areas are located for access to the upland. The Hardware is stocked three times a year with rainbow and brown trout, from the beginning of October to May 31 in a 2.6-mile section of the river from Muleshoe Bend, according to the VDGIF. Anglers fishing the Hardware within this section are required to have a trout license from October 1 to June 15. No trout may be harvested, and only artificial lures may be used from October 1 to May 31. After that, trout may be creeled according to state regulations.

Before beginning this hike, a few words about WMAs, as they are not all created equal and most are not heavily managed: First, always know the hunting schedule at a WMA before visiting, and second, remember that WMAs are usually designed to be friendlier to wildlife than to humans. My visit here was in the middle of July, at the peak of the growing season for wildflowers and weeds. At least half the trail was covered or hindered by overgrowth, making for a slow hike at times. I would have been wise to pack a machete. Perhaps a Sunday in late fall or early spring would have been a better time for a hike.

Hardware River Wildlife Management Area

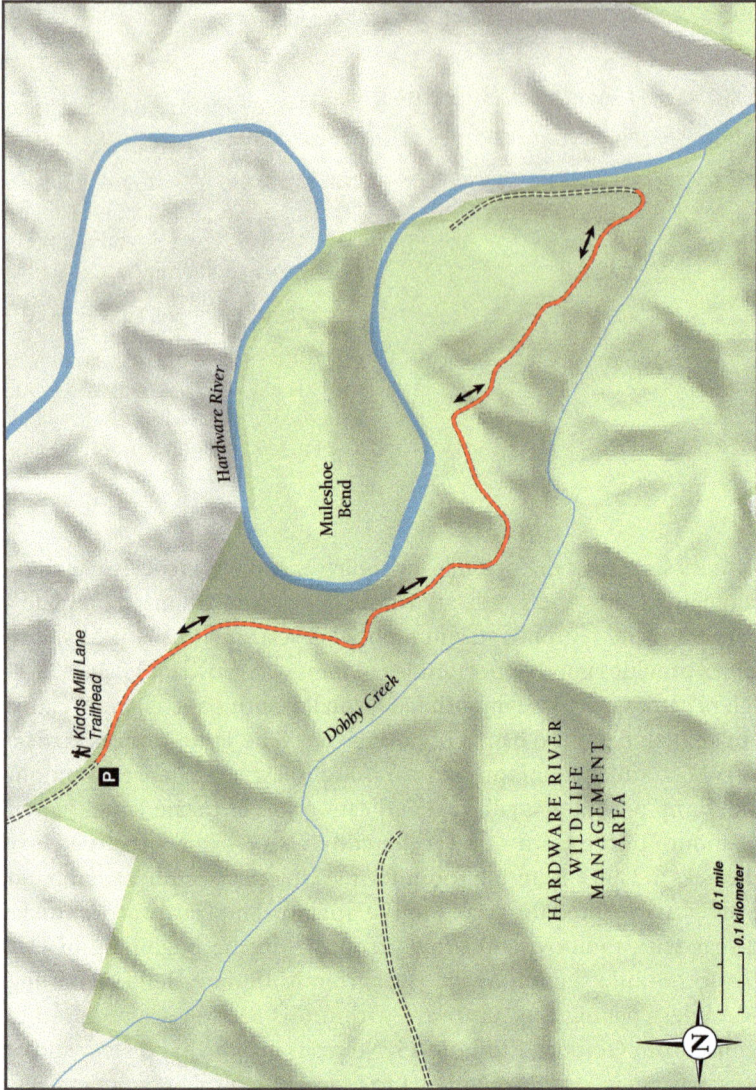

Start from the Kidds Mill Lane trailhead. This out-and-back that covers approximately 2.3 miles, including some exploration along the Hardware River and Dobby Creek, was devoid of many obvious markings on my visit. But unless you leave the main trail, you should have no trouble with orientation.

The trail begins as a doubletrack roadway covered with small chunks of slate gravel. The appearance of the slate gravel is interesting considering the geological makeup of the region. Across the James River in Buckingham County, my family has taken excursions on the Buckingham Branch Railroad from Dillwyn to New Canton/

Bremo Bluff with the Old Dominion Chapter of the National Railway Preservation Society (buckinghambranch.com). The train line passes a slate quarry, and much of the rockwork, walls, and landscaping in the area comes from that location. Seeing the slate on this roadway got my hopes up that Hardware River WMA might have some bands of the same rock layered along the trail, but it eluded me if it exists.

The mixed hardwood forest appeared thick and somewhat walled off from the trail as it began a gradual right turn on the descent toward the river. The trail was mostly crowned with cut drainage on the sides along the way, but in a handful of low areas it was wet, and the vegetation covering the path was thick.

In the first 0.5 mile of the hike, the trail travels atop a steep bluff and occasionally allows glimpses of the Hardware River and Muleshoe Bend, a nearly circular route the waterway follows as it trickles down to the James River. The rest of the hike is relatively sheltered due to the tree canopy or dense forest floor, but this short 100-foot section was a welcome sight.

About a mile into the hike, the trail enters a clearing with a single tree at the center. On the day I visited, a fallen tree had blocked the trail and the weeds were thick, but the path flows to the right in the clearing before continuing downhill about another 0.25 mile to the riverbank.

At the time of my visit, the flat, open area along the bank of the Hardware was not mowed, so a quick push through the weeds and the riparian buffer along the waterway revealed a beautiful and serene setting. Despite a 30-minute fight through waist-high weeds, this was still worth it. I walked along the shoreline under a canopy of sycamore trees to enjoy the peace and quiet, looking for fish and crawdads among the plethora of small, round rocks along the riverbed. In this section of the WMA, the river is the boundary, so if you get into the shallow waterway, do not cross the banks, as it is posted NO TRESPASSING.

A brief walk up Dobby Creek revealed thousands of interesting rocks. Multitudes of colors, textures, and sizes—the perfect place for kids of all ages to play for a while, build a dam, or look for tiny aquatic life. Farther up the creekbed, I caught a couple of deer spying on me. After a few minutes reliving childhood, I began the hike back up the trail to the Kidds Mill Lane trailhead.

• •

GPS TRAILHEAD COORDINATES N37° 45.849' W78° 25.862'

DIRECTIONS From Richmond, follow VA 6 (Patterson Avenue) west to Fork Union. Take a right to continue on VA 6 (West River Road). Just beyond the small town and after crossing the Rivanna River, turn right onto VA 611. After about 1.3 miles, take a left onto Kidds Mill Lane, a gravel road with a small street sign. Follow this road slowly about 0.25 mile, passing homes and farm entrances, to the WMA parking area, gate, and kiosk.

The High Bridge trestle is more than 2,400 feet long and towers 125 feet above the Appomattox River.

THE MORE THAN 30-MILE High Bridge Trail follows an old railroad bed through forests and farms. This bucolic trail is particularly favored by equestrians and cyclists. As it approaches and bisects Farmville, runners and walkers are more the norm. At the center is Farmville's historic downtown. Heading east out of town, the trail crosses the Appomattox River and soon returns to a forested corridor. After another road crossing at the River Road trailhead, the path continues southeast to its namesake High Bridge. This towering railroad trestle also crosses the Appomattox and is the highlight of the trail.

DESCRIPTION

High Bridge Trail State Park is one of Virginia's newest state parks, but not in the traditional sense. The multiuse rail trail is open to hikers, cyclists, and equestrians. Be sure to bring plenty of water, because none is provided along the trail. Even though a portion of the path bisects Farmville, most of the route is isolated, with few stores along the route to restock.

Named for the High Bridge trestle, which towers 160 feet above the Appomattox River and is more than 2,400 feet long, the trail was first proposed when Norfolk Southern announced plans to discontinue rail service on its Pamplin–Burkeville line in 2004. Two years later, the company deeded the line to the state for development as a recreational trail. Enthusiastic local residents helped push the project ahead.

DISTANCE & CONFIGURATION: 8.1 miles, with options to shorten

DIFFICULTY: Easy

ELEVATION: 310' at trailhead, 390' at high point

SCENERY: Upland woods, riparian bottomland, Appomattox River, trestle bridge

EXPOSURE: Mostly open

TRAFFIC: Moderate

TRAIL SURFACE: Wide, mostly crushed-limestone path; some pavement

HIKING TIME: 3 hours

SEASON: Year-round during daylight hours

ACCESS: Parking at 9 lots along the route (some charge a fee) plus public lots in Farmville

WHEELCHAIR ACCESS: Yes

MAPS: At trailside parking lots and dcr.virginia .gov/state-parks/high-bridge-trail

DRIVING DISTANCE FROM CAPITOL: 64.7 miles

FACILITIES: Picnic tables; pit toilets at River Rd. trailhead; full-service restrooms in Farmville

CONTACT: 434-315-0457, dcr.virginia.gov /state-parks/high-bridge-trail

LOCATION: Trailhead next to 318 N. Main St., Farmville

COMMENTS: The Civil War driving trail connects to High Bridge. The trail is open to horses, bicyclists, runners, and walkers, and it is busiest from the River Road trailhead and High Bridge, which is a Virginia Historic Landmark and on the National Register of Historic Places.

High Bridge posed interesting challenges to trail designers at the state's Department of Conservation and Recreation. The first 4 miles of the linear park were opened to the public in the summer of 2008, with 12 additional miles opening the following summer. As of this writing, the trail stretches 31 miles. It could someday extend to 34 miles, from Burkeville, south of US 460 at the eastern terminus, to the small town of Pamplin at the western end.

A hike of this length might be too much to ask of the typical hiker, so allow me to suggest splitting it into segments by using the multiple parking lots along the route. The hike mapped here takes you from west to east along the trail from Farmville, with a brief out-and-back at the end to see the namesake bridge. According to park rangers, the majority of hikers in the park walk from River Road to the bridge and back, which covers approximately 3 miles round-trip. Views of the epic trestle make for a dramatic crescendo to your day on the trail. To get back to Farmville after this hike, I locked up bicycles at the River Road trailhead bike rack and rode back to my car once I had hiked enough. If your time is limited, consider biking instead to see more of the countryside and trail.

Beginning at the Farmville trailhead, you will set out past a large LOVE sign, part of the well-received Virginia Tourism campaign. The trail is approximately 10–12 feet wide, and there are no steep climbs or descents—remember, trains once traversed these hills, and engineers don't design steep climbs and descents with railways. Also, there is little available shade at this initial stage. A trail marker shows that High Bridge will be 4.4 miles from this point, so come prepared with sunscreen and lots of water if you hike on a sunny day. The marker also indicates the next restroom will be 2.5 miles away.

High Bridge Trail State Park

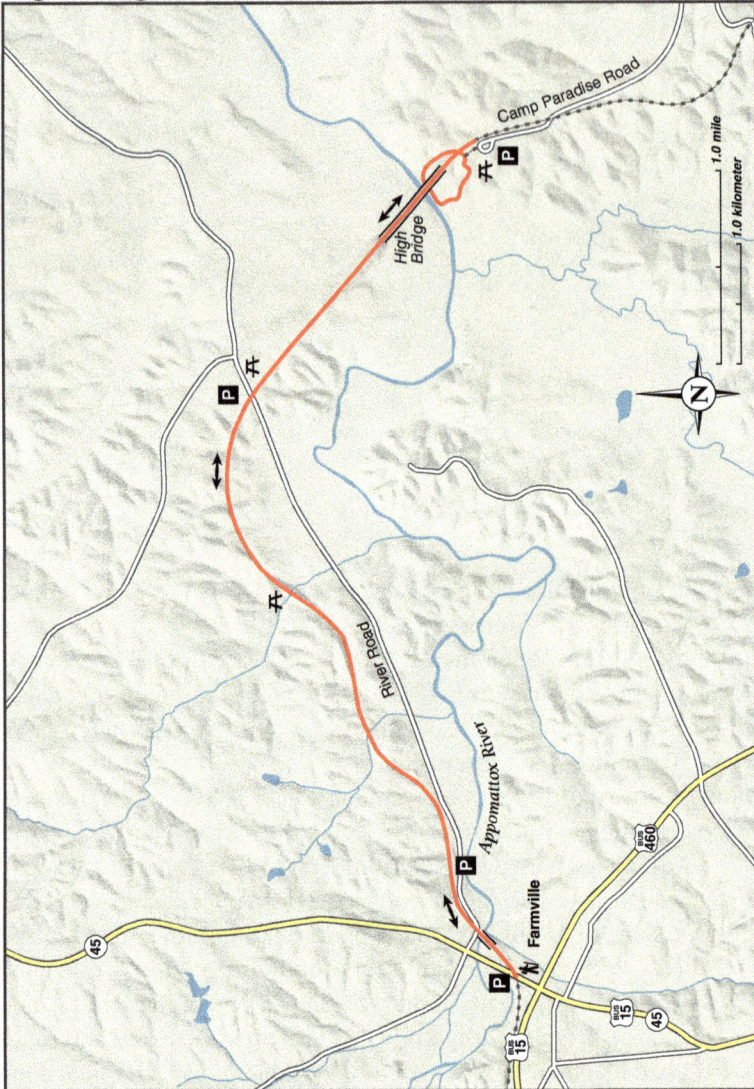

Watch for remnants of the infrastructure of the former rail line: concrete bases, occasional concrete distance markers, and more. There will also be horse-mount blocks, benches, and picnic tables along the trail. The most frequent users of the trail are cyclists, so perhaps stay to the right of the path on busy days. Cyclists are expected to yield to pedestrians, but be prepared to move aside if needed.

You'll enjoy views of the smooth-flowing Appomattox River as you cross it on a wide bridge. Sweet gum and sycamore trees flank the shore. The bridge also crosses

River Road (VA 600), then the trail briefly parallels that road to the north. The trail will next cross this same roadway at the River Road trailhead.

This section of the trail is bucolic in character. Trees line the path of the former rail line, but farm fields stretch to the right of the trail, and dense forest occupies the left. Pine woodlots alternate with stands of hardwoods such as oak and hickory.

Consistent with other Virginia state parks, it is easy to know where you are at all times, as the trail is signed, with distance markers every 0.5 mile. Tall hardwoods line much of the corridor and may provide shade, depending on the position of the sun, and there are few road crossings due to the power that railroad companies have always had in minimizing interruptions to safe passage for their trains.

About 2 miles into the hike, notice the line of old poles running along the right side of the trail. The old lines droop in many sections, indicating they are no longer in service. Note the multitude of blue glass insulators, which were used for telegraph, telephone, electricity, and other applications over the past 150 years. The bright turquoise blue color contrasts with the green and brown hues of the dense forest.

As the steady march uphill from Farmville approaches River Road, rounding the last bend at about the 3.5-mile mark, you'll see an electric power station and the River Road trailhead, which is on each side of the roadway. Take care when crossing the road here, and then continue southeast through a tree-lined stretch to reach High Bridge. The view of the valley below and the Appomattox from the bridge is fantastic and certainly the highlight for most visitors.

The most significant feature of the linear park is High Bridge itself. At more than 2,400 feet long and 125 feet above the Appomattox River, it is the longest recreational bridge in Virginia and among the longest in the United States, according to Virginia State Parks. For safety, the railings were built extra tall, at approximately 5 feet. If you visit with children, they may need a boost to see over the top. Along the bridge are two long shelters with benches to allow more time to enjoy the view.

The steel bridge that stands today was built in 1914 to replace an earlier stone-and-wood bridge built in 1853 as part of the South Side Railroad. That first bridge was partially burned during the Civil War. On April 6, 1865, Union soldiers attempted to burn it to trap Confederate soldiers east of the Appomattox. However, the Union detachment was rebuffed. Later that day, General Robert E. Lee's Army of Northern Virginia suffered a major defeat at the Battle of Sailor's Creek, the precursor to his surrender at Appomattox Court House three days later.

The next day, Confederate reinforcements under the command of General William Mahone arrived, and it was they who attempted to burn High Bridge. The green timber burned slowly, though, and Union troops managed to extinguish the blaze. The bridge was rendered impassable but did not collapse. It was partially repaired during the Reconstruction before being entirely replaced.

In late 2016, the Camp Paradise Trail opened on the south end of the bridge, allowing access to its substructure along the banks of the Appomattox. Camp Paradise is an earthwork fortification that covered High Bridge during the Civil War. According to park signage, the soldiers were "feasted" and "pampered" by the local families, so the post came to be known as Camp Paradise. This artillery detachment took part in the Battle of High Bridge on April 6, 1865, after which they joined the Army of Northern Virginia's retreat and surrendered with Confederate general Robert E. Lee at Appomattox on April 9, 1865. For my visit, this well-signed loop trail added 1.5 miles to the hike from the eastern end of the bridge and back. Seeing the massive bridge from below was amazing. It has been through many upgrades and repairs. After marveling at the steel span and stone pillars—and this river's unique place in American history—retrace your steps to the trailhead in Farmville to complete the hike.

NEARBY ACTIVITIES

If you plan to spend more time hiking near Farmville, consider visiting **Sailor's Creek Battlefield State Park** (804-561-7510, dcr.virginia.gov), accessible from US 360 east of Twin Lakes via VA 307 and VA 617. The Overton-Hillsman House, a Civil War field hospital, is open for tours June–August. At Sayler's Creek—corrupted to "Sailor's Creek" by troops who had only heard it spoken—General Lee's Army of Northern Virginia suffered 7,700 casualties on April 6, 1865, known as the Black Thursday of the Confederacy. The defeat precipitated Lee's surrender three days later. The site of that surrender, **Appomattox Court House National Historic Park** (434-352-8987, ext. 226; nps.gov/apco) is northwest of Twin Lakes and offers a 6-mile trail through a history-rich landscape.

• •

GPS TRAILHEAD COORDINATES N37° 18.263' W78° 23.462'

DIRECTIONS From Richmond, travel west on US 60 (Midlothian Turnpike) about 50 miles to the hamlet of Cumberland. Approximately 2 miles outside town, turn left onto VA 45 southbound. Continue approximately 15 miles into Farmville and park near the trailhead. Or to hike the section at the bridge, from VA 45, take a left on River Road before you cross the Appomattox River. The River Road trailhead is visible where it crosses the road approximately 3.1 miles east.

From Richmond via US 360, drive about 60 miles to Jetersville, and take a right onto VA 307. Drive about 9 miles and take a right onto US 460. Drive approximately 4.3 miles then take US 360 Business 2.5 miles into Farmville. Take a right onto Main Street and look for the Farmville trailhead.

The majority of the trails in Ivy Creek Natural Area are heavily wooded.

MUCH OF THE LAND now protected by Ivy Creek Natural Area was farmed by freed slaves and their descendants for nearly a century. A then-modern barn, built in the 1930s, remains as testament to the land's agricultural heritage. It now hosts environmental-education exhibits, and the surrounding 215 acres, largely reforested, are home to a host of native wildlife.

DESCRIPTION

Established in 1989, Ivy Creek Natural Area is a model of environmental conservation and education in a growing city. An exemplary partnership between the natural area's eponymous foundation, the City of Charlottesville, and Albemarle County ensures that the land will escape encroaching suburban development. Pedestrian-only trails crisscross the hillsides above the Ivy Creek arm of the South Fork Rivanna Reservoir, and an education building hosts programs for schoolchildren.

Located across the quiet, parklike observation area from the trailhead signboard, the education building was designed in the style of the larger Depression-era barn that stands just to the north. Erected by Farm Bureau extension agent Conly Greer during the decade that saw both the Dust Bowl and the New Deal, the barn was a showplace for contemporary farming techniques. If you wish to tour the barn, contact the Ivy Creek Foundation, as it is open only by arrangement.

DISTANCE & CONFIGURATION: 4-mile loop, with additional options; 7 total miles of trails in the park

DIFFICULTY: Moderate

ELEVATION: 496' at trailhead, 390' at low point

SCENERY: South Fork Rivanna Reservoir, Ivy Creek drainage, wooded ridges, open meadows, 1930s barn

EXPOSURE: Well shaded

TRAFFIC: Moderate; highest near the education building

TRAIL SURFACE: Dirt, optional paved trail

HIKING TIME: 2 hours

SEASON: Year-round, 7 a.m.–sunset

ACCESS: No fee

WHEELCHAIR ACCESS: At restrooms, education building, barn; on 0.7-mile paved trail; wheelchairs not recommended on loop

MAPS: On signboard and at ivycreekfoundation .org/trail-map

DRIVING DISTANCE FROM CAPITOL: 74 miles

FACILITIES: Restrooms with water and pit toilets, wildlife-viewing area, education building

CONTACT: Ivy Creek Foundation: 434-973-7772, ivycreekfoundation.org

LOCATION: 1780 Earlysville Rd., Charlottesville

COMMENTS: Ivy Creek is managed by its namesake foundation for wildlife-viewing and preservation. Dog walking, jogging, cycling, swimming, camping, and of course hunting and fishing are prohibited.

Today the barn is the most visible reminder of a century of African American–owned enterprise at River View Farm, as the land was long known before a dam on the South Fork Rivanna River flooded the surrounding valley. Greer's father-in-law, Hugh Carr, was born a slave. A sharecropper in the wake of the Civil War, he and his wife, Texie, managed to scrape together sufficient savings to purchase the farm piecemeal between 1870 and 1889. Their daughter, Mary Carr Greer, served as an Albemarle County school principal, and a nearby elementary school was named in her honor.

Leaving northeast from the parking area, you will pass the cemetery on the right before reaching a covered signboard, where you can pick up a map brochure. Stay straight on the paved trail to pass between the observation area on the right and an area of thick brush on the left. Upon approaching the barn, bear right to encircle the adjacent meadow, walking beneath a broad red oak. From the rear (north) of the barn, turn right to set out on the lavender-blazed earthen Field Trail beneath hackberry and hickory trees.

The trail runs northeast to the right of a field of tall grass and woods. Look for songbirds in the grass and raptors circling overhead. The trail soon ducks left into the forest, making a rocky descent, but wait to follow its second, sharp descent to the left. Continue on the singletrack path downhill through yellow poplar, red oak, and thickets of Virginia pine toward an arm of the South Fork Rivanna River Reservoir. Take a short spur down the bluff to the Hydraulic Mills Overlook, and read about the history of the mill from the post–Civil War years and late 1800s. "The mill complex became the commercial center for a growing African American community of farmers and tradespeople," the sign reads.

Ivy Creek Natural Area

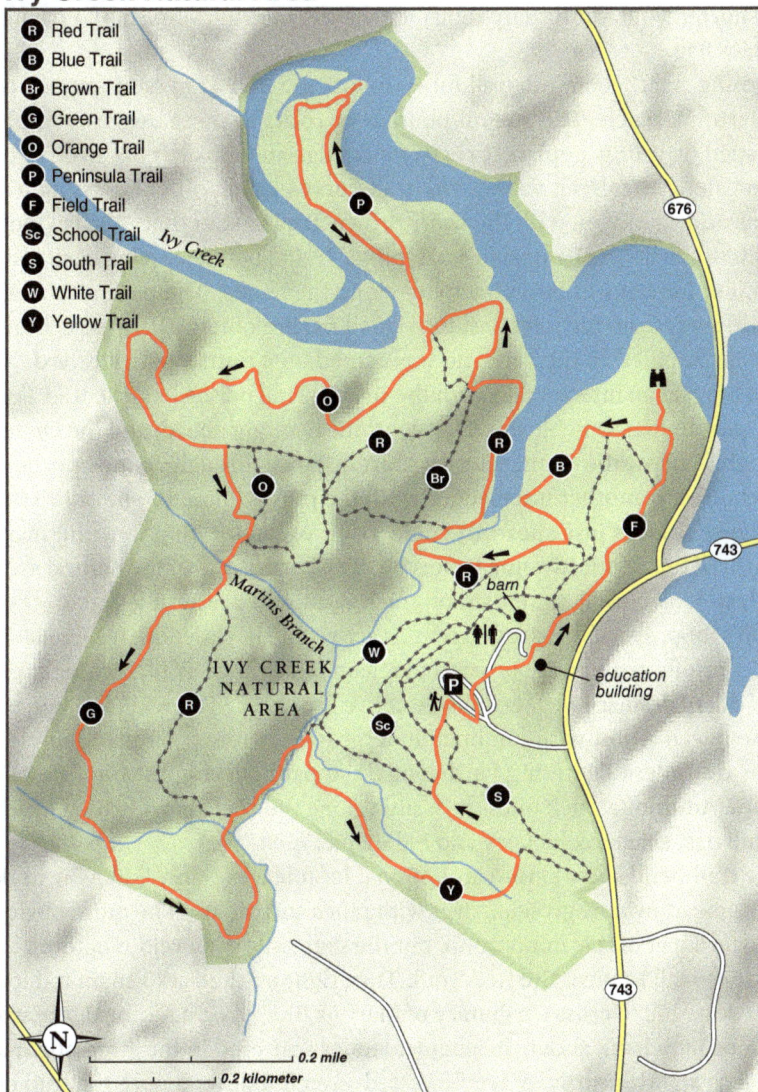

- **R** Red Trail
- **B** Blue Trail
- **Br** Brown Trail
- **G** Green Trail
- **O** Orange Trail
- **P** Peninsula Trail
- **F** Field Trail
- **Sc** School Trail
- **S** South Trail
- **W** White Trail
- **Y** Yellow Trail

Ivy Creek

Martins Branch

IVY CREEK
NATURAL
AREA

barn

education building

676

743

743

0.2 mile

0.2 kilometer

N

Starting back on the trail, take a right to follow the Blue Trail. Hornbeam and beech trees dominate the forest nearer the water's edge and line the root-laced path, which veers left and uphill beside a feeder streamlet on the right. Look for a rocked-in spring at the head of the rivulet. Nearing the hilltop, turn right at an intersection. This level stint of the Blue Trail leads to the central Red Trail, which is a sort of backbone loop from which most other trails spur. The route mapped here uses several trails to make a wider loop but traverses the Red Trail intermittently, allowing you to shorten your venture by returning via the interior loop should daylight fade or muscles flag.

Turning right where the trail forks, follow the Red Trail west as it descends to meet Martins Branch. The stream pours over rocks to meet the reservoir at a still inlet shaded by yellow poplars. Cross a footbridge and look left for an old stone wall that runs along the creek valley. The trail curves briefly uphill, passing a gnarled black oak and a junction with the short Brown Trail (a spur that can also loop to the same junction with the Peninsula and Orange Trails) before veering back toward the water. Look for signs of beaver activity along the banks. The path ultimately turns left to rise away from the inlet past the signed Bartholomew oak. Two centuries old, this tree is the oldest in the park and was named for a former park steward.

Just beyond an intersection with the Brown Trail on the left, the Red Trail veers left, the purple-blazed Peninsula Trail continues straight ahead, and the Orange Trail leaves right. Follow the Orange Trail a short distance through young hornbeams and then hickories to another intersection with the purple-blazed Peninsula Trail. Turn right; the trail forks just ahead to circle a spit of land jutting into the marshy Ivy Creek arm of the South Rivanna Reservoir. The path is one of the natural area's least traveled, so look closely to remain on track. From the western length of the Peninsula Trail's loop, sycamore-shaded islands are visible in widening Ivy Creek.

After briefly retracing your steps to regain the Orange Trail, turn right to follow it in and out of drainages on the hillside above Ivy Creek. The wide trailbed traverses a mature beech wood with minimal undergrowth before mountain laurel thickets reappear trailside. Reentering hardwoods, the path curves past the first of several rock piles. Additional rock piles are visible along the trail ahead, which heads south and uphill past shagbark hickory and red maple.

The trail bends east before an optional loop leaves right. Follow it to descend through a meadow now growing over with pines and cedars. The more obvious path is the eastern half of this minor loop, but the segments soon rejoin before breaching an old stone wall to meet the Red Trail. Turn right on the park's main red loop, and follow it downhill to cross a tributary of Martins Branch on a footbridge. Ferns grow from a foot-high bank above the angular stones scattered in the streambed; a mammoth beech stands nearby. A brief forested stretch follows before the trail emerges into a pipeline right-of-way about 30 feet wide.

The Red Trail turns left with the clearing, but follow the Green Trail straight ahead. The Green Trail gets off to a lackluster start, passing through pine-dominated recovering forest then bisecting a power-line clearing. A more open beech glade follows, then a mix of hardwoods characterized by chestnuts and white oaks. The path descends to cross a small streamlet just as it passes underground and then continues to span another stream-fed creek on a modest bridge. Beyond a hedge of pawpaw, a private home is visible on the right as the path turns from south- to eastbound.

The Green Trail soon turns again, heading north to recross the creek just upstream of its junction with Martins Branch, which is visible in a wide culvert on the right. The trail promptly terminates at the Red Trail, and a right turn takes you northwest along Martins Branch. The path curves right to cross the stream, channeled under a stone bridge through a pipe. Soon thereafter, bypass the Yellow Trail as it extends right, beneath the right-of-way. A slow-moving, rocky streamlet runs in the valley on your left. Though dotted with young beech trees, this forest is relatively mature, with red maples interspersed among the more common beeches and chestnut oaks. Cross the streamlet on a footbridge before the trail curves around a smaller drainage.

A short distance ahead is the aforementioned power-line clearing, and this hike takes a right to follow the Yellow Trail. This 0.4-mile section loops back to reconnect with the Red Trail. Turn right at this intersection, the last of your hike, and bypass the School Trail (designed for school groups). Passing beneath the power lines, the Red Trail descends along then crosses a meadow to return to the parking area.

• •

GPS TRAILHEAD COORDINATES N38° 05.463' W78° 29.609'

DIRECTIONS From Richmond, follow I-64 west to Exit 124 onto US 250 (Richmond Road). In 4.2 miles, turn right onto VA 743 (Hydraulic Road). Turn left in 2.2 miles, staying on VA 743 (now Earlysville Road). Just over 0.5 mile ahead, the entrance to Ivy Creek Natural Area is on the left. Pass a private dwelling on the right to park in the gravel lot just south of the trailhead signboard, restrooms, and education building.

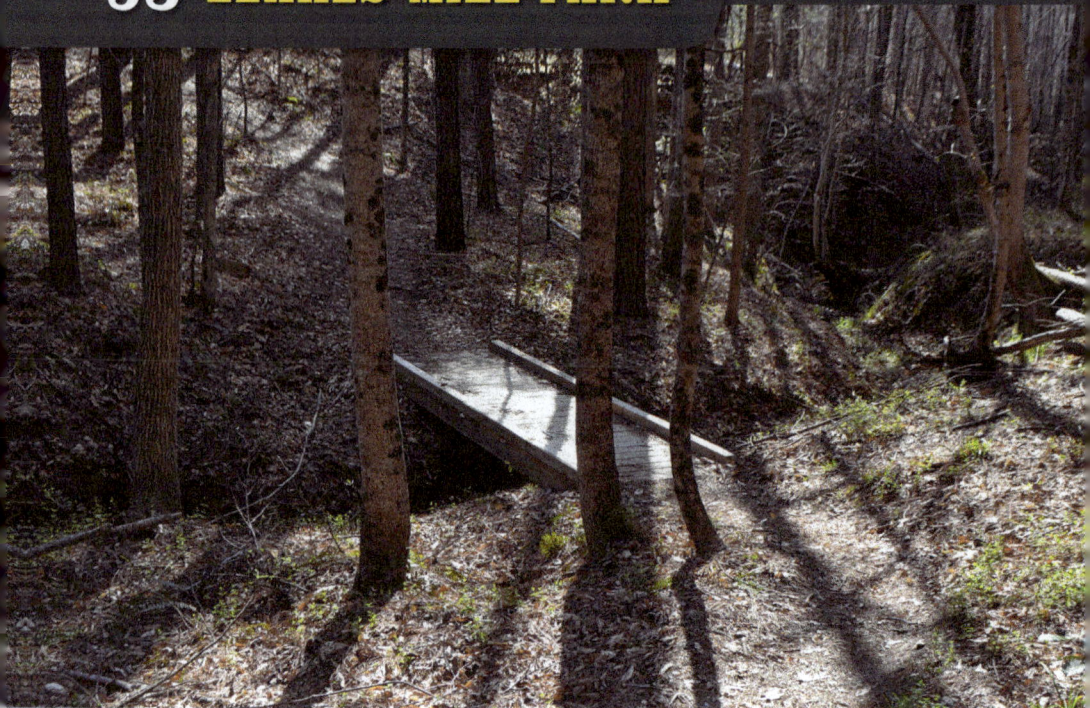

The hilly trail network at Leakes Mill Park has several water crossings that require footbridges.

LEAKES MILL PARK is a 167-acre facility located approximately 3 miles west of Goochland Courthouse. The county plans to build additional mountain bike trails, multipurpose fields, a bicycle skills park, additional trailheads, and additional parking.

DESCRIPTION

The 167-acre Leakes Mill Park opened in 2013. As of this writing, the park was undergoing improvements and volunteer trail-building crews were in the midst of laying out and sculpting a few miles of trail into the ravines and wooded outer boundaries of the park. Portions of that trail were complete when I visited, especially the northwestern and western sections. The terrain creates many excellent climbs and switchbacks for mountain bikers, trail runners, and hikers.

The land was once owned by the Leake family, prominent in Goochland County in the 1700s and 1800s. The Leakes owned the property and the land adjacent to it south and north of VA 6 (River Road). There is a family cemetery north of the road (outside the park boundaries) with headstones dating back to the early 1700s.

Birds one may encounter at the park include cardinals, blue jays, robins, bluebirds, woodpeckers, wild turkeys, ospreys, and red-tailed hawks, according to park signage. Other identified wildlife includes gray squirrels, eastern cottontail rabbits,

DISTANCE & CONFIGURATION: 1.6-mile loop, plus optional spurs and fitness trail

DIFFICULTY: Easy

ELEVATION: 247' at trailhead, 164' at high point

SCENERY: Big Lickinghole Creek, old mill site, woodlands, athletic fields

EXPOSURE: Mostly shaded except along fields and at parking area

TRAFFIC: Low

TRAIL SURFACE: Dirt, gravel

HIKING TIME: 1 hour

SEASON: Year-round during daylight hours

ACCESS: No fee

WHEELCHAIR ACCESS: Wheelchairs not recommended

MAPS: At trailhead kiosk

DRIVING DISTANCE FROM CAPITOL: 41 miles

FACILITIES: Restrooms, picnic shelters, playground, soccer fields, fitness trail, Leakes Mill access

CONTACT: 804-556-5854, goochlandva.us

LOCATION: 3951 River Rd., Goochland

COMMENTS: The park and trail network will have changed dramatically by the time you read this book, but expect an expansive trail network and more ballfields in this park located just west of Goochland Courthouse.

box turtles, garter snakes, black snakes, copperheads, red and gray foxes, raccoons, opossums, white-tailed deer, and even black bears.

We begin this hike from the parking lot and will take a clockwise route. At the time of my visit, construction blocked a part of the access to the trailhead, but there is a kiosk on a bluff along the treeline, south of the playing fields, that is visible from the parking lot. The kiosk has a map and brief details about the history of the park. There is also a fitness trail, and native wildlife can be found in the area.

Follow the brown sign pointing to the Leakes Mill Trails, and enter the forest along the doubletrack path. You will find guidance along this main trail by following the brown markers. The park is small, so you should not get lost. As the trail descends toward the lower flat area along Big Lickinghole Creek, notice the many crossings laid out for the trail network. At the time of my visit, some of the trails were already in use but had not been marked and officially opened. This downhill walk is largely through tall stands of loblolly pines, and the forest floor was covered with pine needles.

As you reach a junction, follow the main trail to the right. A few pieces of exercise equipment are nestled among the trees through this section. There are also many tree identification signs, which are always a welcome sight in a park along a nature trail. Among the assorted trees identified in the park are sycamore, river birch, sweet gum, American beech, loblolly pine, dogwood, white oak, black oak, southern red oak, pignut hickory, and black cherry.

Hike about 0.2 mile, until you find a large brown sign directing you to take a left to the ruins of Leakes Mill. Follow the trail as it winds slightly to the right down the creek bank. You'll find a sign that gives the history of the mill site and a narrow singletrack trail that leads around the ruins, down to the dam, and along the creek.

Leakes Mill Park

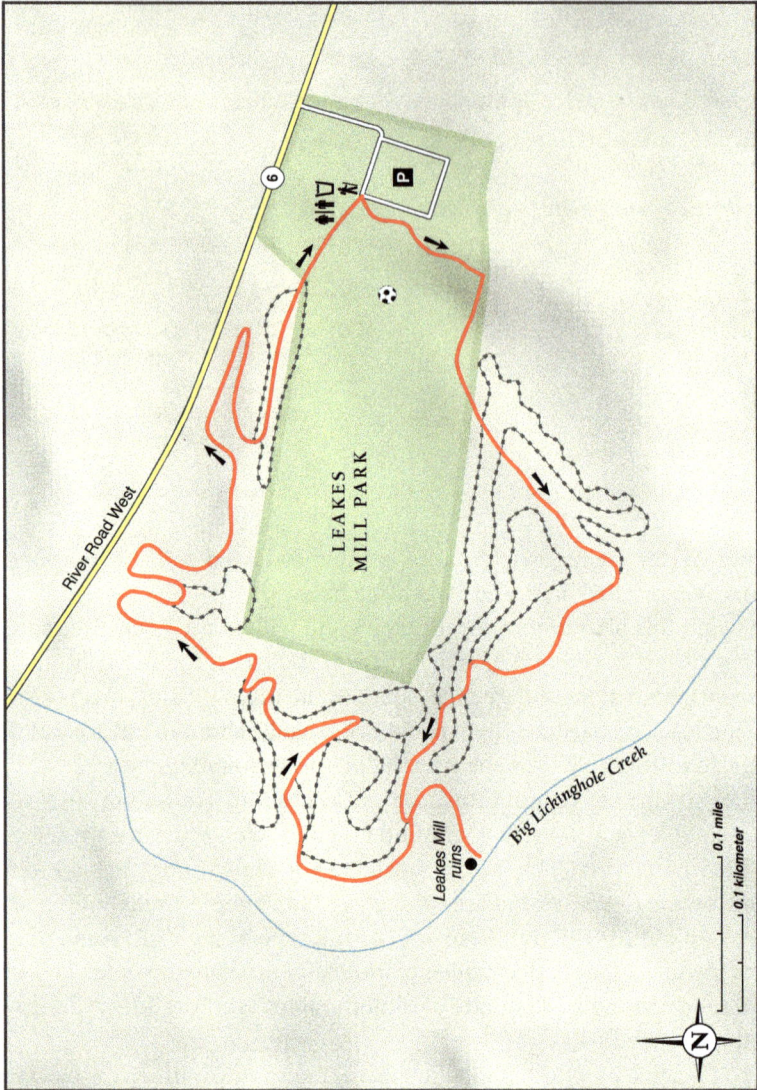

Big Lickinghole Creek plays a big role in Leakes Mill Park. The attractive waterway forms the western boundary of the park. The remains of the old mill, milldam, millhouse foundation, and tailrace that were documented to be on the Leake family property can be found here. The milldam created a wider area of the creek, called Leake's Mill Pond. The area where the old mill remains sits in the floodplain along the creek and is surrounded by sycamores and river birches.

If you're curious about where the name for the creek comes from, there is a farm/brewpub in Goochland County called Lickinghole Creek Craft Brewery, about 4 miles northwest of the park, whose website says that the creek has been known since pre-Colonial times as "the lickinghole where wildlife stopped to drink from the nourishing waters." I'll drink to that.

Once you've satisfied your curiosity at the mill ruins, retrace your steps back to the main trail, and turn left to continue to the western portions of the park. The trail markers indicate through this area that hikers should expect to share the path with mountain bikers, and there are many more crossings along the path as the more developed sections of the trail network develop. The singletrack is marked with round orange blazes that have directional arrows in the center.

As the trail follows along the western portions of the park, look for the maintenance road, and take a left. This will lead toward VA 6, and you will likely begin to hear cars as you get closer. The gravel road dips down to a low drainage area and then begins a gradual climb. Begin looking to the right for entrance points to the singletrack trail in the northwest corner of the park that will wind its way through a mostly hardwood forest. Once you get on the trail, follow it on the north side of a ravine as it skirts below the road along VA 6. After a series of switchbacks, the trail will eventually cross the ravine with a wooden footbridge and then begin another series of switchbacks to climb toward the level of the forest edge, which is about 20 feet away from the playing fields.

Follow the trail along this section until it exits the woods not far from a kiosk, a maintenance shed, a park concession stand, and the restrooms. The parking lot is just a few steps from there.

• •

GPS TRAILHEAD COORDINATES N37° 42.480' W77° 57.456'

DIRECTIONS From Richmond, take I-64 west to Exit 167 for Oilville. Turn left on VA 617 (Oilville Road). Take a right onto US 250 (Broad Street Road), then another left onto VA 632, and continue 5 miles. Turn left onto US 522 before taking a quick right onto VA 6 (River Road). The park entrance will be on the left about 4 miles down the road. You can also take VA 6 (Patterson Avenue) for a more scenic and rural route through the Goochland countryside.

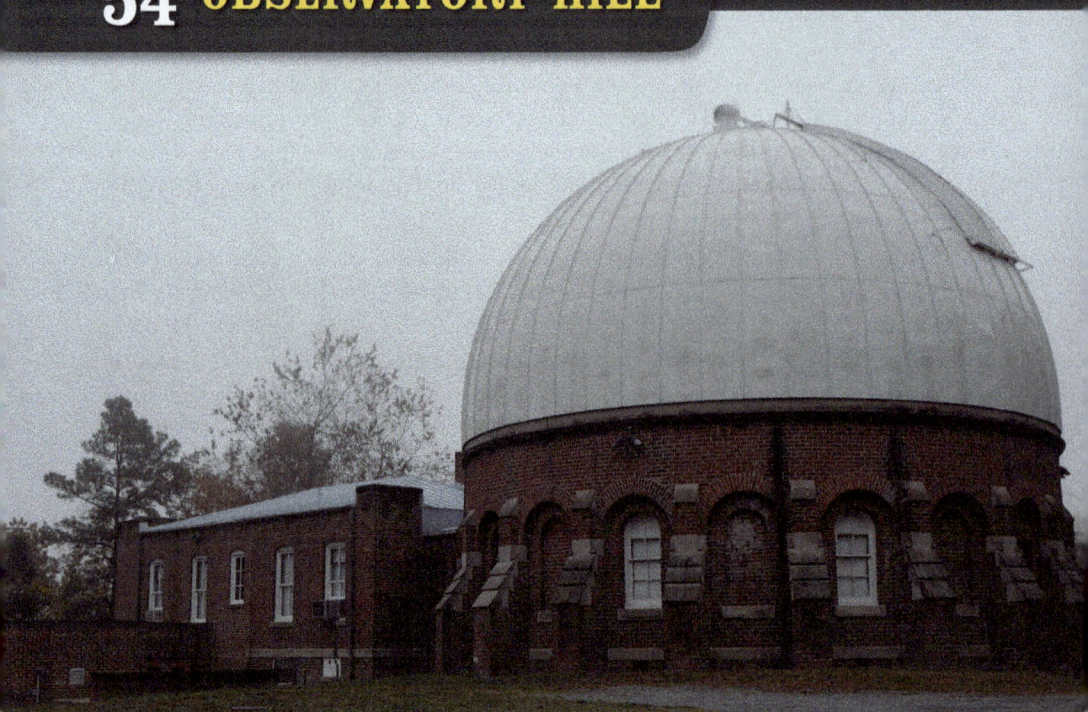

McCormick Observatory in Charlottesville, constructed in 1883

ON THE UNIVERSITY OF VIRGINIA CAMPUS, this dense trail network makes the most of limited acreage on the slope below McCormick Observatory, for which the trail is named. The trail lures dog walkers and hard-core mountain bikers alike and is understandably popular with students. The jumble of unmarked trails offers many options, so use this hike as a starting point.

DESCRIPTION

How apropos: scaling Jefferson Mountain while on a visit to the University of Virginia. Though our third president designed this campus, the observatory was not constructed until 1883, more than 50 years after Jefferson's death. However, he certainly knew this prominent mountain even before it became his namesake. It looms above the main campus to the east.

Be forewarned that there are few reliable trail markers on Observatory Hill. As of this writing, most of the signs at the trailheads were faded and long ago had lost the ability to relay information. The park is small, so there is not much chance of getting lost. The droning of automobiles from US 29 and the whir of machinery at nearby campus office buildings should help keep you oriented.

The mountain rises north from this hike's starting point at Fontaine Research Park on Ray C. Hunt Drive. After crossing Fontaine Avenue, turn left on a gravel

DISTANCE & CONFIGURATION: 2.1-mile loop, plus numerous other options in a compact network

DIFFICULTY: Moderate on the climb up; easy on the way down

ELEVATION: 513' at trailhead, 791' at high point

SCENERY: McCormick Observatory, hillside hardwood forest

EXPOSURE: Mostly shaded

TRAFFIC: Moderate

TRAIL SURFACE: Dirt, gravel, paved

HIKING TIME: 1 hour

SEASON: Year-round during daylight hours

ACCESS: No fee

WHEELCHAIR ACCESS: Wheelchairs not recommended

MAPS: No official map; older version available at cambc.org/images/OHill_Trail_Map.pdf

DRIVING DISTANCE FROM CAPITOL: 74.1 miles

FACILITIES: Roadside parking areas

CONTACT: University of Virginia Community Relations: 434-924-1400, communications.virginia.edu

LOCATION: 525 McCormick Rd., Charlottesville (hike begins from Ray C. Hunt Dr. across Fontaine Ave.)

COMMENTS: To view the night sky through McCormick Observatory's 26-inch-lens telescope, attend one of the UVA Astronomy Department's public nights. These free events are held the first and third Friday nights of each month (visit astronomy.as.virginia.edu for details).

pathway at a large Osage orange tree, which on the midfall morning I visited was still dropping a multitude of large, lime-green hedge apples. Stop for a moment to sniff the sweet smell of the sticky, milky fluid the fruits secrete. The trees are not from the orange family but rather belong to the mulberry family. They are usually covered in orangish bark, and the wood was primarily used by Native Americans to make bows because it was considered strong, flexible, and durable.

Follow a singletrack path up the small hill—this is the Rivanna Trail (see page 291). Atop the slope, turn left on a dirt trail heading north. Set off uphill on one of the mountain's gentler slopes. The trail curves slightly to the right. Chestnut and northern red oaks dominate this hillside, which is spotted with white pines. Also look for a smattering of cucumber trees, a deciduous relative of the magnolia easily distinguished by its large leaves.

Climbing to the west of the observatory, take a trail junction to the right, and follow along the singletrack in a series of short switchbacks designed for mountain bikes. This is still part of the Rivanna Trail. The path soon reaches a wide gravel roadbed. Take a right to follow the old road uphill along rooted and eroded pathways as it continues to climb the mountain. At a trail junction, take the wider trail to the left along a rocky section that winds to the right, below the peak of Jefferson Mountain and the observatory.

The trail soon reaches the lightly trafficked Edgemont Road, which services the observatory from the west. Cross the road and continue along the trail, which runs alongside a clearing for power lines. A steep hillside is visible across the lengthy vista. On the autumn morning I hiked here, the hillside was still covered in a foggy mist and haze, giving it a sinister look. The trail crosses the clearing below the hillside

Observatory Hill

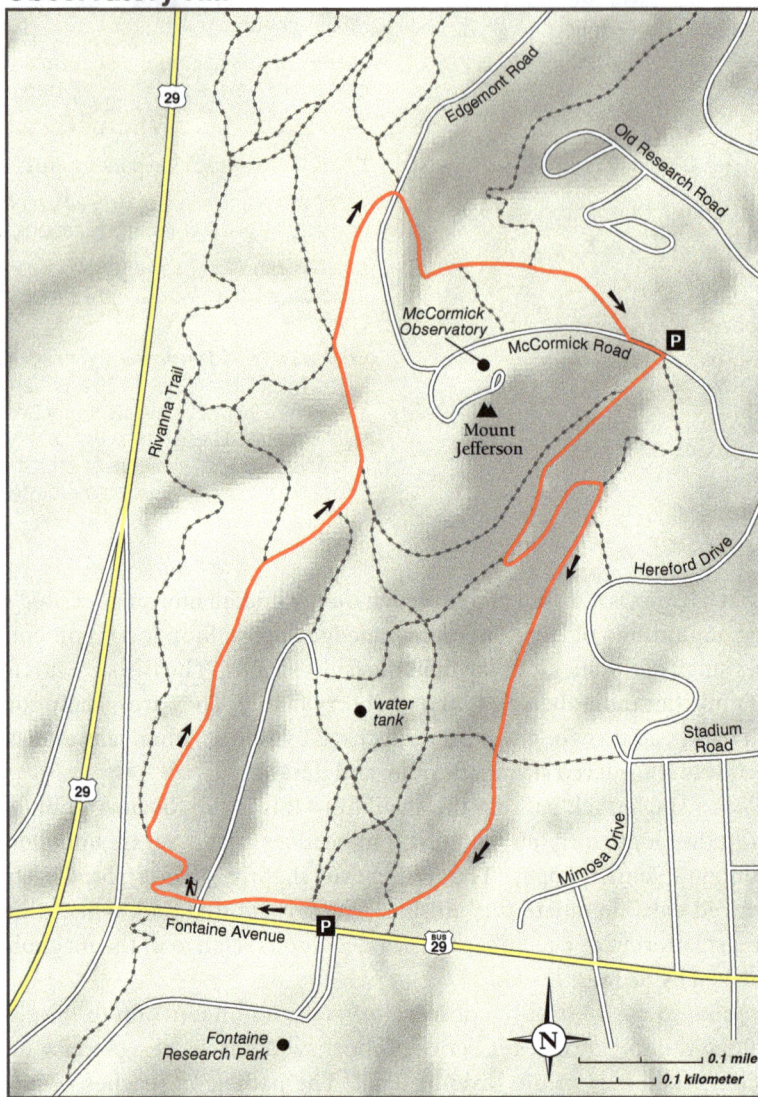

before reentering the forest and winding along to a chain-link fence. The trail follows this fenceline for a few hundred feet before reaching McCormick Road.

This hike does not pass by the observatory, but it is just a few hundred steps up McCormick Road from this spot. The University of Virginia's mountaintop observatory is named for Leander McCormick, who in 1877 donated to the university what was then the largest telescope in America. Leander made his fortune as the business partner of his brother Cyrus, who perfected the scheme for a mechanical reaper first conceived by their father, Robert. The Virginia Reaper, as it was known, dramatically increased farm efficiency and is widely credited with spurring agrarian development of the American West.

Another tycoon, Cornelius "Commodore" Vanderbilt (who built his fortune on a New York ferry route), helped fund construction of a metal-domed brick building to house the telescope. It was completed in 1884 along with a residence for the observatory director. Now known as Alden House, after a former keeper of the telescope, that brick abode stands a short distance south of the observatory.

Though the site was chosen for its vertical rather than horizontal views, today's persistent hiker is rewarded with the sight of the surrounding Appalachian foothills. Obstructed by treetop foliage in the summer, views are best in the winter, particularly after a dusting of snow. Consider a return visit to the observatory to gaze through the university's telescope.

Walk along McCormick Road briefly before reaching an optional trailhead. White oaks and mountain laurel grow more abundantly along this loftier stretch of trail, and modest boulders dot the forest floor. Pass a rusty gate to begin your descent along a rocky doubletrack service road for the park.

The rocky roadbed meanders as it passes far downhill of the observatory, which is not visible, as the forest canopy is too thick.

A series of side trails are visible to the left, dropping sharply away from the gravel doubletrack. Take a left onto a singletrack path about 0.2 mile from the alternate trailhead that follows several humps and turns through a patch of invasive privet and English ivy before connecting to another doubletrack. A right at this lower trail junction leads you past a retention pond protected by a chain-link fence.

The trail then connects to a paved multiuse path in a wide ravine that connects Stadium Road with Fontaine Avenue around the apartments and homes in Mimosa Court. Take a right to follow this path down to the Osage orange tree and the Fontaine Avenue crossing to return to the parking lot.

NEARBY ACTIVITIES

East of the University of Virginia is Jefferson's famed **Monticello** estate (434-984-9800, monticello.org), accessible via the Saunders-Monticello Trail (see page 295). Tours of the restored manse and grounds leave from the western trailhead of that trail, which also passes above Michie Tavern, a late-18th-century inn that still offers a daily lunch buffet, as well as tours led by interpreters in period garb. About a mile from Monticello stands **Highland** (434-293-8000, highland.org), where guests now tour the former home and garden of President James Monroe.

• •

GPS TRAILHEAD COORDINATES N38° 01.610' W78° 31.602'

DIRECTIONS From Richmond, follow I-64 northwest to Exit 118B, and head northbound on US 29. Drive 0.7 mile before turning right onto Fontaine Avenue (US 29 Business). Take another right on Ray C. Hunt Drive into the Fontaine Research Park.

If you prefer, there is a trailhead near the top of Jefferson Mountain on McCormick Avenue. Continue on Fontaine Avenue, then take a left on Mimosa Drive. Continue right on Mimosa to Stadium Road, where the road becomes Hereford Drive. Continue straight as the road winds up the hill. Take a left onto McCormick Road, and the small trailhead will be on left. There is a small parking area at the observatory as well, just a bit farther up McCormick Road.

The rocky trails at Observatory Hill are mostly shaded.

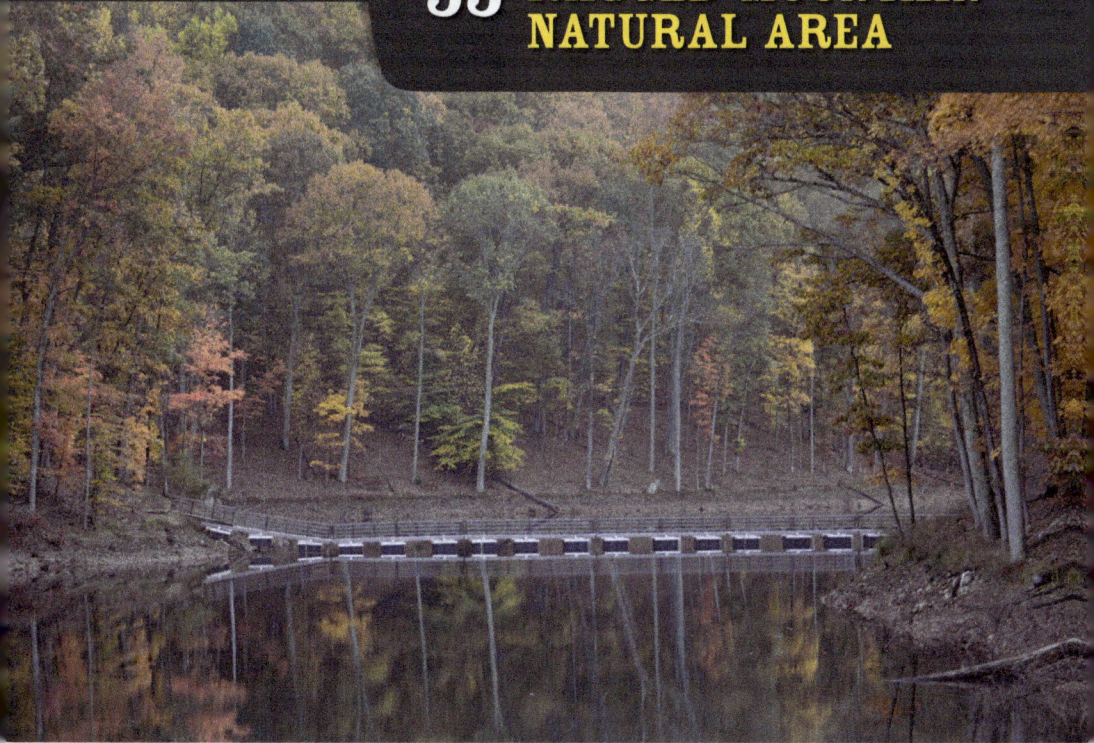

The floating bridge was installed in spring 2016 after the capacity of the reservoir was increased.

BEFORE ENCIRCLING CHARLOTTESVILLE RESERVOIR, the trail at Ragged Mountain Natural Area gets off to a rough start, gaining more than 300 feet in the first 0.5 mile. A round-trip includes several switchback climbs and descents. A scenery highlight is the floating bridge, the first of its kind in the state. Seemingly remote despite the proximity of I-64, the natural area protects both boulder-studded slopes and a creek-fed marsh.

DESCRIPTION

A string of peaks reaching south and west from Charlottesville, the Ragged Mountains remain true to their name: boulders jut from the hillsides, and roots crisscross the earth. Cloaked in mature forest, the hillsides must appear today much as they did when Edgar Allan Poe hiked them while studying at the University of Virginia—woodland ambles that inspired his short story "A Tale of the Ragged Mountains."

In the 1820s Poe could have explored a steep-sided stream valley where modern visitors find Charlottesville Reservoir. In 1885 Charlottesville partnered with the university to dam the creek flowing southeast below Round Top, creating a public water supply. Twenty-three years later, the impoundment was tripled in size. Then in the 1920s, a 13-mile-long cast-iron aqueduct was laid underground to siphon water from

287

DISTANCE & CONFIGURATION: 6.5-mile loop, plus optional spurs

DIFFICULTY: Strenuous

ELEVATION: 570' at trailhead, 855' at high point

SCENERY: Reservoir, hardwood-forested hillsides, creek-fed marsh, floating bridge

EXPOSURE: Well shaded

TRAFFIC: Moderate; highest near the education building

TRAIL SURFACE: Dirt, gravel

HIKING TIME: 3 hours

SEASON: Year-round during daylight hours

ACCESS: No fee

WHEELCHAIR ACCESS: Wheelchairs not recommended, except along reservoir from waterside parking area

MAPS: At trailhead and charlottesville.org /home/showdocument?id=55696

DRIVING DISTANCE FROM CAPITOL: 76 miles

FACILITIES: Portable toilet at waterside parking area, trailhead kiosk

CONTACT: 434-970-3260, charlottesville.org

LOCATION: 1730 Reservoir Rd., Charlottesville

COMMENTS: Ragged Mountain is managed for wildlife viewing and preservation only. Dog walking, swimming, and camping are prohibited. Additional trails are under development to allow bicycles and runners. Fishing is allowed and requires a valid state fishing permit (visit dgif.virginia.gov/licenses). Only nonmotorized boats are allowed on the reservoir. There is not currently a public boat ramp, so smaller boats are encouraged.

Sugar Hollow Reservoir. The pipe still carries 4 million gallons daily; this hike crosses the stone flume that channels that torrent toward its final cascade into the reservoir.

Our trail starts with a steep climb from the lower parking area. It is advisable to take a map with you, as the trails were being worked on as of this writing and many of the junctions were not fully marked. The route departs uphill (northbound), beyond the trailhead signboard. The rock-studded path weaves beneath yellow poplars, red maples, and dogwoods, ascending steadily toward the crest of Round Top. The surrounding vegetation indicates moist soil due to runoff from the rocky hill. After passing through a modest boulder garden and beside a mammoth chestnut oak, the trail forks to offer a spur loop to ascend Round Top or continue along the main trail.

Turn left at a junction along an old doubletrack road. The main trail enjoys a wide, level treadway as it heads gently downhill to the lakeshore. Pass the wooden "Mountain Man" feature, one of a handful of sculpted wooden statues along the trail. When you reach the sculpture of two painted black bears, there is an optional Peninsula Trail loop. Another carving can be found along the lakeshore. If you choose this 0.3-mile diversion, take a left to continue north at the trail junction as you loop back.

The main trail passes through white, northern red, and chestnut oaks to reach a stream. One of numerous tributaries that empty into the reservoir, the trickle has worn a deep gully into the hillside. After passing a carving of a bald eagle with a fish, cross on a footbridge (built by an Eagle Scout in 2015), bear left, and follow the fern-clad rivulet along the lakeshore.

The trail follows above the banks as it curves from west to north. Depending on the water level, granite walls may be visible across the water. Cross a small runoff

Ragged Mountain Natural Area

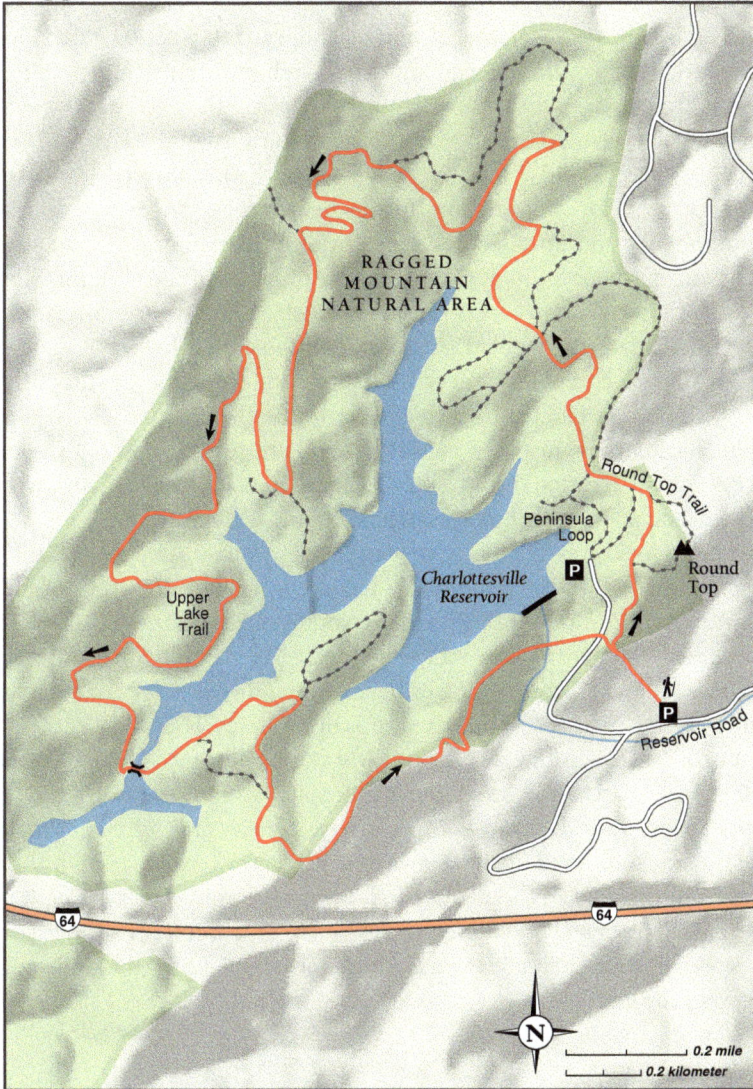

RAGGED
MOUNTAIN
NATURAL AREA

Round Top Trail

Peninsula
Loop

Round
Top

Charlottesville
Reservoir

Upper
Lake
Trail

Reservoir Road

64

64

N

0.2 mile

0.2 kilometer

culvert with the aid of railroad-tie steps after passing through a stand of Virginia pines. Not far ahead, mountain laurel thickets crowd the path. Descend a slope before rounding the northernmost arm of the reservoir, which is fed by two small creeks. Look for shagbark and bitternut hickory growing in the moist soil here.

As the path turns south, across a seasonal stream, the trail rises on wood-beam stairs through a boulder-strewn stretch of forest. Large rocks abut the lake ahead and invite sunbathing or picnicking. Upon reaching an intersection with Upper Lake Trail, take a right to continue along a newer bench-cut trail that generally follows above the shoreline.

Traversing a creek-fed marsh at the southwestern tip of the lake, look for sourwood trees growing along the water's edge. Tread lightly through this marsh and you may spot waterfowl, otters, and turtles before they spot you. The trail turns away from the lake and up the creek valley, where riparian grasses and vines grow beneath young hardwoods, including vibrant red maples in the autumn. Step over a small rivulet, then rock-hop across the larger creek. A tall river birch shades a third, small feeder, while a fern-dappled hillside rises opposite a fourth.

Trail work was completed in early 2018 to connect to the floating bridge that crosses the reservoir. The bridge, which Charlottesville planners called the first of its kind in Virginia, was installed in spring 2016 after the capacity of the reservoir was increased, which raised the water levels in the lake. It provides a new wrinkle for repeat hikers and an interesting vantage point of the waterway.

The bridge measures 220 feet across and 5 feet wide. It is made of planks of ipe, a Brazilian hardwood, selected for its maintenance-free properties, according to the Rivanna Water and Sewer Authority. The wooden planks are held in place by an aluminum frame anchored to six concrete blocks placed at the floor of the reservoir during construction of the dam. The bridge floats by the buoyancy of the foam-filled floats and is designed to accommodate drops in water level up to 10 feet.

After crossing the bridge, the trail slowly climbs up another ridge on the south side of the natural area. You are about a mile away from completing the circuit at this point. The trail winds down to the spillway, a grassy area with high rocky bluffs (blocked off by chain-link fencing) on each side from where the center of the ridge was blasted out to allow an escape for water if the reservoir overfills. The trail meets the dam, and a long gravel doubletrack takes you to the reservoir parking area. A step into the woods and a right back down the trail finish the hike for those who parked in the lower parking lot.

• •

GPS TRAILHEAD COORDINATES N38° 01.607' W78° 33.351'

DIRECTIONS From Richmond, follow I-64 northwest to Exit 118B, and head northbound on US 29. In about 0.5 mile, turn left onto Fontaine Avenue (US 29 Business in the opposite direction). Proceed 0.75 mile, then turn right onto VA 702 (Reservoir Road). The road soon becomes gravel and winds 2 miles to the trailhead on the right, shortly before the road's terminus, at the lower parking area. There is a second parking lot farther along the road, next to the reservoir.

Numbered posts in the Riverview Park section identify nearly 20 tree species that grow along the trail.

THIS TRAIL IS A VALUED RECREATIONAL RESOURCE for Charlottesville residents, but it's somewhat doubtful that many complete the almost 20-mile loop on foot in one attempt. Fortunately, the ring trail passes numerous access points as it wends its way through parks and suburbs, so it's easy to customize a point-to-point or out-and-back that suits you.

DESCRIPTION

In 1992, Charlottesville hikers founded the Rivanna Trails Foundation with an ambitious goal: to encircle the city with a footpath. They chose primarily riparian corridors—along the Rivanna River and Moores and Meadow Creeks—although on the city's western edge, the trail runs nearer roadways.

Having secured landowners' permission, cleared brush, built bridges, and blazed more than 19 trail miles, the foundation's volunteers have almost realized their vision. There are still improvements to be made, but you can hike a loop around Charlottesville via the Rivanna Loop if you try. The foundation's stated focus has been to maintain the trails of the loop to be at least suitable for hiking, but many sections may not yet be suitable for mountain biking or other users.

Rivanna Trail began with the city-owned Rivanna River Greenbelt, which follows its namesake waterway north from Riverview Park to US 250 at East High

DISTANCE & CONFIGURATION: 3-mile out-and-back, plus other options; 19.5 total miles in Rivanna Loop

DIFFICULTY: Easy–moderate, depending on length of hike

ELEVATION: 318' at trailhead, no significant rise (from Riverview Park)

SCENERY: Riparian bottomland along Rivanna River, wildflowers, hardwood and recovering forests

EXPOSURE: Mostly shaded

TRAFFIC: Moderate

TRAIL SURFACE: Paved along 1.5-mile Riverview Park; dirt and paved elsewhere

HIKING TIME: 1 hour for this segment

SEASON: Year-round during daylight hours

ACCESS: No fee

WHEELCHAIR ACCESS: At Riverview Park

MAPS: At major access points and rivannatrails.org

DRIVING DISTANCE FROM CAPITOL: 72 miles

FACILITIES: Portable toilets, playground, parking area for 30 cars at trailhead

CONTACT: City of Charlottesville Parks: 434-970-3589, charlottesville.org/parks; Rivanna Trails Foundation (for tree information): rivannatrails.org

LOCATION: Riverview Park, 298 Riverside Ave., Charlottesville

COMMENTS: A good educational tool for children, numbered posts refer you to an interpretive handout (available at the trailheads) that identifies almost 20 tree species growing along the trail.

Street (Free Bridge). The greenbelt's popularity fueled construction of the longer trail, which uses the greenbelt footpath.

On its own, this section of the trail makes for an out-and-back hike of about 3 miles. The 10-foot-wide paved surface is more conducive to casual strolling than most of Rivanna Trail, and trailside fishing in the river is also a popular draw. An additional 0.4-mile trail offers a loop back to the parking lot, or a short loop hike is possible within Riverview Park.

Begin this hike from the trailhead in Riverview Park, and pass the playgrounds on the way to the river. The trail follows the riverbank, about 15 feet above typical water levels. The path is lined by a variety of hardwoods. Numbered posts refer you to an interpretive handout (available at the trailhead) that identifies almost 20 tree species growing along the trail. The guided walk points out many floodplain species along the initial sections of the trail, including white ash and green ash, box elder, and scattered eastern red cedar. It also identifies sycamore, hackberry, red oak, white oak, chestnut oak, basswood, hickory, ironwood (hornbeam), American holly, eastern hemlock, and pawpaw. Invasive species that likely washed down from old homesites upriver include catalpa and mimosa, which is generally considered a weed.

About 0.25 mile into the hike, the trail crosses an open field cleared for power lines. It quickly reenters the riparian buffer and continues to wind westward, following the riverbank in an S shape. Along the way, sandy beaches and rock outcroppings allow water access. Many brief openings in the tree cover also give glimpses of the river.

The trail passes below Riverview Cemetery, which sits high on a bluff above the river. A brief clearing in the tree canopy reveals a wide trail with a bench, where you can rest and enjoy the scenery. Another 100 yards down the path, the trail takes a

Rivanna Trail

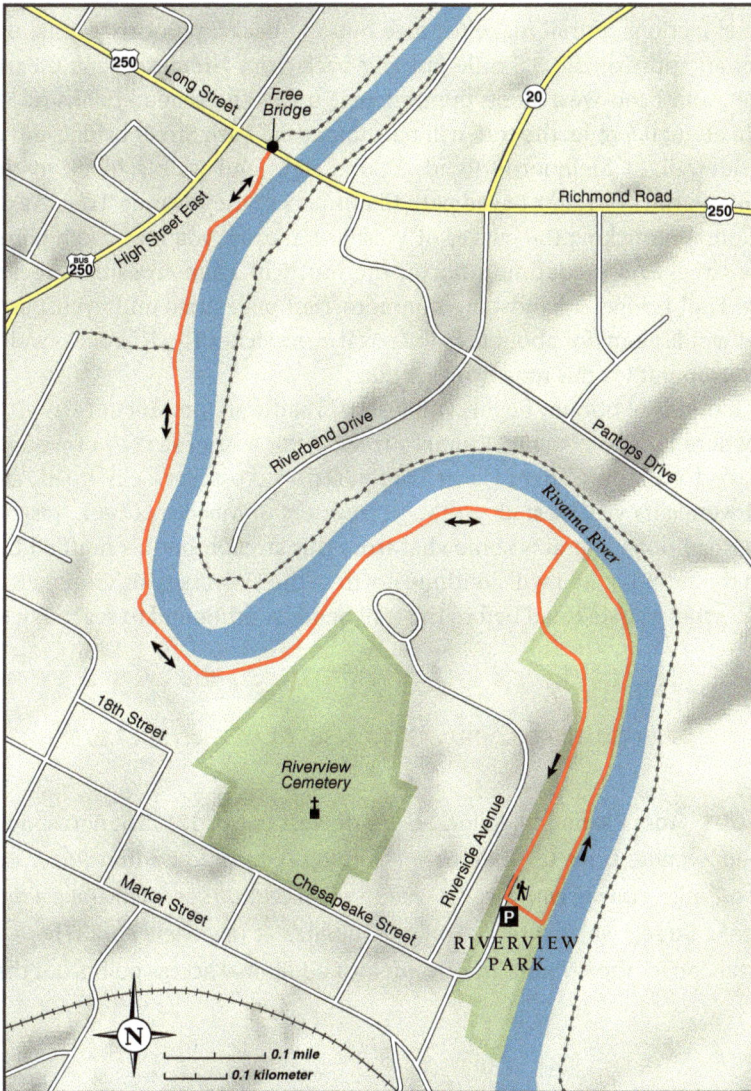

right onto a wide wooden bridge over a creek and then twists back to the left to run north to the Free Bridge, about 0.5 mile from this location. For this hike, we chose to turn around at this point and return to the Riverview Park trailhead.

If you wish to continue, from the Free Bridge the trail travels north of US 250, along the Rivanna about a mile to Meadow Creek, then veers left along the tributary. The trail covers another 1.6 miles to Holmes Avenue.

Other sections of trail make for nice out-and-backs, point-to-points, or loops. Consider an approximate 3.5-mile out-and-back from Holmes Avenue. Park along the street, and head west along the trail as it traces the shaded banks of Meadow Creek. In about 0.5 mile, the trail will pass under the Park Street bridge and emerge onto a sidewalk at Melbourne Road. Take a right and walk a block to the John W. Warner Parkway Trail, a paved path that is part of the Rivanna Trail. As the path winds along, mimicking the curves of Warner Parkway, you may catch glimpses of Meadow Creek. As it continues north, the trail will again cross the creek on the Parkway Trail bridge, a handsome nonmotorized pedestrian and cyclist structure. The trail winds along for about 0.25 mile as it approaches Rio Road. Consider this a good return point for this mostly urban hike.

For a one-way option, begin with a short road walk on Morton Drive/Earhart Street, where it crosses under Emmet Street. After a brief stretch of woods to the west, a road walk on Cedars Court is required to cross Barracks Road, and then the trail wends its way west along the headwaters of Meadow Creek, just south of US 250. Road noise detracts somewhat from this stretch, but it's muffled by dense forest in the summer. You will continue north of the University of Virginia School of Law then cross Massie Road before the trail bends southbound to reach Ivy Road.

• •

GPS TRAILHEAD COORDINATES N38° 01.443' W78° 27.278'

DIRECTIONS From Richmond, follow I-64 northwest to Exit 121. Exit northbound onto Monticello Avenue. Drive 0.7 mile before turning right onto Carlton Road. Continue another 0.7 mile, staying with Meade Avenue when Carlton veers left. Take a right onto Chesapeake Street, which after 0.6 mile terminates at Riverview Park. There you will find a trailhead for the Rivanna Trail. Numerous additional access points dot the route.

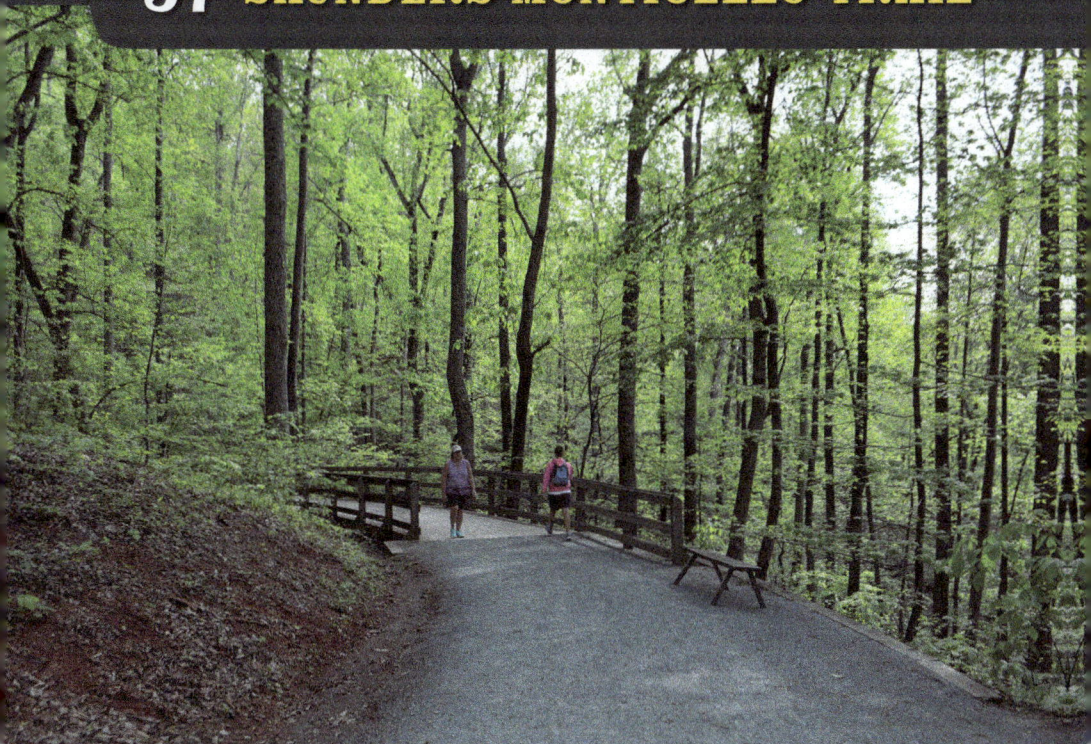

The shaded trail has several long wooden boardwalks as it climbs the mountain to Monticello.

THE WELL-BUILT SAUNDERS-MONTICELLO TRAIL allows Monticello visitors to augment a trip to Thomas Jefferson's famous home with an amble along the hillside of Carter Mountain. However, the path's wide gravel surface and winding boardwalks are most frequented by locals out for a pleasant stroll or an invigorating run. Singletrack trails accessible from the Kemper Park trailhead allow you to expand your visit with a secluded climb among towering oaks and yellow poplars.

DESCRIPTION

Few American homes are more widely recognized than Jefferson's Monticello. But few people recall that it fell into periodic neglect during the 19th century. Though Thomas Jefferson himself designed Monticello and oversaw its construction—an ongoing exercise in perfectionism that spanned four decades—it remained in his family for only five years after his death in 1826.

It was at Monticello that Jefferson likely romanced his slave Sally Hemings (and verifiably freed her offspring), yet he also consented to slavery there because it gave a plantation at the rocky periphery of Virginia's Piedmont some prospects for economic viability. Nevertheless, upon his death, Jefferson left his estate $100,000 in

DISTANCE & CONFIGURATION: 4.3-mile out-and-back, plus other options

DIFFICULTY: Easy

ELEVATION: 411' at trailhead, 663' at high point

SCENERY: Mature hillside forest, small pond, arboretum, native-plant garden, views of neighboring foothills

EXPOSURE: Mostly shaded

TRAFFIC: Moderate

TRAIL SURFACE: Crushed gravel, extensive curving boardwalks

HIKING TIME: 2 hours

SEASON: Year-round during daylight hours, but easternmost section closes with Monticello.

ACCESS: No fee; tours of Monticello from $20 adults, $9 children

WHEELCHAIR ACCESS: Yes, but trail has a steady, steep slope

MAPS: At trailhead and monticello.org

DRIVING DISTANCE FROM CAPITOL: 71 miles

FACILITIES: Trailhead parking, benches, Monticello gift shop at eastern trailhead; restrooms only at Monticello visitor center

CONTACT: Thomas Jefferson Memorial Foundation: 434-984-9800, monticello.org

LOCATION: Kemper Park, 931 Thomas Jefferson Pkwy., Charlottesville

COMMENTS: Dogs must be leashed in Kemper Park, and pets are not allowed on the trail. The main trail is open to runners and cyclists (10 mph speed limit).

debt. The 1,000-acre plantation acquired in 1735 by his father, Peter, had proven unable to sustain Jefferson's costly vision of agrarian gentility.

Within a year of Jefferson's burial at Monticello, the home was denuded of art and furniture. Many of the pieces he had selected while abroad during his tenure as minister to France, as well as the natural-history specimens given to him by, among others, Lewis and Clark, were auctioned to pay off debts. The home soon followed.

Its first savior appeared in the garb of a US naval commodore, Uriah Levy. His curiosity was purportedly sparked by an inquiry from the Marquis de Lafayette as to "the most beautiful house in America." Levy acquired a dilapidated Monticello in 1833 (for $2,700). Recognizing its historical and architectural value, he set about restoring the home. It is often speculated that Levy's Jewish heritage (his ancestors fled Portugal during the Inquisition) had moved him to reverence for Jefferson, chief agitator for the Bill of Rights and thus America's official secularity.

Decades of restoration were undone in a few short years after Confederate troops confiscated Monticello in 1861, a year before Levy's death. The home was later returned to his descendants, who began 17 years of legal wrangling over his will, which offered the property to the federal government for the establishment of an orphanage and agricultural school. Finally, in 1879, his nephew, the aptly named Jefferson Levy, ended the dispute by buying out the other contenders. Meanwhile, Monticello was near ruin. Cattle were housed in the basement and grain stored in the drawing room. Another Levy generation set about restoring the home at great cost.

Far from being lauded for his preservationist impulse, Jefferson Levy was subjected to a nationwide campaign, at times anti-Semitic in tone, to have Congress acquire Monticello by legislation. After years of intransigence, he finally relented in

Saunders–Monticello Trail

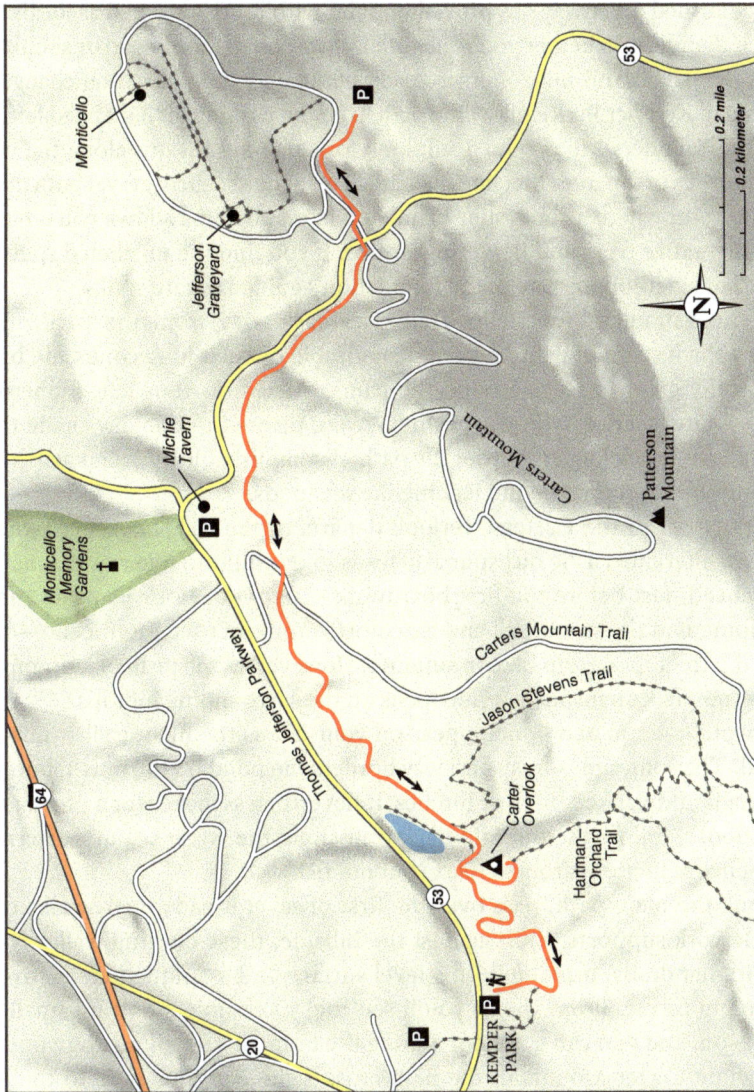

1923, selling the estate to the private Thomas Jefferson Foundation. Today the foundation maintains the property and supports Jefferson-related research and education.

In the past decade the foundation has made ambitious improvements to the VA 53 corridor between Charlottesville and Monticello, known as the Thomas Jefferson Parkway. Eighty-nine acres at the base of Carter Mountain were landscaped and dubbed Kemper Park, and the 2-mile Saunders-Monticello Trail rose up the mountainside on sturdy boardwalks. A stone bridge linking the forested corridor with Monticello completed the project.

The finished greenway has proved popular with tourists as well as locals looking to stretch their legs. Whether you're augmenting a visit to Monticello or simply out for an afternoon stroll, this hike offers a steady but invigorating elevation change (252'). Beginning in Kemper Park, follow the path from the parking lot, and head left. As you ascend the Saunders-Monticello Trail, look for small metal signs along the way that identify dozens of the trees that line the path. The wide crushed-gravel path curves by the arboretum, where a short spur blanketed in wood chips allows you an up-close view of the native trees and flowering shrubs. If you find the unlabeled spur hard to identify, consider joining one of the foundation's guided nature walks.

As the Saunders-Monticello Trail rises east away from the park, it passes through a thick stand of white pines, recognizable by their long cones and branches that typically grow in rings around the trunk. Ahead on your left, numerous oak species—white, scarlet, willow, chestnut—were planted to one day shade the trail. Beyond those, black locusts border the path, distinguishable by their small leaves on long fronds, modest thorns, and legumelike seedpods.

A spur trail to the Carter Overlook departs to the right, curving as it climbs 50 feet. An alternate rustic dirt spur also leads to this hilltop; it leaves the main route farther ahead, just before the first boardwalk. After your brisk jaunt up the knoll, rest a moment at the stone wall and gaze north. You can't see Monticello—or much besides the treetops—from here in summer. However, at the peak of autumn or after a winter snowfall, an inspiring vista opens on the surrounding hilltops.

Downhill, views of a pond appear on your left as the main trail winds around the knoll. The sometimes-busy parkway borders the pond on the north, but, fringed with cattails and flanked by river birches, it nevertheless makes for a pleasant scene. If you choose, follow the out-and-back trail along the water's southeastern shore, where benches invite visitors to relax (but not fish).

Along the main path, pass over the first of several wide boardwalks elevated by trestlework supports. Built against the hillside, these curving walkways, complete with handrails, provide both a level surface and a unique perspective of the surrounding forest. From them, you'll see rocky streamlets cutting small valleys beneath you, and you can stare out among the branches of young dogwoods.

Hugging Carter Mountain, the path crosses the entrance road to the popular orchard. As it continues uphill, it soon passes a water tank in the woods below. The parkway is audible and intermittently visible through the trees at your left. At roughly its halfway point, the trail bisects an old gravel road but continues straight to pass above Michie Tavern. Though the tavern was constructed in 1774, it was moved to its present location in 1928. Before that, the two-story, wood-frame structure stood in northern Albemarle County.

As it continues west, the Saunders-Monticello Trail alternately employs gravel tread and wide boardwalks. Chestnut oaks thrive on this steep hillside and buffer the trail before it emerges into a clearing. Visible ahead, the stone Saunders Bridge links the trail's longest stretch with its final stretch to Monticello. Note that the bridge is also used by vehicular traffic. Once across, bear right, back into the forest. The trail wends a short distance farther, along Monticello's entrance road, to reach its eastern trailhead. Nearby are the Monticello gift shop and café. Don't expect to catch a distant glimpse of Jefferson's landscaped estate, though—for that you'll have to take the tour.

More adventuresome hikers may prefer to stay on the trail, adding distance to their hike by exploring the mowed paths that lace the meadows south of Kemper Park or taking the more strenuous singletrack that continues halfway up Carter Mountain. To reach these trails from Kemper Park, follow signs for Secluded Farm Trails. Stay left after crossing the gravel doubletrack, and you'll find the mulch and red-clay trail that climbs the side of Carter Mountain beneath towering hardwoods. If you're winded, bear left, when the trail forks to descend to the overlook on the Saunders-Monticello Trail. If you're feeling brisk, bear right to keep climbing before making a hard left. A level stretch takes you just below Carter Mountain Orchard and beyond Secluded Farm onto the foundation's Hartman and Montalto tracts. You'll switchback down the mountain to arrive on the Saunders-Monticello Trail just below the overlook. This longer return adds almost 1 mile.

NEARBY ACTIVITIES

History and architecture aficionados will find plenty more to see in the vicinity. **Michie Tavern** (434-977-1234, michietavern.com), one of the commonwealth's oldest homes, serves a daily lunch buffet and seasonal dinners at its dining room, the Ordinary. More than a restaurant, however, the tavern doubles as a museum of 18th-century life, complete with costumed docents and rotating exhibits. President James Monroe's onetime home, **Highland** (434-293-8000, highland.org), circa 1799, is just a mile south on VA 53 and is open for house and garden tours. A visit to **Carter Mountain Orchard** (434-977-1833, chilesfamilyorchards.com/orchards/carter-mountain-orchard) is recommended during apple-picking season.

• •

GPS TRAILHEAD COORDINATES N38° 00.183' W78° 28.686'

DIRECTIONS From Richmond, follow I-64 northwest to Exit 121. Exit southbound on VA 20 (Scottsville Road), following signs for Monticello. After 0.5 mile, passing the Monticello Visitor Center on your right, turn left onto VA 53 (Thomas Jefferson Parkway). The parking lot fronting Kemper Park (western trailhead) is a short distance ahead, just off the road to your right. Additional parking is available off VA 20 northbound and linked to the park via a tunnel under VA 53. To reach the Monticello lot (eastern trailhead), continue on VA 53 for 1.5 miles, then exit the parkway north into the Monticello grounds at the stone Saunders Bridge.

58 SCHEIER NATURAL AREA

The ponds from the Scheier family fish hatchery are still intact.

THREADING THROUGH REFORESTED PASTURE and cropland, the trails at Scheier Natural Area descend well-drained hillsides to a northbound creek. Rising away on tapering ridges and twice bisecting a feeder stream, they're an example of how hydrology shapes topography in these Appalachian foothills.

DESCRIPTION

The 100-acre Scheier Natural Area has nine ponds and more than 3 miles of wooded trails for hiking, enjoyment of nature, and environmental education. The land was bequeathed to the Rivanna Conservation Society (RCS) by Howard and Neva Scheier in 1997. RCS has helped to maintain the trail network and provided an educational kiosk, a parking area, and an outhouse. A pavilion for educational events and programs was in the works as of this writing.

After all the work the Scheier family put into the farm, it is good to see that they were able to secure its preservation. I was inspired reading about their efforts and the work of volunteers to create the natural area. It reminded me of a quote from conservationist Aldo Leopold: "Conservation is a state of harmony between men and land." Their work paid off.

The bulk of Scheier Natural Area is west of the parking area; however, the cluster of ponds, created as a fish hatchery, lies east of VA 639 (Long Acre Road). Today

DISTANCE & CONFIGURATION: 2.7-mile figure eight, plus out-and-back spur

DIFFICULTY: Easy

ELEVATION: 470' at trailhead, 369' at low point

SCENERY: Tributary of Cunningham Creek, wooded ridges

EXPOSURE: Well shaded

TRAFFIC: Low

TRAIL SURFACE: Dirt

HIKING TIME: 1.5 hours

SEASON: Year-round during daylight hours

ACCESS: No fee

WHEELCHAIR ACCESS: Wheelchairs not recommended

MAPS: On park signboard and at rivannariver.org

DRIVING DISTANCE FROM CAPITOL: 71.9 miles

FACILITIES: Parking area, trailhead kiosk, educational kiosk

CONTACT: Rivanna Conservation Society: 434-977-4837, rivannariver.org

LOCATION: 1259 Long Acre Rd., Palmyra

COMMENTS: Scheier Natural Area is managed by the Rivanna Conservation Society. Dog walking, cycling, swimming, camping, and, of course, hunting and fishing are prohibited. Hunters do use the adjacent property, though, so wear blaze orange if you hike during deer season (see dgif.virginia.gov for dates).

the ponds are fringed with bullrush and are home to amphibians, such as frogs. A brief out-and-back to reach them serves as a warm-up to your hike at Scheier, so begin by crossing the road to follow the Green Trail southeast through mixed forest. The doubletrack path is blazed in its namesake color, as are most at Scheier (though some share treadway, complicating matters). Appropriately named, as it is carpeted in bright-green moss and pale gray-green lichens, the path curves to the right after passing a five-trunked chestnut oak. Upon reaching the tiered pools, trace a few of the earthen berms, just 3 or 4 feet wide, that separate them. These ponds, fed by springs and rainfall, stair-step down so that when one overflows it fills another. They ultimately drain east to the South Fork of Cunningham Creek.

Retrace your steps across VA 639 and through the parking area beyond the kiosk to begin your hike in earnest. The trail begins on level ground, part of a broad ridgetop along which VA 639 runs. In the winter, pine saplings and cedars color an otherwise deciduous wood dominated by southern red, northern red, chestnut, and post oaks. Mockernut hickories, red maples, and young beeches fill out this maturing second-growth forest.

Turn right onto the Red Trail at a T intersection with the Yellow Trail, and follow it as it bends from north to west. Moss-covered logs line some stretches of the path—a sort of deadfall recycling—and a field will be discernible through a veil of younger pines on your right. Join an older, wider path by veering slightly left, then pass a thicket of young cedars guarded by an old barbed-wire fence on your right. Pass through a smattering of young white pines, and continue straight on the Red Trail when the Yellow Trail leads left. Young beech trees signal a weaving descent. The path departs the finger ridge it has traveled to descend toward a northbound creek, a feeder streamlet running in the small valley to your left.

Scheier Natural Area

Identified on the park map as the South Branch of the Middle Fork of Cunningham Creek, the larger stream is a tributary of the Rivanna River. The RCS maintains this natural area not merely for watershed protection but largely as an educational forum. A map of the Rivanna River watershed at the trailhead signboard reinforces the notion that this small drainage is interwoven into a much larger ecological tapestry. (Contact the group to learn more, and consider volunteering for its cleanups.)

From a bench facing the creek, you can see mountain laurel clinging to a bluff upstream. Mossy, water-smoothed stones lie below; a pebble-strewn, sandy shoal waits downstream. A footbridge continues the trail over the feeder rivulet; look left to see ferns clinging to the striated-rock channel it has eroded. Then follow the trail on its short but steep rise to a pine-dotted ridge, the laurel now cascading downhill on your right. Continue upland beyond a series of windblown trees, and keep straight as the Blue Trail intersects your path on the left. Just ahead, take the White Trail as it heads right to curve north and runs a somewhat fruitless out-and-back along a finger ridge above the creek. Numerous white pines crown the ridge, most descendants of a lofty parent still watching over the grove. On this visit, the trail ended too far away for me to see the creek.

After retracing the White Trail, turn right on the combined White and Blue Trails. Soon after the path curves west, the White Trail heads left. Continue west, though, to take in one more view of the creek.

After descending the hillside, the trail makes a sharp left. A brook is visible downhill, and if you go a short distance beyond the junction, you will see its junction with another. From here the creek flows northeast toward the spot where you first encountered it. The rock-bottomed stream runs against an eroded rock bank on the west, with sandy, beech-studded bottomland stretching eastward. Be aware that venturing to the water's edge entails leaving the natural-area boundary.

Beyond the sharp turn, the trail heads southeast, running gradually uphill and away from the brook. Mountain laurel abounds downhill then gives way to a stand of young Virginia pines. A potentially muddy spot where runoff crosses the trail precedes another hard left. The singletrack path then continues rising through a forest of white oak and red maple, the latter of which brightens the forest with red and yellow displays each fall. Barbed wire was long ago strung along cedar posts on the right. Upon reaching a junction with the White Trail, turn left to follow the stretch of it you bypassed earlier. Note that by veering right through a break in the barbed-wire fence, you can opt for a shorter loop along the periphery of the preserve rather than the interior figure eight described here.

The White Trail runs level through more maples before reaching a T intersection. Turn right and retrace your steps past the other half of the White Trail on the left. Next, make a right onto the Blue Trail, the path tacking east as it descends past a dense cluster of young beeches. Young hardwoods and slightly taller pines soon border the trail on either side, indicating a past fire or timber harvest here. Ground pine grows along the trail as it curves left. Then a small rivulet briefly runs along the trail on your right before meeting a larger branch—the first you crossed. The water is channeled through a pipe beneath the trail, which ascends away past young piney forest on the right and more-mature open woods on the left.

The path soon meets the Yellow Trail, a mossy doubletrack that appears to be a well-worn old farm road studded with granite. Turn right for this hike's return leg. Continue ascending, sandwiched between old and young trees. The recovering wood on your left momentarily yields to older trees, which then give way to a meadow of tall grasses. Yellow blazes guide you past a junction with an old roadbed before the Blue Trail meets the path to curve left and back toward the connector. Make a right at the next junction to return to the parking area.

• •

GPS TRAILHEAD COORDINATES N37° 50.657' W78° 22.831'

DIRECTIONS From Richmond, follow I-64 northwest to Exit 136. Take VA 15 (James Madison Highway) south about 9 miles to Palmyra. Just beyond the small town, VA 15 crosses the Rivanna River. About 0.75 mile from the river, turn right onto VA 640 (Haden Martin Road) and drive 3.6 miles. Turn right again onto VA 639 (Long Acre Road). Follow the narrow road, which makes one sharp bend left, 3.7 miles to Scheier Natural Area, marked by a granite roadside sign. Parking spaces lie on the outside of the gravel drive that encircles the park kiosk.

From Charlottesville, take VA 53 for 13.5 miles past Monticello. Turn right onto VA 660/619, promptly veering left to stay with VA 660 for 3.2 miles. Make a right onto VA 640, then another quick right onto VA 639 (Long Acre Road). From there, follow the directions above.

Prince Edward Lake at Twin Lakes State Park

AS ITS NAME SUGGESTS, water-based recreation is the main draw at 548-acre Twin Lakes State Park. Goodwin Lake, the smaller of the two at 15 acres, is the epicenter of activity, with a swimming beach, a floating deck, paddleboat rentals, and onshore amenities. The first part of this hike encircles the larger of the aquatic siblings, 36-acre Prince Edward Lake, a quiet fishing lake save when a particularly boisterous group rents the adjacent conference center.

DESCRIPTION

How did Twin Lakes State Park come to have two modest artificial lakes a stone's throw apart? For decades the two were operated as separate parks. The surrounding land was purchased by the US government during the Great Depression and subsequently deeded to Virginia. The smaller twin, Goodwin Lake, was the centerpiece of a recreation area established in 1939. But Twin Lakes' larger impoundment, Prince Edward Lake, did not open until 1950, following a rather sad episode in the commonwealth's history.

In 1948 an African American banker named Maceo Conrad Martin sued after being denied access to Staunton River State Park (located on Buggs Island Lake). In response, Governor William Tuck approved the construction of Prince Edward Lake Recreation Area for Negroes along the whites-only Goodwin Lake Recreation Area. The parks remained segregated, with a black superintendent and staff at

DISTANCE & CONFIGURATION: 4.7-mile figure eight, with optional spurs

DIFFICULTY: Moderate around Prince Edward Lake; easy around Goodwin Lake

ELEVATION: 483' at trailhead, 531' at high point

SCENERY: Upland woods, riparian bottomland, Prince Edward and Goodwin Lakes

EXPOSURE: Mostly shaded; sometimes open along lakeshores

TRAFFIC: Low; higher near beach

TRAIL SURFACE: Dirt, gravel

HIKING TIME: 2 hours

SEASON: Year-round during daylight hours; high season Memorial Day–Labor Day

ACCESS: Parking $4; campsites from $30; high-season canoe, kayak, and rowboat rentals vary

WHEELCHAIR ACCESS: Restrooms, snack bar, conference center

MAPS: At park and dcr.virginia.gov/state-parks/twin-lakes

DRIVING DISTANCE FROM CAPITOL: 62 miles

FACILITIES: Restrooms; picnic shelters; playground; campground; cabins; showers; beach on Goodwin Lake; rowboat, canoe, and kayak rentals; boat launches on both lakes; snack bar; conference center

CONTACT: 434-392-3435, dcr.virginia.gov/state-parks/twin-lakes

LOCATION: 788 Twin Lakes Rd., Green Bay

COMMENTS: For a more robust day of hiking, the park is enveloped by the 6,496-acre Prince Edward–Gallion State Forest, which offers a designated multiuse trail and a network of forest roads. Overnight accommodations include a 33-site campground and 11 climate-controlled cabins.

Prince Edward Lake, until passage of the Civil Rights Act of 1964. The two parks were merged to form Twin Lakes State Park in 1986.

Though established under the auspices of providing "similar and equal facilities in lieu of access," it's noteworthy that Prince Edward Lake is twice as far from Mr. Martin's hometown as Staunton River State Park. Family, church, and civic groups hold cookouts in the shaded picnic area, and parents sunbathe on the sandy beach. The formerly "colored only" facilities on Prince Edward Lake are today part of Cedar Crest Conference Center, which includes displays on the park's history but is open by reservation only. Following the route set out here, you'll see the center across the lake but will bypass it on an upland stretch of the otherwise lakeside loop.

Begin your hike southbound on Goodwin Lake Road toward the boat launches, but turn left into the woods before the intersection that provides access to them. The wide, aptly named Between the Lakes Trail is distinguishable by a timber barrier that prevents vehicular access. Small moss- and lichen-covered boulders lie among the trailside cedars, Virginia pines, and post and black oaks, both of which favor dry, sandy soil. White oaks tower over the lakeshore as the trail bears right.

Just beyond a bench overlooking the water is a T intersection. This is the orange-blazed Otter's Path Trail, which encircles Prince Edward Lake. Turning left to hike the loop clockwise will take you over the dam and into the forest, saving the scenic lakeside section for last. Pass over the sycamore-shaded concrete spillway on a boardwalk about 20 feet long. The rocky streambed below leads north to join the Sandy River, which in turn wends its way to the Appomattox.

Twin Lakes State Park

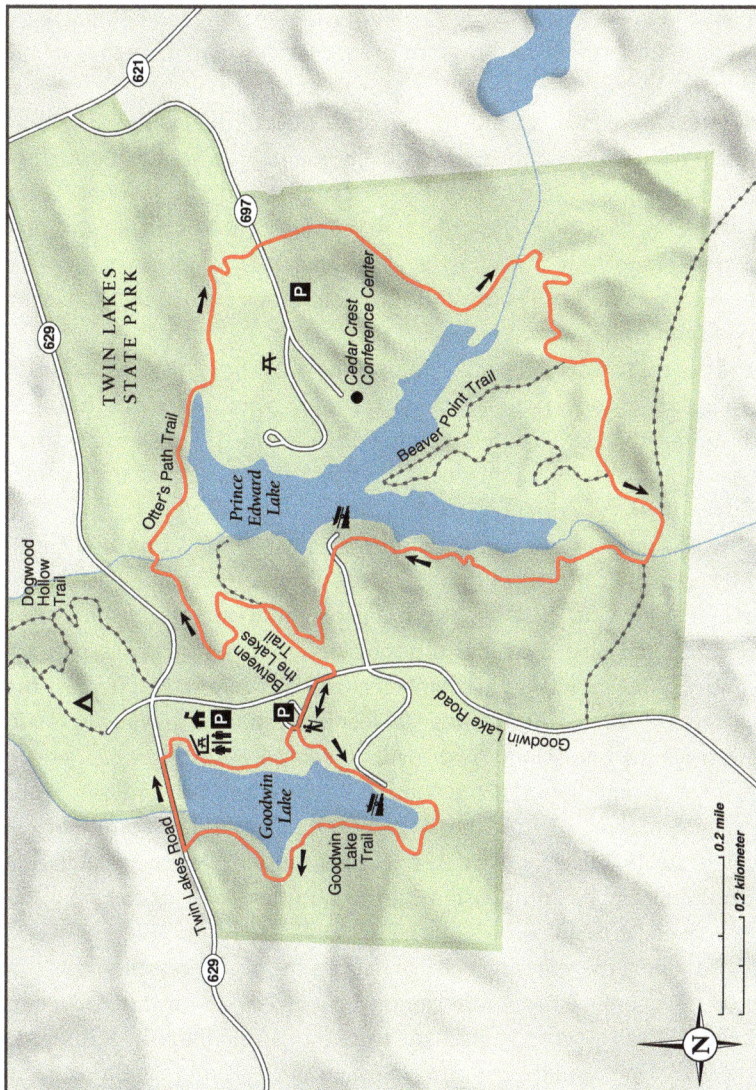

Continue east across the grassy earthen dam, then bear slightly right to bypass a wider trail heading uphill in favor of a sandy singletrack. Roots show through the path as it traces an arm of the lake, crossing feeder streamlets on concrete planks. You'll immediately note a different character to the woods here, which include river birches and red maples. In low-lying plains and on shaded hillsides, the forest floor is carpeted in ferns, sometimes interspersed with the round, lobed leaves of mayapples.

Turn left at the upcoming trail intersection, as the path leading straight ahead enters the conference center grounds. The trail parallels a meandering stream with

307

eroded banks then bears right to wind uphill. After cresting the hill, the path crosses an asphalt road into a glade of pines. An orange Otter's Path marker is visible ahead. Pass into a power-line clearing to enter a forest of hardwoods.

As the trail descends, swaths of the forest floor grow lush with ground cedar. True to its name, the verdant ground cover resembles a stand of 4-inch-tall evergreens. This variant of club moss, often associated with ferns, favors moist, middle-growth forest. Reproducing by spores, club mosses spread along the ground through lateral underground branches. Fossils show that their ancient ancestors towered 40 feet high. The club-moss bogs of the Carboniferous era 300 million years ago are the oil fields and coal mines of today.

Ahead the trail skims the trunk of a sizable yellow poplar. More are visible down the trail, where a seasonal rivulet running on your right turns to briefly join the path. The path soon arrives at a T intersection, with a wooden beam obstructing the trail that heads right to the conference center. Otter's Path turns left to trace a finger of Prince Edward Lake after passing through an airy stand of pine.

Boardwalks augment the trail as it bears right (south) around this marshy lake inlet fed by a small brook, itself draining from a pond upstream. This far end of the loop sees less traffic than the lakeside path; grass and weeds growing in the moist soil may crowd the trail. Bearing right, the trail soon makes a steady ascent, and as the small marsh recedes from view, hardwoods give way to pines, their needles blanketing the trail. Crest the hill, having ascended 90 feet in 0.1 mile, to join an old roadbed.

Begin tracing an oak ridge. The roadbed soon descends to cross a brook. Your route, however, bears right to reach another intersection. Beaver Point Trail, an out-and-back spur totaling 0.5 mile, heads right. Otter's Path crosses the brook before curving right itself. The shallow water is easily forded in an inviting glade where a bridge would merely be an intrusion. In the summer, look for the small flowers of orange jewelweed growing here.

Proceed along the gurgling, clear-running brook. The trail zigzags, rerouted by downed trees, before the southernmost arm of Prince Edward Lake comes into view. Ahead the trail ascends steps made from the sawed limbs of another past windfall. As the lake widens on the right, the path undulates along the shore, occasionally drawing along the water.

Shortly after crossing a small feeder stream on wooden planks, the trail passes the boat launch. From here the conference center is visible on the opposite shore. Otter's Path continues across the gravel vehicle-turnaround area, just slightly uphill. The final leg of the loop continues along the lakeshore, traversing some small, seasonal streamlets and numerous tree roots to reach the Between the Lakes Trail on which you first set out (signed CONNECTION TRAIL here). Retrace your steps to the parking area.

You can end your hike here, satisfied with 3.5 miles, or you can add another mile by hiking the Goodwin Lake Trail loop, which is dotted with wooden benches and is rated as easy. Begin at the trailhead in the southwestern corner of the parking area near Goodwin Lake. The blue-blazed trail passes the boat launch and a gravel trailer turnabout before reentering the woods, rarely venturing far from the banks of the lake. The trail crosses two creeks with a couple of recently constructed footbridges before reaching an older footbridge with an observation deck, offering a new vantage point of the beach, located on the opposite side of the lake. When the trail reaches the main park road, cross the dam along this route and continue walking around the lake along a gravel path, passing picnic shelters, the boat rental stand, and the roped-off swimming area. The park also includes a 1-mile hike on the Dogwood Hollow Trail, which begins east of the main campgrounds.

NEARBY ACTIVITIES

Twin Lakes State Park is enveloped by the 6,496-acre **Prince Edward–Gallion State Forest** (434-977-6555, dof.virginia.gov), which offers a multiuse trail and a network of forest roads. Venturing into the forest is easy with Twin Lakes as your base camp. In 1919 Emmett O. Gallion planted the seed that sprouted into Virginia's state-forest system when he bequeathed 588 acres in Prince Edward County to the commonwealth, stipulating that it be preserved undeveloped. That tract is now a wildlife sanctuary within Prince Edward–Gallion State Forest. The adjacent acreage, like most in the state-forest system, was purchased from struggling farmers by the federal government during the Depression then deeded to Virginia in 1954.

The official route of the Prince Edward–Gallion Multiuse Trail stretches southwest from VA 612 to VA 696. It's possible to park in roadside clearings along the route but not at either end. The only designated parking, signed TRAILER PARKING, is a mile into the hike at the southern end of Stony Knoll Forest Road. The road doubles as the trail for a mile, but you may wish to forgo the northernmost stretch. Mountain biking and horseback riding are also permitted on the multiuse trails.

• •

GPS TRAILHEAD COORDINATES N37° 10.370' W78° 16.811'

DIRECTIONS Twin Lakes State Park is in Prince Edward County, south of Farmville. From Richmond, take US 360 west (Hull Street Road). Stay on US 360 through Burkeville, where it briefly meets US 460 then dips southward. Pass the first signed turn for Twin Lakes State Park (this leads to the conference center), then turn right at VA 613 and travel 4.25 miles beyond Burkeville. Drive north 1.5 miles to VA 629, and turn right at the park entrance sign. Head downhill on a road lined with kudzu to pass Goodwin Lake on your right. Make the first right onto Goodwin Lake Road (the park office lies at this intersection), then pay your fee and proceed to the opposite end of the parking area on the right.

The recommended short loop at Walnut Creek passes over the lake's dam.

CHOOSE FROM A SHORT LOOP southeast of Walnut Creek Lake and its longer counterpart northwest of the reservoir. The former, popular with trail runners, leaves the main parking area near the beach; the latter departs from a trail-head parking lot closer to the entrance. The two can be linked using one of two short connectors.

DESCRIPTION

Walnut Creek Park offers a wide range of outdoor recreation to residents of Albemarle County and nearby Charlottesville. Anglers cast from boats or the shore, with good odds for landing largemouth bass, channel catfish, and sunfish in the stocked 45-acre lake. Disc golfers hone their skills on the park's 34-acre, 18-hole course, built and maintained by the Blue Ridge Disc Golf Club. In the summer, families crowd the beach and nearby playground.

But Walnut Creek Park is best known for the 15 trail miles that lace its 480 acres. The Charlottesville Area Mountain Bike Club, a chapter of International Mountain Biking Association, built most of the trails, with many switchbacks and frequent ups and downs for better trail sustainability (and fun). However, the network sees roughly as many pedestrians as cyclists, notably trail runners. A tapestry of at least 10 distinct paths, the trail system offers many permutations, but the scant signage

DISTANCE & CONFIGURATION: 7.9-mile linked loops (one 5 miles, the other 2 miles), plus connector and numerous spurs

DIFFICULTY: Strenuous on long loop; moderate on short loop

ELEVATION: 487' at trailhead, 714' at high point

SCENERY: Walnut Creek Lake, rocky creek, pine and cedar thickets, mature chestnut and oak forest

EXPOSURE: Shaded, except along lakeshore

TRAFFIC: Moderate; trail also allows bikes

TRAIL SURFACE: Dirt and rock singletrack

HIKING TIME: 3 hours for long loop, 1 hour for short loop

SEASON: Park: Year-round during daylight hours; beach and facilities: Memorial Day–Labor Day, daily, 11 a.m.–7 p.m.

ACCESS: Adults from $3, children from $2

WHEELCHAIR ACCESS: Wheelchairs not recommended on trails

MAPS: At park in season and albemarle.org /parks

DRIVING DISTANCE FROM CAPITOL: 80.5 miles

FACILITIES: Restrooms, picnic tables and shelters, grills, concessions, disc golf course, swimming beach (seasonal), boat launch, canoe and kayak rentals

CONTACT: Albemarle County Parks: 434-296-5844, albemarle.org/parks

LOCATION: 4250 Walnut Creek Park Rd., Charlottesville

COMMENTS: Not every trail intersection is blazed. Look out for mountain bikes along the trail, but remember that pedestrians have the right-of-way. Swimming and watercraft fees apply on the lake.

complicates matters. To keep things simple, you can choose one of the two loops outlined here. For more mileage, you can use a connector trail and hike them both.

SHORT LOOP

This 2-mile outing begins at the main parking lot, which is just uphill from the swimming beach and concession building. A paved service road loops down to the beach from the southwest corner of the parking lot. The blue-blazed trail, dubbed The Blue Wheel, heads southeast from this asphalt surface as a gravel doubletrack descending toward the lake's dam. The path narrows to dirt and grass singletrack as it runs along the lake to traverse the dam. After crossing the dam, you can hike the trail in either direction, but for the route described here, begin on the path to the right, staying along the lake.

Young mountain laurel bushes climb the mossy slope on your left, while the lake stretches away on your right. The trail rises slightly as it curves inland through pine-dominated woods to reach a trail junction. Turn right here. The trail now twists with the topography to remain generally level, twice leaving the lakeshore only to return.

The trail veers decidedly inland to traverse a parcel of pines, many felled by disease, then winds beside multiple piles of granite stones, perhaps amassed here by trail builders or farmers before them. Follow the blue blazes to the right, or continue straight for a shortcut. As you head south, a barbed-wire fence runs to your right, marking the park boundary. Bike traffic has exacerbated trail potholes in a few spots, but the singletrack remains passable.

Walnut Creek Park

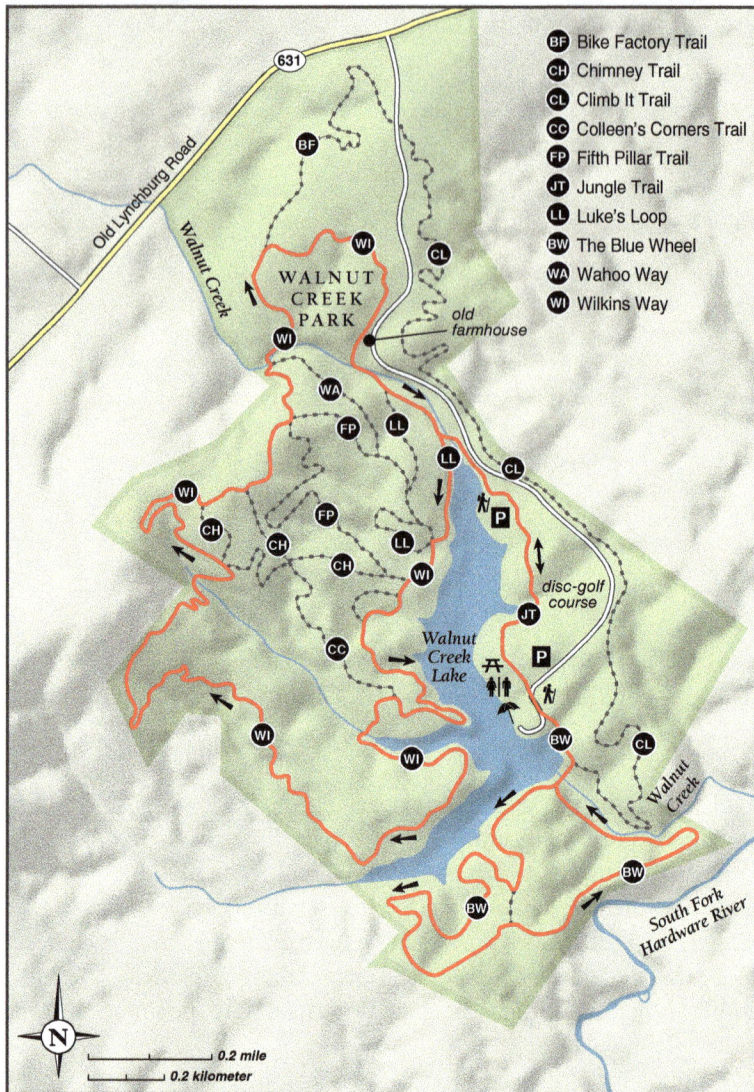

Walnut Creek Park

BF Bike Factory Trail
CH Chimney Trail
CL Climb It Trail
CC Colleen's Corners Trail
FP Fifth Pillar Trail
JT Jungle Trail
LL Luke's Loop
BW The Blue Wheel
WA Wahoo Way
WI Wilkins Way

631

Old Lynchburg Road

Walnut Creek

WALNUT CREEK PARK

old farmhouse

disc-golf course

Walnut Creek Lake

Walnut Creek

South Fork Hardware River

N

0.2 mile
0.2 kilometer

Ahead a cluster of red cedars signifies an old homesite, where you will find the remains of a stone chimney and foundation on the right. Now bear right again upon reaching a second junction with the shortcut trail. Another fence appears on the right as you proceed along a bluffline to crest a small knoll. At the base of the steep hillside across the fence flows the South Fork Hardware River. Walnut Creek drains from the lake to its confluence with the river about 0.2 mile beyond the trail.

As it descends from the ridge, your path curves left to draw along the creek. Proceed upstream amid abundant hornbeams. A bend in the trail grazes the creek just as great sheets of rock thrust skyward from the opposite bank. Perpendicular to the streambed, these successive walls of lichen-spotted rock force the water into a narrow channel. Look for additional rock formations ahead as you proceed through a grassy floodplain studded with poplars. The trail ultimately veers left and rises away from the creek to rejoin the dam-top path on which you arrived.

CONNECTOR

Hikers can walk the 0.5-mile, black-blazed Jungle Trail from the parking lot, past the playground, shelter, and disc golf course and across a meadow and another small wood, to link the two loops. Or take the orange-blazed Climb It Trail, a singletrack connector that runs east of the park road. To follow the Climb It Trail, take the trail leading southeast (downstream) on the northern side of the dam. The path runs beside Walnut Creek then makes a sharp left uphill within sight of the vertical rock walls in the streambed. Crest the hill, and bear left to an overlook. The trail then proceeds north, staying close to the road. It grazes the asphalt near the northern parking lot; you can cross the street to pick up the long loop.

LONG LOOP

Before setting out from the designated trailhead parking lot (north of the beach lot), study the map on the central signboard. The trail departs from the northern shore of the lake below the park road. This stretch of singletrack tends to be muddy. Use the footbridge to cross Walnut Creek before it empties into the lake, then take your first left onto Luke's Loop to head south along the shoreline.

Successive lefts will keep you close to the shore, ensuring that you stay on the main loop, Wilkins Way (red blazes). Your first inland stint entails several ups and downs intended to amuse cyclists, but by following the trail clockwise, you retain the option of retreating after 3 miles and a major climb. Opting to press on, you'll have made the widest loop available.

Crossing numerous laurel-clad runoff gullies, the path generally follows the lakeshore then curves right to trace a small inlet of the lake. You'll double back and cross a feeder stream shortly beyond a trail junction. Bypass the trail that heads right to an old log cabin site, a hub for many of the paths crisscrossing the interior of this loop.

Following the red blazes, the trail reapproaches the lake on a narrow, clubmoss-carpeted peninsula opposite the beach. The path then bends westward, running between an arm of the lake and a pinewood. A slight rise precedes a definitive right, away from the tapering inlet. The trail soon begins a steady climb 250 feet up Ammonett Mountain. You won't top the peak, which crests at 974 feet, but you will switchback beside lichen-dotted boulders and beneath mature chestnut oaks.

The mountaintop is visible uphill on the left as the trail levels out. Numerous windblown trees lie scattered in the woods. The trail temporarily veers east as it dips to cross the upper reaches of a streamlet. Another appreciable climb follows. As you ascend, look for an old stone chimney, the remains of a former farmstead, on your right. A right at the chimney leads downhill to the log cabin. The larger loop, however, rises on, briefly heading west then doubling back. Catch your breath on the downhill stint that follows.

The trail soon forks at Chimney Ridge, descending on either side of this tapering ridge. Continue left along the red-blazed Wilkins Way on a long descent, passing Wahoo Way just before crossing Walnut Creek. The forest is dotted with piles of iron-red stones as the trail parallels the park road. This path curves around a hillside as it passes an old farmhouse on a downhill loop back toward the creek.

After rock-hopping across the wider and shallower creek, follow the trail downstream. The path tunnels through dense thickets of pines then cedars on its twisting ascent from the creek. The trail will soon reconnect with Luke's Loop. The rocky trail descends to bisect the remains of a stone wall ahead. Continue to return along a grassy, cedar-dotted power-line clearing. The creek meets the lake just ahead. The parking area is visible a short distance on.

• •

GPS TRAILHEAD COORDINATES N37° 55.361' W78° 35.282'

DIRECTIONS From Richmond, follow I-64 northwest to Exit 120 and head southbound on VA 631 (Fifth Street/Old Lynchburg Road). Continue southwest for approximately 8 miles before turning left into the park on Walnut Creek Park. Upon entering the park, wind downhill on the paved road to reach the main trailhead parking area, on the right next to the lake. This is the trailhead for the longer loop. To reach the beach and most facilities, continue along the park road until it terminates. This is the trailhead for the shorter loop.

APPENDIX A: Local Shopping for Hikers

You can find anything you want online, but you can't try on boots.

BASS PRO SHOPS
basspro.com
11550 Lakeridge Pkwy.
Ashland, VA 23005; 804-496-4700

CABELA'S
cabelas.com
5000 Cabela Dr.
Henrico, VA 23233; 804-340-7300

COLUMBIA SPORTSWEAR
columbia.com
5711-37 Richmond Road
Williamsburg, VA 23188; 757-564-7604

DICK'S SPORTING GOODS
dickssportinggoods.com

- **Chesterfield Plaza**
1520 W. Koger Center Blvd.
North Chesterfield, VA 23235; 804-897-5299

- **Creeks at Virginia Center**
9940 Brook Road
Glen Allen, VA 23059; 804-261-1853

- **Fifth Street Station**
120 Wegmans Way, Bldg. 200, Ste. A
Charlottesville, VA 22902; 434-270-7117

- **Hancock Village**
14629 Hancock Village St.
West Chesterfield, VA 23832; 804-639-1107

- **The Marquis**
120 Gristmil Plaza
Williamsburg, VA 23185; 757-258-3364

- **Short Pump Town Center**
11800 W. Broad St., Ste. 1096
Henrico, VA 23233; 804-360-8165

- **Spotsylvania Mall**
137 Spotsylvania Mall, Unit 290
Fredericksburg, VA 22407; 540-548-1200

- **Southpark Mall**
324 Southpark Circle
Colonial Heights, VA 23834; 804-526-2745

- **Willow Lawn**
1601 Willow Lawn Drive
Richmond, VA 23230; 804-237-0849

FIELD & STREAM
fieldandstreamshop.com
120 Wegmans Way, Bldg. 200, Ste. B
Charlottesville, VA 22902; 434-270-7117

GREAT OUTDOOR PROVISION CO.
greatoutdoorprovision.com
Barracks Road Shopping Center
1125 Emmet St. N.
Charlottesville, VA 22903; 434-995-5669

GREEN TOP SPORTING GOODS
greentophuntfish.com
10150 Lakeridge Pkwy.
Ashland, 23005; 804-550-2188

HIGH TOR GEAR EXCHANGE
hightorgearexchange.com
1717 Allied St.
Charlottesville, VA 22903; 434-260-4026

L.L. BEAN OUTLET
llbean.com

- **The Shops at Stonefield**
2015 Bond St.
Charlottesville, VA 22901; 888-660-1569

- **Short Pump Town Center**
11800 W. Broad St., #2072
Richmond, VA 23233; 888-534-5803

THE NORTH FACE
thenorthface.com
5715-66A Richmond Road
Williamsburg, VA 23188; 757-253-8620

NORTH RIVER OUTDOORS
northriveroutdoors.com
10384 Leadbetter Road
Ashland, VA 23005; 877-465-4634

ORVIS OUTLET
orvis.com

- **Short Pump Town Center**
11800 W. Broad St., Ste. 1650
Richmond, VA 23233; 804-253-9000

- **River Road Shopping Center**
6235 River Road
Richmond, VA 23229; 804-282-0492

REI
rei.com
2020 Old Brick Road
Glen Allen, VA 23060; 804-360-1381

REPUBLIC OUTDOOR EQUIPMENT
republicoutdoorequipment.com
5825 Plank Road, Ste. 113
Fredericksburg, VA 22407; 703-216-5482

RIVER ROCK OUTFITTER
riverrockoutfitter.com
915 Sophia St.
Fredericksburg, VA 22401; 540-372-8708

WALKABOUT OUTFITTER
walkaboutoutfitter.com

3015 W. Cary St.

Richmond, VA 23221; 804-342-5890

YAMA MOUNTAIN GEAR
yamamountaingear.com

1304 E. Market St., Ste. V

Charlottesville, VA 22902; 434-202-9717

APPENDIX B: Clubs and Organizations

In addition to hiking clubs, this list includes some running clubs that support trail runs and conservation groups that sometimes lead educational outings. There are also numerous local "friends of" groups that support the parks and public lands described in this guide; inquire with management at your favorite park.

BIKEWALK WILLIAMSBURG
bikewalkwilliamsburg.org
757-810-3102

CHARLOTTESVILLE TRACK CLUB
cvilletrackclub.org

THE CHESAPEAKE BAY FOUNDATION
cbf.org
Capitol Place
1108 E. Main St., Ste. 1600
Richmond, VA 23219; 804-780-1392

COLONIAL ROAD RUNNERS
colonialroadrunners.org

FREDERICKSBURG AREA RUNNING CLUB
runfarc.com

FRIENDS OF JAMES RIVER PARK
jamesriverpark.org

FRIENDS OF THE LOWER APPOMATTOX RIVER
folar-va.org

IVY CREEK FOUNDATION
ivycreekfoundation.org
434-973-7772

JAMES RIVER OUTDOOR COALITION
jroc.net

NORTHERN NECK AUDUBON SOCIETY
northernneckaudubon.org

OLD DOMINION APPALACHIAN TRAIL CLUB
olddominiontrailclub.onefireplace.org

PENINSULA TRACK CLUB
peninsulatrackclub.com

POTOMAC APPALACHIAN TRAIL CLUB
patc.net
118 Park St. SE
Vienna, VA 22180-4609; 703-242-0315

RICHMOND AREA ROAD RUNNERS
rrrc.org

RICHMOND SPORTS BACKERS
sportsbackers.org
100 Ave. of Champions, Ste. 300
Richmond, VA 23230; 804-285-9495

RICHMOND AUDUBON SOCIETY
richmondaudubon.org

RIVANNA TRAILS FOUNDATION
rivannatrails.org

RVA MORE
rvamore.org

TIDEWATER APPALACHIAN TRAIL CLUB
tidewateratc.com

VIRGINIA CONSERVATION NETWORK
vcnva.org
103 E. Main St., Ste. 1
Richmond, VA 23219; 804-644-0283

INDEX

ABOUT THE AUTHORS

Photo: Marsha Frith

Philip Riggan spends much of his free time outdoors and considers his hikes in Montana at Glacier National Park his favorites, although he has enjoyed hiking along the Appalachian Trail in Virginia as well. Since he hung up his soccer cleats, he has devoted more time to riding bikes, hiking, and paddling. He is lucky enough to have his family join him on many of his outings. He also volunteers in Richmond-area parks and public spaces and appreciates all the wonderful and generous people he has met who share a common goal to increase respect for our natural environment.

Phil holds a bachelor's degree in journalism from the University of Richmond and a master's degree in urban planning from Virginia Commonwealth University. After 23 years in the media business, he switched careers in 2016 and became a transportation planner for the Richmond Regional Planning District Commission, focusing on bicycle and pedestrian infrastructure and improving connections to mass transit.

Photo: Elizabeth Lott

Nathan Lott holds a journalism degree from Samford University in Birmingham, Alabama. The son of an Air Force officer, he has lived and traveled widely in the United States, Europe, and the Near East. He credits his parents with fostering the appreciation for history, culture, and the natural world that serves him well as a writer.

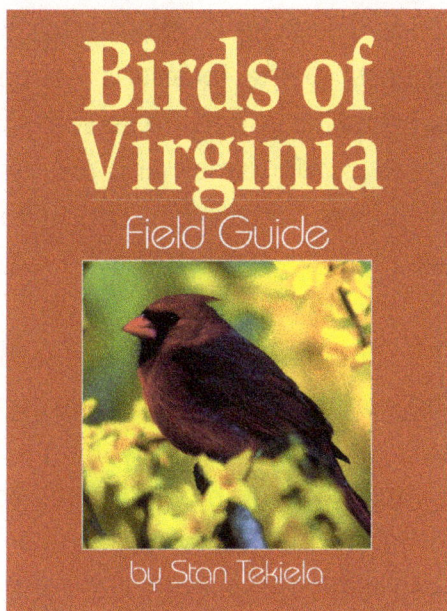

DEAR CUSTOMERS AND FRIENDS,

SUPPORTING YOUR INTEREST IN OUTDOOR ADVENTURE, travel, and an active lifestyle is central to our operations, from the authors we choose to the locations we detail to the way we design our books. Menasha Ridge Press was incorporated in 1982 by a group of veteran outdoorsmen and professional outfitters. For many years now, we've specialized in creating books that benefit the outdoors enthusiast.

Almost immediately, Menasha Ridge Press earned a reputation for revolutionizing outdoors- and travel-guidebook publishing. For such activities as canoeing, kayaking, hiking, backpacking and mountain biking, we established new standards of quality that transformed the whole genre, resulting in outdoor-recreation guides of great sophistication and solid content. Menasha Ridge Press continues to be outdoor publishing's greatest innovator.

The folks at Menasha Ridge Press are as at home on a whitewater river or mountain trail as they are editing a manuscript. The books we build for you are the best they can be, because we're responding to your needs. Plus, we use and depend on them ourselves.

We look forward to seeing you on the river or the trail. If you'd like to contact us directly, visit us at menasharidge.com. We thank you for your interest in our books and the natural world around us all.

SAFE TRAVELS,

Bob Sehlinger

BOB SEHLINGER
PUBLISHER